WIN YOUR PERSONAL TAX REVOLT

by Bill Greene

Published in San Francisco by
HARBOR PUBLISHING

Distributed by G. P. Putnam's Sons

For information contact Harbor Publishing, 1668 Lombard Street, San Francisco, California 94123

Printed in the United States of America.
ISBN 0-936602-10-4
Composition by Abracadabra
Printed and bound by Fairfield Graphics
Cartoons by Charles Fleischmann, San Anselmo;
and Edward Barker, London, England

Win Your Personal Tax Revolt is a revised and updated edition, previously published as *Welcome to the Tax Revolt*

Recent Books by Bill Greene

Think Like a Tycoon: Two Years for Freedom
(How to become financially independent in two years)

How to Buy Distress Property (California oriented) Success
ful selection and bidding at foreclosures, probates, bankrupt
cies, etc.

Tycoon Newsletter

Any of the above may be ordered
by sending a check to
Bill "Tycoon" Greene
P.O. Box 810
Mill Valley, CA 94942

Phone orders accepted with Visa or Master Charge
(415) 383-8264

Please add $1.50 for postage on each item except news-
letter. For fast U.P.S. delivery, add $3.50. California residents
add 6 percent sales tax.

Our books come packed 13 to the carton; standard bookstore discount is allowed for carton purchases. Sorry, no
C.O.D. orders.

All prices listed in this book subject to change without
notice.

Bookstore orders to Harbor Publishing Co.
1668 Lombard St., San Francisco, CA 94123

Dedication

to
Dale and Larry,

tireless I.R.S. special agents who are still spending countless hours trying to find something wrong with my 1973 income tax return.

You traveled the far corners of the hemisphere, spending perhaps a million in public funds investigating my affairs. You carefully interviewed my ex-girl friends. When no dirt was uncovered, you sought out *mothers* of ex-girl friends. You declined to come to my free public lectures, but you cleverly infiltrated my $250 Tycoon Classes with undercover agents. You paid full price and didn't apply for the couple rate.

Finding nothing sinister, you had the government pay for a 4,000-mile trip to interview my childhood playmates. You induced an uninformed informant to mail you a false "tip," then used it to justify an expanded investigative budget. You harassed my parents, friends, tenants, employees, and relatives. You intimidated my accountant and banker. You issued summonses and subpoenas in paper blizzards that caused my lawyers and others to lose another million in productive time and money.

When I think of the 500 homes or other useful products lost to society by this diversion of resources, I consider what might have been: You might have found an error on my 1973 tax return. You might have had me indicted for tax fraud. You might have won a conviction. You might have won the appeals. You might have had me sentenced to a one-year retreat in Southern California. During the six months until my parole, I'd have improved my tennis and horsemanship at the Lompoc Correctional Facility (cost to government, about $200 per day). There I'd have enjoyed the company of Nixon's White House Aides and other soon-to-be-famous authors.

I'd have finished this book a year earlier.

Thanks, Dale, Larry, and successors for trying to help!

Contents

San Francisco Examiner

Friday, April 20, 1979   **20¢**

CITIZEN TYCOON

HE CALLS HIMSELF "Tycoon" Bill Greene. His boyhood hero was Scrooge McDuck, Donald Duck's tight-fisted uncle.

"That goes back to the time when I was 6 or 7 years old," Greene says. "I promised myself that when I grew up, I'd have a Scrooge McDuck room, full of wadded-up bills, and when I got to feeling low, I'd throw that money up over my head and let it cascade down all around me."

Greene doesn't have a Scrooge McDuck room in his Mill Valley digs, I'm sorry to report. But he has worked out a compromise.

"Anytime I withdraw money from petty cash and put it back, I say it's going to my S-M account," Greene says. "That doesn't stand for sadoma-sochism. It stands for Scrooge McDuck."

He doesn't say so, but there might be as many wadded-up bills in Bill Greene's petty cash drawer as there were in McDuck's vault.

Greene reportedly is a multi-millionaire, most of the money having come through judicious real-estate deals.

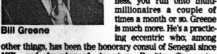

Bill Greene

But in my kind of business, you run onto multi-millionaires a couple of times a month or so. Greene is much more. He's a practicing eccentric who, among other things, has been the honorary consul of Senegal since 1971, and founder of American Equities Group (an international detective agency that tracks down missing heirs and lost stockholders); he hopes to become the Libertarian Party's candidate for vice president of the United States in the 1980 elections.

HE ALSO TALKS about 300 miles a minute, which makes understanding him somewhat difficult at times.

People from all strata have been listening, however, and learning how to become tycoons. That includes some inmates up at San Quentin.

"It was my idea to go to the prison," Greene says. "I figured maybe some of the guys there couldn't afford to take a real-estate course, but needed a way to make a living other than holding up a gas station and hitting someone over the head. In the real-estate field, your past isn't held against you."

In two days of work at San Quentin, Greene says, "I was aiming the course at people about to get out. But I had some surprises. A lot of the 50 or so inmates who showed up for the classes had 20 or 30 years to go on their terms. And well over half of them owned real estate on the outside. One has a shopping center in Palo Alto. There's a new prison policy that allows inmates to do business like that."

Greene generally speaks to classes that number 200 or so. "I asked that it be limited at San Quentin," he says. "I was afraid that if they didn't like what I was saying, they might get violent. San Quentin isn't where they put guys for traffic tickets, you know."

But everything went smoothly. "They were very polite, and interested," Greene says, "and asked pretty much the same questions I'm asked on the outside."

In the purest Howard Cosell tradition, Greene says he told it like it was to the convicts. When he talked about real-estate corruption, he says, his audience wasn't put off at all, as a more traditional audience might have been. "These guys would get up and cheer," he says.

ONE INMATE WROTE a note that said: "Bill Greene, you have showed me the light. I am going to lay down my guns and my life of crime and be a real-estate tycoon when I get out of here."

It's possible you could be similarly motivated if you attend one of Greene's coming free lectures —

at the Jack Tar Hotel. You might even reach tycoon status.

"In America," Greene says, "a tycoon is a person who doesn't make a living at a 9-5 job but by running his own empire of deals — big or little. I'm a medium-sized tycoon by that standard."

He concedes the image isn't one that puts him up there with, say, a man of the cloth.

"Generally, capitalists and tycoons are thought of a little negatively in the United States," he says, "very negatively in places like England. There was a time — maybe 1860 to 1935 — when they were admired here. But the Depression brought on a shift of attitude toward people of wealth. Now, in some areas, rich persons are kind of universally disliked, but I think that will change."

I don't have the space here to detail how Greene has made his millions. I can offer one of his real-estate tips, however. Something he calls "the yuck rule." If you look at a piece of property and your first inclination is to say "yuck," Greene thinks, "that's probably the best investment you can make."

by Dwight Chapin

Warning!

Until now, many of the ideas in this book have been closely
guarded secrets, available to the highest of high rollers. They
seldom appear in print because of the annoying tendency of
Congress to close tax avoidance loopholes once they become
known. Obviously, if tax lawyers or C.P.A.s discover something good, they often want to keep it for their own high-
paying clients. Go over the ideas in this book with your own
consultant. Your tax lawyer or accountant may or may not
have known a particular idea, but he should be able to recognize it as a good (or bad) one for you when he hears it.

Your adviser might say, "It'll never work," when he
hears a novel plan. If this happens, don't let the matter drop.
Accountants are not very creative—that's why they work for
a living and pay high taxes themselves! When your accountant vetoes what you think is a good maneuver for you, *you*
must ask, "How can we vary Greene's approach to *make* it
work for me?"

Accountants and lawyers by nature are deal killers. As a
group, they are very conservative. They reject new ideas. If
you took all their advice, you would spend your life in bed,
lock the doors, and never do anything. *Remember:* It is up to
you to tell the "experts" what *you* want to do. You must insist that they give you the best and most legal way of doing
it. The slightest variation might take a transaction from the
"gray area" into the black, or vice versa. Your accountant's
job is to keep you on the right side of the law with his advice,
and, more importantly, to let you accomplish your aims by
effectively getting around unfair laws.

This book is meant to stimulate thought, not to provide
a detailed plan you can follow without expert counsel. With
that warning, here comes your ticket to a tax-free ride on the
American system.

Welcome to the taxpayers' revolt!

Bill Greene

*Twenty years ago, money really was laundered
in coin-operated laundries—but not any more.*

1.
Welcome to the Taxpayers' Revolt!

Long before I began teaching my Tycoon Class or writing on the subject of tax avoidance, I had a friend: Terry the tax lawyer. Terry represented people in disputes with the Internal Revenue Service. Terry's tax practice was different from that of the average tax lawyer because he usually went to bat for people accused of crime. They were gold dealers before the ownership of gold was legalized, abortion doctors before abortions were legalized, and other individuals who supplied human needs with temporarily "illegal" products or services. As might be expected, Terry's clients also included honest hookers and friendly marijuana dealers.

Terry's clients were put in a bind by the I.R.S. If they reported their true income and its true sources, the I.R.S. made their tax returns available to other government agencies as evidence for prosecutions. If they didn't report "illicit" income, the I.R.S. could prosecute for tax evasion.

Trying to do his best for established clients, Terry established "money laundries." In the 1950s, they were literally laundries: coin-operated wash and dry machines. A client who earned say, $10,000 per year from his "illegal" business would report an *extra* $10,000 per year in coins from the laundries. That way he could sleep soundly, knowing that he wouldn't be prosecuted by the feared I.R.S. for tax fraud.

The world being what it is, the I.R.S. soon learned about "laundered money," and bright young I.R.S. agents decided to bring criminal tax fraud actions against one of Terry's clients for paying *too much* tax. The government decided that reporting *too much* income from a business was criminal— "filing a false tax return." The I.R.S. in these instances was obviously not trying to collect taxes anymore, but was pursuing its social goals theory. U.S. tax-collecting mechanisms have for years been used to jail "bad" people even if they paid their proper taxes or more. Most Americans seem to approve of using the I.R.S. to "catch crooks." "After all," thinks the man on the street, "How else could you get Al Capone?"

The only problem with this prevailing attitude is that it brought about the present practice of "selective enforcement." Selective enforcement is the procedure whereby some nameless, faceless cog in the bureaucracy decides that pediatricians, headwaiters, gamblers, or *you* and your colleagues are "bad guys." Some luckless individuals are arbitrarily selected from the group for criminal prosecution. The full resources of government are then thrown into an unequal battle. The indicted individual is financially and mentally exhausted—and the government gets exactly what it wants: Lots of publicity. The ordinary person like you or me is, according to I.R.S. theory, terrorized into shaping up and cheating less. The present standard operating procedures allow the I.R.S. to attack *anyone it pleases* by using any small error in a tax return as the basis for prosecution. Even a $2 error, even an overpayment, could be the basis of a criminal tax fraud prosecution. On that basis, we are all criminals . . .

Without income tax laws, how could they have caught him?

What does this all mean to you? It means that if the I.R.S. is "out to get you" it can make your life mighty uncomfortable. Can you minimize your chances of an unpleasant encounter with the I.R.S.? Yes. Besides presenting a myriad of clever ploys to avoid taxes, I try to remind you at every opportunity of what goes on in the real world. I believe that the present tax system in the United States is grossly unfair and unjust. But it exists. Fortunately, there are ways to operate within the present system so that you pay zero taxes, year after year. There are ways to arrange your affairs so that you not only pay zero taxes during your lifetime but you can also leave a big estate to your heirs—totally tax free. All this is my subject for the next few hundred pages.

On a deeper and more philosophic level, the little stories

I tell should make you think, "What an absurd system we live under!" It should also stimulate you to want to change the laws—but in a way that never seems to occur to our politicians. There has been a big change in how people view the government and the tax-collecting mechanism. In my opinion, during the 1950s a majority of people didn't mind paying taxes, viewing them as a necessary evil. Taxes were considered a contribution to "our" government. And by and large our government was pretty fair, effective, and civilized.

As we moved into the 1960s, I detected a marked change in attitude both among my friends and in myself. The regimes in Washington after John Kennedy were becoming less and less a government that I could identify with or defend. Could I continue to pay taxes that were used for social goals I couldn't support? For me and many of my contemporaries, the last straw was the betrayal of the Nixon Administration. Nixon, Agnew, and Company mouthed platitudes about "law and order" and prayed on television with Billy Graham. But underneath prayers for public consumption there was corruption of the greatest magnitude. Like the tin-horn dictatorships of Central and South America, like the barbarous regimes of black Africa—Nixon's boys observed only one law: The law of winning the next election. The Drug Enforcement Agency became a corrupt gang of thugs who protected some dope dealers and were generally available to the highest bidder. The General Services Administration, which handled all public buildings, procurement, etc., was also staffed by the best people money could bribe. The main role of the I.R.S., F.B.I., and C.I.A. was to harass and sometimes assassinate "political enemies" of the Nixon Administration at a cost of billions to the taxpayer. At federal, state, and local government levels, more and more taxes were collected to create a vast army of government dependents, until today welfare recipients and government employees begin to approach 50 percent of the working population. The inevitable happened. With the majority of people taken out of production, the amount of goods and services fell, inflation soared, and the middle class—the productive elements of society—began to feel a squeeze that actually lowered its standard of living for the first time since the Great Depression.

Dangers of Cooperating with the Feds

I could cite a million stories about federal government employees who fall all over each other in luxurious offices, with nothing else to do but collect bloated salaries. Some of them feel from time to time that they must "get out and *do* something." The doing something involves mucking up the lives of private citizens—at great cost to all concerned. The worst bureaucratic offenders are always agents of regulatory agencies and tax collectors. Here is a typical tale. Something like this goes on every minute of every day, day after day.

Background: There is a law on the books to the effect that original artworks and antiques may be imported to and exported from the United States without limit. But all such importing and exporting should be reported to customs officials. One day, some U.S. Treasury agents in San Francisco with time on their hands and a big budget to "enforce the law" decided that there must be some unreported art imports and exports going on. They must have decided that a flashy series of arrests would strike a little needed terror into the hearts of the citizenry. It could be played up in the papers and on the 6 o'clock news! In their personal promotion files, it would make the agents look good to have made waves instead of merely holding down seat cushions with their backsides.

According to a deposition filed by the Seattle First National Bank on November 20, 1976, the U.S. Treasury Department, in the person of agent Leslie G. Kinney, requested the assistance of the bank in apprehending some alleged criminals involved in an art-smuggling "racket" between the United States and Canada. At his request, Kinney was allowed to pose as the bank manager, and in this capacity he accepted a $260,000 cash deposit from, and gave a receipt to, one Sam Angel, alleged to be a Canadian art smuggler. A year later, the bank was sued for $260,000 by Angel. The bank spent over $13,000 on legal fees defending the case but eventually lost and had to give Angel his $260,000.

This is Sam Angel's strange story. It was accepted as true by the U.S. Federal District Court in Seattle, which awarded Angel $260,000 in October 1979.

Angel, a legitimate Canadian businessman, accumulated an art collection over the years and had proper purchase receipts for all works in his collection. He had no criminal record, and no charges of any kind were ever made against him. In 1976 when Angel was approached by an undercover U.S. Treasury agent who called himself Mark Hartman, he agreed to sell a painting and some of his Eskimo carvings. The agreed price was $260,000.

Although there is no duty on original artworks bought in Canada and exported to the United States, failure to declare them to U.S. customs when crossing the border constitutes "smuggling."

The undercover U.S. Treasury agent pleaded with Angel to accompany the artworks in his private plane to California without declaration to U.S. Customs. Angel refused. Angel told "Hartman" to pick up the art himself only after he had deposited the purchase price in a bank. Angel agreed to accept a bank manager's receipt to verify that the $260,000 was really deposited in an account for him.

That's where the Seattle First National Bank came in.

The deposit and verification was made, and other secret agents posing as business associates of "Hartman" then picked up the artworks. U.S. Treasury agents then hired a Canadian flying instructor to take them in his private Canadian plane, across the border, into the United States. At the request of the agents, he didn't stop for a customs inspection. When they landed in California, the flying instructor was arrested by the undercover agents for smuggling. Angel was then indicted by a Fresno, California, grand jury for conspiracy to smuggle. The flying instructor, threatened with confiscation of his plane, plea bargained. He got a $500 fine and a year's probation. Angel was never arrested, but when he asked for his money or his artworks back, the U.S. Treasury served notice on him that, as an indicted smuggler, his artworks and

Even an angel can get screwed if he trusts a "G"-man.

any money due him were forfeited to the U.S. government. Remember—Angel never left Canada at any time! He believed he had sold part of his art collection to two Americans who deposited payment for him in Seattle. That's when Angel sued the Seattle Bank.

The bank, through its lawyers, pleaded that it was "caught in the middle" for its good-faith cooperation with U.S. Treasury agents. Angel's lawyer in his complaint alleged that it was the agents who deprived Angel of his artworks in a swindle that seemed to have been taken directly from the movie *The Sting*. As government agents, they claimed immunity from all suits. But the bank had no immunity and had to pay Angel $260,000, plus attorney's fees.

Angel stated that as a result of the bad publicity resulting from the indictment, he suffered a heart attack.

The Royal Canadian Mounted Police, in a press release to the *Vancouver Sun* (October 16, 1979) said that the undercover U.S. Treasury agents advised them of a plan to recover "stolen property" from Angel. "We were satisfied that nothing (illegal) was occurring in Canada." Tell that to the Seattle First National Bank, which lost $260,000 plus a lot of time and attorney's fees.

Oh, how about the artworks? They are in the Customs Warehouse in San Francisco with tens of millions of dollars worth of other confiscated objects. They will be sold off at the annual Customs House auction in San Francisco. A San Francisco art expert estimated that Angel's artworks would sell for $13,000 at auction. The U.S. Treasury will keep the $13,000 unless the Seattle First National Bank can collect from the Feds.

It's likely the Seattle bank will recover its entire $260,000 loss, but only because big-shot bankers always have friends in the Congress who can apply pressure or even pass special laws for them—but you can be sure that, if asked to cooperate in nabbing thieves or smugglers again, these bankers will think twice. *You* think twice too, and when asked to help, remember who the enemy *is*.

And the undercover agents? The government won't say, but they probably got a raise and a promotion!

The tax protest movement materialized first in California, and against the stiff resistance of almost every elected politician in California, Proposition 13 quickly got on the ballot and reduced local California real estate taxes by 60 percent. The dire predictions of disaster by the politicians didn't materialize, and, economically, California is doing better than ever. Other states followed the California lead. But the federal government is not subject to the initiative process and is therefore less receptive to the will of the public. And not everyone wants tax cuts and less government. The people with their hands out for a handout are an effective lobby for more taxes and more free goodies.

Where does that leave you today?

One element of the tax revolt involves some 6 to 20 million people (according to whom you believe) who never file their returns or file so-called Fifth Amendment returns, which are essentially blank. Joining this group has some advantages and one risk—you might spend a few months in the pokey. More on this in my chapter "How to Become a Tax Rebel."

Another element pays some taxes and gives political support to the various formal groups that are the cutting edge of political change: The Libertarian Party, the National Taxpayers' Union, the American Tax Reduction Movement, and Americans to Cut Taxes Now. Get involved with one of these movements. You'll make interesting friends and work toward desirable social goals.

Finally, without risking your freedom, or spending much time or wealth, you can quietly plan your affairs to make more money and pay less tax. At the same time, you can give yourself a "computer profile" that will reduce or

An investment, or business deal, properly structured,
can be the magic wand that eliminates your
state and federal income taxes as long as you live!

eliminate the chance of your having any major problems with the I.R.S. What's the big secret? Nothing that self-employed people or property owners don't already know: Investments or business deals, properly structured, can be a magic wand to eliminate taxes. One rule of the income tax game, as it now stands, allows a taxpayer to shelter any amount of salary or other income, *up to infinity* by the simple method of acquiring a business or income real estate with little or no down payment. "Paper" losses and tax credits allow you to eliminate or postpone taxes into an indefinite future. Because it's all *legal* and the amount of tax shelter can be infinitely expanded to cover all your income for life, I always tell my seminar students there is no good reason to ever risk fines or jail for tax fraud. Using my preferred methods, you can have all the moral outrage and good feelings of the "tax rebel" and at the same time file a legal, accurate, and unassailable income tax return—with *zero* due the government, year after year. If you are ever selected for an audit, by having far more "paper losses" than you need, you should be able to convince the I.R.S. that even if you secretly earned many times the income you reported, there still would be no tax due. Having more artificial or paper "losses" than you needed to shelter all your income is your key to avoiding I.R.S. hassles. Having good counsel is also important. There is plenty of "bad" tax advice floating around, and a licensed, practicing Certified Public Accountant (C.P.A.) or tax lawyer should—at least once a year—review and give his or her written approval to the manner in which you handle your affairs. Even if your accountant or lawyer is dead wrong—the fact that you followed the advice in good faith is enough to keep you absolutely immune from any criminal prosecution.

I honestly wish that it was not necessary to write this book. Why? Because I would much prefer to live in a society that had a tax law all on one page: "Thou shalt pay as tax 10 percent of all thy gross receipts of income from all sources." Period. No exceptions!

The thousands of pages of tax code and millions of pages

18

of annotations and case law on the books today are totally incomprehensible to the average person. They are so full of contradictions that no one on earth really understands the code. I would be much happier to support a small government that protected my person and my property against fraud, violence, and external enemies. But until that happens, until we get back to a limited government, this book will show you the way to pay no taxes, ever, legally.

The tax code has become so long and complicated that no human being can even begin to understand it any more.

2.
Pay No Taxes Ever Again, Legally!

If someone told you that Bill Greene could wave a magic wand to help you manage your financial affairs so that you would never need to pay income taxes again, you'd say they were crazy. But I'm going to show you how to do just that: Pay no taxes, ever again, for the rest of your life—legally!

In spite of intensive scrutiny by the Internal Revenue Service, I've paid only minimal taxes, while accumulating several million dollars in assets. The methods I explain in this book will show you how to do it too, in simple, non-technical terms. With minimal effort on your part, you can not only eliminate all future income tax liabilities but also get a refund of taxes you have paid during the past three years.

This chapter on using real estate to avoid taxes is reprinted from Bill Greene's book *Think Like a Tycoon*.

Our well-intentioned but somewhat naive former President, Jimmy Carter, claimed during his presidential campaign that "The income tax laws of America are a disgrace to the human race." He frequently maintained that our income tax laws were unfair and unduly complicated. He promised vast reforms that were necessary. Yet after his election the "reforms" he introduced—the so-called Tax Simplification Act—only made things more complicated. Accountants and lawyers lovingly call it *their* "Full Employment Act"!

Accountant and tax lawyer celebrate 1976 "tax simplification," which added several thousand pages to our already incomprehensible tax code and will take a decade for the courts to figure out.

In many ways, the Carter reforms made taxes even more burdensome to the ordinary middle-class wage slave. More than ever, productive working people are getting taxed to death by a system nobody likes. The I.R.S., in its collection

*The wage slave, without any tax shelters, gets hit
the hardest by the income tax these days...*

and enforcement proceedings, often operates like the Gestapo or secret police, incorporating in its methods midnight raids, rewards to informers, burglars, and female secret agents who use sex to pry out information from suspected tax evaders.

These days the I.R.S. is even trying to pass regulations taxing people for such things as the "value" of the parking space they get when they park! Our Constitution and Bill of Rights have been so eroded by I.R.S. practices that our founding fathers must be turning over in their graves.

We might as well be living in a totalitarian dictatorship for all the voice we have in our tax system. Certain politicians express wonder that overtaxed, basically honest citizens are turning to any device in their fight for survival. Even the lunatic fringe tax rebels who refuse to pay any taxes and file blank returns have over a million supporters these days. The growing subterranean economy of nontaxpayers who earn money but don't file any returns or even officially exist "on paper" is estimated to produce one-tenth of our gross national product. It's all cash, no questions asked. No W-2 forms, no checks, please.

The C.P.A.'s Secret

Arthur, a former I.R.S. high official, is a tax lawyer and a Certified Public Accountant. He is now the senior partner of a major accounting firm. When I interviewed him for this book, he provided unique insight into the mentality of a former tax collector who has joined the "other side."

Question: Do we really need income taxes?

Arthur: Yes, taxes are the most important product we as a nation produce.

Question: How do you figure that?

Arthur: After all of society's work is done and all the sound and fury has subsided, taxes are the "pure surplus" that society makes available to spend on its most important projects.

Question: What is that?

Arthur: Whatever the people who run things decide it shall be. Sending rockets into outer space, providing medical care for the poor, national defense. Society's most noble purposes and aspirations are paid for by taxes. Taxes are tangible expressions of man's highest goals.

Question: Does that include exorbitant costs of government and graft for the people who run things—our elected representatives and our tax collectors. And bombs? What's noble about chemical warfare and destruction of lives? Doesn't the most tax money go for war materials?

Arthur: It goes for what the people or their elected representatives vote for.

Question: Do you think it's proper that half of our gross

national product goes for taxes?

Arthur: I think you'll find that the percentage is closer to 15 percent. What you may find more thought-provoking is that the cost of tax collecting including the functionaries, lawyers, and accountants on both sides is far more than the amount of taxes collected.

Question: I never heard anything like that before—you are saying that more money is spent collecting, processing, and paying taxes than the tax collected?

Arthur: Yes. All accountants know that.

Question: I may have stumbled onto something. You are then saying that about 15 percent of all the products and services we produce are redistributed by government for "noble purposes" but it costs over 15 percent of the GNP to do it?

Arthur: Exactly. The costs of creating and maintaining all the equipment and personnel involved in the processing of taxes are more by far than what is collected.

Question: If that is true, why does government have so much money to spend?

Arthur: Because a lot of money is involved even though well over half the money spent is spent by the "other side," the taxpayers who employ people like me to create methods and procedures to pass taxes on to others or to pay less tax. The people who buy your book, for instance, are diverting time and financial resources away from producing useful products and services. The printer, bookseller, and many others play a role in this diversion. Tax avoidance, when combined with the costs of compliance—or keeping the records required by government—is the biggest business in the United States. Government employs far more people and resources than all business enterprise combined.

Question: Do you like the present tax code?

Arthur: Without a complex tax collection code, I'd be out of a job. Just as long as the tax code is amended and confused every year or two and stays comfortably beyond the comprehension of the average business executive, I stay the high priest of the most important religion in America. I tell my clients what they can and cannot do. In a way, I'm like God.

Question: But you don't *make* the rules, you just interpret them.

Arthur: Just like Moses and the Pope.

Question: Let's cut the delusions of grandeur. Do you think the tax revolt people and their program of tax simplification and tax elimination will ever get anywhere?

Arthur: No! People talk about wanting to eliminate taxes, but, like you, those who feel strongly enough about not paying taxes simply don't pay. They can do that legally under our present system. We don't need any major changes. The present system is just fine. It suits the majority.

Question: What percentage of individual taxpayers cheat on their taxes?

Arthur: When I worked for the I.R.S., I used to think it was about 50 percent. Now that I'm out in private practice, I'd say 99 percent.

Question: How about business and corporation tax returns?

Arthur: About 110 percent.

Question: Why did you leave the I.R.S.?

Arthur: Mainly because I make four times as much money on the outside. But that wasn't the only reason I left. I began to identify with some of the people I was hounding down. The I.R.S. literally *persecutes people at random* to throw a scare into the rest of us. Some poor cab-driver who is also a bookie cheats by not reporting all his income, then is stupid enough to buy a Ferrari and leave a paper trail of his expenses. He gets turned in by an ex-girlfriend, prosecuted for tax fraud, and makes some special agents of the I.R.S. a lot of brownie points. What the I.R.S. wants in its compliance prosecutions is to create a lot of awareness in the community that they are on the job. The result is, they succeed most with dumb slobs who have inadequate representation and who become easy marks for the Service. There's no fairness in it at all. The bad guys always get away from the I.R.S. I didn't mind matching wits with other good tax lawyers and accountants, but when we got some guy who represented himself and screamed about the Constitution and his "rights" the other agents laughed at him all the way to the jailhouse. The businesspeople with good representation, no matter what they had done, almost always got off with a compromise adjustment and a minor fine. The I.R.S. lost the real cases. So I simply wanted to join the winning side—and make more money too. It was no fun socking it to losers. I couldn't identify with that. I can identify with helping intelligent clients. Together we can wind our way through the tax law minefields without getting blown away.

Question: What do you think of all the books, like mine, that tell people how to avoid taxes?

Arthur: They are wonderful. People read them and come to us to apply the ideas they read about to their own situations.

Question: How about the tax rebels who don't pay any attention to the laws and just don't pay taxes?

Arthur: They are wonderful, too. Eventually, if they get caught, they must come to us for a defense, and after they get out of jail, they employ us to keep them out.

Question: You love everyone, don't you?

Answer: As God's representative on Earth, I have to.

Question: I know you are putting me on. You don't really believe that there is any divine inspiration for the tax laws, do you?

Arthur: Just as much as there was for the Ten Commandments.

Question: Oh Lord!

Arthur: Yes, my son . . .

Of course, the members of the subterranean economy are tax evaders. They risk actually going to jail if they are informed on and caught. But legal tax avoidance—what we talk about here—is for many people a game with no risk. The rules guarantee you will win. You simply learn the rules. Find a good coach and manager—your lawyer and your accountant—and get on with the game. Look for openings. Never give up. Hang tough. Play to win. Beat your opponent. You can't lose. You don't have to pay any taxes again, ever! You never go to jail in this game unless there is an *intent to defraud.* Everything I'm going to tell you about and everything I do in my personal life involves *no intent to defraud* the I.R.S.—I am merely using the present laws as they stand, the same laws our former President declared a disgrace to the human race. These same unfair laws allow big corporations like Syntex, the oil companies, the coal companies, and rich guys like me, to earn millions and pay no taxes whatsoever.

When the I.R.S. heard that Bill Greene was teaching sophisticated tax avoidance classes to the Johnny Lunchbucket crowd on his front lawn, they tried to shut him down. But that made Greene angry enough to buy television time.

The I.R.S. doesn't like the Bill Greenes of the world telling Mr. Average Taxpayer these secrets. They've tried to shut *me* down, instead of the loopholes. But I contend that the loopholes I talk about will stay. Why? Because most senators and congressmen use them. They pay no taxes. If you play by their rules, you won't pay taxes either. When Ronald Reagan was governor of California, there was a flap because he paid no federal or state income taxes. Nixon managed to keep his taxes at zero by falsifying deductions (clearly tax evasion), for which he quietly received a full presidential pardon.

You might remember from the papers that during his first year in office Jimmy Carter made a small cash gift of $6,000 to the U.S. government because he was so "embarrassed" at having no taxes due. As if he hadn't planned it that way! I submit that a large proportion of our senators and congressmen enjoy allowances and incomes of $500,000 a year from the public, and most of them pay little or no tax. *I* certainly pay no taxes. If after reading this you ever pay income taxes, you deserve a dunce cap. America today is like France before the French Revolution; a few aristocrats and politicians control 95 percent of the wealth, and they pay no taxes. The workers and small businessmen pay all the taxes. But you can get smart and join the tax-free class now!

I'm going to show you how to get on the bandwagon. In just one book I can't cover every detail, but by making you aware of the opportunities, the different tax shelters, the books and literature available, I can enable you to get out in the world to ask the right questions. Then you will be able to apply these tax avoidance principles to yourself. Remember, you can only become a millionaire quickly if you don't pay any taxes.

Let's run through a basic outline of one way to eliminate or at least save substantially on your taxes. It will also make you considerably richer, because the main focus of the plan saves taxes but represents a very good investment. Let's take an example. We will assume that it is January 1981. You're a working person, or couple, and you make around $25,000 a year. You don't own a small business or investment property. You are that unenviable person—the wage slave, the consumer, the taxpayer. You are a person who goes to a regular job at 9 A.M. and gets out at 5 P.M. You get a paycheck and find that about one-third of it is deducted for federal tax, maybe 10 percent for state tax, another 10 percent for Social Security, and other deductions. Little or no chance to finagle. What do you take home? Less than half your earnings. A large part of that goes for sales taxes, gasoline taxes, property taxes on your home, and so on. Worse than that, even if you get a salary raise of 10 percent every year, the extra wage throws you in a higher tax bracket resulting in more tax than ever.

Combine the ever-growing tax burden with the fact that inflation continuously reduces the purchasing power of every dollar you receive. The net effect of all this is that your standard of living declines every year—even with cost of living raises from the boss. What can you do about it? A hell of a lot!

Following the procedures taught in my Tycoon Class and explained in this book or on my cassette tapes, you can negotiate your way into the no-money-down purchase of income property. You'll end up reducing the tax on your $25,000 regular income to zero. For example, say you buy a $100,000 fourplex, located in Anytown, U.S.A. This fourplex you select is old, grungy, and in need of lots of cosmetic work, like painting, repairs, and maintenance. It has worn carpets and drapes and, if you're lucky, perhaps some scruffy furniture. These physical defects are the ideal ones you are seeking. Financially, the closer you can get to a no-money-down deal on the fourplex, the better your tax benefits will be.

In connection with our $100,000 fourplex example, let's assume you bought it with no-money-down because you got an $80,000 first mortgage from a savings and loan association. You got a $24,000 second loan from the seller of that property. The extra $4,000 over cost was to provide enough to cover the closing costs. So, on January 1, 1981, you take title to this income property without taking a dime out of your pocket. We'll assume that rents cover expenses during 1981, your first year of ownership. Now, let's skip to April 15 of the following year, 1982, and look at your tax return. Remember that tax return is a summary of your income and expense for the year ending December 31, 1981. Let's see what the effect of buying this one property has had on your income tax.

First of all, you must be aware that the I.R.S. has a concept known as *depreciation*. Even though the value of your building may be going up by 20 percent per year in the real world, the I.R.S., for tax purposes, will let you write off as tax-deductible expense between 4 and 10 percent of its value per year, as if it were losing cash money. The I.R.S. ties in allowable depreciation with the concept known as "useful life." This means that the I.R.S. allows you to take a loss based on your original cost of $100,000 spread over each year of the "useful life" of property. The fact that you did not spend a dime of your own money, but used only borrowed money to buy this property, is totally irrelevant to the depreciation you're allowed to take.

Depreciation

Question: Please explain *depreciation?*

Answer: Depreciation is an abstract concept that can put you in a position where you never have to pay another cent in income taxes. You might even be able to get a refund of taxes you have paid for the past three years. This is how it works.

The I.R.S. allows you to deduct a portion of the value of a building, car, or other property owned and *used* by you *in business* over what they call its "useful life." What the I.R.S. feels is the useful life, and what in reality is the actual useful life, may be totally different. But you have to play by their rules. Any I.R.S. office will give you suggested depreciation schedules on items of interest to real estate tycoons. Drapes, carpets, and furniture in rental units would have a useful life of about three years. A brand new "tilt-up" concrete-wall warehouse would be assigned by the I.R.S. a useful life of as much as 50 years. Everything else is in between. Depreciation on property is determined largely by the type of building materials used and the type of use anticipated. Thus, assuming a warehouse building cost of $50,000 you could deduct from your income $1,000 per year for 50 years as a "reserve for depreciation."

Even though you did not lose or spend $1,000, if you claim the $1,000 depreciation for accounting purposes in figuring your income tax, you would be treated exactly as if you spent $1,000 cash per year on repairs or on any other expense that could be deducted from income. If your warehouse were subjected to unusual wear and tear, you could claim a shorter useful life. The I.R.S. ignores the reality that our 10 percent per year inflation is probably increasing the value of your warehouse by at least 10 percent per year.

For a different example, assume that you were able to buy a wooden *rental* house and rent it out.* Say you assign $25,000 of the price to the land value and $50,000 to the building. Further assume you were able to borrow $75,000 to make the purchase. An older wooden house would have a useful life of, say, 10 years, and this useful life of 10 years divided into the structure's cost of $50,000 would allow you to get a depreciation deduction of $5,000 per year, even though you didn't put up a dime of your own money for the purchase of the property. Assuming you earned $5,000 per year at your regular job for the next 10 years, you'd pay no income tax because each year you would have a $5,000 depreciation "loss" to offset against your $5,000 of earned income. You are never allowed to depreciate land because the I.R.S. feels its useful life is infinite.

There are lots of technical variations, but I hope this explains basic depreciation.

Let me show you how this first property (and others like it that you might buy this year) will be a magic wand to eliminate your taxes. Because of depreciation allowance and a few other goodies you can legally claim, you won't have to pay *any* taxes this year or ever again. In fact, if you do two or three real estate deals this year, you'll get a refund of all the taxes you have paid for the past three years as well. I'll run

*You can't take depreciation on a home used solely as a personal residence. But if you have roommates who pay rent, or if you use your home for business purposes, you can depreciate that portion of your residence used "solely" for business purposes or for the production of income.

through it now to show you exactly how the system works.

The first thing you do after you have closed your deal is set up depreciation schedules. You select a "useful life" for each component of the property—that is, the structure, the roof, the carpets, drapes, stoves, furnishings, and so on. These depreciation schedules must be reasonable, and the I.R.S. does publish certain guidelines. But it is up to you to either use these schedules or to create shorter ones if you feel you can justify selecting a shorter "useful life." The I.R.S. will try to change your figures only if they are judged unreasonable. Of course, if you're not audited within three years your figures stand and can't be challenged. This is due to the three-year statute of limitations.

Now, as I said, I like to buy older, run-down structures because with such buildings the "useful life," in my reasonable opinion, may be as little as 10 years or less. Of course, you as a taxpayer always want the shortest possible life because that generates maximum depreciation. In one case, I actually bought a building so run down that it was condemned one week after I bought it. In that instance, I gave it a "useful life" of one year. I don't see how the I.R.S. can complain about that, because I did in fact have to rebuild it completely in order to get a permit of occupancy.

The "useful life" concept does not mean the time remaining until the place will fall down but rather the time span during which it will lose its useful or economic value. For instance, if you have a run-down, worn-out building that will have to be substantially remodeled within a 10-year period, then a 10-year useful life on that property for tax purposes is fine. It is strictly a matter of opinion. *Your* opinion, if at all reasonable, is just as good as an I.R.S. agent's opinion. They want a long life. You want a short life, to get the largest possible depreciation deductions.

Now, the purchase price of the example property was $100,000. You must break it down into various components. First estimate what represents the value of the land. You want it to be a low percentage—say, 10 percent of the total.

The I.R.S. would like it to be high, because you can't depreciate land. In our example, let's give the land a value of $10,000, the structure $70,000, and the furnishings (drapes, carpets, stoves, and refrigerators) another $20,000. The important thing to remember is that you want to choose a value for the structure that is relatively high as compared with the land value. Obviously, you couldn't get a ratio of 10 percent land to 90 percent building if you were dealing with a little old farmhouse on a 50-acre farm. The value of the land would probably exceed the value of the building by far.

What do you look for to get the best depreciation? Small lots with tall buildings, not too much land, plenty of bricks and wood. With urban property where a structure occupies most of the lot, you will find that the I.R.S. will go along with your setting a land value of around 20 percent of the price you paid, with 80 percent allocated to the buildings and furnishings. Who sets up this allocation? *You do.* This allocation will be challenged by the I.R.S. only if you are audited, only if they look at it, and only if it is unreasonable. Once you come up with any evidence showing that your estimate was based on a reasonable set of assumptions, the burden is on the I.R.S. to show that your estimated useful life and allocation of land value to building value is unreasonable. If you want to be totally on the safe side and allocate in a way that will never be challenged, your county *property tax bill* generally values the structure and the land separately. If you use that ratio, the I.R.S. will seldom question a ratio set by independent county "experts."

However, with many properties I feel the ratio arbitrarily selected by the county assessor is wrong—often in our favor (with a low land value), sometimes in favor of the I.R.S. You are free to develop a ratio more favorable to you. What's all this for? Once you've estimated the land and deducted it from the cost of property, the remainder is the value of the structure and contents. Valuing the structure itself at, say, $70,000 and setting the useful life of that structure at 10 years, then straight-line depreciation on your tax return gives you a $7,000 per year depreciation loss that you can use to offset other income on your tax return. Even though the building may be going up in value by $10,000 or $20,000 a year in the real world, for tax purposes you're allowed to *depreciate* the building—that is, take a loss on your tax return—just as if your salary were reduced by $7,000. Depreciation gives you a loss that isn't really a loss. It is a loss for accounting purposes only.

Let's assume that with the deal you got drapes, carpets, furniture, and removable fixtures (such as refrigerators) that you and the prior property owner by contract agreed were worth another $20,000. Getting a high value on any personal property is best for you. You can also depreciate these fixtures and furnishings, but the estimated useful life of personal property is much shorter than the useful life of a structure. So let's say you bought this fourplex and allocated $70,000 to the value of the structure and $20,000 to the value of the personal property inside the building.

You will notice that this leaves $10,000 for the value of the land. Land, according to the I.R.S. rules, does not depreciate at all. Therefore, one thing I like to look for is real estate on leased land. Actually, if that lease at a reasonable "ground rent" runs for a very long time such as 99 years, you then have the use of that property for as long as you live but you get maximum depreciation. Why? Because the entire cost of the deal was all for depreciable assets.

Let's get back to the depreciation on personal property. Say you give the personal property a life of six years. Actually that's a very conservative (long) estimated life for used carpets, drapes, stoves, washers, and dryers. The I.R.S. would probably let you get away with three years. But for the sake of this example let's use six years. The cost or basis of the personal property is $20,000. On any personal property with an estimated life of at least six years, the I.R.S. will let you take 20 percent extra depreciation the first year. Why? I guess the I.R.S. wants to encourage the purchase of used junk. That's the rule. That 20 percent of $20,000 obviously gives you an extra $4,000 in first-year depreciation on the personal property. That too will be a loss deductible from your regular other income even though it's all on paper. So you see how a $11,000 depreciation loss was created: $7,000 on the structure, $4,000 plus regular depreciation on the contents. (This "bonus depreciation" is limited to $4,000 per year per couple as of 1981.)

The next thing to do toward the year's end is to arrange for an improvement loan. You borrow $10,000 for repairs and painting on your fourplex.

Borrowed Money Is Never Taxable Income

You can do what you want with it, but by definition, borrowed money is not income and therefore not taxable. So here we are on December 30. You borrow $10,000, and on the same day you write out a check to the Victorian House Painting Co. for a $10,000 interior and exterior paint job. Guess what that accomplishes? You've got a $10,000 deduction for the money you've borrowed to repair, cosmetically improve, or paint the property. Out of pocket, you've spent nothing. But now, in addition to the $11,000 depreciation deductions, you've got another $10,000 deduction: total, $21,000!

That's only the beginning. Perhaps you bought a new car or pickup truck. Before you got into the real estate business, a car used for pleasure or driving to and from work wouldn't have resulted in any deductions at all. But now that you're in a business where that car is used, you will not only be able to deduct most or all of your car expenses, you'll also be able to get an investment tax credit! What is an investment tax credit? Very simply (and brushing aside a lot of the bull), an investment tax credit gives you a bottom-line deduction from your taxes of approximately 10 percent of the cost of that car. Your accountant will do the paperwork. So, assuming you bought a relatively cheap car, a nice economical Honda for $5,000, to use in connection with looking around for properties and managing the properties purchased in 1980, you get $500 off your tax bill *plus* 20 cents per mile. If you drove 10,000 business miles, that's $2,000. (More about your car a few pages later.)

So here it is, December 30, and you have generated these deductions—$10,000 repairs, $11,000 depreciation, $2,000 car expense, and $500 tax credit—and you have reduced the tax on your $25,000 regular job income to zero. If you had earned more than $25,000, you would have just bought a more expensive building or two or three more properties.

As you see, the acquisition of one small piece of real estate generated enough deductions to save you around $7,000 in taxes. What was the secret? What was the formula? Acquire run-down buildings, not vacant land, but income property, putting as little as possible of your own money into the deal. You'll get the same deductions even if you put your own money into the deal, but from an investment point of view (aside from tax considerations) the less money you have put into a project the less you can lose, and the less risk you have. For that reason, I emphasize making no-money-down deals. These deals can usually be structured so you have no personal liability. As a result, if the project doesn't work out you can always walk away from the property and you will have lost nothing except your credit rating.

Once you own property, you will collect rental income. You will use rents to pay your loans and expenses, and in a year or two all sorts of magical things will happen in terms of making tax-free money. First, when a tenant moves out and you get another one, you're going to get from the new tenant a very big security deposit. The old landlord probably made the mistake of getting a deposit for what he called "first and last month's rent." Thus, for example, he got $300 for the first and $300 for the last month's rent and that counted as taxable income to him. But you put in your rental agreement that you'll give the tenant the first month free. Then you take an amount equal to the first and last months' rent plus $150 as a security deposit (in this case, $750). Guess what?

Any security deposit you take in is tax-free money. Why? Because it's not income you are collecting. At least as far as the I.R.S. is concerned, you're going to have to return it some day!

In the real world, will you ever have to return it? No! "Some day" will never come! When that first tenant moves out and a new tenant moves in, the new tenant's security deposit will replace the deposit you have to return. In other words, when Tenant 2 moves in many years from now, he'll be obliged to give you an even larger security deposit and you'll use that new deposit to pay off the $750 that's due Tenant 1. Result? All security deposits collected by you will, in effect, be tax-free money.

Tax Deferral

We live in a short-term world. In the long term, we're dead. If I can put off tax liability for a decade or more, it will give me the use of my money during that period. Once money is gone to pay taxes, there is no return, no nothing, it's just gone.

I'd rather bank on the fact that if I can hold on to a dollar's worth of real estate, art, antiques, or gold coins—an asset that in a few years will be worth $3 or maybe $300—I'll owe the government a maximum of $1 in back taxes. Reducing or eliminating current taxes by deferring them into the distant future is, in my opinion, *always* a good thing—*if* the money saved is put into wealth-building investments. Debts due in the future can be paid off with cheaper dollars. Deferring taxes and then *spending* the tax savings is like living on borrowed money. You can live on borrowed money today and let the paying back be tomorrow's problem. Unfortunately, tomorrow does eventually come—unless you die first. Waking up to debts I can't meet, even in an era of $10 local phone calls, isn't a tomorrow I want to look forward to. The only sensible strategy as I see it is to shelter your income with deals and investments over which you and only you have total control. You must control the cash flow. Hopefully the income from your profession or trade, plus your investment

---

income, will continue to rise dramatically, at least in terms of today's dollar.

When local phone calls cost $10, tax and loan obligations you incurred when calls were 10 cents will look very small. They can be satisfied out of petty cash. But you must invest and plan to have the petty cash. In the unlikely event of deflation and depression, everybody will be selling apples—and survival, not the collection or payment of old debts, will be on everybody's mind. If that happens, paper money and securities will be worthless. You'll need the stash of gold and silver coins in your vault in Switzerland. You should, in my opinion, plan for the hyperinflation that is probably coming. But if you also hedge your bets with a contingency plan to stash away a year or two's income in hard assets, you'll do fine no matter what happens. No one can predict the future exactly—but my plan should allow you to prosper in either inflation or deflation. If things stay the same and present trends continue, we get more inflation. And that, in my opinion, is 20 times more likely than deflation.

One I.R.S. agent, auditing a friend of mine, took the very unreasonable position that for security deposits to be tax-free money, the landlord had to keep them in a separate segregated trust account. Such bullshit! But, if you want to be super conservative and meet the I.R.S.'s latest brainstorm, setting up a trust account really doesn't cramp your style much. All you have to do is put that money in a savings and loan association at 6 percent interest, say, and keep it nicely segregated from your operating funds and play money. As a matter of course, the savings and loan will allow you to borrow against that money immediately. They'll give you the money right back at one point higher than they pay you. So, if you deposit in the savings and loan at 6 percent, they'll lend you that money back indefinitely at essentially 1 percent a year. In the case of our $750 security deposit example, the 7 percent loan cost of $52.50 a year will be fully deductible, of course, so you get the use of $750 indefinitely as your play money. The interest income isn't taxable because it is held "in trust" for tenant claims while you borrow and use it. The tax benefits of a property owner are just beginning for you now.

Let's go back to auto expenses. When you were a wage slave, you drove your car to and from work; you got no benefits and no deductions whatsoever. But now that you are in the business of owning and operating property a certain large percentage of the use of your auto will be applicable to your business. The I.R.S. makes it easy for you. It says take, say, 25 cents per mile as a deduction. Once again, this mileage allowance is an arbitrary figure set annually by the I.R.S., just like the depreciation figure that you set. Let's say that in the course of a year's time you drive 20,000 miles in your car. A certain amount of that will be for personal use. You have a social life, and you drive over and pick up Suzy to go dancing. That is not business mileage. However, if it is reasonable to assume that you use your car 50 percent for business (which you should document in some way, either by keeping records in a diary or however you want to do it) then you take 25 cents a mile or $2,500 as a deduction allowed off your other income. Now we assumed that you bought a Honda. Remember? That particular car at 45 miles per gallon is cheap to run and doesn't need any repairs. The cost of the gas and oil and very minor repairs may average 8 cents a mile. In our inflation-ridden world, Hondas don't go down in value when you sell—their value usually goes up 20 percent per year. The real cost to you in running that car for a business is possibly 8 cents × 10,000 miles or $800. The real cost doesn't make any difference to the I.R.S. If the government says you can take $2,500, and of course you should take it. The rule as I understand it (and I always stand ready to be corrected) is that you get a mileage allowance as set by the I.R.S. regardless of the fact that your actual costs may have been far less and your car appreciated in value during the year. When you were a working stiff, there was no way that you could deduct car expense as a business expense. Now, with a high-mileage

40

inexpensive car, you can legally deduct more than you actually spent. With a low-mileage Rolls Royce or Porsche, you can do the same thing by using actual expenses plus depreciation.

Another good deduction is your telephone bill. Most of us get phone bills of $40 or $50 a month. Once into real estate or any small business, you can deduct a reasonable percentage (shall we say half?) of your phone bill. Why? Because you've been calling tenants. You've been calling plumbers, suppliers, and workmen, all in connection with your business. Those are all deductible business calls. As a result, a reasonable portion of your phone bill is now also deductible for income tax purposes.

There are lots of other deductions, such as depreciation and investment tax credits on that portion of your home furnishings set aside exclusively for your property management office. These deductions are limited only by your imagination and resourcefulness. As long as they come within the I.R.S. definition of having been ordinary and necessary to the sort of business you are in, they are legal and you should take them. When you were a working stiff, you had a shop in your basement. Suppose you wanted to buy a lathe or expensive woodworking equipment to make yourself a desk or piece of furniture. You spent $5,000 on the woodworking equipment—hammers, nails, drills, and that sort of thing, none of which was deductible because it was a hobby. Now it is all deductible, because you use the tools and supplies to fix up your investment property. The costs of small tools are immediately deductible. If you were to buy a $5,000 Shopsmith drill press, lathe, and band saw, you could possibly borrow the entire purchase price and have the loan payable over a long period of time. You'd get an immediate investment tax credit and a deduction for tax purposes that would save you several thousands in taxes.

You can even deduct the cost of some clothes. The I.R.S. can get a little picky on this. You can't deduct the cost of a suit, tie, vest, and white shirt. The rules say you can't deduct the cost of clothes you can wear outside the particular requirements of your profession or trade. Thus you still can't deduct the cost of a new suit you could wear to church on Sunday. However, if you bought a pair of studded bib overalls—which are very fashionable with the Disco set—for the specific purpose of working on your building, this clothing expense is (in my opinion and according to cases I've studied) another deductible expense as "work clothes." Then, of course, there's the carpeting, furniture, and all the supplies you would need in the course of running your real estate business.

Can you deduct your groceries? Lunches? Certainly you can deduct cleaning supplies, soap, and what you feed prospective tenants and business contacts. I'll tell you how. At Christmas time, if it is your custom to give your tenants a bottle of wine there is no reason why you can't deduct a case of wine as a business expense. If it is your custom to invite prospective tenants to your home for lunch to gain their goodwill before renting an apartment, there is no reason the wine or lunch you serve them at home (or pay for in a restaurant) can't be deductible. Certainly if you invite your handyman out to lunch or entertain a potential secretary or a person who might be interested in renting your property, these outlays are all deductible business expenses.

How about a trip to Mexico? Unfortunately if you fly to Puerto Vallarta with the idea of looking at property that you *might* buy, the I.R.S. won't let you deduct the cost as a business expense. However, you do get the deduction if you go to a meeting of the California Apartment Owners Association, or a Bill Greene Tycoon Class, that happens to be held in sunny Puerto Vallarta. Many organizations hold conventions or educational seminars in resorty locales. With certain minor limitations, these travel expenses for "education" are deductible.

Now let's assume you purchased another fourplex or even two fourplexes in the course of the following year. That shouldn't be too hard. You can acquire three properties in a year with ease. During my very active period, I did as many as three deals a *week*. Most of them required little or no money. Sometimes I was able to walk away from a closing with the proceeds of overfinancing. It was as easy as falling off a log. Every deal generated more and more tax losses until I had far more than I needed.

You'll note that even if you buy property on the very last day of the year you still get the extra 20 percent first-year depreciation on personal property. In our example, that was a $4,000 bonus depreciation loss you took on carpets, drapes, furniture, and appliances. The $10,000 loss you generated by borrowing money for repairs or painting could have been done on the last day of the year. Also, there are the investment tax credits on basement power tools or the car used in your business. All these tax benefits can be obtained by purchasing "capital assets" up to the last day of the year. Straight-line depreciation on the *structure itself* must be allocated equally throughout the useful life of the property, so you get the *most* depreciation if the property is purchased on January 1, and only one-twelfth as much if you bought on December 1. How to account for all this is explained in my book, *Think Like a Tycoon—Two Years for Freedom*.

In my hypothetical example, I presumed that your job-related income was $25,000 per year. You saw how easy it was to shelter that entire income from tax by merely acquiring one property. If you bought three more properties, assuming the same facts, you'd generate tax losses in excess of $74,000. Why bother? What can you do with excess or "overflow" depreciation that more than shelters all your current income? Simple! You can use the excess depreciation generated by real estate acquisitions to get a refund of all taxes you've paid in the past three years. Here's how: Let's suppose that in your first year you bought several small buildings to generate accounting "losses" of $75,000 more, for a total of $100,000. If you earned $25,000 a year during the past three years, guess what? That $100,000 of losses not only can shelter your current year's income of $25,000 but can also be *car-*

ried back three years. You don't pay any tax this year, and you also get back every cent you paid in income taxes for the past three years. Not only that, you get *interest* from the federal government along with your tax refund. The interest varies with the market rate, but is in the area of 12 percent per year. The I.R.S. form used to obtain a three-year carryback refund is at the end of this chapter.

So let's review the assumptions:

1. You earned about $25,000 this year and for the past three years.
2. You expect to pay $10,000 federal income tax this year. You paid $10,000 income tax in each of the past three years.
3. This year you acquired (with little or no investment) one or more older income properties that break even financially but generate a total of $100,000 in overflow depreciation or "tax shelter."
4. You file your current year's tax return showing the $100,000 "loss."
5. On your tax return, you use your paper losses to cancel out your taxable income for the current year and for the past three years.

Result?

1. No tax due for the current year. The $10,000 that was withheld or prepaid is returned to you in full.
2. The $10,000 that was paid in income taxes last year comes back to you in the form of a U.S. Treasury check for $10,000, plus over $2,000 (two years') interest.
3. The $10,000 in income taxes you paid two years ago comes back to you with over $3,000 in interest.
4. The $10,000 in income taxes you paid three years ago come back to you with around $4,000 in interest.
5. The grand total you get is $40,000 in tax refunds, not

even counting interest. And the best part is that this $40,000 is TAX FREE INCOME. Why? By definition, a tax refund is *not* income. The interest (calculated by the I.R.S. computer according to complex formulas mere mortals cannot understand) will come out to be something like $9,000. Unfortunately, the interest on tax refunds is taxable. But once you get your nice green treasury check for $49,000 you will probably invest in more property to shelter the interest too.

Plan and structure losses so they always just balance your income. In the beginning, you'll need to take maximum allowable depreciation and create deductions that can carry back for three years. After a while, though, what you want is just enough losses to cancel out your income. That way, total earnings from your outside job and rents will just equal losses and you won't waste depreciation you might need in the future. In other words, why take more than you need?

In my own case, because of the large number of properties I owned, I could (by taking shorter lives or accelerated depreciation) generate two or three times as much depreciation as I needed to shelter all my income. By taking less depreciation than what was legally allowed, I saved it up to shelter future profits. Accounting is not a science, it is an art. At first you'll need the help of a Certified Public Accountant. Later you'll develop all the required talents yourself. The art of filing a proper tax return lies in constructing reasonable depreciation schedules that will be honored by the I.R.S. and that at the same time will put you in a position of not having to pay income taxes.

Everything I have been talking about so far is *strictly legal* tax avoidance. Some people would call it *tax deferral*. It's very different from tax *evasion*, which is *illegal*. You can go to jail for evasion if the blue meanies catch you. Let me give you an example of tax evasion: Assume that you collect $25,000 in fees, and you *intentionally* do not report it. If you really owe a tax on that money (because you don't have any tax shelters) and your lover or spouse gets very mad at you, that person could report you for 10 percent blood money reward. For this money, the ex-lover might testify in court that you *intentionally* didn't report $25,000 in income. With an informant's fee at stake, he or she may even amplify or lie for the I.R.S. That's the sort of thing you could go to jail for. That's tax evasion.

Avoidance is legal! Taking a 10-year life on a property on which the I.R.S. feels you should have taken a 15-year life is not tax evasion, it's just a matter of differing opinion. You're not anywhere near the gray area of criminal prosecution. If you are audited, the I.R.S. likes to argue almost every aspect of your return. Once you become a large-scale property owner, expect to be audited almost every year. I.R.S. agents will probably fiddle around with your depreciation schedules and suggest all kinds of inane and typically bureaucratic changes they want to make on your return. However, the rules of the game are on your side. If you take straight-line depreciation for, say, 10 years, and the I.R.S. insists on a 15-year life, then you can take component depreciation. Component depreciation is where you set up a separate useful life for the roof, the windows, the floors, the pipes, etc. You can then get exactly the same total deductions as before.

If the I.R.S. does get tough about your taking too short a life on property, you can always increase deductions dramatically by "breaking up" property into its various components. For accounting purposes, you would get up on the roof and say, "This roof is already 10 years old and probably has only a 12-year life." So you take the value of that roof—say, $4,000—and break it down so that you take $2,000 (2-year life) depreciation on that. You can use this method with every window, stove, and floorboard, carry it to any extreme, and always come out with the desired deductions. As I mentioned, in your first year of operations high deductions may be more significant because you want to generate enough depreciation losses to carry back three years in order to get that big refund. But once you've got a substantial number of properties you will find that overflow depreciation will be so much that you can become very conservative and still have all the depreciation you need. Strangely enough, the I.R.S. never fights when you use conservative figures. If the I.R.S. says the life of the building is 20 years and you take a 30-year life, they don't argue. But if they say it's 20 and you take 10, they may give you some static. When push comes to shove, if you really need that high depreciation and they do knock out the figures you chose, then threaten to use either component depreciation or accelerated depreciation to come out with the same result you had before.

In the example I just gave, you'll have many other deductions, too:

1. Interest paid on money borrowed
2. Real estate taxes
3. Maintenance expenses.

The taxpayer in the real estate business is in a game rigged in his favor. *If* he knows the rules. In the course of being in this business, a lot of other tax opportunities will come your way if you keep up with the latest gimmicks by reading books such as this one, taking courses like mine, and keeping up with all the current literature in the field. *The Wall Street Journal*, for instance, has a tax tips column once a week. Read it! Apply it!

I'm assuming that in all the buildings you get rents and expenses which are just about even. Thus for tax purposes it's the depreciation figures that really loom important. This depreciation never catches up with you. Conventional wisdom goes something like this: You can shelter your outside (non-real estate) income with the real estate overflow depreciation. Your ordinary income from your job or outside earnings would have been taxed at ordinary income rates, but you sheltered all the income. Later on when you sell the property, you must recapture the tax savings, but you do so at the (lower) capital gains rates. For instance, if after 10 years you sell the property for what it cost ($100,000) and you had depreciated it to zero, you would have to pay a tax on the whole $100,000 received as capital gains. However, as I say, this is conventional wisdom. The $100,000 profit would be theoretically taxed at capital gains rates or half of your ordinary income tax rate. The I.R.S. rules say that each year you take $10,000 in depreciation, your "basis" goes down by $10,000. So if you sell it in Year 1 for $100,000 after taking $10,000 depreciation, you would have a $90,000 basis and a taxable capital gain profit of $10,000. If you sell it in Year 2 after taking $20,000 in depreciation, you'd have a capital gain (profit) of $20,000. This is, of course, if you sell at the price you bought it.

Most accountants will agree that the net effect of investing in real estate is being taxed at capital gains tax rate. But I say you'll never have to pay any taxes during all of your life because, like Vincent Astor, you should never sell your properties. Ever. You can pull money out by tax-free refinancing, or the I.R.S. will allow you to go through a maneuver called "trading up." This is covered quite clearly (for a refreshing change) by Internal Revenue Code Section 1031. For all practical purposes, this law allows you to find a new property and arrange for the sale of old property to close the same day. If you do the paperwork right, there is no tax consequence whatsoever. I cover this in great detail in the chapter on exchanges. But for now let me show you how it works. Let's assume that a few years ago you bought a fourplex for $100,000. You depreciated it to zero, but it's still really worth $100,000. You now find a building worth $1,000,000 that requires a $100,000 down payment. You arrange for the sale of your $100,000 building to be simultaneous with your purchase of the million-dollar building. The $100,000 cash you get for your old building goes to the seller of the million-dollar building as a down payment. If you do it just that way, there is no tax consequence to you.

Instead of starting depreciation at $1 million on the new building, you start at $900,000 because you carry over the used-up ($100,000) depreciation or basis from the old property into the new. In real life, the figures would never be simple, but I'm giving you this only as an example.

Let's recap. The original property bought for $100,000 you depreciated to zero, so $100,000 depreciation was used up. When you buy that new million-dollar building, the depreciation that you took on the original property is taken off the price you pay for the new building. This is called a $100,000 *reduction in basis*. Your depreciation starts at $900,000.

When you trade up, you should try to trade up in value as dramatically as in this example. Let's look at what happens if you go from a $100,000 building to a $1,000,000 building. From the $100,000 building, you took $10,000 a year depreciation each year for 10 years. At the end of the 10 years, if you buy a million-dollar building (without a dime out of your pocket) you begin to generate $90,000 a year depreciation, assuming a 10 year life on the trade-up property. Can you see how trading up gives you new depreciation every time you do it? The depreciation in the new deal can be many times more than what you had before. That's why any real estate investor who has been at the game for a while keeps trading up regularly.

Actually, the rules of the tax game as they now stand *force* you to trade up. If you don't trade up and your depreciation runs out, all those rents coming in become taxable income. A tycoon wants to shelter *all* his income *all* the time. Real estate is tax shelter that you can create for yourself.

Now that I have given you the basics, let's get a little more sophisticated and go into the subject of generating maximum deductions in real estate.

Suppose that one of your tenants puts an unsightly chip in the bathtub. You have to spend $60 to replace that broken bathtub with a new one. Because it's a relatively small expense, I'm quite sure the I.R.S., even if fully informed, would not make you capitalize the bathtub and depreciate it over six years at $10 per year. As picky and unreasonable as they are, they'd still probably allow you to write off the entire $60 in the year the broken bathtub was replaced. Likewise, if in a later year the same thing happened to a commode or a toilet fixture, you could probably replace it and write it off immediately.

Bear in mind that if you were to do a major remodeling job all at once—take out the fixtures, retile, put in new fixtures, and basically build a brand new $5,000 bathroom—the I.R.S. would say that's a capital improvement. Remodeling must be depreciated over the life of the new bathroom, which might be 20 years. Therefore, remember to get maximum deductions you want to "expense" the costs of improvements; that is, write it off immediately as a repair. However, once you have all the losses you need you may want to drag out those deductions by capitalizing them. The I.R.S. will never argue if you capitalize a repair, but they *will* fight you if you are trying to expense something they think is a capital improvement.

The I.R.S. does issue guidelines, and there are books to help you decide what's a capital improvement and what's a repair. In those years you need deductions, be sure to classify expenses as repairs, not capital improvements. Is there a choice? Let me give you one example: If you have a house with a four-sided roof and you repair or replace all four sections at once, that's clearly a new roof, a capital improvement. If you put on a brand new roof that will last 10 years, you can write off only one-tenth each year. But, suppose only a quarter of the roof was leaking, and you just got that quarter fixed, and the roofing bill said clearly "Roof Repairs, $200." The I.R.S. couldn't get you to capitalize that because you didn't get a whole new roof. You only took care of one section needing an emergency repair. Of course, if it is an old roof the chances are that next season another section will leak and you can fix that up. It can then be expensed as another repair. If, in the third year you have another leak, you'll expense that. In the fourth year, the same. The net result is that in four years you have a brand new roof but you've been

50

able to expense it off right away instead of writing it off over 10 years. Remember, if you want write-offs, do repairs and do them piecemeal, not as part of a general remodeling plan—or at least not as part of a plan the I.R.S. can ascertain.

I think I should now introduce you to the concept of the lottery system. It works like this: The I.R.S. does not audit everybody. It does not even audit all landlords. Often audits are aimed at one specific enforcement problem that the President has thought up in that particular year in order to get a few votes. For example, a directive may come down some year that property owners should get a rough treatment because it is thought that they are expensing too many four-martini business lunches. The I.R.S. will pull your tax return to see if you wrote off a lot of lunches. That year, taxmen may not even look at your depreciation schedules because they are only interested in one little area—how many martinis you drank. The agent may say you should have charged off only $500 of your expenses. Most taxpayers don't argue because they don't want the agents delving into every single accounting entry. As I told you, accounting is an art, not a science, and the I.R.S. could take you to court over every single expense if it wanted to be nasty. Because court lawyers and accountants are expensive ($50-$100 per hour) even if you win and keep your $500 expenses, it would probably cost you a couple of thousand dollars thrown away in legal costs. Not to mention fooling around for months and going to countless meetings and conferences. Generally if you are audited, give in, settle fast, and keep expenses down. If possible, keep the I.R.S. agents out of your hair. If you are argumentative, they may start going over everything. But remember—not everyone is audited. The I.R.S. uses the lottery system. If your name is not pulled and three years pass, you're home free. The statute of limitations says that the I.R.S. can question your return for only three years after it's filed. However, if they suspect you of tax evasion, they have up to seven years to investigate.

If you've been audited once for a particular year, they

generally don't come back at you for the same year. Perhaps during the first audit they just asked about one very narrow issue (such as the yacht you kept to entertain your tenants). If you give in on the yacht, maybe they will let you keep your 10-year depreciation schedules.

Once you own real estate, there are many gimmicks you can use that are entirely legal. Let me give you one more: Suppose you have a teenage kid who goes to high school. I'm not sure what teenage kids get as allowance these days, but let's say you give him $100 a month. If you give your kid $100 a month for his record albums, gasoline, and baseball uniforms, of course there is no deduction—you don't get any tax benefit. So, why not *hire* your kid instead of just giving him that money? Let him do minor jobs around the property you own. Keep a record of what those duties are: washing the windows, painting the walls, vacuuming, cleaning up the yard. Give him $100 a month for that. What can happen here? What if you had your own kids or three or four kids to whom you previously were giving money without getting any tax benefit. Suppose you now *pay* those kids $750 a year? That $750 × 4 kids is now deductible to you as an expense! It's not taxable to the kid however, because people don't have to pay income taxes if they earn under $3,300 a year. Of course, this figure changes every year.

Tenants' Leasehold Improvements to Your Property Are Tax Free!

Let's suppose that you own an apartment house, office building, or even a piece of vacant land. My goal is, and your goal should be to increase your net worth without paying any taxes. When you buy income property, rental income is usually sheltered by depreciation—for the first few years, but after that your rents may become unsheltered taxable income. How can you increase your net worth or your cash flow on vacant or depreciated property you own without

*Instead of just giving your kids an allowance,
you can hire them to work in your side business,
deduct their salaries as a business expense,
and still keep the dependents' deductions.*

producing taxable income? Get the tenant to put in some expensive improvements!

Here's a strategy many real estate owners use. With variations, it might fit your needs. Let's assume that you own a rental house formerly rented for $500 and now worth about $1,000 per month. A tenant comes along and says, "I'd give you $1,500 a month if you build me an extra 'guest house.'"

You could build the guest house, write it off over its useful life (20 years?), or you could say to your tenant, "For tax reasons, I'd like *you* to build the improvement. It will cost $20,000. Get a contractor to do the work and a construction loan to pay for it. I'll keep your rent at $500 per month for a two-year lease term." Assuming that the addition or improvement is made, your property value is increased by $20,000. The tenant pays you $500 rent per month. This reduces your taxable income from the $1,500 per month you would have received if you made the improvement yourself and charged more. Your taxable income is kept low. The value of your assets—your net worth—goes up $20,000.

Under your deal with the tenant, the tenant can advance

the cost up front and pay about $1,000 per month on his two-year construction loan—which isn't income to you. At the end of two years, the tenant moves, and you get the $20,000 improvement, tax free. Why? Because that's the rule! (See Regulations Section 1.109-1 or Section 769, Improvements by Lessee—U.S. *Master Tax Guide*, a Commerce Clearing House publication.)

Over the two-year period, you had only 24 × $500, or $12,000 of taxable income instead of 24 × 1,500 or $36,000. Because your improved property is worth $20,000 more, presumably you can borrow more against it if you need cash—or you'll get a higher price when you sell. In any event, your net worth went up by $20,000, and it was tax free.

What about the tenant? The cash and tax net effect to him was nil. He paid $1,500 per month—the figure he was ready, willing, and able to pay in the first place. If the property was a residential rental, he received no tax benefit. But if the new room was used solely for some business related enterprise the tenant gets to deduct the entire $20,000 from his income over two years. For the tenant, that would be a much better deal than taking, say, 10 percent of the rent for the portion of the premises solely used for business purposes.

Obviously, on vacant land, you'd always be better off trying to get a tenant who would build you a warehouse or other solid commercial structure and lease it back for a relatively short term. A lease of 15 years or less is good for you. When you don't get the improvement for 15 or more years, it doesn't matter a heck of a lot (taxwise) who does the building. The only way to figure out what gives you the most tax benefit is to do a cash and tax projection on paper covering the period of the proposed lease. But because the rules of the game change and inflation can make mincemeat out of any projections you may do, my recommendation is to keep all leases as short-term as possible, give no renewal options, and, if a lease is for more than a year, be sure to have automatic annual increases based on changes in the cost of living.

It's important to remember that you should never make

a decision solely because of the tax aspects of a deal. The economics are just as important! Don't make a deal just to save on taxes. All deals should *make you money, and make economic sense.*

It's just common sense to make money *and* save on taxes—but there's still another reason: If you ever get into court with the I.R.S. and they can show that there was *no economic justification—no possibility of profit* from a course of conduct you entered into, they can simply disregard any elaborate deals or contracts that gave you some tax benefits. I bring this up in this section because an audit is always triggered by something suspicious on your tax return. Merely reporting the same rental income next year that you made this year would not raise any red flags. Reporting a drastically lower income on the same property could be noticed. If it were, you'd have to come up with an explanation as to why the rent was reduced. If it turned out you *reduced the rent in return for* a tenant making *improvements* on your property, then you might have problems.

Why? As with so many tax gimmicks, it's what you appeared to be thinking that counts for more than what you did. The regulations indicate that if the landlord gave a reduction in rent in return for expected tenant improvements, then the improvements are to be considered "taxable income" to the extent of their fair market value, in the year constructed. That's why in our example the property owner gave no concessions in "lieu of rent." The thing to remember is that if you the taxpayer give any sort of discount on rent in exchange for getting the tenant to make improvements, those improvements are taxable to you as the owner. Obviously, all agreements (at least all *written* agreements) should state that any rent being paid by the tenant is believed to be "fair market value" and that no concessions are being given for any leasehold improvements to be made by the tenant.

How about repairs by the tenant for which the tenant takes off something from his rent? Although I haven't found any regulations on point, if one of my tenants repairs a faucet and takes $30 off his monthly rent, I simply report $30 less rental income. Some of my peers report $30 less and take an expense deduction for the $30 repair bill as well. This latter approach is creative—but will definitely be disallowed if noticed in an audit. You can't get a deduction for money you didn't spend. If your income was reduced by the cost of the repair, you're not supposed to get a double deduction by reducing income $30 *and* raising expenses $30. But some people do it, and I guess they get away with it. Personally, I have so many more losses, credits, and deductions than I need, it's not necessary to resort to petty chiseling. Own a few pieces of real estate and it will make an honest man (or woman) out of you!

Here's another advantage to owning real estate: If you have a windfall in your non-real estate business (whatever that business may be), there are a few maneuvers to shelter that unexpected income. They are legitimate and at this point perfectly legal and ethical. Owning real estate makes it possible for you to shift income and losses to different years. Suppose you got a $5,000 bonus in December from your regular business. You hadn't planned on that, right? Now you need to generate a $5,000 loss if you want to avoid paying tax on that bonus. One thing you can do is prepay your real estate taxes, insurance premiums, or any other expenses in connection with real estate. That way you generate a $5,000 loss when it's needed. Another way to do the same thing is to prepay any legal or accounting fees. Or almost any expense, for that matter. Of course, if you don't happen to have the cash you can always borrow to prepay bills. Once you are a real estate owner, lenders realize that we do this sort of thing and are quite accommodating about making loans in December to be paid back the following year. As a result, you shouldn't have any difficulty shifting expenses (or income) back and forth between the years to keep your income tax at zero, regardless of unexpected factors.

A logical question at this point is "Since you have now exposed all these loopholes to the unwashed masses, don't you think this in itself might cause Congress to clamp down and make it impossible to do in the future what you have done in the past?" There is that risk, of course, but if any logic or sanity exists in Washington (and I usually doubt there is) they must realize that housing and construction are two of the most vital sections of the economy, right up there with food production and distribution. Farmers get all sorts of subsidies and benefits to encourage them to work long hours at physically difficult and somewhat unpleasant tasks. Likewise, real estate has to get some special encouragement from government if money and effort is to flow into buildings and homes. There are negative factors involved with real estate (just wait till you get a deadbeat or problem tenant!) so there must be something to make it more attractive than Swiss bank accounts, gold, fine art, or antiques. That "something" exists in being *left alone* and being able to defer taxes. Without the benefits of overflow depreciation and tax-free trade-ups, you can be sure I'd walk away from my holdings tomorrow. I'd let the lending institutions take over my empire, or the government, if it wanted it. If the rules were changed, money would flow out of real estate in a flood the likes of which haven't been seen since Noah's days. We'd follow England down the tubes—creating the European situation where there is virtually no new construction except for inefficient public housing erected at government expense. Of course, "government" expense is always taxpayer expense. Congress has often enacted British socialistic legislation here almost exactly a decade after it proved to be unworkable in England. This proves that there may be no logic or sanity in Washington.

The present system of no government meddling, plus tax breaks for real estate investors, works. Whole cities could be housed in the projects built by wealthy investors who backed ventures solely for their tax shelter features. The present system of a relatively free economy in real estate works. It delivers reasonably priced dwellings, factories, warehouses, offices, and stores to the people who use them.

The United States is the only country in the world with no housing problem. Housing here is abundant, with an existing housing stock supplying per person double the square footage of other developed countries. Our low costs for finished housing is a marvel to the world. In Denmark, Sweden, France, and England there are 10-year waiting lists for apartments. All but the most expensive housing is built wastefully by governments at substantial cost to the taxpayers. Homes or apartments are simply not available.

In the United States, the only problems exist in such places as Manhattan where *local* governments have instituted high taxes or rent controls or both. In New York, no new residential construction takes place unless it is super-luxurious condos or public slums erected and maintained at enormous taxpayer expense. Some areas of New York look like Dresden, Germany, after the bombings. The strangulation of private real estate in New York has made it the most unlivable city in the world and has played a large part in bankrupting the city. Even *talk* by politicians of the elimination of the tax shelter features from real estate will cause a rapid outflow of capital from this industry, just as surely as presently existing tax incentives have caused wealthy people to invest in real estate tax shelters.

I feel that the unhealthy socialistic trends of the past 50 years are finally being reversed. The election of Ronald Reagan with his "reduced government" program is one manifestation. The successful taxpayer revolt in California—led by property owners—reduced real estate taxes by two-thirds. If that can be done nationally, you and I can spend less time working on loopholes and more time being productive. With income taxes at a maximum of 20 percent, I'd be more than happy to pay my share—wouldn't you?

Until then, let's play by the present rules, take advantage of the laws as they stand, and pay no taxes at all—legally.

3. How to Write Off All Your Personal Expenses

The main trick in writing off *all* your personal expenses is to combine business and pleasure inextricably. In my world, I do not make a phone call unless it is business related, nor do I have a meal, take a trip, or even make love to anyone but a client, employee, employer, or other person in a business relationship to me. This makes all related expenses totally deductible on my income tax return. I wouldn't dream of having my office anywhere but my home. For tax purposes, I sleep away from the office, so that my home (oops, *office* expenses) can be claimed as a 100 percent tax write-off. This way I'm able to deduct 100 percent of my office expenses as a business expense.*

---

*Internal Revenue Code Section 280A allows the deduction of home expenses for premises used exclusively as an office. In the case of *Curphey*, 73 Tax Court 61, a physician who used part of his home for running six rental units was allowed to deduct home office expenses plus travel expenses in connection with all his upkeep and rental activities.

You needn't be quite such a fanatic to get plenty of deductions. Merely begin to integrate a second or third business into your personal life. If you are a professional of some sort, you no doubt already write off substantial business mileage on your car at 20 cents per mile. You can get a lot more expenses to write off by owning income real estate. Business related expenses include phone calls, work clothes, furniture, carpets, fixtures, education, travel, gifts, and so on. If you also owned a delicatessen, restaurant, or farm, a substantial amount of your food costs might be written off on the principle that "good cooks have to sample the soup." The samples could feed your family, with food costs being attributed to the business.

More Piddly Little Stuff

Business gifts worth under $25 are tax-deductible business expenses to the donor (giver) but not income subject to tax to the donee (recipient).

Let's see how the well-lubricated tax avoider's mind can use this general rule to good advantage. Around Christmas time, you buy a few dozen cases of champagne for distribution to your tenants and business associates that you'd like to present with small gifts. The cost is fully deductible to you as an ordinary and necessary business expense: advertising and promotion. If the recipients reciprocate (or can be convinced to reciprocate)—that could be worth a few thousand in tax-free gifts of groceries to you. Everybody in business does that one, with variations. But did you ever consider this possibility: Your mother-in-law gave you a gorgeous $25 tie with a hand-painted hula dancer and palm tree on it. Instead of chucking it in the garbage, why not generate a $25 deduction by giving it to a tenant? Up until now you probably threw away unwanted gifts and accumulated junk without realizing that you can give away your personal property as deductible business gifts. You get a write-off for the fair market value (as set by you).

Your secretary or anyone who works for you would rather have tax-free compensation than highly taxed income. For National Secretary's Week, Valentine's Day, Mother's Day, and any other holiday, you can give her up to $25 in cash as a nontaxable gift that is also deductible to you. Naturally your *intent* is supposed to be gift giving and not substitution of tax-free income for what would otherwise be taxable income. But now that you know what your intent is supposed to be, you can work at developing the appropriate intent.

The Reciprocal Lunch Date

Entertaining clients, prospects, or other business guests always results in generating a business deduction for the lunch. Everyone with their own business knows that trick and does it regularly. Only problem is, if you are always buying people lunch, it's money out of your pocket, even with the tax deduction. But suppose you are a real estate investor, and you often eat lunch with your lawyer. In the past, you went dutch treat and each paid your own way. The I.R.S. won't let you deduct a single lunch (unless it's away from your usual area on a business trip). But they will let you deduct the full cost of lunch for two where there was a business discussion. All you have to do is keep the receipt (if over $25). If it is under $25, you make a note of the restaurant, the date, what was discussed, and what was paid. (The best place to keep your contemporaneous expense records is in your daily desk diary.) You can toss a coin with your lawyer to decide who picks up the tab for two. Or decide some other way how to arrange all your meal checks to be paid for on a rotating or reciprocal basis—so you only end up paying for half your lunches but are able to deduct what amounts to all your eating out food costs—it can come to thousands per year! Every little bit helps.

Hobby Business

The I.R.S. will disallow deductions that recur year after year in a "business" they regard as a money-losing hobby. My friends Charlie and Harriette were just wild about being part of the horse-racing set. They blew a fortune on hydroponic grass, vitamins, vet bills, and all the other things necessary to keep their horse Ramjet in racing silks. They sheltered all their income with the horse expenses, but these losses probably would have been disallowed if they were audited. Why? For two years, Ramjet didn't come close to winning a race. The I.R.S. would say, "Hobby losses are not deductible, you didn't intend to make a profit—ever." The next horse Charlie and Harriette added to their racing stable was a lot better. Clover's winnings plus his stud fees in their third year into racing amounted to more than their expenses that year. Charlie and Harriette got to write off all their current and prior expenses without I.R.S. challenges.

The secret of getting a write-off for your hobby is to see to it that, over the long run, the hobby business makes an overall profit. If that can't be arranged, the I.R.S. seems to allow a business deduction if in two calendar years out of five you have profits. That shouldn't be hard to arrange if income fees and sales can be bunched up in the year you want to show a profit. At the same time, expenses are prepaid or deferred to other tax years. I understand that former President Dwight D. Eisenhower did that with a model farm he owned in Pennsylvania for many years. With the proper "intention"—that is, an intention to make a profit—you can do what turns you on, and write off all the expenses.

Do you like collecting stamps, coins, old snuff boxes, artworks, classic cars? A little imagination can allow you to have a good time collecting and also getting write-offs. The late Bill Harrah of Harrah's Casino in Reno had the most magnificent auto collection in the world. I am sure he wrote off the million dollars a year or more he spent going to the Concours d'Elegance in Monte Carlo and other glamour spots. Many of his friends were taken along as "consultants," mechanics, and experts. The auto collection was never profitable *per se* but hundreds of thousands of people paid a dollar to see it. They got back their dollar in the form of a free gambling chip usable at the Casino. It appears that Harrah convinced the I.R.S. that his classic cars served as a lure to bring potential gamblers into his Casino. Result: Harrah was able to have fun with his hobby and write it all off as an expense.

If you are interested in cars, *antiques* are those dating back prior to World War I. *Classics* date between the two wars, and *milestones* are post-World War II models. The best deals tax-wise are the milestones, because the I.R.S. will accept your classifications of them as "used cars" that depreciate and not as antiques that can't be written off. You could, for instance, depreciate your 1955 Packard Clipper over a two- or three-year "useful life" and get away with it. Cars of the 1950s can be picked up for under $10,000, and rare convertibles like the Hudson Hornet or 1955 Corvette should provide extremely rapid appreciation over the next few years. Seeing them double in real value while you write them off to zero and then trade up under Section 1031 offers a particularly satisfying prospect. For a wide selection of fascinating old cars, see *Hemming's Motor News*, available in many magazine stores. Classic and milestone cars are almost as good an investment as real estate, but unfortunately, do not provide much income while you hold them. But you can register them with movie-casting agencies and get huge rental fees if they are used as props.

People who like to breed race horses, raise fancy pedigreed dogs, put together computers, race cars, or even collect stamps and coins can usually develop their own do-it-yourself at home tax shelter by following some of these suggestions:

Step 1. Create the *appearance* of a business:
a. Stationery and business phone

b. Advertisements in trade publications
c. Membership in trade organizations
d. Listing in Yellow Pages of phone book
e. Consider forming a Subchapter S corporation and channel all income and expense through the corporation bank account.

Step 2. Create the *reality* of a business:

a. Arrange finances to create occasional profitable years (two out of five) in which a nominal income tax would be due. No actual tax need be paid because you will no doubt have *other* shelters.
b. In your mind, form the proper intention—obviously, that will be the intention to make a profit sooner or later. Let the world *know* your intention. You might have a framed motto made for your office wall: "This is a profit-making enterprise (I hope)." Send out Christmas (Hanukkah?) cards with a photo of yourself in front of the motto. Write the cards off as a business expense, and keep a few copies for your audit.

The funny part of all this is that you may create a friendly Frankenstein monster! What if your businesses actually do make money?

I started out to have a little fun and a few deductions by restoring an old Victorian home in San Francisco. I made so much money that I had to look for a new hobby to shelter the profits from my real estate. So I bought expensive sound equipment and a swell hi-fi system that I wrote off because I made some cassettes on "How to Buy Your First Investment Property With No Money Down." Once I advertised the tapes, I was collecting so much money that I needed a new tax shelter. So I took expensive trips to the tropics, where I gave seminars and lectures on the subject. But the Bill Greene Tycoon Classes made so much *more* money that in the following year I bought an expensive I.B.M. word processor, a ton of paper, and wrote this book. I hope to heck it doesn't make a million!

If you become a multimillionaire and your tax shelters start to mushroom into giant conglomerates of casinos, stables, fish hatcheries, bestsellers, publishing plants, and international real estate holdings—don't blame me!

Just keep asking yourself, as I often do . . .

"Where did I go right?"

Are Any Politicians Listening?

I hope you are, because there are a few observations I want to pass on to you.

As a rational human being, I will spend an amount of time equal to my tax bracket looking for ways to avoid taxes. If my possible maximum tax bracket is 85 percent, then I will be spending 85 percent of my time not on productive activities but on ways to save taxes. The more you raise tax rates, the more time and effort I will spend planning ways to lower my taxes. And if the rates get high enough and the loopholes few enough, I probably won't pay any taxes at all.

So, Mr. Politician, take note: *Increasing tax rates will always eventually yield decreasing tax revenues.*

I have always harped on the fact that America waits a few years to repeat all the mistakes of England. British politicians have assumed for years that their constituents would bear almost limitless taxation. And Britain literally taxed itself to death. The productive classes have largely emigrated to other countries. England experienced double-digit inflation long before we did. And England—which started out with the most conscientious, obedient group of taxpayers in the world—now has an organized subterranean economy of tax dropouts second to none in the world. In England, they call tax evasion "fiddling." And *everybody* fiddles in England. Why don't you cut tax rates by about 75 percent? You might find that the collections and our general level of productivity will go up dramatically!

A Frequently Asked Question . . .

"Dear Bill: At several points in your books and tapes you mention that it is theoretically possible for the wage earner to get a 'refund plus interest' on all taxes paid during the past three years, as well as sheltering all wages and salary income for the next seven years. My accountant says that he never heard of such a provision in the tax code. Could you please, in your famous *baby talk*, explain exactly how to do it, referring to exact sections of the tax code, and exact lines on the tax forms. Thanks a lot."

Answer

Loopholes are never spelled out in the tax code as a simple "how to avoid taxes" instruction statement. It is by combining various code sections that you get the result you want. Here is how to get the three-year refund of taxes:

1. Money spent on repairs and maintenance of property has always been recognized as a deductible expense. Borrowed money has never been classed as taxable income. Thus it is possible to generate deductions without any "out-of-pocket" expenditures.

2. Depreciation allowances have always been recognized as deductions that can be used to shelter cash income whether ordinary, unearned, or capital gain (Internal Revenue Code, Section 167).

3. A combination of deductible expenses and depreciation in excess of taxable income will produce carryovers or carryback losses that, according to the code, may be carried forward seven years or backwards for three years (Internal

---

Revenue Code, Section 172(b) Reg. 1.172-4).

4. These losses are indicated on the front page of your tax return, in the space set aside for "Income." Net losses are shown in parentheses; i.e., *(Loss)*. The summary figure from the front page is calculated on a "schedule," which may be entitled "Business Income and Loss," or "Rents and Royalties," or "Partnership Income and Loss," or "Other Income and Loss." What you title your "schedule" depends on how you want to characterize your participation in the real estate business and if you are combining it with other ventures.

If and when the various deductions exceed your taxable income in a particular category, a (loss) is shown on the front page of your tax return. If your loss from "Rents and Royalties," for instance, is $50,000, and your income from wages has been $10,000 for the past three years (and the current year), you would come up with a total income for this year of "Loss .... ($40,000)."

This $40,000 loss would entitle you to a refund of all taxes paid for the past three years on your $30,000 of income (three years at $10,000 per year). It would also give you another $10,000 loss to be carried forward to the following year.

On the second page of your tax return, in the section marked "Tax Computation," you would show an adjusted gross income of *zero*. Thus no tax would be due.

On the same page, in the section marked "Payments," you would indicate the amounts withheld in the current year, if any, and make a note indicating "$XXX paid in taxes for the past three years."

In the section marked "Refund or Tax Due," you would enter the current year's withholding plus the amount of taxes paid during the past three years. You would also put in a big asterisk, preferably in color, with the notation: "See Form 1045, attached." Form 1045, which you obtain from the I.R.S., is the proper form for explaining to the I.R.S. how you calculated your refund of the prior year's taxes, and requesting a refund. These refunds are normally paid very promptly, with the I.R.S. figuring up the interest due you.

The refund itself is *not* taxable income. The interest is taxable in the year received.

Form **1045**
(Rev. December 1979)
Department of the Treasury
Internal Revenue Service

Application for Tentative Refund

(From Carryback of Net Operating Loss, Unused Investment Credit, Unused
Work Incentive (WIN) Program Credit, Unused Jobs Credit, OR Overpayment of Tax Due to a Claim of Right Adjustment Under Section 1341(b)(1))
▶ For use by taxpayers other than corporations.

Do Not Attach to Your Income Tax Return—File Separately to Expedite Processing

Please type or print

Name	Employer identification number
Number and street	Your social security number
City or town, State and ZIP code	Spouse's social security number

1 Return for year of net operating loss, unused investment credit, unused WIN credit, unused jobs credit, or overpayment under section 1341(b)(1) . . . . . ▶

(a) Tax year ended	(b) Date filed	(c) Service center where filed

2 This application is filed to carryback . ▶

(a) Net operating loss (See instr.—Attach computation)	(b) Unused investment credit	(c) Unused WIN credit	(d) Unused jobs credit
$	$	$	$

3

(a) Preceding tax year(s) affected by carryback	(b) Did spouse file a separate return?	(c) Service center where return(s) filed (City and State)
3d	☐ Yes ☐ No	
2d	☐ Yes ☐ No	
1st	☐ Yes ☐ No	

4 If you changed your accounting period, give date permission to change was granted ▶

5 Have you filed a petition in Tax Court for the year or years to which the carryback is to be applied? . . . . ☐ Yes ☐ No

Computation of Decrease in Tax	3d preceding tax year ended ▶		2d preceding tax year ended ▶		1st preceding tax year ended ▶	
	(a) Before carryback	(b) After carryback	(c) Before carryback	(d) After carryback	(e) Before carryback	(f) After carryback
6 Adjusted gross income as last determined .						
7 Net operating loss deduction resulting from carryback (See Instructions—Attach computation)						
8 Subtract line 7 from line 6						
9 Deductions						
10 Subtract line 9 from line 8						
11 Exemptions						
12 Taxable income (subtract line 11 from 10) .						
13 Income tax						
14 General tax credit						
15 Foreign tax credit						
16 Investment credit (see instruction I) . .						
17 WIN credit (see instruction I)						
18 Jobs credit (see instruction I)						
19 Other credits						
20 Total credits (add lines 14 through 19) . .						
21 Subtract line 20 from line 13						
22 Tax from recomputing prior year investment credit						
23 Minimum tax						
24 Self-employment tax						
25 Other taxes						
26 Total tax liability (add lines 21 through 25) .						
27 Enter amount from line 26 { column (b) .						
column (d) .						
column (f) .						
28 Decrease in tax (subtract line 27 from 26) .						

29 Overpayment of tax due to a claim of right adjustment under section 1341(b)(1)—attach schedule (see instruction J) . . . . . .

Under penalties of perjury, I declare that I have examined this application (including any accompanying schedules and statements), and to the best of my knowledge and belief it is true, correct, and complete.

(Your signature and date)   (If application is filed jointly, both you and your spouse must sign)   (Spouse's signature and date)

c70—313-308-2

Form **1045** (Rev. 12–79)

General Instructions

(Section references are to the Internal Revenue Code unless otherwise specified)

A. Purpose of Form.—An individual, estate or trust must use this form to apply for:

(1) A quick refund of taxes from carryback of a net operating loss, unused investment credit, unused WIN credit, or unused jobs credit.

(2) A quick refund of taxes from an overpayment of tax due to a claim of right adjustment under section 1341(b)(1).

Do not attach Form 1045 to your income tax return.

B. Special Rules.—

Carryback. If you filed a joint return for some, but not all, of the tax*years involved in the carryback, see section 1.172–7 of the regulations before applying the carryback.

You may elect to carry forward a net operating loss instead of first carrying it back by attaching a statement to this effect on a timely filed return (including any extensions) for the year of the loss. Once you make such an election, it is irrevocable for that tax year. The carry forward is limited to 7 years, whether or not a carryback is used first.

C. Time and Place for Filing.—This form must be filed with the Internal Revenue Service Center where your tax return is required to be filed. It must be filed within 1 year after the end of the year in which the net operating loss, unused credit, or claim of right adjustment arose, but only after the return for such year is filed.

If a net operating loss carryback, an investment credit carryback, or a WIN credit carryback eliminates or reduces the investment credit, WIN credit, or jobs credit, that can be applied in a prior year, the unused credit that arises may be carried back 3 additional years. When an unused credit created by the net operating loss, or unused credit affects the taxes of a year or years before the 3 years preceding the loss year, or unused credit year, a second Form 1045 must be used for such year(s). In such case, the second application must also be filed within 1 year after the year of the net operating loss or unused credit. To expedite processing, both Forms 1045 should be filed together.

D. Allowance of Adjustment.—The Internal Revenue Service will act on this application within a period of 90 days from the later of:

(1) The date on which this application is filed; or

(2) The last day of the month in which falls the due date (including any extension of time granted) of the return for the tax year of the net operating loss, unused credit, or claim of right adjustment.

Additional Information.—We may need to contact you (or your authorized representative if you have one) for additional information in order to be able to act on your application within 90 days. If you wish to designate a representative for us to contact (for example your accountant or tax return preparer), please attach a copy of your authorization form to Form 1045. Form 2848 or Form 2848–D may be used for this purpose.

E. Disallowance of Application.—The Internal Revenue Service may disallow any application which contains material omissions, or errors of computation which it deems cannot be corrected by it within the 90-day period. This application for a tentative carryback adjustment is not a claim for credit or refund. If it is disallowed in whole or in part, no suit may be brought in any court for the recovery of that tax. You may, however, file a claim for refund before the expiration of the period of limitation, as explained in instruction G.

F. Assessment of Erroneous Allowances.—Any amount applied, credited, or refunded on the basis of this application which is later determined by the Internal Revenue Service to be excessive may be assessed as a deficiency as if it were due to a mathematical or clerical error appearing on the return.

G. Form 1040X (or other Amended Return.)—If you are an individual, you may obtain a refund by filing Form 1040X. An estate, trust, or fiduciary may file an amended return. Generally, Form 1040X (or amended return) must be filed within 3 years after the due date of the return for the tax year of the net operating loss or unused credit.

In filing a Form 1040X or an amended return, show a computation of the net operating loss deduction. A separate form must be completed for each year you request an adjustment.

H. Supporting Data and Explanatory Material.—In addition to supplying the information called for on page 1 of this form, you must submit with this application, all adjustments required to compute a net operating loss which is carried back to any prior year.

I. Carryback of Unused Investment Credit, Unused WIN Credit, or Unused Jobs Credit.—If you claim a tentative carryback adjustment based on the carryback of any of these credits, attach (1) a detailed schedule showing the computation of the credit carryback and (2) a recomputation of the credit after application of the carryback. Make the recomputation on the appropriate credit form (or on an attachment which follows the format of such form) for the tax year of the tentative allowance.

If the refund is only from a credit carryback, skip lines 6 through 12 when figuring the decrease in tax on page 1.

J. Overpayment of Tax Under Section 1341(b)(1).—If you apply for a tentative refund based on an overpayment of tax under section 1341(b)(1), enter it on Form 1045, line 29. In addition, attach a computation which shows the following:

(1) The tax for the tax year without the deduction described in section 1341(a)(2).

(2) The tax for all prior tax years for which a decrease in tax is figured under section 1341(a)(5)(B).

(3) The decrease in tax for each prior tax year figured under section 1341(a)(5)(B), including any decrease resulting from a net operating loss described in section 1341(b)(4)(B).

(4) The decrease in tax under section 1341(a)(5)(B) treated as an overpayment of tax under section 1341(b)(1).

K. Computation of Net Operating Loss.—Your net operating loss is figured the same as your taxable income except that:

(1) You may not deduct a net operating loss carryover or carryback from any year.

(2) Your capital losses cannot be more than your capital gains. Your nonbusiness capital losses may not be more than nonbusiness capital gains, even though your business capital gains are more than your business capital losses. See section 1.172–3(a)(2) of the regulations.

(3) You may not take any deduction for the excess of a net long-term capital gain over a net short-term capital loss.

(4) You may not claim any personal exemptions or exemptions for dependents.

(5) Your nonbusiness deductions may not be more than your nonbusiness income.

(6) Your "zero bracket amount" for 1979 and subsequent years is $3,400 if married filing joint return or qualifying widow(er) with dependent child, $2,300 if single or head of household, or $1,700 if married filing separately. This is allowed as a nonbusiness deduction in figuring a net operating loss if the election to itemize deductions has not been made. Itemized deductions, if elected, are usually nonbusiness also, but may include some business deductions.

Salaries and wages you received are trade or business income.

Gain or loss on sale or other disposition of real or depreciable property used in your trade or business is to be taken into account fully in figuring a net operating loss without regard to the limitation on nonbusiness deductions.

Loss on the sale of accounts receivable, if such accounts arose under the accrual method of accounting in your business, is included in figuring your net operating loss as a business deduction.

Casualty losses and theft losses are considered attributable to your trade or business. This is true even if it involves nonbusiness property.

A partnership is not allowed to claim a net operating loss deduction, but as a partner you may use your proportionate share of the partnership's loss in figuring your individual net operating loss.

Losses on stocks in small business corporations which qualify as ordinary losses are business losses and allowable in figuring the net operating loss.

Shareholders of an electing small business corporation (Subchapter S) may treat their allowable pro rata share of the corporation's net operating loss as a business loss in figuring their individual net operating loss. Any share of the income or gain, other than salaries, from a subchapter S corporation is treated as nonbusiness income or gain.

Loss resulting from the sale or exchange of small business investment company stock which qualifies as an ordinary loss, is considered as a loss attributable to your trade or business and is allowable in figuring your net operating loss.

c70—313–308–1

69

4.
Tax
Avoidance
Is Legal

Tax avoidance is the lowering of your tax bill by what you in good faith believe to be legal means. Almost anything except hiding income or inventing deductions is legal if you are making an effort to abide by the tax code as you understand it. The regulations and cases interpreting the tax code are so long and complex that there are a thousand ways to interpret them. This chapter is not about illegal means of not paying taxes, called *tax evasion*. It is only about legal methods, or at least quasi-legal tax avoidance techniques that some courts have approved. Where there is judicial disagreement (cases going both ways) or where your tax avoidance is thought to be "questionable" by the I.R.S., you can not be criminally prosecuted. The I.R.S. in rare cases will attempt to collect the back taxes for up to three years after the date you filed your return. They have seven years to prosecute for tax fraud.

Before we go on to discuss legal tax avoidance, let's focus

on how the I.R.S. sometimes catches people guilty of crimi nally *evading* taxes. The most common way they get convictions is with an informer. Informers are almost always ex-employees or ex-lovers. Without an informer, the I.R.S. has only two ways to proceed against a taxpayer they suspect of tax fraud. Both are exceedingly difficult for them to prove.

The first is the net worth test. The government tries to show that the taxpayer started out broke (or with X dollars) in a certain year; that he received no gifts or other tax-free assets; or that he paid little or no income taxes. Then they try to prove that as of a certain later date the taxpayer owned assets (bank accounts, stocks, and property) worth, say $10 million. It then becomes the taxpayer's responsibility to prove how this wealth came to be accumulated without a tax being due. The usual defense is to prove that he had money or assets at the start. Or perhaps that he borrowed money and still owes it. Perhaps small investments have appreciated dramatically and are now worth $10 million, and the investments, not having been sold, are tax exempt until they are sold.

Another I.R.S. method of nabbing tax evaders is to show a lot of unexplained deposits in bank accounts, unexplained cash used for investments, or a lot of consumer-type expenses, or other expenditures—the total far exceeding reported income. It then is up to the taxpayer to show where the money came from to support all these expenditures. The defense could be savings, gifts, inheritances, or many other things. If *you* are planning to avoid run-ins with the I.R.S. there are obvious rules to follow.

First, don't allow anyone, including and especially spouses, lovers, and employees, to know you are intentionally doing anything questionable.

Be able to provide the I.R.S. with proof (or a convincing story) of where you got the money you didn't pay any tax on. If you are going to be a big spender of untaxed money, do it discreetly and in cash, not by check or credit card. Spending $100,000 on a new custom-made Ferrari or Rolls Royce Corniche would be a big mistake, because the high cost is obvious. Flaunting wealth is certainly not discreet. High visibility and envy invite the I.R.S. to investigate your affairs.

The same rule (keeping a low profile and being discreet) applies even if you are an avoider—not an evader. In the present-day world, the consequences of being criminally accused or investigated, even if you haven't done anything wrong, are nearly as unpleasant as a trial or conviction for tax evasion. If an I.R.S. special agent starts an investigation and begins riding and raiding you and your business associates, they can quickly put you out of business. Government pressure can cause you to be shunned by lenders and friends. The I.R.S. can tie up your bank accounts, tie up all your time with questioning and demands for old records, and drive you to drink. Worst of all, there is no recourse against the government for wrongful investigation or prosecution. They may cause banks to cut off your credit, cost you thousands in attorney's fees, and merely by their investigation and harassment hound you into bankruptcy. They may arrest you and hold you in jail—but when the ordeal is all over and you are acquitted, you have no right to recover costs, damages, or anything else from the I.R.S. This is true even if the particular special agents involved were dead wrong. There is no recourse even if they knew they were dead wrong but were just out to harass you for personal reasons. Thus, the best advice I can give you is to keep a low *profile* and don't do anything to raise a red flag or antagonize the I.R.S. if at all possible. You may remember the picture of the Czechoslovakian youths throwing rocks at the Russian tanks in the 1968 rebellion there. Well, if you don't want to be like the Czechs, fighting heavy artillery with your bare hands, keep a low profile. With that advice, I'll show you how to beat the tax man discreetly.

Certain categories of income or cash flow are, by I.R.S. definition, *not income*. If you can arrange for money coming your way to be designated as tax-free receipts, *you don't have to report it on your tax return at all*. Nontaxable, nonreport-

You can't fight heavy artillery with your bare hands,
but this book ought to give you a few Molotov cocktails.

able receipts include gifts to you of up to $3,000 per year
from any one individual. The obvious gimmick is that if an
individual wants to give you a tax-free gift of more than
$3,000, he or she should give the amount over $3,000 to a
third party and suggest that the third party give it to you.
This could be as simple as your father and mother each giving you a tax-free $3,000 instead of your father giving you a
taxable $6,000.

Inheritances can also be tax free. The Feds tax the estate
but not the recipient. Some states tax the recipient. The
gimmick there is to try and arrange your inheritances from
non-U.S. relatives and live in a state like Nevada or Florida
that has no state inheritance tax. If you could do that, there
would be no tax at all on your inheritance. Your rich uncle
just has to move to the Bahamas or any other tax haven before he dies. You must move to a domestic or foreign tax
haven before you inherit.

Annuities are (with minor limitations) tax free. One

gimmick involving annuities would be to pay, say, $100,000 in cash to a Swiss insurance company that pays you an 8 percent annuity in Swiss francs. As the annuity goes up to $16,000 or $20,000 per year, due to the increased value of the Swiss francs, your annuity still remains largely tax free to you.

Pensions and Social Security benefits are tax free. Gimmick? Early retirement or a cozy arrangement with your employer, who could be a closely held company you've set up yourself to provide for your early retirement.

Welfare, unemployment compensation, and sick pay is tax free. What can you do? Don't be too quick to go back to work, because your after-tax earned income may be a lot less than tax-free welfare, unemployment, or sick pay benefits.

Military and veterans benefits are tax free. That doesn't do you much good if you weren't in the military, but if you

Don't be in too much of a hurry to get back to work,
Sick pay is generally tax free!

were, fight for every dime. It will have double value because of the tax-free feature. Consider joining the National Guard or Navy Reserves. Once you get some rank, the pay and benefits are probably a lot greater than you think. Besides tax-free cash allowances, P.X.-subsidized merchandise, free food, untaxed liquor, an enormous pension, and free medical care, you get to play with million-dollar toys like jet fighters and to hop free military transport planes to exotic places—all tax free.

Workmen's compensation and most lawsuit damage recoveries or settlements are tax free. (I've got a long story on this coming up later.) Same tax-free treatment with academic scholarships and fellowships.

If you live abroad, you can earn up to $25,000 tax free, and as of 1981, President Regan said he would raise that to $50,000. Funny thing is, if you change your citizenship to something other than American, you can live in the United States for up to six months a year, earn fifty billion a year, and pay no U.S.A. taxes. Details to follow: I'll tell you about the "three-flag theory," which will show you how to become a tax-exempt "foreigner" for tax purposes.

Then there's good old welfare, food stamps, and other government giveaways that are the main cause of the high taxes we are trying to avoid. They are all tax free to the recipient. So you just have to get on the receiving end of Uncle Sam's largesse—not the paying end.

Also tax free are reimbursements from your employer for all job-related expenses. These include the three-martini lunch, the convention in Paris, and the delightful secretary you employ to sit on your lap. All tax free. There is lots of room for creativity with the business expense account.

Gambling gains are tax free up to the amount of your losses. You can deduct reasonable expenses in perfecting your game and getting to and from the casino if you list "gambler" as a profession on your tax return. Borrowed money is always tax-free. Bond interest received on city, state, and county bonds is nontaxable and nonreportable.

Money that comes your way, but that you don't actually get control of, is often tax free. This would include an escrow deposit in your name that you can't take out for a certain period of time. That brings up the "incomplete transaction doctrine." You get a commission but the understanding is that you may have to return it if the deal falls through. The money so received can usually be considered an advance or loan, which is always tax free, until it is finally yours without strings.

Return of capital is not taxable. Example: You put up money to help Cousin Adrian start a cosmetic-importing business. The first money you receive from Adrian should be structured as return of investment or repayment of loan. That's tax free. When you put money into mining, oil, or gas production deals, a part of what you get back is sheltered by the depletion allowance. It ranges from 5 percent to 22 percent. That percentage is considered a tax-free return of capital. The same sort of thing happens in many types of real estate investments where the return of your investment and even your profit is sheltered by depreciation.

Another tax shelter device is the reserve for losses or bad debts. If you go into any business that has risk, you might be better off accounting for that particular business on the "accrual" basis, which means that the cash you take in or pay out is irrelevant to your tax obligations. The "accrual method of accounting" allows you to take profits at the time you send out a bill or to deduct expenses when you incur liabilities. Depending on the type of business you are in, the accrual system could be a real tax saver. For example, in a small loan business, retailing, or an insurance venture, you could take out millions in cash but have it all sheltered by deducting not-yet-paid expenses or setting up bad debt reserves.

Certain prizes and awards are tax free. Suppose you were awarded the $50,000 Nobel Prize—that would be tax free. So are scholarships, fellowships, government, and most private research grants. Medical care, group life insurance, or educational benefits provided as a fringe benefit by your employer or your own personal corporation is a legitimate and common tax-free "perk." Dividends or interest payable to you in forms other than dollars—for example, a stock dividend, will be tax free, as may interest on your foreign bank account. (More details coming up on this overlooked loophole.)

Finally, there is what you gain through barter transactions. Whole clubs have been set up to help you eat, sleep, vacation, and have all your needs met tax free.

So far I've given you all the tax-free income or benefits I can think of. If you have any more, please let me know. Our Founding Fathers were part of a taxpayers' revolt against England. Today our own unresponsive government has levied taxes far more oppressive than England levied on the colonies. If you are reading this book, you're a member of the new tax-rebel movement. Let's hang together. I have a series of live and taped lectures and a newsletter on how to make money and save taxes. To get on my mailing list, drop me your tip with a self-addressed stamped envelope (SASE). If I use your ideas, I'll put a smile on your face with a swell present. As Ben Franklin said, "We can either hang together, or we'll hang separately." So share your thoughts with me.

Having talked about tax-free income or the equivalent, I'm now going to the other side of the coin—deductions, sometimes called *write-offs*. There are some deductions you can use to offset your taxable income. If you can find enough deductions to totally cancel out your current year's income, you pay no income tax at all. You can also carry back losses for up to three prior years. That allows you to get a 100 percent refund of taxes you paid in the past, plus interest. If you've gone back three years and still haven't offset all your income, you can carry deductions forward to offset income in future years.

What are these deductions? If you have your own business, trade, or profession you can deduct all *ordinary and necessary business expenses*. Who decides what's ordinary and necessary? *You do.* You can deduct depletion and depreciation allowances in excess of the return that an oil well, mine, or real estate investment gives you. Often these create "overflow deductions" that shelter your wage or "earned income." This overflow depreciation or depletion is said to "shelter" your other income, and that's why so many investments are called *tax shelters*.

You can deduct losses caused by thefts, acts of God, vandalism, and disasters, even if you do not spend money to replace or repair the damage. You can deduct bad debts, business losses, charitable cash contributions, interest on borrowed money, all business expenses, political contributions, and alimony. Here's one you might not have thought of: the appreciated value of charitable contributions. Example: You bought a watercolor for $50. You give it to your local museum, and they value it at $1,000. The $950 deduction you get could be worth far more to you than the cash you'd get by selling the artwork. The same appreciation in value could be present in the furniture or old clothes you give to charity. Libraries, museums, and charities all are very accommodating in setting relatively high values on donations. According to *The Wall Street Journal*, as of May 1980 even in blatant cases the I.R.S. had never prosecuted a single art donor for tax evasion.

Biggest of all deductions are the special tax incentives the government gives you for doing—or not doing—things. There are a million government rebate or credit programs. One is the investment tax credit. If you buy a new Mercedes Benz or any capital asset for use in your business, you can borrow the entire $30,000 cost and without spending a dime get a *tax credit* of $3,000. Tax credits are a lot better than mere deductions. You can use a tax credit exactly as if it was a cash I.O.U. from the government. You deduct the credit in full from any tax that may be due. A deduction merely reduces income. Thus, a $100 deduction is usually worth only half as much as a $100 tax credit.

A few years back, if you bought a new house, even with all borrowed money, you got up to a $2,000 tax credit. In 1978, if you hired a new employee you got a tax credit of half his or her wages. Childcare expenses result in tax credits. Keep your eyes and ears open for the latest government giveaway or tax credit program. See if what you were going to do anyway gives you a tax break. If not, consider modifying your planned activities to qualify for tax credits, special deductions, or tax-free benefits.

The latest giveaway is an extra-fast write-off on "historic" structures. Besides actual "historic" buildings, everything built before last week in a designated "historical area" stands a chance of being considered a historic structure.

That covers the outline of deductions and credits. Remember, if you think of anything else, drop me a line. If it's something I haven't heard of, I'll send you a present that will put a smile on your face.

Now I'll talk a little about tax deferral. These techniques do not technically eliminate taxes, but they allow you to defer taxes into the distant future. In real estate, the most important deferral is accomplished by trading up or exchanging, pursuant to Section 1031 of the Internal Revenue Code. It is such an important subject that one whole chapter in this book is devoted to just that. Briefly, trading up allows you to sell real or personal property that has appreciated; if you do the paperwork right, to use the entire value of the sold asset as the down payment on a bigger and better similar property without any tax consequences.

Then there are depreciation reserves for bad debts and the use of nonrecourse loans in real estate deals. With most tax deferral schemes, if you defer taxes till you die you've beaten the I.R.S. because your heirs will probably be allowed to take over your assets, with the I.R.S. totally disregarding cost or depreciation previously taken. The law is in a state of flux now, but at least for the moment I believe it is possible to use depreciation to defer taxes till your death, and pass appreciated property to your heirs free of capital gains taxes.

Can you get into trouble by deferring taxes? *Yes!* If a property you have depreciated goes into foreclosure, the I.R.S. will try to treat the situation as a "sale" at the foreclosure price. As a result, when you're short of money and segments of your real estate empire begin to collapse, you may generate what tax lawyers call "phantom income." Depreciation and loans you took out in earlier years become "taxable income." You may be going broke, and just when you don't need further aggravation the I.R.S. demands its pound of flesh. To understand this "phantom income" concept, let's look at the following example.

Many years ago, you bought the Lakeview Apartments for $10,000. You depreciated the property down to $1,000. As the property got more valuable, you were able to refinance for $50,000. You spent the money on high living. Now times are tough. Your bank foreclosed and took the property back for the unpaid $50,000 debt. You gave them a deed to avoid a deficiency judgment. The I.R.S. comes to you during the following year and says the forgiving of the $50,000 debt constitutes $50,000 in taxable "phantom income" now that you have "sold" the property. Not only that, the I.R.S. might claim that, since there was a "sale" at $50,000, you also owe tax on a capital gain of $40,000. Result? The I.R.S. says you owe a tax on $9,000 (recapture of depreciation), $50,000 (forgiveness of debt), and $40,000 (capital gain). The tax on those items could be as high as $50,000. If you had had $50,000 cash lying about in the first place, you'd have paid the loan off and not let it go into default. Thus "phantom income" is triggered by the foreclosure or involuntary sale of appreciated property.

Finally, our last general category of tax-avoiding maneuvers involves using or taking someone else's deductions or shifting to someone else your income. This is a delicate situation in many instances and, unless done exactly right, could result in your scheme being disallowed by the I.R.S. One common and legal method of shifting income is by giving your spouse or children stocks, bank accounts or income property, either outright or in a 10-year "Clifford" trust. The kids then get the income and report it on their tax returns. If your two-year-old daughter has a total income of under

$3,500 (or whatever the minimum currently required is), the child is not required to pay a tax on the income you've transferred.

It's also possible to transfer your income to corporations that you own, foundations you set up, a church or other non-profit corporation controlled by you, or foreign entities. It's also possible to channel income that might have come your way to deserving friends, dependents, or a spouse who is in a lower tax bracket or has excess tax shelter.

That gives you an outline of what I'll be talking about next in more detail.

Before going into that detail on how to beat the taxman, let's bring the whole subject of tax avoidance, or tax planning, into proper focus. Who needs the tax advice in a book like this?

Low-income people need these techniques more than high-income people because low-income people are on a taxation/consumption treadmill that keeps them from building assets to the point where they have any financial freedom. High-income people need shelter because they are on a similar treadmill. Although their incomes may be much bigger, their taxes are a much higher proportion of that income. To keep that high-paying job, appearances must be maintained, so expenses are higher. Neither rich nor poor can save much today. So I'm going to show both the $10,000-a-year man and the $1,000,000-a-year man how to scheme a little and hold on to more of that hard-earned money so that it can be used more effectively than it is by the politicians, who just throw it down bottomless pits.

Marilyn Monroe, after a decade as one of the world's most famous movie stars, left an estate of under $300,000. Even adjusted for inflation, this amounts to far less net worth than what can be accumulated by one of my average Tycoon Class graduates in a few years. Monroe paid tremendous income taxes. I'm not exactly original when I say it's not what you make, but what you keep that counts. When you're old and flabby and nobody needs you as a sex symbol—or anything else—a few good investments will be a great comfort. As Mae West said, "I've been rich and I've been poor, and rich is better." The truth of the matter is that the vast majority of older retired people—even those who earned huge incomes in their prime—don't manage very well as senior citizens. Most are broke. They subsist in retirement city rooming houses. Too often the only thing going for them is a Social Security check. That pays for four walls, bath down the hall, and meals of dog food. Poverty is easy to avoid if you start saving on taxes and put those savings into good investments.

Before going any further, I have a special message for fanatics on the subject of tax avoidance. If you are like me, you want to make a big game of beating the system by registering a "paper" loss every year. You'll go miles out of your way to pay no taxes. You even have lots of philosophical justification. Your script goes something like Ayn Rand's hero said in *Atlas Shrugged:* The more power politicians have to tax you or to jail you, the less freedom you have. If the politicians have the power to put innocent people in jail, they can control every aspect of your life. But the politicians (read *government*) already have the power to take all your money and to put you in jail if you become a threat by being too visible or by talking too much. The government has already made so many things a crime that it has become impossible to live without breaking laws. The reason there are so many laws is that the government needs a nation of lawbreakers. It needs laws that are so abundant and so contradictory that they can't be observed, enforced, or objectively interpreted. That way, government can select you (or anyone) as an object lesson and break you. Then government can justify and perpetuate itself, its power based on guilt and fear!

American tax laws are a great example of this. No one can earn any money outside of a deducted-at-the source wage slave job without running the theoretical risk of going to jail for a tax fraud. Why is this? Aren't there rules to the tax game that will keep you out of jail if you stick to the rules? The

If they don't see you, they won't harass you. Nothing will keep you out of trouble better than a low profile.

answer is yes and no. If you keep a low profile and never incur the wrath of government agents, as a practical matter the odds are that you can cheat your heart out, and there is less than a 10 million-to-1 chance you'd ever go to prison for it. But if for some reason the government wants to "make an example of you," then, with their unlimited resources, they could probably convict 98 percent of all taxpayers for the crime of tax fraud. The reason for this is that the laws are so voluminous and complex that it is impossible to live without breaking at least some of them. Further, there is the general principle that if you have the *intent* to pay less (or *more*) taxes than you "should," this can be interpreted as a criminal intent to defraud. As a result, any minor error on a tax return, even an overpayment of $2, is a technical criminal violation. What many people do not know is that even an intentional *overpayment* can be considered a crime. The result of all this is that sophisticated criminals and tax avoiders are always busy manufacturing evidence of their noncriminal non-tax-avoiding intent.

Tax avoidance is the structuring of financial transactions to lower income or increase expenses in such a way that it appears your intentions in a given deal were purely profit oriented and that you had no knowledge of or interest in tax considerations. If you made a deal "just" to save taxes, the transaction will be disallowed. "Structuring financial transactions" or "casting the deal in its most tax advantageous light" are tax lawyer euphemisms for manufacturing evidence to show that your intention to avoid taxes was not what it really was. Realize this: The Great Truth is that the multibillion-dollar tax-planning and tax shelter investment industry, employing millions of lawyers and accountants, is daily forced to engage in a colossal fraud. By reading this book and using some of the ideas or investing in any *tax shelter*, you become a part of that oppressive system, giving the government power over you. But don't let it get you down. At least you'll probably get rich. And if you're very rich, you can always leave the country.

My more sensible friends play the game like this. They go out of their way to create a tax return in which some small tax is usually due and paid. What is small? Between 1 and 5 percent of your adjusted gross income. They also save up and do not report at least one well-documented loss or deduction that would totally cancel out the minimal tax they have paid. If and when they are ever called in for audit, they open the interview by exhibiting documents to support and prove up a loss they "forgot" about. The apparent overpayment of taxes never ceases to have a disconcerting effect on the enemy, and, with you having won something with the first salvo, the agent may wonder if it was a good idea to bring you in at all.

Well, that's one point of view. I prefer to structure my affairs so that my "paper losses" *exceed* my income each and every year. But do it quietly! Don't go on television. The I.R.S. got on my case a few weeks after I was written up in the local papers for giving tax avoidance seminars on my front lawn. I had not paid any taxes for many years—and in all those years I had nothing but friendly cursory audits. Only when I exercised my constitutional right of freedom of speech did the government retaliate. So, unless you want grief, don't be a pioneer. Don't be the cutting edge of social change! Leave that to me and other fools like me. Reformers are driven by irrational impulses to do what's right and change the world for the better. Czar Alexander of Russia had the situation sized up correctly when in the late nineteenth century he said, "Show me a 19-year-old without radical idealism, and I'll show you someone without a heart. But show me a 40-year-old who hasn't stopped trying to change the world, and I'll show you someone without a brain."

Sometimes I wonder if it was smart of me to get into public speaking and writing on tax avoidance. Until recently, the I.R.S. had two special agents who did nothing but check out all my deals. It took me half an hour to make a deal and

Once I made a real estate deal in half an hour. It took three I.R.S. agents two full days to figure out the tax implications and challenge my accounting. They were wrong.

took them two days at the taxpayers' expense to figure out what I did. Then, when they tried to nail me, I had to spend a fortune on lawyers and accountants to keep me out of trouble. So far, I've won every encounter with the I.R.S. But those darn I.R.S. agents wouldn't have come around at all if I hadn't gotten this high profile. I guess I'm the 40-year-old without a brain that the Czar was talking about.

Take my advice, be a *closet* tax rebel. It's cheaper! The I.R.S. can be a tough adversary. Don't invite conflict with them!

Getting Your Team Together

In the tax avoidance game, two different taxpayers may make the same moves. Both might be selected for a detailed audit. Both may be accused of tax fraud. Ultimately one may be commended by a judge for his ingenuity and be given a hefty award against the I.R.S. for costs and expenses. The other (although this would rarely happen) might be fined or even sent to jail for doing the same thing. Why does this happen every day in a country where all people are supposed to be equal before the law?

The answer is one of the two had good representation. A top-notch tax lawyer or Certified Public Accountant can take whatever you did and present it to the I.R.S. (or if worst comes to worst, a jury) and make you seem as pure as the driven snow.

Few Tax Offenders with Good Lawyers
Ever Get to Trial

Without good representation, the I.R.S. with its unlimited, and sometimes unsavory, methods can often get a conviction. The tax code is vague and contradictory. All tax "crimes" are so dependent on your "secret intent" that if you don't have a good lawyer you can be accused, railroaded, and convicted so fast you won't know what hit you. Top business

executives who can afford good counsel are rarely punished for tax offenses. The I.R.S. follows the very sensible admonition of Lenin for battles with capitalists: "Probe with a bayonet. If you feel fat, push; if you hit steel, pull back."

A good lawyer and accountant will be your steel. You need them as a buffer. Before you do *anything* in this book (even if you *are* a lawyer or accountant), run the idea by another creative accountant or lawyer. Every tax avoidance scheme must be hand-tailored to fit your own particular situation and the degree of risk you feel comfortable with. Creative thinking on the part of your tax specialist may be stimulated by the ideas you get in this book, but, whatever you do, you need good advice. Don't make a move without clearing it with your "team." In the American legal system, the fact that you relied on the advice of a licensed professional should be a complete defense to any charge of tax fraud.

How to Find a Good (Cheap) Lawyer or Accountant

At my tax lectures and in the letters I get from readers, this is probably the most frequently asked question. If the truth were known, most lawyers are irresponsible incompetents. And because of the changing of the tax law from year to year, most accountants—five years out of school—have no more idea of what is going on "out there" anymore than you did before you read this book. How do I know this? I studied accounting at the Wharton School of Finance and many of my friends from those days are C.P.A.s today.

Old school chums discuss things among themselves that clients must never know. And what clients don't know is that *they must supply the tax-saving ideas themselves.* All an accountant can do is to provide record-keeping services—after the facts are in. Very few accountants suggest tax shelters and exciting tax avoidance gimmicks to clients. Why should they? There is no incentive. They get their $50 per hour for keeping the books. If they recommend a move that doesn't work out for the client, they get wrath and anger—and if they make a good suggestion that saves the client thousands of dollars they don't get paid any contingency fees.

After Wharton, I went to the John Marshall Law School and a few other places where I eventually picked up a law degree and was admitted to the bar in two states. As a beginning lawyer, I worked for established practitioners, and what I saw was shocking. Lawyers, in general, literally didn't know what they were doing. They didn't know the law or bother to research it thoroughly before their case came up. They failed to file cases or documents on time (thereby losing a case for their client) but told the client a cock-and-bull story—and charged the client for their bumbling. The client usually didn't know what went wrong, and in rare instances where he found out, other lawyers refused to sue a "brother" for malpractice.

As a young lawyer, I went before a number of judges (who are only lawyers who, because of political activities, are elected or appointed to decide cases). With few exceptions, the motivation of the judge was *expediency,* not *justice.* In all fairness, with a backlog of four to six years of cases, maybe expediency *has* to come before justice. But in any event, I seldom found any judges at the trial level who were willing to put any intellectual depth (if they had any) into a decision. It was just "Decide in favor of the lawyer who made the least mistakes and took up the minimum of the court's time." The reason I gave up practicing law—before I came to California—was that in every single winning case in my experience, I felt deep down I should have lost, if justice were done. And, as you might expect, I was even more upset by the fact that every single case I felt strongly about—every case where an important principle of justice was involved—I *lost* the case on a fluke of technicality.

The moral I want you to draw from this—and it has nothing to do with taxes—is that lawsuits are like *wars.* They cost a lot of money, waste a lot of time, and when the smoke clears, almost always both sides have lost far more than if there had been a settlement at the beginning. The people who profit most by lawsuits, besides lawyers, are the next biggest winners—criminals, swindlers, thieves, deadbeats, and tax cheaters. Defendants who are sued often find it a smart move to hire a lawyer who specializes in continuances and delays. Normally, *any case* can be won by a defendant who will drag it on and appeal the hell out of it until the other side is worn out or financially exhausted. In tax cases particularly, the government—who is usually the plaintiff—tends to stay on top of a case, but a determined defendant can usually get a favorable decision by fighting every step with procedural matters—continuing, appealing, and outmaneuvering the government. As the years go by, due to high turnover in government staff, new employees take over old cases. They are usually more interested in pursuing fresh matters that they have initiated. If the government fails to move or file papers at the proper time, the statutes of limitation run out and a case cannot be filed. Or, if a filed matter has been dormant long enough, your lawyer can claim "*laches.*" That is a legal word meaning that the other side has been dragging its feet and for that reason the case against you is so old that it can't be properly defended anymore, and should be dismissed.

As to accountants, my own accountant a couple of years ago had all of the papers necessary to file my income tax return on time—but didn't. He filed seven months later. As a result, I am still fighting with the I.R.S. over penalties that they insist are due for the late filing. When I fired the accountant and threatened to punch him in the nose, he had this answer for me: "I am so overworked that I didn't have time to file my own tax returns for the past three years!"

One more little thing that isn't generally known to the man or woman on the street: Suppose you are considering doing something really nasty or illegal. Or perhaps you have already done it. Can you be honest and spill the beans to your own lawyer or accountant? The answer is simple. To your lawyer, yes. To your accountant, no. Reason? If you tell your lawyer "What I am about to tell you is in confidence," he is bound by the code of his profession not to reveal that information. I wouldn't count on it, but if he *ever* reveals a confidence in a court proceeding he has violated your right to give your own lawyer privileged information. That information cannot be used against you in any court proceeding. The same is true of documents, letters, or objects entrusted to your lawyer. They cannot be obtained by court procedure with rare exceptions such as murder weapons or bags of heroin.

The rules for accountants are entirely different. An accountant must produce all papers relating to your case, and he can be forced to answer, under oath, questions such as the location and number of your secret foreign bank accounts.

To summarize: About the only person on earth you can confide in and not have it used against you is your lawyer. No other person, including your clergyman or confessor, has this privilege.

So what does this all mean to you? Basically you can't and shouldn't trust lawyers, accountants, and for that matter most licensed professionals. As a sidelight, for years I had a girlfriend who was a physician. Over and over again I told her of professional incompetence I kept running into in business. The answer she usually gave me was "If you think *that's* bad, let me tell you what So-and-So did at the hospital today." Her horror stories were even worse than mine. To this day, I stay away as long as I can from any treatment that goes on when I am not awake to ask questions. And I ask questions at every stage of any medical treatment. What is needed? What are my alternatives? What could happen if this or that goes wrong? If a doctor tells me something like "It's too technical, you wouldn't understand . . ." I tell him that if I don't understand, he isn't going to do it. If my "professional" doesn't want to explain things to me in "baby talk" that I can understand, I want another doctor.

You should be the same way with your lawyer or accountant. Ask for your alternatives and options. Explore: "What if this happens or that happens?" What are the risks to you? Particularly with lawyers, get copies for your own file of every paper filed on your behalf, and every document filed by the other side. They are in English, after all, and you should be able to read and understand them. If you can't, ask more questions.

But I still haven't covered how to *find* yourself good professional representation. Let me tell you, it's difficult. If faced with a specific problem, as I was when the I.R.S. was out to get me, I simply asked the Department of Justice prosecutor the names of his two immediate predecessors. Then I made an appointment with them (one was in a different government job and another was in private practice) and asked for the names of the best defense counsel. Eventually I was put in touch with another former district attorney who has represented me well ever since. In accounting, I looked for the best hard-nosed, mean, son-of-a-bitch I.R.S. agent who was now in private practice. I figured he'd be the best person to represent me against his own kind. When I was the defendant in a divorce proceeding, I asked several "divorce lawyers" who was the toughest, most unyielding opponent they'd ever had.

It turned out to be a real snarling bitch of a woman lawyer whom I hired. I was thankful I did because she knew and used every dirty trick in the book. It was a delight to have that despicable person on my side instead of against me.

Now the title of this chapter was how to find a good (cheap) lawyer or accountant. I've told you how to find a goodie—but how do you find a cheapie? *The most important thing to remember is that incompetence is not cheap at any price.* Would you want open-heart surgery at $2,999 from a bumbling idiot with a *zero* success rate, or would you spend every dime you had on the best in the business? Get the best, and forget the price, and you will have the lowest-cost representation in the long run.

For ordinary run-of-the-mill work that is not too important, you can rely on social connections, chance meetings, lawyer referral services, or the accounting equivalent. But for important stuff, do a little research and seek out the best. Having excellent representation in accounting or lawyers may *by itself* intimidate the other side so much that they cave in. I can make a few recommendations for people in the San Francisco area, but outside of my home base I'm afraid you're on your own.

One more thing. In legal matters, the best lawyers can't do much for you if you have a lousy case. To keep your affairs in order, these are the most important three rules to win lawsuits:

Get it in writing.
Get it in writing.
GET IT IN WRITING.

If the other side refuses to put it in writing, send what lawyers call a confirming letter:

Dear *Deadbeat:*
This will confirm our conversion of *2 PM* at your home on *123 Cedric Drive, Brentwood,* where my assistant *Alice* was present. You will deliver the *seven ceramic spark plugs* by next *Tuesday,* and failing that, you will pay me *$7,000.*

If this is not your understanding, please let me know at once, by letter.

If this is your understanding, please sign and return the enclosed copy of this letter.

Sincerely,
Paul Potential Plaintiff

Judges love confirming letters because it gives them something clear and in writing to look at and ascertain the "facts." Every letter you write, you should realize, is potential evidence in a lawsuit. Accordingly, foul language, threats, or anything that could put you in a bad light should be avoided. Anything the other side does that puts them in a bad light should be saved and commented on in your letters to them.

For your accountant, always save or keep records of all receipts or expenditures. When you make a bank deposit, always keep a record of the *source* of the funds that you have deposited. Unless you can prove that it was a gift, transfer from another account, or other nontaxable item, the I.R.S. can say it was taxable income.

Now go out and *win.*

5.
The
Gray
Area

This chapter is about the gray area—situations where, if the I.R.S. took a close look, it could challenge the way you handled things. The odds are that it will never take a close look at you if you file an average-looking return. American audit and enforcement procedures are like a lottery. In the United States, you are "on your honor" to prepare and file an accurate return. All returns are theoretically checked for mathematical accuracy. If an arithmetic error is found, a refund check or bill is sent to you. Otherwise your tax return is accepted as filed.

    Some tax returns are selected for a detailed audit at random. To determine who gets special scrutiny or an audit, a group of Social Security numbers are pulled from a hat and these (unlucky few) taxpayers get a thorough going over. Your chances of getting such an audit in your lifetime are about the same as winning the Irish Sweepstakes. Aside from this random selection, other returns are culled for special scrutiny only if the taxpayer has been specially targeted for prosecution.

Targets are selected because of an extremely unusual return or informer's tips, or because a certain occupational category has been chosen for the hot seat. The government may want to get publicity by going after tax avoidance authors, prominent Republicans, or dope lawyers. The theory is that selective enforcement, plus a lot of I.R.S.-generated publicity, will act as a general deterrent to socially undesirable activities in general and suspected tax evasion in particular. In the past, this theory might have worked, but lately, as almost all occupational groups feel the tax system is oppressive and everyone begins to chisel on taxes, I.R.S. policy often backfires, as it did in the recent Margulies case in San Francisco. There the accused was acquitted by a sympathetic judge and jurors, who decided that the tax collector was the bad guy and the accused taxpayer was the victim.

The atmosphere in courts today is much like it was in colonial America when local judges and juries refused to convict accused violators of British tax laws. In spite of my personal feelings and the ever-growing odds against a criminal conviction, I wouldn't advise anyone to do something that's clearly tax fraud. In most instances, I will be showing you a legally acceptable way of doing the same thing that you might have been tempted to do illegally.

Before proceeding further, you should know what criminal tax fraud is. It's popularly known as *tax evasion*. Let's look at a few examples. You are a doctor. You collect two-thirds of your fees in cash. You never deposit them. You use the untaxed cash receipts to support your buxom, gorgeous nurse-receptionist in a palatial seaside condominium. You intentionally never report the cash fees on your income tax return. Your wife finds out about the nurse, and during the divorce she squeals to the I.R.S. You do not pass Go. You may go to jail. That's because what you did was clearly tax evasion. There is probably no way out, unless you have a

WRONG! X

good lawyer who can get you off on a temporary insanity plea.

But you take the same situation: This time the doctor sets up, in advance, the Pismo Beach Health Research Foundation—perhaps as a Caymanian nonprofit legal entity. The same untaxed fees go into a foundation account that spends the money for advancing the charitable purposes of the foundation, as determined by the doctor. Headquarters are in a luxurious condo at Pismo Beach. The doctor hires a lawyer to set up a foundation and a C.P.A. to handle the books. The foundation then advances the cause of mankind with an occasional research grant to the same worthy buxom and beautiful nurse. The I.R.S. can always argue that the foundation was a sham for the doctor to support his mistress. But since the doctor followed prescribed forms and wasn't concealing anything, there is no question of criminal fraud. There was tax avoidance, certainly—but it was legal tax avoidance, not fraud. *The only difference between right and wrong is that you tell a lawyer or an accountant what you want to accomplish and let him or her handle the details of structuring it to be legal!*

RIGHT!✓

Creating deductible business expenses out of thin air on a large scale might also result in criminal prosecution. But taking a short 5-year useful life for depreciation instead of the 40 years the I.R.S. feels you should have taken is not criminal. It's only a difference of opinion—normally settled out of court by compromise.

The I.R.S. is said to have some rules of thumb on tax fraud. They go something like this: If provable income is not understated by more than 25 percent or deductions are not overstated by more than 33 percent, they will not presume criminal fraud. Unless, of course, they are out to get you. A $2 error might be sufficient to bring a suspected Mafia don or other target to trial. But for the normal, run-of-the-mill tax cheater, the I.R.S. wants you to have been awfully blatant before they'll set the special agents on you.

The Subterranean Economy

What's this subterranean economy of tax evaders you've been reading about? Briefly, in 1977 a bright college professor did a study of the paper money in circulation in America over the past few decades. He noticed that in times of price controls and known black market activities (such as during World War II), the amount of cash in circulation grew drastically. Cash was needed, presumably to finance illegal transactions where no records were desired. The professor noticed that in the past few years, although more and more economic activity should logically have been handled by checks and credit cards, the amount of cash in circulation increased drastically. His startling conclusion was that at least 10 percent of the gross national product is produced, sold, and distributed illegally or underground. Since few black markets exist except for dope, the use of cash appeared to be in connection with tax avoidance. He figured that the equivalent of 1 in 10 employed people was not officially in existence as far as the government was concerned. That person was taking it all in cash—neither paying Social Security nor income tax. Or looking at it another way, everybody was cheating by not reporting 10 percent of their income and by spending that 10 percent on illegal merchandise or unreported transactions.

The professor concluded that the number of Americans engaged in massive tax evasion involved infinitely more people and infinitely more money than our government could dare admit. And the 10 percent figure appeared to be a rock-bottom minimum! He suggested that research indicated that the vast majority of self-employed people engaged in tax evasion. The bottom line seemed to be that the honest American taxpayer depicted by the I.R.S. in news releases disappeared from the scene several years ago—perhaps around the time that Nixon got a presidential pardon for his own tax evasion. The backdating of Nixon's personal tax return documents and affixing of phony notarizations by Nixon was clearly fraud. If white is 1 and black is 10 on a scale of 1 to 10, our recent President was operating in a 10½ black area.

More Gray Area

Certain portions of the tax law can be referred to as "black and white" areas. Here, your activities can be clearly distinguished as "right" or "wrong." The majority of our activities are in the gray area. Perhaps 95 percent of all tax cases that get to court because of a concept that is wholly unique to American tax law. The I.R.S. idea is that whatever the regulations say, or whatever the tax law allows you to do, if you do it with the sole *intent* of avoiding tax then a tax *is* due. As a result, the I.R.S., like the priest at confession, as part of its job looks not just at what you did but what was in your secret heart. Its agents will usually ascertain a tax avoidance intention if they start poking around. The result is that a great many gray-area situations are produced. To clarify, let's talk about a hypothetical case.

While your friend Mr. Wong of Hong Kong was visiting the United States, you helped him out. You showed him property and introduced him to certain business contacts. You had no prior understanding about pay for your services. In the company of your true love Pigeon (always a potential informer), Mr. Wong tells you he wants to give you a present of $10,000 for your services. He hands you $10,000 cash. You tell Mr. Wong that you don't want a penny for your services, but since you are a little short of cash you will take the money and *consider it a loan*. Orally you promise to pay him back someday. He says, "That isn't necessary."

You keep the money but don't pay any income tax on it. You are considering it a loan, or maybe a gift. Whatever it may have been, you don't report it. It doesn't show up as a deduction on Mr. Wong's U.S. income tax return because he's a foreigner and he doesn't file a U.S. income tax return. You spend the money and forget about the whole transaction. Later, after an argument, your girlfriend Pigeon turns you in for her standard reward of 10 percent of the tax you didn't pay. She tells the I.R.S. you made $10,000 in unreported income. In a *civil action* (noncriminal) to recover the income tax on $10,000, there is no question that the I.R.S. would recover the tax you didn't pay. The reason? You can't unilaterally (all by yourself), turn fee income into a loan or gift by just calling it that.

In a *criminal action* against you for tax fraud, there's a definite grayish tinge to the matter. Did you call the matter a loan to *evade* taxes or because in your heart of hearts you really intended to pay the money back someday? The I.R.S. will always claim that whatever you did was done intentionally, solely to evade taxes and defraud the government. But if you can convince a judge or jury that you truly considered the $10,000 to be a loan, and if there is any corroborative evidence to back this up you probably wouldn't bear any risk of criminal prosecution.

What would be good evidence? A canceled $500 check to Wong showing that *before* Pigeon turned you in you had treated the transaction as a loan. If I were a judge or juror, the fact that you started to pay back the money would be convincing proof that you regarded the $10,000 as a loan and were in the process of paying it off.

Now, let's assume the exact same facts. This time you wisely left Miss Pigeon at home. Wong is again to leave for Hong Kong. He hands you the same envelope full of cash. I won't ask what's going on in your heart of hearts and suggest you don't tell me or anyone else. If you keep your mouth shut, the world must rely on objective evidence of what happened, even if in your heart you are an "evil tax evader." So you say to Wong, "Sir, I appreciate the generous gesture, but due to American tax laws I would be honor bound to report any cash you gave me to the I.R.S. In my bracket, I would then have to pay 50 percent of your money to the I.R.S. as taxes. Accordingly, would you allow me to structure our transaction in such a way as to save me some taxes?" Mr. Wong naturally says, "What can I do to help you?"

You take out a note form and pledge agreement that says,

> I, *Walter Wong*, hereby acknowledge receipt of a valuable *diamond ring done in gold dragons with inset ruby eyes and seven flawless diamonds* as security for an *$11,000 loan*, advanced today in cash to *Tom Taxpayer*. It is agreed between the parties that this loan shall be repaid within *18* years, together with interest at the rate of

10 percent per annum, with no prepayment penalty. It is agreed that if the loan is not repaid when due, the pledged article shall be forfeited. Dated *1/1/1980.*

You, Tom Taxpayer, sign, and Wong accepts the note. Wong delivers $11,000 cash to you. You then give Wong a priceless family heirloom ring that, if pressed, you'd value somewhere between $5 and $11,000. A month later, you mail Wong a check for $1,000 marked "Principal payment on $11,000 note dated 1/1/80."

As you recall, Wong gave you an envelope with $11,000 cash in it. You didn't put the cash in your bank because you didn't want the bank to report it as an "unusual cash transaction," which the I.R.S. requires all banks to do. Why raise any red flags? Naturally you did not report it on your income tax either, because you regarded the $10,000 as a loan. Even if the I.R.S. (as it does to one in a million people), gives you a full Mafia-style audit in which they actually examine all your bank accounts, they won't find the $11,000 deposit.

Let's assume they find out about the $11,000 in some other way. Then they ask you why you didn't report it as income. What do you do? You observe the "Keep Your Mouth Shut" rule. *Never* talk to an I.R.S. agent personally. Have your lawyer or C.P.A. show them the note to Wong and the cancelled check for the $1,000 repayment. The I.R.S. cannot prove the Wong money was anything but a loan, and a secured loan at that.

Tax lawyers set up transactions of a similar nature for clients every day of the week. Semifictitious loans are made. Properties and shares that never existed change hands. All sorts of transactions designed to bamboozle or mislead the I.R.S. are the stuff of which the multibillion-dollar per year tax shelter, tax planning, tax avoidance industry is made. I don't consider it honest, but that's what goes on in the real world. They may call it "tax planning" and "tax accounting," and the lawyers and accountants setting up the deals may be the most respectable in town, but if the I.R.S. really could ascertain the "secret intentions" as the I.R.S. is supposed to do by law, it would all be revealed as cleverly disguised tax fraud. Without it, private industry would grind to a halt in a week—because present tax rates, if honestly paid, would put everyone out of business. The Great Depression of 1930–1935 would appear to be a Sunday School picnic if everyone really paid their taxes at today's rates.

In our example with Mr. Wong, since he is a foreigner from a very low tax jurisdiction (Hong Kong), he does not care one way or the other whether he gave you a loan, a gift, cash, or whatever. He does not need the write-off on his own books. When engaged in international deals, there are always many alternatives to choose from.

6.
The Tax Code Can Make You Rich

This book is concerned with avoiding taxes. But for some of us, the immediate problem is *making* enough money so that we can someday be in the enviable position of using all these neat little tricks to keep it from the tax man. In my earlier book, *Think Like a Tycoon*, all I did was talk about ways to make your fortune within two years. But one method I saved for this book should be obvious! You all remember that the best way to get rich was to identify a common need or problem. Then, you as an opportunist, could create an appropriate product or service. As noted in *Think Like a Tycoon*, all the great fortunes made in the past 10,000 years were amassed by people who could

Find a need and fill it.

As a reader of this book you must be painfully aware of the great need felt by millions of Americans and citizens of other countries having high tax rates. They want to avoid taxes. Information on how to avoid taxes is a multimillion-dollar business for many companies and individuals. But you don't have to write a book like this or become a Certified Public Accountant to cash in. There is a far better way, and the people who go into that end of the business make far more money than you have ever dreamed of. By the time you finish this book, you will know more about tax avoidance than 99 percent of the population. That puts you in the unique position of being able to help other people invest their "funny money" or pretax dollars in *tax shelters*.

Have you ever seen an article like the one on page 107? Is there any reason you couldn't be like Klaus Hebben? In this chapter, I will show you how to start out with virtually no money—in your own home town! By next December, you could be in control of millions of dollars worth of property.

More money will be made in the second half of the twentieth century by people who set up what I call "Superterranean" or tax shelter investments than in any other form of enterprise!

This is the age of the rapacious thieving government, and the only people on the other side may be *you* and me. Here is the way to not only join, but to *lead* the tax revolt in a way that will make you filthy rich.

Obviously there is a tremendous need for good tax shelters—investments that make economic sense and can at the same time take the pretax dollars of people in the higher tax brackets and put them to work generating tax deductions, investment tax credits, and other "paper losses" to

106

WRITE-OFFS AT HOME

Resources attracting German money

CALGARY (CP) — A cosmopolitan crowd of investors has been pouring money into Alberta, lured by its resource industries.

Challenging the U.S. dominance as the primary non-Canadian source of venture capital is West Germany, which has a highly-attractive tax-writeoff legislation for investing abroad.

Klaus Hebben, a youthful, self-effacing entrepreneur, is one of the new breed of West German investors.

In the last six years, Hebben has put more than $500 million of German venture capital to work in North America, mostly in junior oil companies in Alberta.

German seed money helped launch, among others, Czar Resources Ltd., Peyto Oils Ltd., Bonanza Resources Inc., Coseka Resources Ltd., Petromark Minerals Ltd. and Canadian Hunter Exploration Ltd.

Canadian Hunter, which found gas in the Deep Basin of western Alberta in 1977, has been an outstanding success story. Hebben liked the unconventional theories of gas occurrence advanced by Canadian Hunter, so much so that he concluded a string of joint venture deals worth more than $40 million.

Hebben said in an interview that the key to the continued flow of German risk capital is appropriate tax legislation at home, which permits 100-per-cent writeoff of all exploratory expenses undertaken abroad by investors, who also get tax deferment on their foreign earnings.

The Munich Group, as the chain of corporate entities stretched between the Bavarian capital and North America is known, will be delivering some $100 million of new financing to North America annually, mostly to Western Canadian resource companies.

"There is still some romance to Western Canada as far as the German investor is concerned," Hebben said. Petroleum prospects provide the best bets for a five-fold return German investors are promised over 25 years.

Hebben said about 80 per cent of the money will be invested in Canada and the rest in the United States.

In West Germany, the Gesellschaft Zur Exploration Von Erdol Und Erdgas, commonly known as the Triple E organization, is the vehicle used by Hebben to solicit private capital in search of a tax shelter.

The money of German investors in due course reaches Bluesky Oil and Gas Ltd., main operating company in Canada.

Bluesky in turn concludes joint venture arrangements with Canadian companies in need of outside financing and willing to give up some of the working interest in a project.

Hebben's companies so far have entered into about 200 joint venture deals with Canadian and U.S. partners. German investors in general are "cautious but ready to take reasonable chances," Hebben said.

He said barring negative Canadian legislation and a massive economic upheaval back home, West German investors will continue to enlarge their presence in Canada.

help the overburdened productive classes keep a little more of their hard-earned money. At my front-lawn classes in Mill Valley, I noticed that there were always two types of individuals in attendance. First, doctors, lawyers, accountants, plumbers, and others who were sick and tired of paying up to 85 percent of their earnings in taxes but who simply had no time to spend looking for suitable real estate investments.

The people in this first group would have been tickled pink if someone else would do all the work in return for up to half of the profits. They all had had experience with investment groups and tax shelter syndicates. That experience was almost always abysmal. Over a four-year period, my own surveys (of approximately 3,000 investors) indicated that more than 97 percent of all "tax shelter" investments were pure garbage. They never returned the original investment (much less any profit) to the guy who put up the money. That was because most of the people in the tax shelter business are flakes, phonies, and promoters who know little about investments and even less about the tax code. The world *needs* honest, knowledgeable originators of tax shelter investments. Are you a young (thinking), hungry (thinking) hustler?

A second group at my lectures was always the "Young Hungry Hustlers." These were usually recent college graduates who were not yet earning enough to worry about their taxes. They had motivation, time, and intelligence—but little or no money. It was possible for the hustlers to make "no-money-down deals," and many of them owned five or six buildings within a few months after taking my classes. But no-money-down deals were available only on relatively small, problematic properties. The hustlers had to pass up the multimillion-dollar deals if even a small amount of cash was required.

Then the inevitable happened. One of the more creative hustlers announced that he would like to take investor partners in on deals on this basis: The hustler would find the deal, do all the negotiations, manage the property, and eventually refinance or resell it. The investor would do nothing but look over the deal and the paperwork at the beginning, put up *all* the money, hold title to the property (if desired), and take *all* the tax benefits. When it came time to sell or trade up, profits would be split 50/50, with the investor getting a minimum of 10 percent per annum annual return on his money before the hustler got anything.

As it turned out, this arrangement turned out to be wonderful for both parties. The hustler didn't get paid unless he produced, and the investor got a minimum return even if the deal didn't work out too well. In the crazy California market, the investors averaged about 50 percent per annum returns on their money—and the hustlers, well, they got an infinite return on no investment at all. Of course, they earned it—they found a good investment and made it work out.

The difference between these deals and the standard real estate syndication was immense. The investment that is packaged by a major investment house is normally the garbage of the real estate market. It may be good property—but the price is double or triple what experienced real estate people would pay. Further, most real estate syndicators are not compensated on the come—or on the contingent fee principle. (They get paid whether or not the deal is successful for the investor.) Typically, little or none of the investor's money finds its way into a syndicated deal. Most of it goes for commissions and advertising. The syndicator is paid "up front," and his profit is already made once the investors are found and the deal is closed. Obviously, there is no incentive to give the investors a good deal, so they get garbage!

In what I am going to call the "minipartnership," there is a close relationship between the investor and the active partner. Usually there are just the two of them in the deal. With proper buyout agreements, if the active partner does not perform the investor can kick him out of the deal and owe him little or nothing. Until the active partner has a track record of successful deals, he will have to operate on the basis that the investor can fire him at any time he flubs up on the job.

To accomplish their objectives, many of my Tycoon Class graduates came to me to draw up a partnership agreement that was fair to both parties. Several partnerships were created for fees of $300 or more. Let me emphasize that this is the form for use by beginners on small deals. If and when

their small deals work out, they come to me for the "advanced course."

Now, you may be a plumber making $175,000 per year—in which case you can use this agreement as a model form for a deal with your son-in-law. Or, if you are not wealthy but think you can put deals together, here is a form you can use to give your investor a fair shake. This partnership agreement, with minor variations, can be used for almost all real estate deals, mineral exploration, and leasing. It is exempt from state and federal regulation, and the agreement is strictly between the partners. Unless you have a disagreement that can't be resolved and the partnership agreement is shown to an arbitrator or a judge, you and your partner are the only people who ever have to see it.

My suggested form is only a guide, and should be modified to suit the needs and desires of you and your partner.

Most people of substantial wealth have this choice: (1) Pay taxes to a thieving, rapacious government, or (2) give pre-tax "soft" dollars to thieving, rapacious promoters of garbage tax shelters.

This agreement may give you a third alternative.

Date: *January 1, 1981*

Partnership Agreement

This agreement is between *Irving Investor* and *Tom Tycoon*, hereafter known as *"I."* and *"T."**

The above-named partners have agreed to acquire a *20-unit apartment building located at 123 Amen Drive, Salt Lake City, Utah*, to be owned and operated by them as the *T. & I.* partnership. The business address of the Partnership shall be *Apartment #1, 123 Amen Drive, Salt Lake City*, the residence of *Tom Tycoon*, who as part of this agreement shall receive said residence rent free and shall manage said *apartment building* without further compensation from the partnership, except as here provided.

This agreement shall be effective as of this date, which is the date title and possession of the said *apartment building* passes to the *T & I* partnership.**

This partnership shall continue for a period of *three* years unless dissolved by mutual agreement or as otherwise provided herein. *Thirty-two* months from this date, the property will be put up for sale by listing it with *Robert Real Estate Broker* at a price to be set by him.

The parties to this agreement agree to contribute to the business as follows: *I.* will contribute all cash needed to acquire the property. Thereafter, in the event of any negative cash flow, repairs, or other contingencies requiring funds, both partners agree to contribute equally; *T.* will contribute *no* initial cash, but as his contribution has located the investment property, negotiated for its acquisition and financing, and by this agreement undertakes to do all physical repair work needed to improve the property, to manage and collect rents, and to the best of his ability take over all problems of running this partnership on a day-to-day basis, including the obtaining of suitable 1031 exchange property within the next *three* years.

---

*Under the laws of most states and the federal government, up to 10 investors may be involved with a deal before it is considered a "public offering." Also it may not be shown to over 25 potential investors. This form is intended for use by no more than a pair of active investors and a pair of passive investors.

**If Tom Tycoon is not a "proven quantity," it is suggested that title to any property acquired be kept in the name of the investor(s) who put up the money.

For their respective contributions, any cash flow including refinancing proceeds is to be used to

1. Return in full the original contribution of *$25,000* made by *I.*
2. Return to *I.* any additional contributions plus a minimum annual return of 10 percent per annum on any cash invested.
3. Return to *T.* any cash invested in the deal plus a return of 10 percent per annum on any outstanding investment.
4. Any balance to be shared between the parties on an equal basis.
5. In the event of losses from any cause, they shall be shared equally.

Books and records of all expenses and receipts shall be kept on the *Safeguard Account System for Real Estate,* by *T.* and shall be available for inspection by *I.* or his designated agent during all business hours.

All funds of the partnership shall be deposited daily at the *Desert National Bank* of *Salt Lake City* in a joint account. Withdrawals of over *$200* shall require the signatures of both parties.

T. shall provide *I.* with regular monthly statements and a year end statement containing all information needed for *I.*'s federal income tax.

DISSENTING REMEDY

In the event that either party wishes to dissolve the partnership, he may offer to buy out the other at a certain price set by him. Thereafter, the other partner shall have *10* days to either accept the offer or pay the other partner the price previously offered to him. Provided however, that if *T.* is making the buyout offer, it must be for at least the amount of *I.*'s investment plus 10 percent per annum. In the event a third-party buyer has materialized and either party does not wish to sell, the partner who wishes to hold agrees to buy out the other party for whatever his share of the resulting profit would have been. The partner selling agrees to convey his interest immediately on payment to the holding partner.

DEATH OR ABANDONMENT

In the event *T.* dies or is absent from the project for more than *five* continuous days, *I.* shall automatically acquire a 100 percent interest in said project with no further obligation or debt to *T.* or his estate.

In the event *I.* dies, T. may (1) complete the project as planned and pay *I.*'s share to *I.*'s heirs, or, at *T.*'s sole option, (2) T. may buy out the interest of *I.*'s estate for the amount invested by *I.* plus 12 percent per annum return.

112

COVENANT NOT TO SUE

T. covenants not to sue *I.* at any time during the life of this agreement, and *T.* expressly agrees that his maximum damages in the event of litigation shall be the amount of his actual investment returned to him.

OTHER ACTIVITIES OF PARTNERS

It is agreed that *I.* is not expected to put in any time or effort running the partnership property, and he is not restricted in any way by this agreement from making other investments.

T. agrees to devote all his spare time to this project and not to undertake the management of any other businesses or real estate ventures without the express written permission of *I.* In the event *I.* gives such permission for *T.* to engage in other spare-time entrepreneurial activities, it is agreed that *I.* shall have no interest in profits from other ventures. In the event that *123 Amen Drive* is fully occupied and is being properly managed, *I.* agrees to give his permission for *T.* to work on other projects.

DEPRECIATION AND TAX BENEFITS

Since *I.* is putting up all the cash, it is agreed that for state and federal income tax purposes he shall get 100 percent of the write-offs and tax benefits, including any tax credits or depreciation allowances generated by this property.

INSURANCE

It is agreed that *T.* will, prior to the closing hereof, insure the property with a comprehensive fire policy in the face amount of *$500,000* and procure liability insurance in the amount of *$1,000,000*, with a waiver of the business risk exclusion, and title to the property shall not be acquired until such coverage is obtained, in writing.

ARBITRATION

In the event the partners cannot agree, both parties shall submit any dispute to *Albert Arbitrator* and agree that his decision shall bind them as a final judgment in a court of law.

MISCELLANEOUS

The parties agree not to endorse any note nor become surety for any person(s) without the written consent of the other. It is further agreed that any contracts or obligations undertaken by either partner in respect of business other than the *123 Amen Drive* property shall in no way bind or obligate the other partner.

In the event that there are more than *three* vacancies in the property for more than *three* consecutive months and/or delinquent rents in *three* units or more during this time period, *T.* agrees to either contribute to the partnership an amount equal to said rents, in cash, or to remove himself from the premises, quit claim the property to *I.*, and renounce any further interest in it to *I.**

On Date: __1/1/81__, the parties have signed this agreement.**

Irving Investor   Tom Tycoon

Now that you have the agreement and an inkling of what I am talking about, you wonder, "What shall I do with it?"

This is my suggestion: Particularly around the year's end, get *The Wall Street Journal*, *Barron's*, and your local newspapers. You might also want to splurge on the Sunday *New York Times* and *Los Angeles Times*. You will see dozens of ads for "year-end tax shelters." Respond to all of them. See what they are offering. Let the salesman come out and call on you. Observe his techniques, note what is convincing and where he leaves you cold.

A lot of wealthy people go absolutely bananas at year end, and they will "invest" in any garbage that gives them a substantial tax deduction and even a glimmer of hope for an eventual profit. Your fortune can be made by giving these people a *decent* investment and tax shelter. How do you find the deals? Simply read *Think Like a Tycoon* or *The Distress Property Workbook* and look at everything that is on the market. There are plenty of deals—far more than you can handle. But the best ones require work and creativity. Money is easy to get. There are thousands of investors with money burning a hole in their pockets.

How do you meet the investors?

---

*This paragraph was included to indicate a type of "minimum performance standard" to be set by I. for T. to live up to. In the event T. does not do his job, I. will, for all practical purposes, be able to fire T. and terminate T.'s interest in the property. A quit claim deed from T. to I. should be executed simultaneously with this document and deposited with an escrow agent to implement this agreement.

**Always use a Notary Public to acknowledge partnership agreements or any contracts involving real estate!

One way might be to put an ad like this into your local paper:

You could give a free seminar for tax shelter investors at your home or at a local hotel meeting room. You could write all the local Certified Public Accountants about your deals. Believe me, a deal "with a good story" is as easy as pie to market. Once you have closed a few deals and made your investors some money, you will have to employ people to beat off the investors.

In my own case, I seldom took in partners because I just didn't want to bothered by a bunch of idiots who would always be telling me how to run a business I knew far better than they did. But to my surprise, when I laid the law down to a few investors and said, "If you want in on my deals, you read your semiannual statements and *keep out of my hair,*" I was left alone. My agreement was a lot tougher on the investor than the sample provided simply because I knew I could and would average about 100 percent return per year for the investor—but only if I made the decisions and wasn't bothered. Today I still do a few syndications from time to time with minimum investments of $50,000. If you want to be on my list, that's fine. My investors get full disclosure at the beginning, regular reports in between, and a full statement when the deal is sold off or (more often) refinanced and traded up. But I don't want any weak sisters or Willy

Worrywarts in deals with me. Those types can be as annoying as fuzzy-thinking, deadbeat-leftist tenants. *You* may have to put up with them at first as a hungry hustler. But after you make your investors a good return, you'll be able to pick and choose new investors from a long waiting list. Word gets around that you are "some kind of financial genius."

You personally can make pots and pots of money as a syndicator. The reason is simple. Suppose you find a million-dollar property that you hope to upgrade and sell in a year for $1.2 million. If it takes $100,000 down to make the deal, you get an outside investor to put up the whole $100,000. A year later, you sell. The investor gets a 100 percent return, and you have a $100,000 profit to trade up into another profitable building. Putting together only one big deal a year can make you a multimillionaire without a dime of your own money at risk. The investor loves you because you do all the work and produce better profits than he can on his own. You can soon take all the deals that come along because you have a following of eager, moneyed investors. Soon you'll have groups of investors. If you don't take your money out in cash—but trade up to bigger and better deals—your own wealth builds up tax free. You live on tax-free refinancing proceeds, as I do. And that's how you can make millions! Now go out and do it!

Another Giveaway

A few years back, the government offered a $2,000 income tax rebate to anyone who bought a new home. With a deal like that, on a "no-money-down" deal, anyone with about $10,000 in gross income wouldn't have to pay any tax at all—just for signing on the dotted line. Let them foreclose the following year! Tax credits aren't tax deferrals. Once you've qualified to take a tax credit, the government can't (usually) get it back.

Most Certified Public Accountants stay on top of the latest government gimmicks and giveaways, and can tell you

Government Giveaways

My high school buddy David, who is as rich as Croesus due to a $20 million inheritance, never pays any tax on his $2 million annual income. He avoids all taxes by watching for the latest government giveaway. "There's always something," he tells me. In 1977 and 1978, it was a combination of W.I.N. and the 50 percent tax credit that good old Dave used.

He borrowed $1.5 million to equip a gorgeous new swinging singles restaurant bar and disco. Normally I would not invest in bars or restaurants. But if the government subsidizes the whole operation and if they are in a super location and can open with a public relations splash that will bring in the local beautiful people, then how can you lose? According to Dave, the Feds, who are interested in stimulating employment, developed a program called W.I.N. (Whip Inflation Now) by which the federal government actually paid 50 percent of the salaries of all new (formerly unemployed) employees taken on during 1977 and 1978. At the same time, a different government program made the other 50 percent of the salaries paid a *tax credit*, not just a write-off. The Small Business Administration guaranteed the $1.5 million loan needed to start operations. The net result was that Dave didn't put up or risk a dime. He took a $150,000 investment tax credit plus depreciation on the equipment. More tax credits came from the salaries paid out. Result? His entire $2 million income from other sources was sheltered.

He also made a small tax-free profit on the operations and got a lot of action and free meals. Ultimately he sold the whole show to another rich friend, who repeated the script the following year.

how to take advantage of them. You can keep up with current programs by subscribing to or reading (at your local business branch library) materials put out by Prentice-Hall and Commerce Clearing House. If seed money is required you can always give an armchair-investor-partner half of the project in return for putting up *all* of the money.

Hope for Disaster

Because declaring an area a "disaster area" gives the federal government an opportunity to play Big Daddy and distribute lots of money and other benefits locally, it seems that every heavy rain or snowstorm, minor flood, drought, hot spell, or cold spell qualifies your home town for disaster area status. In the area north of San Francisco where I live, we seem to be either a flood or drought disaster area every other year. People wait for the next disaster to get new driveways or retaining walls. Why not wait for the next dry year or flood to replace all landscaping with the aid of government grants or super-low-interest loans?

Even if you don't feel quite right about taking your share of all the federal handouts, you might as well learn about and take the tax benefits. All damage, direct and indirect, caused by a disaster can be an immediate write off, whether or not you have it fixed. If you get it fixed, instead of depreciating the "improvement" over its estimated useful life, you can write off the entire cost as a repair in the year done.

Let's look over what a friend of mine did to take advantage of this situation. Gerry had a rotten little add-on alcove at his personal residence. He was about to tear it off when, as luck would have it, a tree fell on a corner of it, causing damage of at least $50. Gerry knew about the "disaster area" rules, so he got a bid of $10,000 for tearing off the room and replacing it with a glass-walled conservatory dining room. For official report purposes, the cause of the damage was the drought in the local disaster area, which damaged the root system of the tree and caused it to topple, doing $10,000 in damage.

The $10,000 was duly deducted on his income tax return as a "disaster loss." In Gerry's case, the local helpful federals arranged to get him a grant (tax free, of course) the following year to defray this loss. For good measure, Gerry deducted another $8,000 as the loss in value to his property caused by the drought killing off his daisies and other rare garden plants. We should all have such disasters!

Remember the principle: Even if you don't repair it, if any act of God damages your *investment* property (disaster area or not), that gives rise to a business loss you can deduct in the year it occurs. But the same is true of your residence when you're lucky enough to be in a declared "disaster area." So pray for a *little* earthquake so you can remodel your home with the aid of tax benefits and tax-free grants.

You Can Be More Equal Than Others

I was taught in law school that the law (imperfect as it is) applies to everyone equally. It did not occur to me that someone could wangle official exemption from taxes or prosecution for crimes just because that particular person was well placed politically or socially. Well, it is true that some are more equal than others.

If you are good buddies with a congressman, senator, President, or someone influential in high places, you can get a diplomatic passport, a pardon, or a "private law" passed just for you. If you or your political friend has pull, your own little law or pardon comes through with the greatest of ease. It can give you a complete pass on convictions, criminal prosecutions, or on any taxes that may be due from you. During the Nixon administration, certain Mafia figures who had actually been convicted and sentenced to jail got Nixon pardons for no particular (or at least visible) reasons. They just walked away from serious raps. *Nixon himself got a pardon for his personal tax evasion.* A Hollywood magnate who had made a bundle in a particular transaction had enough political pull to get a law passed exactly describing his transaction and exempting it from tax. Good friends in the right places can make you more equal than others.

Why newspapers don't expose this sort of thing as a major scandal is simple: The establishment always has and always will favor its own members in good standing with special consideration. You can even read these federal private laws at major law libraries. Private laws and pardons are just favors for people.

Another big boondoggle is "secret" C.I.A. money. Billions of our tax dollars are channeled to private citizens tax free for various outlandish schemes of the C.I.A. There is absolutely no accountability for these funds to anyone, including the I.R.S. If the I.R.S. starts poking around in a C.I.A. deal, their special agents get a call from the C.I.A. and they lay off the case. Problem: How can you, just an ordinary nobody, gain immunity from laws in general and taxes in particular? The name of the game is *developing contacts. Knowing the key person in the right place delivers all the goodies.*

How can you get to know foreign or domestic political figures? How can you cultivate friendships with them? The answer is "Find a need and fill it." You can be a power behind influential politicians by supplying money, information, votes, or whatever they need. *Being "needed" by politicians will pave the way for you to be above the law.*

Special "deals" have been made before and since the Nixon Administration, but, because Nixon got caught, extensive literature and films of that era provide a glimpse of how privileges, pardons, and passes are dispensed. Giving votes, love, loyalty—whatever up and coming politicians are turned on by—has long been a practice of successful tycoons. Howard Hughes, for instance, always contributed large cash sums to both sides in campaigns. There is evidence that he was rewarded with complete immunity from federal prosecution and became a major conduit for C.I.A. funds.

"Very good," you say, "but how do I personally infiltrate these high places and gain intimacy with powerful people?" Simple. Let me spell it out. In your own home district, pick a likely winner in the next campaign for mayor or national office. Call the guy up. Offer your services in delivering the vote in a certain area. He will accept. Then go around visiting voters in their homes. There is no rule saying you can't pick up a few real estate deals at the same time. If your candidate wins, you call him again to make sure your help is remembered. A political favor is owed to you. It may be collected with an appointive no-pay or low-pay position to the airport authority, or the parole board, or some similar quasi-government agency. As you pick up appointments like this, at the same time as you are forging ahead as a tycoon, you meet the up and coming powerful people and become a respected member of the establishment.

The choice between remaining at a low local level and rising quickly to national stature as a behind-the-scenes power broker is up to you. The same techniques used to become a tycoon and gain wealth are used in obtaining political power. You never have to stand up for election—you merely have to make yourself useful, perhaps indispensable, for those who do. It starts with a phone call or letter. Do it now!

7.
Family Trusts
and Other
Ripoffs

My uncle Hermann, a former German paratrooper, is a most unlikely candidate for tax rebel. He has far too much respect for authority! If his government told him, as it once did, to get ready to jump out of a plane into a pack of bloodthirsty Russians, he'd jump as directed. And if a superior officer told him to shoot a bunch of unarmed civilians, as they once did, he'd do that too. But the war is over, and these days Hermann is a florist in a typical American suburb. Every few years I drop in to visit him and his kids—my cousins. His idea of a good time is getting together with the local chapter of Wehrmacht veterans. They drink Löwenbrau, sing German marching songs, and talk about the good old days at Stalingrad. One of his old war buddies came by the florist shop last year and told Uncle Hermann to come to a lecture about how to save income taxes. Since I was there visiting, he invited me along.

So I went.

It was at the Holiday Inn. When we went into the standard meeting room, there was a silver-haired 70-year-old guy who had already started his talk and was rambling on about God, Christ, and George Washington. These were apparently the "good guys." It was like an old-time revival meeting. Down in hell there with Satan were the socialists, communists, and the Internal Revenue Service. The speaker was dressed in a red, white, and blue "Uncle Sam" suit, complete with top hat and cutaway coat.

"The blacks and Mexicans get food stamps, welfare, and subsidized housing, and rich Jews get all the deductions, but what do we productive working people—we loyal, patriotic, Christian Americans—get? We get a kick in the ass, that's what! The government takes our tax money and gives us *nothing. . . .*

I thought to myself, "This guy is a real kook. Can anyone take him seriously?" I wondered. Sensing that the audience was lapping up this speech, I was surprised at the generally favorable reaction. Uncle Hermann applauded with the others. Being half-Jewish, I was getting uncomfortable and made a move to get up and leave. Uncle Hermann, sensing my discomfiture, raised his hand and said bravely, "I don't like you saying bad things about Jews—some of my best friends are Jews."

The speaker in the Uncle Sam suit answered without losing a beat: "I have nothing against Jews, blacks, and Mexicans. Some of them are good Christian Americans, just like us. I am talking about the welfare recipients and the rich communist Jews in government and the blacks on welfare who take all the benefits for themselves, and don't leave us anything."

That seemed to satisfy Hermann. He smiled at me, having done his duty to the family. The red, white, and blue man then took off his stovepipe hat and got to the point.

> The reason I am here tonight is to tell you about the benefits of the family trust. The family trust that can eliminate

124

your estate taxes, gift taxes, and income taxes. It can give you *privacy* and insulation from creditors and government agencies. . . .

Karl Marx—the Jewish father of communism—told his Bolsheviks that the best way to destroy a free nation is to lay heavy taxes on the people. His partner, Lenin, said in the *Communist Manifesto* that the *key* to establishing communism is to destroy the middle classes with tax and inflation. And that's what's happening here in the United States. The present government is a bunch of Pinkos and Communists that are in a plot to destroy us. That great American, Judge Learned Hand, said, "Taxes are not voluntary contributions. There is not a patriotic duty to pay more than you have to and there is nothing sinister about arranging your affairs to keep your taxes as low as possible." You can read that great decision in the law books! 60 Federal Second 809!

Having a family trust of your own is moral, it's patriotic. It's anti-communist! All millionaires have them, and you can get the exact same benefits starting immediately. "How?" you ask.

You can't get these same trusts set up by your family lawyer or accountant because they don't know how to do it. All our forms are copyrighted, and nobody but the Family Circle Freedom Foundation can sell a family trust to you. Your trust records are *strictly private.* Nobody can see them! Nelson Rockefeller had a trust like this, and when he was being nominated for Vice-President, a Senate committee wanted to see his trust records. Rocky refused, and even the senators agreed that trust records are confidential.

The Father of our Country, George Washington, had a trust like *this* to protect his estates in the event King George won the American Revolution and tried to seize his estate at Mt. Vernon. But the secret of this "Pure Trust" was lost over the years, until our own Family Circle attorney figured out how to give its benefits to the great middle-class American worker. Our organization, the Family Circle Freedom Foundation, with its millions of dollars of resources, will stand behind people who use our family trusts with a free attorney for the life of the trust in the event there is any challenge by the I.R.S. We will defend your trust, *unconditionally,* for the life of the trust—which is *forever*—at our expense. The cost to you for a family trust is nothing! If you want to have one of our representatives meet with you personally to discuss your own family trust you just fill in the cards being passed among you.

The audience cheered, stayed around for a few questions, and on the way home, Uncle Hermann asked me what I thought of the talk.

"Personally," I answered Uncle Hermann, "I am sure that guy was more full of crap than a bag of horse manure."

Hermann said, "You are just mad at him because he doesn't say nice things about Jews."

"Listen, Uncle Hermann, almost everything he said was baloney. I'll tell you just a few things that were wrong with his talk. Anyone with brains should run in the other direction." I pulled out the spiral pad I had been using to take notes. "First of all, when anybody starts talking about Jesus, I put my hand over my wallet. I'm convinced that these Born-Again financial saviors are a lot more interested in the coins they can shake out of you than in your welfare. And since Jesus was big on tolerance and loving your neighbor, I get doubly worried when a preacher-man starts disparaging Jews, blacks, Mexicans, or other minorities. It's a small man's nature and very unChristian desire to see yourself as inherently better—born superior to other groups of people. Your old leader Hitler did an awful lot of mischief with that appeal, Hermann, and you ought to know better! But getting back to Uncle Sam, it's true many judges have said that you can take some legal steps to reduce taxes—but waving unrelated court decisions around doesn't mean that any tax quackery will fly."

"But," interrupted Hermann, "They had an attorney right there at the table."

I thought about it. "Either that attorney is disbarred or soon will be. There are attorneys who are slippery crooks or just plain ignorant lawyers around who will lend their names to pure ripoff schemes for a piece of the action. Ask around.

Ask other attorneys what the reputation of that guy is. I'll bet you find if he's a lawyer at all, he is thought of as a town shyster. Some lawyers will say or do anything if you pay them enough."

"Still," said Hermann, "You can't condemn a family trust without knowing what they have in mind—and he never really did say how it works or what the trust would do."

The next day I left for home, and didn't hear anything more about family trusts for two years, when I got an urgent call from Uncle Hermann. He offered to pay for a round trip ticket to his place if I'd help him out of a jam. What had happened?

When I got to his house he told me. After the family trust talk, because he'd filled in the address card requesting further information, he received a visit from a representative of the Family Circle Freedom Foundation. They looked at his personal situation—a florist shop earning about $60,000 per year net, a wife, and three kids. He had a good chunk of savings in the bank, a nice home, a station wagon for deliveries, and a personal car. He paid about $15,000 per year in income taxes.

Red, white, and blue Uncle Sam—this time in a business suit, with a younger aide introduced as a Certified Public Accountant—declared that Hermann was an ideal candidate for a family trust. They began to refer to him as "the Creator," which made Hermann feel kind of like God. They claimed the cost of setting up the trust would be "free," since Family Circle would get paid just 1½ years tax savings, or $22,500 for doing all the work. After the salesman made the pitch, Hermann agreed that if the deal wouldn't cost him any money and could be fully paid for out of tax savings, he would go along with setting one up. He looked forward to being the Creator of a family trust.

Over the next few weeks, Uncle Sam prepared deeds and other documents transferring the title of the house, cars, florist business, and Hermann's lifetime income to the Hermann Krauss Family Trust. The documents made Hermann and his wife the trustees and beneficiaries of the trust together with the three kids who were also beneficiaries. As the kids became 21, they also were to become trustees. Eventually, the salesman explained, their grandchildren would become trustees, and the trust could go on as long as there were any descendants of the Krauss Family—just like the Rockefellers, Kennedys, and other dynasties.

The family trust salesman pointed out that the income from his new family trust was not taxable at all, and that what used to be Hermann's $60,000 per year income should be all used up in "business expenses," a part of which could be paid to a foreign bank account for "flower seeds and other florist supplies" that were never really purchased. The salesman pointed out further that trust records, being confidential, need never be shown to anyone, and therefore the I.R.S. could never find out about the foreign accounts. What's more, since Hermann never got the money, even if they did find out, it wouldn't be taxable to him.

The $22,500 for setting up the trust was to be paid for by taking out a second mortgage on the flower shop, and (the salesman said) since it was a business expense of the trust, it would be one of the deductions used to reduce the income of the trust—even though it didn't come out of Hermann's pocket. Hermann agreed to this, and the Family Circle Organization got a check for $22,500. That's the last he saw of them!

Hermann stopped paying his quarterly estimated taxes, and, in line with the instructions of Family Circle, filed a tax return for himself and his wife the following year, showing *zero* income and, of course, no income taxes due.

In due course, a special agent from the I.R.S. showed up at Hermann's florist shop, and asked how come a business that grossed over $100,000 and netted $60,000 in the prior year all of a sudden had no sales and no expenses? Hermann, confident that his family trust was all legal, explained to the I.R.S. agent the basics of what he had done.

The I.R.S. agent said, "Mr. Krauss, I think you have been taken. We don't care in the least whether you have a trust or not. The I.R.S. is entitled to a full accounting as to the profits and losses of your business, and if you have any control whatsoever over the assets of your trust, or if you get any benefits from it, or if you assign any of your income to it, or if the earnings of the trust are used to maintain and support your spouse or kids, then from an income tax point of view we treat the situation just exactly as if there were no trust at all. Now, having said all that, if your trust beats all of those tests the I.R.S. is still entitled to a Form 1041, which is an annual income tax return for the trust itself. And if the trust had any income at all, it is required to pay a tax at the same rates as a married person without any dependents, filing singly, which would be more than you pay without a trust. And if the I.R.S. wants to audit that trust's tax return we are entitled to *all* backup books and records of the trust's income and expenses.

"There is no tax savings of any sort to be obtained by using the Family Circle Freedom Foundation Trust as marketed throughout the United States," the I.R.S. agent stated flatly.

"Hermann, you have been conned, pure and simple," said the I.R.S. agent.

When Hermann called me, he indicated that he had first called the Family Circle Office. He was going to ask for the free legal representation to defend his trust. But the number had been disconnected and the office closed. "Naturally," I told him, "Did you think that a guy who dresses up in an Uncle Sam suit was a representative of the Bank of America? Responsible organizations are not represented by bigots or clowns."

Ultimately, in Hermann's tax audits, all books and records were subpoenaed and produced, and Hermann ended up paying the tax he would have paid, $15,000, plus a $7,500 fraud penalty, plus his own attorney's fees and all the government costs to prosecute Hermann. The government generously waived another few thousand dollars of interest they felt was due. In the next year's return, Hermann sought to deduct the $22,500 that he had paid the Family Circle for "tax advice," plus $7,500 in attorney's fees. In a later tax court case, this was disallowed. (Note: Hermann is not a real name, but the same case has come up many times. In a similar actual case, the court imposed a penalty on another victim of the family trust racket by not only disallowing the deduction of all costs and fees in connection with the family trust, but also by finding that the taxpayer was negligent and intentionally disregarded valid I.R.S. rules and regulations. See *Johnston* v. *Commissioner*, #37 Tax Court Memo 544, Commerce Clearing House, Decision No. 35,065M.)

What the judge said and what any judge in a family trust case would say is that there is no way to shuffle a few papers, then go on as you had before, and pay no taxes. The family trust, as marketed by seminars and direct mail, is a con game, pure and simple.

How, then, you may well ask, *can* trusts be used as a tax dodge? There is one way, although it has a lot of restrictions. For some people, the "Clifford Trust" may be an answer. The name "Clifford Trust" grew out of the fact that during the 1930s one George Clifford drew up a document giving his wife title to and income from some property he owned. (This arrangement was to last only 5 years. At the end of that time, if he were still alive, title to the property was to go back to him, and the wife was to get no more income.) Mr. Clifford thereafter did not report the income from his property, but his wife did. The I.R.S. claimed that Clifford's trust, (sometimes referred to as a *temporary trust,* a *trust-for-years,* a *reversionary trust,* a *short-term trust,* or a *family trust*) made no change whatsoever in Clifford's tax status, and any income from the property was still Clifford's. The U.S. Supreme Court in a 1940 case (390 US 331) agreed with the I.R.S. but in its opinion said that *if* Clifford had made his trust for *10 years* he could have successfully transferred the taxable income to someone else. I.R.S. Regulation 671-678 clarified and codified this Clifford Trust. Why was 10 years "good" and 5 years "no good?" Don't ask me! The tax law is very arbitrary and capricious, but today all tax lawyers know that if Mr. Richman gives property or other assets to a trustee with the income to go to someone else for *10 years or more*, and the property returns to Richman at the end of the trust period, the taxable income can be transferred and Richman's tax avoided. Of course, he gave away the income! Would this be a good deal for you? Assume you were a highly taxed professional, and you had an investment earning of $10,000 per year. Assume also that you had ten kids who earned nothing. You could deed income property to a trustee with instructions to give $1,000 each to the ten kids for 10 years, then to return the property to you. The net result would be that each kid gets $10,000 over a ten-year period. The income is no longer yours. Ten years later, you get the property back. In the meantime, the kids got $1,000 apiece per year, tax free.

Naturally, the I.R.S. can't keep things simple, so they restrict the use of the $1,000 given to the kids to "nonnecessaries" that the grantor of the trust wasn't legally obligated to provide as support. Ballet lessons, cars, parties, and ski trips or deposits to a savings account would be, of course, nonnecessary. One doctor transferred title of his medical equipment to a ten-year Clifford Trust, then leased it back from the trust, taking the lease payments as deductions. The doctor's kids got the monthly lease payments and paid little or no tax on the income because they had no other income or were in a very low tax bracket (as infants). The I.R.S. challenged the arrangement, and in U.S. Tax Court (1978) Dr. Lerner won.

Things to watch out for in setting up your trust:

1. Local state laws on trusts vary, and tax cases changing the rules are being decided every day. The services of a C.P.A. and/or a tax lawyer who keeps up with it all are absolutely essential. Even if your own lawyer or accountant flubs up and does not follow the latest rules, it is likely that his

errors would never be as blatant as setting you up with a worthless family trust. The fact that you were guided by a licensed and presumably competent professional will always be almost complete protection against criminal charges, fines, or penalties. The reasoning of a court (or even the I.R.S.) is that a taxpayer can't be held criminally accountable for something his own lawyer told him was legal. A stranger in an Uncle Sam suit is a horse of a different color.

2. I.R.S. agents assigned to poke around your tax return will probably know less about twists and exceptions in the law than your own lawyers and accountants. A judge hearing the case, not being a specialist, will know even less. To predict in advance what a court would do about any particular set of facts is like trying to outguess the stock market. Nobody can tell. The unsettled nature of the tax law is frightening to some people. Others feel it is an advantage because most returns are never audited, and, if you took an aggressive position and it isn't questioned, after the three-year statute of limitations runs out it is incontestable.

3. Someone will have to file an income tax return for the trust in each year that it exists. This Form 1041 must show all the income and expenses received and paid out by the trustee. Income retained by the trustee is taxed at the same rate that would be applied to a married individual filing separately. Income distributed by the trustee is taxed to the recipient as unearned income at a 70 percent maximum federal rate, but the trust is not taxed if it distributes all income to the beneficiaries.

4. The I.R.S. can and will attack a trust and call it a sham unless the trustee is an independent, adverse party to the grantor or person setting up the trust. Thus an unrelated friend or independent trust company should be selected to run the assets owned by the trust. Naturally, this costs money, because nobody works for nothing.

5. A gift tax may be due if the property transferred to

the trust is worth more than $3,000 or more than $6,000 per couple.

If all this is somewhat discouraging, take heart. It was planned that way! The tax laws have been revised since 1913 to close loopholes. Trusts are simply not much use any more. The person with unlimited time to spend in the law library, or unlimited funds that allow him to buy the time and research of others, can ferret out little quirks and unique exceptions to allow him to beat taxes entirely. For the middle-class working stiff unable or unwilling to do the research, there is no legal way out except perhaps what I cover in this book. If and when the last tax avoidance redoubts are eliminated, the only alternative will be putting up with the confiscation of our income earned from Monday to Thursday, or going underground into the subterranean economy. But aside from shifting very limited amounts of income from very high-bracket taxpayers to low-bracket taxpayers, to save at most a few thousand dollars a year in taxes, trusts are simply not useful.

8.
Avoid
Estate
Taxes

Once upon a time, Clarence, a 69-year-old crusty business-man, went to visit his Certified Public Accountant. He said, "I've been in business in this town for five decades, and in that time my net worth has increased to a comfortable $6 million. During my life, I've always arranged my affairs to pay little or no tax. I've got two married sons with their own businesses and families. I want to see to it that when I die they get $3 million each—with as little tax on their inheri-tance as possible." The businessman asked Irving, his ac-countant, to prepare an "estate plan" to accomplish this goal.

After thinking about it, the accountant gave the busi-nessman conventional wisdom: "A few years ago we might have been able to pass your estate on without too much tax. But these days the Feds have hit us with the Unified Estate and Gift Tax, which makes the first $250,000 of your estate pass tax free, but after that the tax hits pretty hard. The tax rate on your estate would mean about 70 percent goes to the government, and 30 percent goes to your kids."

Clarence, the businessman, got angry: "There's no way I'm going to let the politicians squander over $4 million of my money—surely there's some way to beat the inheritance tax—just like I've been beating the income tax all my life."

The C.P.A. said, "See those bookshelves over there? That's my tax library. The tax code is 2,500 pages of fine print that nobody understands. Cases deciding what the code means, and scholarly commentary, and all sorts of interpretation fill an entire room. But you are welcome to study here in my little tax library. Perhaps you'll come up with something. I don't think you will, but *try*. And if you get any ideas, let me know. Welcome to the tax revolt!"

With that, Irving went back to his other work, and the old businessman, being retired, put in all his spare time trying to find a loophole in the federal estate tax law. Naturally, it wasn't an easy job, because beating the tax is not in the table of contents as a recognized index classification. The old man concentrated on the sections of the code annotations and cases that dealt with "receipts not classified as income." He saw that the possibilities for passing money to his kids without tax to them were almost without limit.

1. Loans, for instance, have no tax consequences to the person who makes the loan and are not income to the person who receives the loan. He could make a loan to the kids and simply not ask for repayment. Hmmm.

2. Up to $3,000 in gifts per year are not taxable to the giver, and gifts of any size are not taxable to the recipient. With $6 million to give away, perhaps he could invite 1,000 people to a New Year's Eve party and at 11:59 P.M. give each of them a $3,000 gift check with the request that they pass it on to one of his two sons. Then at 12:01 A.M. he'd pass out another 1,000 checks, each of $3,000, and express the wish that his 1,000 guests pass the checks on to his other boy. It would all be legal, and that way he could give each of his kids $3 million, tax free. Hmmm.

136

3. Another possibility: Installment *sales* are tax free to the seller if the seller of property takes back a note and no cash. He could "sell" his $6 million in property to his kids and take back notes or I.O.U.s for $3 million each. The kids could then go out and borrow against the property to raise tax-free money in cash for themselves. The possibilities and combinations seemed endless—for someone with a little imagination. "Can't accountants read?" Clarence thought to himself.

4. Clarence could also buy a life insurance policy, and on his death the proceeds would pass entirely tax free to his two kids as his beneficiaries.

5. If Clarence formed a corporation to hold his $6 million in assets, and the kids formed a corporation to hold their much smaller assets, and he could swap his stock for some of their stock, then that swap would be tax free. When Clarence died, it could be arranged, with options and such, that his stock wasn't worth much in his estate.

All those possibilities were fascinating and seemed to be only the tip of the iceberg. He kept digging. Finally, about two weeks later, with a twinkle in his eye and a smile on his face, Clarence the businessman told Irving the C.P.A. that he had the information he needed.

"I never knew how important a few weeks in the library could be," said Clarence.

The accountant asked, "Did you find anything you could use?"

The old man smiled like a cat that had just swallowed a parakeet and replied, "You'll see!"

A few weeks later everybody in town got an invitation to Clarence's 70th birthday banquet. Not really everyone, just everyone who was *anyone*. The mayor was there, the fire chief, prominent politicians and businessmen, the entire Kiwanis Club, and all Clarence's buddies from the Knights of Columbus. It was a great party, and just as the dessert was about to be served Clarence clinked on his glass for attention

137

and began his speech. He thanked everyone for coming to help him celebrate and led the group in several toasts—to old business competitors, his dear departed wife, the mayor, the district director of the Internal Revenue Service, and his "two fine daughters-in-law, the mothers of my fine grandchildren." The little tykes were then introduced and cheered.

Then Clarence said something that shocked and startled everyone and put a real chill on the party.

"And," went on the 70-year-old birthday boy, "I would drink a toast to my two sons, but they are such a disappointment to me, I just can't do it."

The assemblage was hushed, everyone was waiting for the funny punch line of some intended joke. But instead Clarence continued in a very serious tone:

"My two boys have treated me terribly—but not nearly as badly as they have treated their wives and families. Did you know they are both carrying on with their secretaries? And before that they cheated on their wives with other women. In business, they are thieves. They have entered into one sharp transaction after another and have robbed me blind. And they have stolen from some of you, my dear friends, too!"

The boys got up and stormed out with their wives. Most of the guests, not wanting to be part of a family scene, began to drift out of the banquet hall behind them. Before dessert was over, no one was left but the old man and a few waiters. Clarence continued on with his tirade against his sons. The room was empty of guests by then.

The next day, the two boys, through their attorneys, filed a $10 million slander suit against their father! After the case came up for trial, the judge looked at Clarence sternly and indicated that from all he'd heard the boys had been grievously wronged. What Clarence said at the banquet had been false! The judge said that he intended to award the boys $5 million each for injuries to their reputations due to the inexcusable defamations uttered by Clarence. Before setting the award, the judge asked Clarence if he had anything to say in his defense.

*The recovery of damages for personal injury, defamation,
or loss of goodwill is not considered taxable income
under the current Internal Revenue Code.*

"Your honor," said Clarence, "What I did was terrible and you are right to throw the book at me—but the problem is I don't have $10 million. I only have $6 million."

The judge thanked Clarence for the information, said he'd take it into account, and then he passed sentence:

"For damages in this case I award each of your boys $3 million."

About four years later, Clarence died with a smile on his face, no estate, and his boys had $3 million each—tax free. Why tax free? Because awards or out of court settlements in libel, slander or personal injury cases are tax free to the recipient.

Lest you think this chapter is entirely fiction and could never happen in real life, remember Howard Hughes? In the years just before Hughes' death, the strawboss of his operations, Robert Mayhew, a former F.B.I. agent, was fired. In those days, it might have cost over $7 million in severance pay to give Mayhew $3 million net after taxes. Howard Hughes fired Mayhew and told the world in a press interview, "He stole me blind."

Mayhew sued for defamation. When Mayhew settled for about $3 million in damages, *tax free,* some people wondered if Mayhew and Hughes hadn't planned it that way.

9.
1031
Exchanges

Knowing how to make a tax-free real estate exchange is extremely important. I'm going to tell you what a tax-free trade is, why you should trade, when you should trade, and how you should trade. As a result of this information, instead of selling property and paying up to 65 percent of your profits in federal and state taxes, you will be able to make deals and save substantial amounts of money. This involves big money that would otherwise have been squandered in taxes. The net result of your mastering the technique of trading up will be to increase your net worth at tremendous speed. This will give you a fast, clear path to financial independence. With financial freedom, you gain control over your own destiny.

What we are covering specifically is the use of Internal Revenue Code Section 1031, relating to tax-free or, more accurately, tax-deferred exchanges. After reading this, you will be able to mastermind your own tax-free trades without a lawyer or C.P.A. at your side. In addition, you will understand exchanging better than a vast majority of lawyers, accountants, and real estate brokers.

First of all, let's clear up the biggest misunderstanding concerning trades of real property. Most people believe that if you own a small property and you want to trade up to a bigger property, you have to find someone with a big property who is willing to take your smaller property in trade. Nothing could be further from the truth. Here is what really happens: You want to trade up from a single family home you own (as a rental unit) to a bigger property—say, a 20-unit apartment building. The owner of those 20 units doesn't want your single family house because it is smaller. He himself wants to trade up. In the real world, the owner of the larger piece of property you want almost always wishes to trade up. He will seldom want to sell for cash and will rarely, if ever, want to trade *down*.

"But," you may say, "You are not talking about trading after all, are you? Because I always thought that when you traded you gave something other than cash and you got something other than cash in return from the person you traded with." Here I will clarify a common misconception about real estate trading. Exchanges or trades under Section 1031 of the I.R.S. code are never *really* trades or exchanges of Property A for Property B. Section 1031 tax-free exchanges are simply paper exchanges done solely for tax purposes. 1031 exchanges are a completely legal, I.R.S.-approved way of legally avoiding taxes when you sell property at a profit and immediately invest in other property. This 1031 exchange really is a way to "sell" your property without paying any capital gains tax, any ordinary income tax, or any tax at all!

There are three main requirements for such tax-free exchanges. The fourth requirement (an immediate reinvestment of proceeds) has some flexibility. First, there must be like property sold and like property acquired. But "like"

*Why is the I.R.S. like the Catholic Church? Both find
"sin" in what you were thinking—not in what you did.*

*"Your lips tell me 'no-no,'
but there's 'yes-yes' in your eyes!"*

*Section 1031 exchanges are one of the few exceptions to
the general rule that a transaction entered into primarily
for tax avoidance reasons is declared void by the I.R.S.*

property has a very special meaning for the I.R.S., as I will
explain later. Second, the property you are buying must have
a bigger price tag than the property you are selling. Third, the
property you are buying must have a bigger mortgage than
the property you are selling. And, fourth (this is where some
flexibility comes in), there should be a *simultaneous* closing
of the two deals. But if you structure the "trade" carefully
you can sell now and reinvest several months or even several
years later.

The "trading" is all done on paper. There is no real trade.
There is just an elaborate fiction to avoid taxes. The Section
1031 deal is an artificial method of selling and buying that
would never exist but for the tax code. It's a way that you and

I can "sell" property by meeting requirements set forth by a certain very important federal law known as Section 1031 of the Internal Revenue Code.

If you have ever looked up anything in the tax code, you know the code is indeed code. It is difficult to understand, uses obscure language, and is almost impossible to read. But, in contrast to most other sections, 1031 is relatively clear and is only one paragraph long. It says, "No gain or loss shall be recognized if property held for productive use in trade or business or for investment is exchanged solely for property of a like kind to be held either for productive use in trade or business or for investment." Specifically excluded from this section is stock in trade, property held primarily for sale, stocks, bonds, notes, claims against other people, certificates of trust, or other securities.

To have your deal meet the code requirements, it is necessary to previously establish an *intent* that the property you own and the properties you are acquiring are for investment, not for a quick resale. Then, all you have to do is adhere to the three main requirements for a 1031 exchange. As I said,

1. It must be a like for like exchange.
2. The new property must have a bigger price tag.
3. The new property must have a bigger mortgage.

The fact that your *intent* in doing a 1031 exchange is solely to avoid taxes cannot be held against you and will not invalidate the tax-free status of your trade. Actually, you could broadcast on national network and place an ad in *The New York Times* saying that your whole, exclusive, and only purpose in doing a Section 1031 exchange was to avoid taxes. And, if the I.R.S. heard that announcement and knew your intention, your exchange would *still* be tax free—as long as you followed the exact provisions of Section 1031. Under existing U.S. tax laws, almost any other tax-saving business transaction could be disregarded by the I.R.S. if tax avoidance was your main motivation.

The only reason for doing a 1031 exchange is to take advantage of a legally approved method of avoiding taxes. This section is one of the few of the tax code that have been interpreted in favor of the taxpayer in many court cases. For perhaps the first time in your "tax planning," you do not have to go through elaborate shenanigans to manufacture "evidence" to convince the I.R.S. that what you did was a bona fide business transaction without tax avoidance motives. It is sufficient that your exchange was done for no other purpose than beating the I.R.S. out of taxes.

Normally, in other areas of tax law, if you arrange almost any transaction for the purpose of avoiding taxes, you will achieve the opposite result. The I.R.S. will say, "Any transaction you did just for tax benefits is not bona fide, and we will tax you anyway." But 1031 is different. Just follow the three rules—like for like, bigger price, and bigger mortgage—and you are home free (free of taxes, that is). You will notice 1031 does not apply only to real estate. Before I elaborate on how to use it in real estate, let's take some other examples. First, gold coins and foreign money; second, antique cars. Last, we'll look at real estate.

Suppose that, in your opinion, Austrian Corona gold coins will go up in value faster than South African Krugerrand gold coins. You have $1,000 worth of rands, 10 coins that you bought for about $100. You swap them for $1,000 worth of Coronas—also 10 coins. In a few days, your prediction comes true, and the Coronas are in fact worth 20 percent more than the rands. By trading, you accomplished what amounts to a tax-free sale of your Krugerrands. You acquired 10 Austrian Coronas with 10 rands. Had you paid a capital gains tax on the sale of your rands, you would only have been able to buy 5 Coronas. Now the rands go up by, say, 20 percent, you trade back for 12 rands. If you had paid taxes, you would be down to 5.5 rands from the 10 you started with. Now, let's say you own Swiss francs today but you feel that German marks will go up at a faster rate. You can exchange your Swiss francs for German marks, tax free.

If what you did was a sale instead of an exchange—what

would your tax situation look like? Say you bought marks for $10,000. They now have a market value of $20,000. If you sold them for dollars, you would have a $10,000 gain and a tax to pay of around 50 percent of that $10,000 gain. You would *lose* $5,000 of your capital and would only be able to spend $15,000 on German marks. So by *trading* your Swiss francs for German marks you keep your profits and do not have to pay any tax! In effect, you have used your entire $20,000 worth of your Swiss francs to get $20,000 worth of German marks. If the marks go up relative to the francs (which is what you thought they would do), you can trade back and forth indefinitely and thereby keep increasing your wealth, at least in dollar terms. In real terms, all paper money is depreciating.

Where do you get the money to live on in the meantime? You could borrow dollars against your foreign money—*tax free!*

Next, assume you had an antique 1910 Buick. Why would you want to do a tax-free exchange? Because you would avoid the capital gains tax that would otherwise be due if you merely sold the car at a big profit, took the money, and then went out to buy another car. So you can do a three-way exchange of the car you own for the one you want to buy—and thus avoid any taxes. But, as in real estate, the owner of what you want probably doesn't want what you have to trade—so a three-way deal is needed. Let's see how a three-way trade works in real estate.

Real Estate Trades

Now, you will recall that the property eligible for a tax-free exchange must be property held for productive use in a trade or business or for investment and cannot be property held primarily for sale. How do you make sure that the I.R.S. cannot establish that you are holding the property—the gold coins, foreign money, antique cars, or real estate—for sale?

At the outset, you should form the required intention

with regard to *every* piece of property that you ever buy or ever consider buying. Your intention must be that you are *buying for the long term;* that is, you *are buying "it" for a long-term investment.* You have no intention of selling. You will not sell. I repeat, you will not *ever* sell that property. That *must* be your intention if you want to own property that qualifies for trading.

It is necessary and essential that at the time you buy the property you write everyone who might possibly be interested in your intentions, and also everyone who isn't interested, that your *intention* with regard to that specific piece of property is to never sell it! Got that? Keep carbon copies of those letters. You tell everyone in sight, and you even write on your offer form, "This property is being purchased for investment and not for resale." Nobody cares except the I.R.S., which you do have to convince that any trading property you own was bought for investment, not stock in trade. It is going to be considered stock in trade if you are willing to sell it at a profit the minute a good offer materializes.

You might consider creating plenty of evidence of your investment intentions by asking a broker you know to write you a letter asking you if your property is for sale. Then you can reply in the strongest imaginable terms that you are outraged that he or she would consider offering you mere money for your property. Rant and rave a little: "I would never consider selling my property to you or to anyone else! I bought this for investment purposes, and I am not of a mind to sell that property just because somebody offers me a quick profit." Be irate. Be firm!

With five or six file copies of similar answers to inquiries about a possible sale, the I.R.S. will be hard put to classify that property as dealer property because, by their definition "dealer property" is property that you bought with the intention of reselling to someone else, not as a long-term investment. So, to summarize, it is very important to form the proper intention at the time you buy any property that you are going to hold that property as a long-term investment and you are not going to sell it—unless your circumstances change drastically. You are going to buy that property for investment.

Another reason acceptable to the I.R.S. is that you bought the property for the production of income and not for resale. As another example, let us say you bought a building for the purpose of manufacturing rubber tires. You buy a tire factory with the intention of manufacturing tires, not to re-sell the building at a profit. Now, of course, "use in trade or business" may be interpreted another way. Your trade or business could and should be owning and operating warehouses or other income property such as apartment buildings or stores. But the important thing is that if the I.R.S. suspects that you were a speculator (shudder) and just bought to re-sell, they will hit you with an ordinary income tax and won't let you do a tax-free exchange. The important thing is, at every stage of your operations, to make very clear to everyone that you are not in the business of buying property to sell at a profit.

Why? Well, to have that intention—to buy property with the intention of selling it at a profit—and then to rein-vest the money would be stupid. These days, *ordinary income* is taxed at up to 50 percent by the Feds.* California state tax adds another 15 percent (you can adjust the figure to meet your own state tax). For example, if you bought property with the intention of selling it for a quick buck, then you would also have the intention of giving 65 percent of your profits away to Uncle Sam and your state. That would be a pretty stupid intention when the law as expressed in 1031 gives you the opportunity to dispose of your property in a tax-free exchange.

The only motive for doing a 1031 exchange is tax savings, and as I've said that is considerable. There is really no

---

*The effective tax rate was reduced from 50 percent to 30 percent for transactions after November 1978. Congress may reduce the capital gains tax even more in 1981-82.

other motive. Naturally it would be much easier, even if you wanted to acquire other property, to merely sell Property 1, take that money and buy Property 2, the bigger and better property, because then you wouldn't have to worry about doing all the paperwork that is required for a 1031 exchange. But, with a big potential tax bite involved, obviously it is better to take the time and take the effort to do a 1031 exchange rather than to merely sell your property, take the proceeds, and invest it in other properties. Why? Because if you do a sale and repurchase, the federal and state governments could take as much as 65 percent of your profits from the sale!

Now you want to know, *when should I exchange?* *When* should I start trying to arrange an exchange under section 1031? The answer is: Any time you find a bigger and better property than the one that you own and it's for sale at a fair price, consider arranging a 1031 exchange.

I have heard some so-called authorities say that you start looking for an exchange only when your depreciation runs out. That may be anywhere from 10 to 15 years after you have acquired the property. Don't tell the I.R.S.—but you should be ready to exchange *one day* after you get the property, just as long as the new deal is better than the one you're getting out of. The prospective trade property must have the magic three factors: (1) like for like, (2) bigger price tag, and (3) bigger loan.

Don't wait until depreciation runs out. If you want to be a tycoon, always keep your eyes open for good real estate deals. Be prepared to use the equity in property that you already own as the down payment on property you hope to acquire.

Are there any alternatives to a 1031 exchange that you should consider? Of course there are. If it's possible to make a *no-money-down deal* for the place you are acquiring and not dispose of the place you already own, then hold on to good investment property. If you are able to acquire Property 2 without trading for a low down payment that you have or can borrow, try to hold on to it. Remember one of the greatest real estate fortunes of all time—that of Vincent Astor—was built on the motto "Never sell the land" (if you don't have to). And he formed that intention even before the tax code made it even more necessary.

With that, I will show you how a classic "1031" trade works. In the real world, every trade involves at least *three* people. There are never just two people because in the real world there has to be a cash buyer; that is, someone who comes into the deal with money and no property to trade. At the other, or upper, end of the trade, there is usually someone who is selling real estate for cash. "He" may be a tax-free entity such as a pension fund, foundation or charity. Or he is cashing in his chips and willing to pay the tax on the sale. More than likely the seller is going to arrange for his own tradeup. Getting all these characters together might seem like a tall order, but we are going to see what happens in a typical trade deal—the 1031 exchange that goes on every day between sophisticated large-scale real estate investors—the likes of which you will be within the next three years.

Let's dissect a typical simple tax-free exchange. There are three characters in our drama. We will call you Mr. Dumpy because many years ago you bought "El Dumpo," a little house in the Oakland ghetto, at a cost of $2,000. Today it is worth $10,000. It brings you $100 per month in rent. You have a potential $8,000 profit or capital gain on the house. If you sold it outright, you would have to pay a capital gain tax on the $8,000 profit you would make. Depending on your tax bracket, that could be up to $4,000 or more.

You have been looking around at various real estate deals, and you've found Mr. Classy who owns a $100,000 apartment house of four units in a nice section of Reno, Nevada. He has it up for sale and will take $100,000. Step 1 is for you to go to Mr. Classy to negotiate price. We will assume that Mr. Classy agrees to sell you his fourplex for the sum of $100,000 payable in cash, within 90 days.

But on your offer to Mr. Classy, after you have put in all

of the other standard terms, you write, "This acquisition subject to buyer being able to find a buyer for 23 El Dumpo Lane, Oakland, at a price of $10,000 or better and structuring this deal as a tax-free exchange under Internal Revenue Code Section 1031." Now, if Mr. Classy is not a sophisticated investor, he will want to know why you put that sentence in this contract. And then you are going to show him this chapter. You show him that if you are able to close the sale of your house and buy Mr. Classy's apartment house on the same day and you do all the paperwork just right, then you will not have to pay any tax on the sale.

Mr. Classy, learning about exchanges, will think trading is so clever that he will want to do a simultaneous trade of his property so that he can get the same benefits. Actually, in the real world, Mr. Classy and people like him have already arranged for an exchange just as you are doing except that Mr. Classy is probably buying a million-dollar property. The owner of the million-dollar property is in turn probably arranging to trade into a $2-million property. And that seller of the $2-million property is moving up to a $10-million shopping center, and so on up the line.

In the real world, when you close your first trade you may well find that not only your trade, but also six or seven or eight other trades all in the same chain must close simultaneously with your deal. Now that, of course, involves a lot of fancy footwork. And if you have ever been in any real estate deals at all, you know that even simple deals seldom close on time. So you can just imagine the postponements that will occur with a large number of closings all having to be done on the same day. Some people have conflicting appointments and medical problems. Spouses have to be brought in to sign papers; some may be involved in divorce proceedings. It should be obvious that in your typical exchange there are normally all kinds of special problems. Exchanges rarely, if ever, close on the day scheduled.

That is one reason why real estate brokers do not like trades. When you mention trading to typical real estate brokers, they will do all they can to discourage it. They will lie and tell you that the tax saving really is not significant. They will advise "just sell your property and forget about the fancy complicated trading business." But what these brokers are really saying is that they don't want their commissions delayed. Because brokers don't like their commissions to be postponed and like a deal to close as quickly as they can, they will discourage you from doing a tax free exchange. Whether you pay zero tax or a half-million capital gains tax is of little concern to a real estate broker. Their commission is the same regardless of your tax liability. Obviously the broker would rather have you do a simple deal and pay a big income tax rather than do what from their point of view is a complicated deal just to save you a great amount of money in taxes. *Moral:* Don't let anyone talk you out of it. It is your money, your future, and your freedom!

Let's get back to our example. Your first trade will be very simple and very easy to understand. Your first step as an exchanger was to go out and find a bigger property that you wanted to exchange into.

Step 2 is to *find a cash buyer for your property.* Now that doesn't mean the cash buyer must have all cash but he must be able to raise a down payment plus financing so that, at the close, he will come up with a total of $10,000 in cash to be able to cash out Mr. Classy.

Now, what do I mean by "cash out" Mr. Classy? Well, look at Mr. Classy's motivation for a minute. He doesn't really want your little dumpy house. If anything, he wants a much bigger and better apartment building than the one he is selling. But for the moment, assume that Classy just wants to cash out. In real life, you will find that cashing out is often the motivation of the person with the bigger property. He may want to cash in his chips and retire, or maybe it is an estate sale. But seldom, if ever, does the owner of a bigger property want to trade down into a little dump.

I won't say it never happens but I have just never seen a "trade down" and I have been involved in a hundred or more trades. As I say, I've never once seen the owner of a bigger property who wants to trade down into a little one. The only time something like that happens is with residences where parents formerly had a large family. The kids went off to school or got married. Now they want a smaller house. When we are talking about residences or owner-occupied homes, a whole different set of trading rules apply, and we will cover those later. Here we are learning about exchanging *investment* or *income* property. It could be vacant land, held for investment, farms, or factories, but not homes or principal residences.

Getting back to our story of Mr. Classy and Mr. Dumpy and Mr. Cash, Mr. Classy wants to cash out by selling you his fourplex. Mr. Cash wants to buy El Dumpo. You are Mr. Dumpy, and you won't sell your property to Mr. Cash just outright because if you did you would have to pay a substantial amount of capital gains tax. So here is what you do.

This is how you arrange your exchange. Go to your favorite escrow company. Tell them that you want them to arrange a tax-free, three-way exchange under Section 1031 of the Internal Revenue Code. Give them the prices, names, and addresses involved, and they will do all the paperwork. As always it is your responsibility to make sure that they don't foul up. So that you know how to check on them, this is what the title company should do. Prior to the day set for closing, they should ask you for a deed to El Dumpo. This deed should transfer title to El Dumpo to Mr. Classy. Then they will get a signed deed from Mr. Classy covering El Dumpo, transferring title to Mr. Cash. They will also need a deed from Mr. Classy for his big apartment building transferring title to you, Mr. Dumpy.

When the smoke clears on the day of the closing, this is what happens. Mr. Classy technically (and always technically) "buys" El Dumpo, but it is done with the understanding that he will simultaneously sell it or deed it to Mr. Cash. Mr. Cash will deposit in escrow $10,000—part of it may be coming from a mortgage and part of it from his own money—but

A three-way tax-free trade

Mr. Dumpy owns
El Dumpo.

Mr. Classy owns
the Classy Apartments

Mr. Cash has
$10,000

Banker has
$90,000 cash

The bank puts
$90,000 in the pot.
Mr. Cash puts
$10,000 in the pot.

Mr. Dumpy deeds
El Dumpo to Mr. Classy

Mr. Classy deeds El Dumpo to Mr. Cash.
At the same time he deeds the
Classy Apartments to Mr. Dumpy.

Mr. Cash owns El Dumpo

Mr. Dumpy owns Classy Apartments

Mr. Classy walks away with $100,000

The bank keeps an i.o.u. for $90,000.

in any event, $10,000 will be deposited with the title company and that $10,000 will be handed to Mr. Classy in exchange for his deed to the apartment building and the deed to El Dumpo. Now, Mr. Classy has to get one other thing: that's $90,000, so that his total receipts for the day will be $100,000.

Where does he get the $90,000 from? Well, you, Mr. Dumpy, have arranged for a $90,000 loan in connection with buying Mr. Classy's apartment house. Perhaps you got $80,000 from a savings and loan association and $10,000 from your mother-in-law or a hard-money lender, or even $10,000 from Mr. Classy himself, who carried back a second mortgage. In any event, Mr. Classy now has the $100,000 he wanted in the first place. Mr. Classy walks away from the deal with money. He does not own El Dumpo. That has been sold out of the trade to Mr. Cash. Chances are, in the real world, Mr. Classy will have arranged a tradeup and his $100,000 will be used as the down payment on a still larger property, but that is no concern of yours.

To summarize, Dumpy, that's you, ends up with title to Classy's $100,000 fourplex. Mr. Cash ends up with the title to, and ownership of, the $10,000 El Dumpo. Mr. Classy walks away with a total of $100,000 in cash or paper he's carried back. As mentioned, more than likely he's arranged his own trade to close the same day. Classy will probably trade up and buy an even bigger and better property, perhaps an eightplex or 16 units.

You saw how, for an instant, Mr. Classy did in fact own El Dumpo. He sold it immediately, to Mr. Cash. Now, it is very important that in an exchange the person with the big property takes title to the property at the bottom end of the trade. There are no tax consequences to Mr. Classy for having bought and simultaneously sold the dump. He bought it for $10,000, and he sold it for $10,000. Whether he was a dealer or not is irrelevant, because there was no profit. He bought and sold at the same price.

You, Mr. Dumpy, were the owner of El Dumpo, and you

This is what the I.R.S. gets in a 1031 exchange!

(The Shaft)

now have achieved your objective, which was to use your entire $10,000 equity in that house (assuming there was no mortgage) as if it were cash, as a down payment to buy the fourplex, the bigger building you wanted. You had a $10,000 property free and clear, and you used that property, just as if it were cash, to make the down payment on the bigger property you are going to move into. If you had not done it as an exchange, there would have been a capital gains tax of up to $4,000 on the profit resulting from a cash sale of the dump. But no tax at all was due, because you did a 1031 exchange. It's really quite simple.

Now that you understand the concept, let's talk in detail about the requirements of a 1031 exchange. First of all, there must be "like property for like property." What does the I.R.S. mean by that? Does it mean you can only trade a fourplex for another apartment building? Not at all. You could have a single family rental home (not your principal residence) that was worth half a million dollars, and you could trade it for an apartment building of 20 units that was worth any amount more than half a million.

You can trade *any* sort of real estate that is held for investment purposes for any other sort of real estate that is held for investment purposes. A farm for a store. Store for office buildings. Offices for land. Land for homes. Don't let anyone tell you that you can't trade a farm for an apartment building, or an apartment building for a shopping center. Shops can be traded for homes, or homes for farms, or apartments for vacant land—all of that is like kind property, just so long as it is held for investment purposes, *or* for the production of income, *or* for use in your trade or business.

What is *not* like for like? Assume you bought vacant land, created a subdivision, and then built 20 homes on it. If you had advertised those 20 homes for sale to whoever came along, then the I.R.S. would say that these homes were your inventory. It would be just like a jeweler's inventory of diamonds. If he made a profit on jewels, he'd have to pay ordinary income tax on his profit. More importantly, because it was stock in trade he could not *trade* that property tax-free at all. Therefore, you cannot trade so-called "dealer property" for investment property.

Is there any other kind of unlike property that you might get in trouble with? Certainly there is. Your primary residence is governed by a different set of rules. You cannot trade your primary residence for an apartment building or for another house that you are not going to move into. How can you get around that rule?

Is there a way to trade your primary residence for income property? Well, that's very simple. All you do is move out of your primary residence and rent it out. Once it has been rented out for a reasonable period of time (at least six months), it is no longer your primary residence. It has been transformed into income property. You can then trade it for other income property. But a residence can be sold for tax-free cash and need not be traded, under a different tax rule. Using that option you'd have up to 18 months to reinvest cash received from the sale of a residence into a more costly residence.

What's the next requirement for a tax-free exchange?

The first was "like for like." The second one is "bigger price." The place that you are trading up to must have a higher price tag than the place you're getting out of.

Supposing in our example you own a $10,000 dump and you are going to trade but you're going to wind up with a $9,000 dump plus $1,000 cash. That would be called "trading down," and in that case you would realize $1,000 taxable cash. That $1,000 cash would be taxable to you, either as ordinary income or capital gain. Had you traded for a $10,000 deal, you could have worked things out so that there was no tax. The whole purpose of making an exchange in the first place is to avoid any tax.

To review, the place that you are trading into should have a bigger price tag, and common sense requires that it be a bigger and better place than the one you are disposing of. Naturally the place you're trading into (not a tax requirement, but just common sense) should be a better *value* than the place you're getting out of. Obviously, if you think you are getting less than fair market value for the place you are getting rid of and you are paying over market value for the place you are getting into, there is no reason to do an exchange. What would the purpose be? Besides tax benefits, always look at basic economics before you exchange—or before you do any deal, for that matter. After the exchange is over, you should make more money. You should be getting more cash flow. Cash flow, remember, is the net money left over after you pay mortgages, expenses, and real estate taxes. If you would have more cash flow from staying in the old property than from the one you're buying, stop and think it over. The improved cash flow doesn't have to be immediate but you certainly should have the prospect of making more money (after taxes) out of the new deal than the one you're getting out of.

The final requirement of a tax-free exchange is that the place you're getting into should have a bigger loan on it than the loan on the place you are selling. That's pretty straightforward. In the case of our example, El Dumpo had an $8,000 loan against it. But the place you're getting into is going to have a $90,000 loan against it. No problem there.

What happens if the loan on the new place, for some reason, is smaller? Then you have to take the smaller loan on the new place and subtract it from the larger loan. The net "loan relief" figure that you get constitutes taxable income to you. How do you avoid that problem? You arrange things so that the place you are going to buy has a bigger loan than the place you are selling. You can do it by refinancing the old place before you trade. Simple!

Can you do an exchange like for like, bigger price, and bigger loan, *and on the day of the closing* take out a lot of cash? The answer is no. If you do that, there will be tax consequences. You always have to arrange your affairs so that you do not take out any cash on the day of the exchange. There are plenty of other ways to get cash out of an exchange.

You can refinance the old property and take out cash before the deal closes. Remember, when you refinance property you already own any money you borrow is tax-free money. The fact that you trade up later, as long as you follow the rules (like for like, bigger price, bigger loan) doesn't result in the money you got in an earlier "refi" becoming taxable.

What if you do not refinance? In a proposed trade, you meet the three requirements: like for like, bigger price, and bigger loan. You close the deal and trade up into the new building. Assume for the moment you had a very big equity in your original property, so the loan on the new property is less than eighty percent of the value. For example, you had a $50,000 free-and-clear duplex, and you are using that equity as the down payment on a $100,000 free-and-clear fourplex. You would have a $50,000 equity in the new fourplex after the deal closed. The way you would get tax-free cash out of that deal is to wait a respectable amount of time (30 days, anyway) to refinance.

After the deal closed, *then* you'd arrange to refinance the new property with an 80 percent or an $80,000 loan, thereby raising $30,000 additional tax-free cash. The I.R.S. rule on the subject is that the refinancing of the place you end up with cannot have been arranged prior to the exchange date. So, even if it is your intention to refinance, you should not tell anyone your intention or arrange refinancing until after you have taken the title. Don't send in any loan applications. Don't start that until *after* you close the deal or the I.R.S. might try to tax the refinancing proceeds. The same rule would apply to refinancing the place you are about to get rid of in an exchange. That should be done on a date prior to the date of any of your negotiating or signing papers with the seller of the big property. The I.R.S. rule is that *if you take money out of a trade as part of the trade, that money will be taxable.*

Refinancing negotiated as part of an exchange can give rise to tax consequences. I will not go into the formula of how it's taxed because I advocate structuring every deal so you don't have to pay any tax at all. You can do that by simply exchanging like for like, paying a bigger price, and taking over a bigger loan. If there is no loan on either property, that's OK, because you can always *add* cash to close a trade-up without tax consequences to yourself.

Suppose that the only property you have is a single family residence and you want to do the equivalent of a Section 1031 exchange, getting yourself a bigger and better residence. Actually, that's covered by a different section of the Internal Revenue Code, Section 1034. That section provides you do not have to go through the rigmarole of a simultaneous trade and transfer of title. These complexities are eliminated. All you have to do is sell your residence. Then you have 18 months to take that money and find another house. The same three rules apply. But with Section 1034, like for like means that when you sell a primary residence you must buy another primary residence. The new place must have a bigger price but the loan amounts are irrelevant with residences. As a result, you can come out of the sale of a residence and acquisition of a new one with a lot of cash.

Let's see how it works: Suppose you own a $100,000 house free and clear. You bought it cheap 30 years ago. You now sell your home for $100,000. Now you've got $100,000 cash. Next, within 18 months, you buy a $101,000 house with a $10,000 cash down payment. Assuming a $10,000 down payment on a $101,000 house, that leaves you with $91,000 cash, tax free, to use for speculating in real estate, or whatever you want to do with it. So you see, Section 1034 is actually considerably more liberal than Section 1031 because you don't have to do any same-day close, and you can pick up a lot of cash by heavily mortgaging your new home. You can sell and have use of the money while you take 18 months to look around for a new place. It's 24 months if you *build* a new home. The 24 months from the sale date applies to the date when you actually physically move into a new property, not when you pay for it. You must be physically residing in a newly built place 24 months from the time you sell the old place. With new construction, you can also move into the new place 24 months *before* you sell the old one and get the same benefits. If you're over 55, the first $100,000 in capital gain on a residence is tax free, even if you don't purchase another house.

If you want to trade from an expensive residence into income property, you have to move out of the residence, rent it, or at least try to rent it, thereby converting it to income, or investment, property. Then, of course, you can do a 1031 exchange by arranging simultaneous closes of escrow, just as we did in our example with Mr. Cash, Mr. Dumpy, and Mr. Classy.

Is there any disadvantage to exchanging? Yes. It's a very minor disadvantage. It results from the rule that you *must* carry forward the depreciated basis of your old property into your new property. Now, that was a big mouthful of words. Let me explain how the accounting works.

In our example, to keep the math simple, assume that the $10,000 dump you bought was on land of little or no value. You bought it 10 years ago for $10,000, and over the years, since it was run-down rental property, you depreciated it down to zero. So, although your original cost was $10,000, your basis (that's what the I.R.S. people use to describe the net figure you get when you take cost less depreciation over the years) was zero. As you remember, if you bought something for $10,000, depreciated it down to zero, and then sold it for $10,000, you would, for tax purposes, have a $10,000 profit. This is the tax consequence even though your actual profit, because you bought and sold at the same price, was zero. Why would you have a $10,000 "profit"? Because the I.R.S. let you use that depreciation—let's say $1,000 a year for 10 years—to shelter your outside or regular income. They do not let you get away with sheltering your ordinary income for 10 years and then selling the property and paying no tax at all. No, they make you recover that depreciation when you sell, giving rise to the accountants' saying, "this year's depreciation is a future year's taxable capital gain."

So, you had a $10,000 property. You depreciated it down to zero. Now you're going to buy a $100,000 property. In an exchange, you must now adjust the basis of the new property by taking the depreciation that you have *already taken* on El Dumpo and carrying it forward into the price of the Classy Apartments. Now this is really pretty easy to do because in our example you're using that fully depreciated $10,000 property as a down payment, just as if it were $10,000 cash on the new property for $100,000.

Because you've fully depreciated that $10,000 property, what you do is treat the new $100,000 property as if you had already depreciated $10,000 of it. You acquired the $100,000 property in an exchange. You used your fully depreciated $10,000 property as your trade-in. Assuming you have a 10-year useful life expectancy on the new place, you start with a tax *basis* on the new property of only $90,000. You do not get to take depreciation on the full $100,000 price because you are *carrying forward* the used-up depreciation. But now you deduct from the depreciable basis of the new property the $10,000 depreciation you already used up on the trade-in. As a result you only get $9,000 per year depreciation on the Classy Apartments, instead of $10,000 per year depreciation.

I hope that teaches you the principle of the "carry forward basis." With multiple properties and the various complicated deals we go into these days, the actual accounting can get a little hairy. But now that you know the principle, you can probably figure out your carry forward basis on a simple deal. On your tax return, I'd advise you to get a C.P.A. to look your figures over!

In most trades, you will be getting much more in depreciation deductions after the trade than you were getting before the trade. If the price of the property you are getting into is much more than the price of the property you are getting out of, you'll always have plenty of overflow depreciation. Let me explain how that works.

If you had a $10,000 property, assuming your depreciation hadn't run out and it was being depreciated on a 10-year life, you were getting a $1,000 per year depreciation allowance. But if you go to a $100,000 property, even if the $10,000 property was fully depreciated, you would get $9,000 per year annual depreciation allowable out of the new property. That means you're exchanging a zero or $1,000 per year depreciation allowance for a $9,000 depreciation allowance. So obviously one advantage of trading up is that you can, without laying out any cash, increase your depreciation deductions drastically. If you own a $10,000 building that had a 10-year life and you were in your ninth year, one of the classic reasons for looking for a trade is to generate new depreciation when your old depreciation schedule is about to run out. You can shelter all your outside salary or professional income with depreciation, as more fully explained in the chapter "Pay No Taxes Ever Again."

Another reason for trading up is to take your profits out of old deals, tax free, acquire new larger properties, and then raise more cash by refinancing the new property after the close of escrow. You don't pay any ordinary income tax or capital gains taxes when you exchange, and, of course, borrowed money is never taxable.

You can also use a trade to get out of three or four small slummy properties into one bigger property. You can consolidate small holdings by trading up into one big project. Just arrange for our Mr. Classy to take title, only for a second, to your three, four, or six dumps. You can get out of slumlording; sell the whole mess at a stroke and move into "pride of ownership" deals. Of course, you must prearrange for the sale of your dumps to Mr. Cash buyers. In this way, you can exchange a lot of little scattered junk properties into one first-class apartment complex or shopping center.

Another reason you might want to do a trade is to generate a larger scale of operations. In other words, on Day 1 you had half a dozen single-family homes you were renting out. Because the rental income was marginal, you had to do everything yourself: maintenance, repairs, and collecting rent. That took up a lot of your time. But if you could trade those small homes up into a 100-unit apartment building, then the cash flow and the rents from that 100-unit apartment building will support a full-time manager and a handyman who could run the place without you. You would then become more of an executive and less of a janitor. No more stopped-up toilets or unpleasant details.

When you trade up into bigger properties, you generate a larger amount of cash flow. There is money for staff and, of course, larger amounts of borrowing power. In a few years, you become a much more important individual to bankers, suppliers, and everybody else when the rents you have coming in are $900,000 a year rather than $9,000.

Some people exchange because they want to change location. For instance, you may think that the property you own in Los Angeles or Boston is overvalued. Property in Palm Springs, Atlanta, or Miami is, you feel, going to increase in price at a much more rapid rate. Hopefully you will be getting much more appreciation by reinvesting in another location. You can trade out of property in one city and go to another city. Not only that, you can trade U.S. property for non-U.S. property, or you can trade your foreign property for U.S. property. There are no geographic requirements under Section 1031! You can trade into or out of any type of investment property in the world. And, of course, if you trade up at regular intervals you will go from being a small property owner to being a tycoon.

Now that you know the basics of exchanging, let me pass on just a couple of warnings so you don't screw up. First of all, there is a good form some folks use called an "exchange agreement." The I.R.S., when it is giving somebody a real thorough audit, likes to review all the papers. If agents find a "buy and sell" agreement (an agreement that shows you are buying Mr. Classy's place and you are selling your place to Mr. Cash) they may try to disallow the exchange because they say you didn't do the paperwork properly. But you are home free if Mr. Classy actually took title to El Dumpo. You should have some sort of agreement covering the mechanics. Here is one suggestion (all contracts should be adapted to your own deals with the help of a competent attorney):

Addendum to Deposit Receipt
Offer to Purchase *The Classy Apartments*
Dated June 1, 19XX

The undersigned *Mr. Classy* does hereby agree to take in trade for *The Classy Apartments* title to *El Dumpo* for the sole purpose of effecting a Section 1031 tax-deferred exchange for *Mr. Dumpy*. *Mr. Classy* agrees to immediately convey title to *El Dumpo* to *Mr. Cash*, or such other buyer out of trade as may be found. It is understood that this exchange is being made as an accommodation to *Mr. Dumpy* and shall not result in any additional costs, risks, or liabilities to *Mr. Classy*. All such costs or risks shall be borne by *Mr. Dumpy*. In the event *Mr. Cash* is unable to complete the purchase of *El Dumpo* by *September 1, 19XX*, it is agreed that on that date

Mr. Dumpy will purchase *The Classy Apartment*s at the price and terms agreed upon in the attached Deposit Receipt.

David Dumpy	Calvin Classy
Signature	Signature

Mrs. Humpty Dumpy	Mrs. Corrinne Classy
Signature	Signature

The crucial thing in a tax-free exchange is the taking of title to the smaller property by Mr. Classy before it is deeded to the cash buyer. To do it exactly right, you should create some sort of exchange agreement making it obvious to an I.R.S. agent what was done. You need only have a letter that you and Mr. Classy sign showing your intention to do a proper 1031 exchange. You both understand that you are really just selling El Dumpo to a third party and buying the Classy place. Mr. Classy understands that he is just taking title to the dump as a convenience to you, but the I.R.S. (if it wants to give you a hard time) will insist on seeing an exchange agreement. The sample exchange agreement just given should do the trick.

Let's assume another problem: For some reason, Mr. Classy at the closing doesn't want or isn't able to sign a proper deed to El Dumpo. The most common reason—he is not getting along with his wife. A divorce may be pending. As a result, Mrs. Classy won't sign papers for him. Under the law of most states, a wife has an automatic interest in any real estate that her husband owns. But if the wife will not sign or Mr. Classy cannot sign the deed there's a solution. It is possible for the owners involved to deed all the properties in the trade to a title company as nominee or straw man. The title company then completes the trade and deeds out El Dumpo to Mr. Cash and the Classy Apartments to you. This is an alternative way of doing a legal tax-free exchange.

Once again: Both properties in the trade are deeded to a title company. The title company, acting as an agent for Mr.

Classy, conveys to Mr. Cash. Remember, in real estate (or in any other business), wherever there is a problem there is always a way around it. I certainly hope that my tycoons never assume that all is lost. If Mrs. Classy refused to sign the trade papers for El Dumpo, you simply ask the title company if they know any other way of doing it. They probably will tell you they could take the title, as just explained. If they don't make any useful suggestions, it is up to you to go to another source for ideas. Never give up until you have exhausted every title company, every lawyer, every accountant, and every trade broker in your city. Get the deal to close—one way or another. It's easy to give up! But tycoons are a different breed. They always close their deals. When the going gets tough, the tough get going. A cliché, but apt!

Another problem that often comes up is that the person taking the role of Mr. Classy in our agreement says, "Look, I'll cooperate with you in doing a tax-free exchange. I'll do whatever you want. I also want a real firm deal on my sale, so if you're not able to make an exchange I want you to personally guarantee that you will take the property anyway." If that happens, you have a decision to make. Are you willing to take the property even if you do not sell your old place? Can you raise the money to close the deal? I would generally prefer to put into my exchange agreement that if I do not sell El Dumpo to a third party I would deed it to Mr. Classy and buy it back myself within a year at the exchange price. Or as an alternative I might try to get a concession from the seller: that he would take back a big-enough second mortgage to cover the smaller amount of cash I would have had to make up for if El Dumpo could not be sold. I would also see how much cash I could get out of a refinance of El Dumpo and try to renegotiate either price or terms to fit the realities of my pocketbook.

The best possibility is that you might be able to talk Mr. Classy into really taking title and possession of El Dumpo, especially if you guarantee rents at a certain level satisfactory to Mr. Classy. You can, if you have to, guarantee to manage El Dumpo. You can further guarantee to sell it for him within a year or whatever time period you both can agree on. If it can't be sold, you can buy it back yourself.

In case you are ever audited by the I.R.S. and they find you've used our sample contract—to the effect that if an exchange could not be arranged you as buyer would pay cash and take over the property anyway—the I.R.S. agent may not know his law very well. *The agent might try to disallow the trade*, saying there really was no exchange. "You just wanted to buy his place and sell your place," says the I.R.S. "All your agreements were buy/sell agreements, not exchange agreements." The I.R.S. agent may wrongly try to disallow the tax-free exchange. If that happens, you just tell the I.R.S. agent that there was a case in 1935 called the Mercantile Trust Case. It was a very famous case for exchangers. In that case, there was an agreement to exchange with a "sale in lieu" provision, just as in our sample form. The deal was approved by the courts as a tax-free exchange! In other words, there was contractual language between the parties in that particular case that if the property were not in fact exchanged the deal would go through anyway and the property would be bought for cash. The I.R.S. tried to say that even though there was an exchange later, the Mr. Dumpy of Mercantile Trust did not really have any intention to do a 1031 exchange. The good old I.R.S. was trying back in 1935 to say that a secret intention to buy rather than trade resulted in a "non-tax free exchange." But the court said as long as the parties go through the motions required by Section 1031 it doesn't really matter what was in their heart of hearts.

There was another interesting twist in 1962 in the Baird Publishing Company case. It involved a delayed exchange. A religious organization wanted to acquire a building that was owned by Baird Publishing Company. A church owned all the property on the block except Baird's factory and wanted it all for their new church. Baird didn't particularly want to sell his little printing plant until the church agreed to build Baird a brand new building nearby. But they wanted to buy the Baird building immediately. Since Baird didn't want to pay taxes, a trade was written up on paper. The deal was to give Baird a new building built to his specifications a little distance from the old one. The exchange contract provided that Baird could stay in the old building rent free until the new one was finished. Only when the new building was finished would Baird move all his publishing equipment over to the new place. So what essentially happened in the Baird case was this: The church bought Baird's property on Day 1. Considerably later, the new building was completed. Baird moved, and title was then conveyed to Baird. He got his new publishing company building, worth considerably more than the old one. The I.R.S., as you might imagine, said this was not simultaneous exchange and disallowed it as a tax-free exchange. When it got to court, the judge decided that even though legal title to the trade-in property passed long before title to the new place passed to Baird, Baird still had the use of the old place rent free and the "equitable" title remained with Baird. In other words, the court felt "real ownership" passed to the church only when Baird finally moved out of El Dumpo and moved into the new building. So they let Baird have a delayed tax-free exchange.

Now, let me tell you how you could possibly use that case to your advantage. You've got a red-hot buyer for some property that you own and they want to tie up your property. They want it badly and are willing to pay you a very good price. You think your building is worth only $70,000, but the buyer is willing to give you $100,000. The only problem is that you haven't found a suitable property you want to trade up into. You could, of course, have the buyer build for you. But here is my suggestion how you could structure a variation on the Baird delayed trade to still come within the rule of the Baird Publishing Company case. You sell your property to the new buyer. We will call them the "Church" just to make the example tiein with Baird. You sell your property to the Church, but do it on a contract of sale. That is, you give possession but keep title. The Church "agrees to buy" but does not close the deal by taking title. You keeping title and giving up possession would probably be construed as you keeping a substantial interest in the property, just like Baird, who in his case gave up title while he kept possession.

I think if you, as seller, kept title to your property and delivered physical possession to the buyer and then had the Church put $100,000 cash or an I.O.U. for $100,000 into a title company escrow to be held until you found a suitable trade property, I believe you would have the makings of a good deferred tax-free exchange. You would go out and find the trade property. *When* you do, whether six months or five years later, shouldn't matter to the I.R.S. Once you have found the trade-up property, have the title company use the $100,000 on deposit as the down payment on the place you are buying. Now, very important: *The Church should take title to the new property* and one second later convey title to you. Simultaneously, you convey a deed to El Dumpo to the Church. Both titles change hands at the same instant. It would seem to me that the Baird rule provides a way for you to take advantage of a situation where you find somebody who really wants your property and will pay a premium price at a time you haven't found "trade-up" property.

Another famous case for traders was the Starker case. Until 1977, every "trader" was going crazy using the so-called Starker rule. Everybody in the business thought it stood for the proposition that if you found a buyer for your property all you did was sell your property to him, transfer title, and tell that buyer to put the money into an escrow company (not to give it to you). Then you both gave the escrow company instructions that that money could only be taken out to buy suitable exchange property. The new trade-up property would be purchased years later in the name of your buyer, who would simultaneously deed it to you, thereby accomplishing a tax-free exchange. That was a pretty good rule while it lasted. But in Oregon, Judge Solomon, who decided the original Starker case, in a different case came to the conclusion that he had made a mistake. The net result was that many knowledgeable people in real estate felt as of 1978 that the Starker rule was dead and that title to all properties in a trade should pass simultaneously. But that was before the Federal Court of Appeals rule in '79 on the appeal of Starker.

The Latest Case on Exchanges

All good real estate tycoons who have attended my lectures know that the single most important real estate tax case ever decided was the famous Starker case, known in the trade as Starker 1. Starker 1 held that as long as a seller of investment real estate carefully avoided getting cash in hand, the proceeds from a sale of investment property could be held by a third party and be invested in another investment property at a later date, without any capital gain (or ordinary income) taxes on the deal.

The events giving rise to Starker 1 took place in the mid-1960s. Starker 1 was decided a number of years later. The I.R.S. did not appeal the case, and it was thought to be a final judgment. Later it turned into a long-running soap opera, with the I.R.S. bringing a similar action against another member of the Starker family involving the same transaction (Starker 2). Strangely enough, the case was heard by the same judge. Even stranger, the same judge (Solomon by name), changed his mind and said his earlier decision would give rise to too much tax avoidance. In a cryptic decision, Solomon seemed to say that a valid, tax-free 1031 exchange required a simultaneous transfer of title.

Almost 15 years after the facts, a three-judge Federal Appeals Court heard the appeal of Starker 2 and *reversed* the decision (the second decision, that is) of Judge Solomon.

Thus, now we have as the undisputed law of the land a relatively clear decision I will call Starker 3. This one gives tax avoidance enthusiasts an even greater victory than Starker 1. Starker 3 is nothing short of an amazing triumph against the I.R.S. Here is what you need to know to have

172

your lawyer or accountant structure a trade. Starker 3 is officially known as *Starker* v. *United States*, 602 F 2d 1341 (1979). The full opinion may be read in any law library. Incidentally, while a victory for all of us, poor Starker had to pay the tax up front and sue for a refund. After waiting 15 years for a decision, he'll get back inflation-eroded dollars worth (in real estate values) about 12 cents on the 1966 dollar. With the court costs and lawyers' fees, it was hardly a victory for Starker. Of course he will get interest from the I.R.S.—but they'll just be a few more 12-cent dollars.

Here is what the decision said, in my view:

1. You can't sell investment property and reinvest in a residence for yourself. If you do, you must pay the capital gain tax on the sale of the business property. Nothing new there—we all know that a 1031 exchange must involve "like kind" properties.

2. After the smoke clears in a complex 1031 transaction, you must end up with *ownership* of property. If you never get title *or* possession of the new trade-up property, but if you direct title to be transferred to a friend or relative, that will be treated as the equivalent of taking cash and making a gift.

3. The "ownership" you end up with does not necessarily have to be *title*. A *lease* of 30 years or more, a life estate, or a contract of sale will be considered the equivalent of title. The court in Starker 3 was not concerned with who held the "bare legal title" to the trade-up property. They looked for who was the "real" owner. It is very nice to have this formerly unclear point straightened out.

4. It is not necessary that the property one sells and the property one ends up with transfer at the same time. In the Starker facts, the time between the sale and the purchase of the trade-up property was several *years*. The key to keeping the deal *tax free* was *not taking any cash in hand*. In Starker, the cash was held in a special trust-type account by the

seller—but if the cash had been held by a broker, title company or any "independent" person with the *intention* of all parties that the funds be used only for purchasing trade-up property, you'd be home free—tax free, that is.

5. The possibility that (if no suitable trade property is located) you can demand and get your cash is not enough to destroy the tax-free nature of the deal. The key is your *intention* that you *prefer* to end up with another investment property and *not* cash. If you do eventually end up with property, the I.R.S. may not challenge the 1031 exchange on the grounds that you had the right to take out your cash without a trade. Naturally, if you received cash, profits would be taxable in the year received. The trade would be aborted. But no tax would be due until *either* the funds were invested in like-kind property (at which point only the accrued interest would be taxed) *or* until the year that the funds were withdrawn for personal use.

6. If you sell a property for, say, $100,000 profit and have the proceeds held by a title company or other independent trustee in, say, a "money market fund" at 12 percent per annum interest, and three years later you buy a property for $136,000 using all the money in your account, the court says that the interest earned *is not taxable* to you until it is taken out and/or spent. It *is taxable* as *ordinary income* in the year received or spent, but not before.

7. This Starker 3 decision applies not only to real estate but also to the sale of almost any investment or property used in a trade or business. Trucks are specifically mentioned in the opinion, but there is no reason to suppose that a sale of coins, diamonds, gold bullion, antiques, artworks, or *any* investment medium would not be covered. Securities are specifically *excluded.*

What this important decision means is that if you want to get out of a bad real estate deal, any declining investment, or just take advantage of a good offer, you can do so—tax free—by leaving the cash in some sort of a trust. You can arrange for the acquisition of trade property at a later date. The mechanics of handling the paperwork probably should be handled by a good lawyer or the legal department of a title company familiar with the Starker 3 case. It also means that unless you have dire need for the cash, you'd be an utter idiot not to arrange for the funds from any sale of assets to go into a special "1031 exchange account," to be drawn out only when you needed the money. Creating such an account will defer indefinitely the tax on *any* sale until you pull out the money (under the reasoning of the Starker 3 decision).

As a conclusion, I would have to warn you that in spite of the court decision in Starker, the I.R.S. does not follow the law in many districts and they try to disallow deferred exchanges. But the law is a very funny thing, and because every case is a little bit different and the intention of the parties is always a little bit different, who knows? You might fight your Starker-type-trade out with the I.R.S. and get your transaction ruled to be a valid tax-free exchange. Disputed real estate trades seem to be one of the few areas of the tax law where the taxpayer often prevails against the I.R.S.

In summary, it is best to follow approved, established procedures. But if you have created something that looks vaguely like a trade, you might as well risk treating it as a tax-free exchange. The worst that can happen is that the I.R.S. will disallow it. If your tax-free exchange is disallowed, you may be able to settle the tax they claim is due for a small percentage on the dollar. If the I.R.S. will not be reasonable, you can fight it out in court, where the odds are the court will side with you. In any event, you have got the use of the money for half a dozen years until your case is decided.

This analysis was prepared by myself, William Greene, J.D., and while I believe it to be accurate, it is not intended as legal advice. Before taking any action in reliance upon it, consult your own lawyer to determine applicability to your particular situation.

Delayed Real Estate Exchange Agreement

Re: Moonglow Lane
Exchanger: Bob Buyer
Owner: Sam Seller
Escrow Agent: Efficient Title Co.

1. The undersigned owner is disposing of his interest in the above property in exchange for the above exchanger depositing cash proceeds that represent the exchange value of the property and agreeing to purchase for him with said funds like-kind property that would qualify as a tax-free exchange under Section 1031 of the Internal Revenue Code. The said escrow agent will hold the funds in a savings account as trustee, and funds will not be available to owner except as provided herein.

2. It is understood that owner would not make a sale nor close this transaction unless it was a tax-free exchange under Section 1031, Internal Revenue Code.

a. The property being disposed of is one that was purchased for investment and is currently being held for the production of income and not for resale.

b. The exchanger does not now own property that the owner wants to acquire, but the exchanger and owner will agree on suitable property within 36 months, at which time the cash balance in escrow will be used by the exchanger to purchase said property for owner.

c. The cash balance in escrow shall not be available to owner, and the interest thereon shall be used to pay trustee and attorney fees, plus closing costs on the trade-up property.

d. Title to the property and cash representing exchange value shall be held by the escrow agent as trustee. If no trade property is located within 36 months, then the exchanger shall have right to close out its books by paying all funds in this trustee savings account to owner and conveying title to the order of the exchanger. But until that time owner shall have no right to the deposit, which remains the property of exchanger subject to this agreement. If no trade property is located and exchanger refuses to approve delivery of cash proceeds, owner can recover possession and title to above property. Until such time, owner shall retain equitable title to the property.

e. Owner would not sell the property to exchanger without an exchange agreement valid under 26 United States Code, Section 1031 of the Internal Revenue Code, and all parties understand that this transaction is an exchange under Section 1031. However, exchanger assumes no responsibility whatsoever for any

176

rulings on the taxability or nontaxability of the exchange value herein.

f. Exchanger will take title to the new property that is selected if this is deemed necessary under I.R.S. rules, before the (new) exchange property is transferred to owner and will fully cooperate in effectuating a tax-exempt exchange for owner.

g. This document shall serve as instructions to the title company to hold all exchange proceeds due owner until suitable trade property is located and proceeds are used to acquire trade property or until property is reconveyed by buyer to seller.

Dated: _____   _____
                                       Owner

                                       _____
                                       Exchanger

In economic reality, it should be noted that the combined state and federal capital gains tax does not just take 50 percent "profits"—it confiscates half the value of everything. Look at it from another angle. You bought a single, family rental property for $25,000 all cash five years ago. You sell it today for $125,000. Your "profit" is theoretically $100,000. But after a 50 percent federal and state tax bite, your net dollar-ahead profit is $50,000. Assuming you had no mortgage, that leaves you with a tax-free return of your original capital $25,000, plus your $50,000 "after-tax profit." Total in hand: $75,000.

The problem is, $75,000 today won't buy what $25,000 would have bought five years ago. You need $125,000 to replace the home you just sold. Obviously, the government has taxed a "capital gain" that wasn't really a "gain" at all. In real or constant dollars of home purchasing power, there was no gain.

Now change the facts! For those rare few who had investments in the stock market and were lucky enough to show a small profit, the capital gains tax is even more grossly unfair. Let's say you bought railroad stock for $10,000 in 1935. You sell it this year for $20,000, leaving you with

$15,000 in capital after paying your $5,000 capital gains tax. In 1980, your $15,000 will buy you less than $1,500 would have bought you in 1935.

What's the solution? The law should exempt capital gains from tax altogether or *at least* provide for indexing so that only "real" capital gains are taxed.

What was $10,000 worth in 1935? Plumbers got 25 cents an hour in those days. Today they get $25. The "capital gain" is strictly an illusion. Any idiot would tell you he'd rather have had $10,000 in 1935 than $200,000 in 1980.

In my opinion, rather than burdening the productive elements of society with need for the time-consuming and wasteful mechanics of the Section 1031 exchange, the capital gains tax ought to be eliminated entirely. Just because an object is sold at a higher dollar quoted price than that at which it was purchased does not necessarily mean there is a gain.

The big winner during an inflationary period is government. It creates nonexistent profits or capital gains and then taxes them heavily. The national debt is about $150,000 per person. That is the amount the U.S. government owes. It is being eroded by inflation. By the time it is paid back (to foreigners and Americans trusting enough to "invest" their money in savings bonds), it will be returned in dollars worth a tiny fraction of the dollars originally borrowed. Yet the government printing presses run on spewing out more and more unbacked paper money. When a dollar could be exchanged at the U.S. Treasury window for a silver or gold coin, there was a modicum of discipline imposed on government treasuries.

Today, if a private citizen or bank attempted to screw customers or depositors in the same way the U.S. government is screwing its citizens and creditors, it would be jailed for criminal fraud. But in the United States nobody seems to care except a few right-wing loonies and the generally ignored Libertarian Party.

If you pay very little tax and have a small business
of your own, driving a Rolls Royce convertible invites
I.R.S. scrutiny. You might as well put a neon sign on it!

"Why didn't anybody tell me this could be a tax shelter!"

10.
Porno Movies and Other Exotic Tax Shelters

If you keep in mind the methods by which shelter is obtained in real estate, the same principles with minor variations apply in all other businesses.

Producing porno movies can be a better tax shelter than real estate. Anything shot in focus seems to return a 100 percent or better profit in a year. Personally I'd rather do a first-class feature film, but due to the high costs and higher risks ($750,000 and up) only a skin flick ($35,000 to $95,000) qualifies for consideration as a one-man tax shelter. A documentary film for television might be equally good—if it is presold to television stations.

Step 1. Decide on the topic. To get the fastest tax write-off, it should be a timely topic where the popularity of the film could reasonably be expected to last no more than a year or two. Under the "timely useful life" rule, these films will qualify for a one-year write-off of their entire cost. Many porno films are "sexploitations" of currently popular movies like *Westworld. Sexworld,* as a result, had a limited life for tax purposes—in theory, for only as long as the major movie was being marketed and advertised.

Tax Shelters Defined

A tax shelter is any investment where an investor puts up his or her own (or borrowed) money to acquire an interest in a business venture. Using accounting procedures permitted by the Internal Revenue Service, the investor (at best) comes out of the deal with cash ahead, at the same time showing a loss for tax purposes. Many ventures advertised as tax shelters cost a great deal of money, provide no return of investment, lead to unlimited liability, and give the investor no tax shelter, but only an expensive lawsuit with the I.R.S.

The family trust arrangement sold by many tax quacks is an example of a "bad" shelter. Here's an example of a good one:

Example

Mr. X purchases an executive jet airplane for $800,000. $700,000 is borrowed from the Teamsters Pension Fund, $100,000 is borrowed from the dealer who sold the plane.

Interest is set at 10 percent per year on both loans for a total annual outlay of $80,000. All other expenses, including insurance and maintenance, are $20,000 per year.

The dealer agrees to lease back the plane for $100,000 per year with annual increases of 20 percent each year for the next ten years.

Mr. X gets an $80,000 investment tax credit against the income tax he owes—in the first year. He also is allowed to depreciate the plane over its useful life (eight years?) to achieve an extra $100,000 per year offset against his other income in future years.

Mr. X breaks even the first year, but due to rising lease payments, makes $20,000 cash the second year, $40,000 the third year, $60,000 the fourth year, and so on.

Assuming that the value of airplanes rises at the same rate as rental values, the plane is worth $160,000 more the first year, $320,000 the second year, and so on. If this is true, Mr. X should be able to refinance the airplane each year, borrowing, say, $100,000 per year in cash. Since borrowed money is always tax free, Mr. X will be able to spend his $100,000 in refinancing proceeds and his $20,000 in lease fees *at the same time he shows a loss for tax purposes!*

And, of course, you observed that at no time did any cash leave the pockets of Mr. X.

This example of an "ideal tax shelter" requiring no investment and utterly without risk has been included for illustration only. They may exist, but are not easy to find. If you get me or my investors "such a deal," I'll be delighted to put a smile on your face with a handsome finder's fee. In the real world, no one can guarantee that the value of an airplane (or anything else) will increase by 20 percent forever. But buildings tend to wear out so slowly that they come close to being the ideal tax shelter in times of inflation: The value and rents tend to rise each year, but for tax purposes a loss is created by depreciating over a short useful life.

Step 2. Go to your bank for a 120 percent loan on the project. You get the larger loan by having previously (in other borrowings) established good credit. The 20 percent overestimate of expenses is done to have cash to take out of the deal (hopefully). Unlike real estate, where you pretend to be paying more than you actually are, cost overruns with movies are to be expected. If your movie production only runs 10 percent over budget, you'll be extremely lucky.

Which bank do you go to? I understand that all of the big banks of California are heavy into porn movie loans. Why? Because they have proven to be exceptionally reliable. Few porno movies made by professional directors fail to make back all costs, and considerable profits too.

Step 3. Film the movie. All costs are usually amortized over the estimated useful life of the film—that normally means about 18 months. But print costs and advertising (about one-third of the total budget) are deductible in the year spent. Thus a porno can be an excellent year-end tax shelter, because advertising and processing costs can be prepaid with borrowed money on December 31 to shelter that year's income.

The best tax feature of a porno is that the producer gets an investment tax credit (in the case of a $95,000 film, $9,500 directly off his tax liability). By law, the tax credit applies only if the producer uses American naked bodies, American locations, and an all-American production crew. Leave it to Uncle Sam to be sure that those foreign pornos don't get the jump on native talent.

Financially, producing a movie, porno or otherwise, works like this: (1) Borrow $100,000 against the cost of the movie, (2) spend $90,000 on the flick, pocketing $10,000 tax free.

When the film is "in the can," which is movie talk for finished, you give a sneak preview for the press and the owners of the Pink Pussycat, Mitchell Brothers Theatre, or a similar chain.

If your film has any redeeming social value at all, a chain will buy it for about $100,000 cash up front against 50 percent of gross ticket sales or whatever you are able to negotiate. You get more money and bigger share of gross if the picture is something special. The owners of the Linda Lovelace film, *Deep Throat,* could ask for and get 85 percent of gross. The theater owner gets the rest.

If the film is received well, you can get more earnings by negotiating for foreign rights in other English-speaking countries. You could then contract for foreign-language dubbing if you want to make sales in Sweden, Italy, and other possible markets.

Without a penny out of pocket, by producing a skin flick as in our example, you can generate a $10,000 investment tax credit and about $30,000 in paper tax losses in Year 1, even if you started the film in November or December. In Year 2, you can probably write off the additional $70,000 cost of the film. Of course, there will hopefully be profits in Year 2. The first $110,000 of income goes to pay off the loan and (assumed) 10 percent of interest. The amount of profit over costs and interest is taxable income. So what do you do? Shelter it with a new film, *Close Encounters with Miss Linda Lovelace.* As taxable profits begin to materialize, starting a new movie is the filmland equivalent of trading up.

Making legitimate feature films used to be a good tax shelter for prosperous Beverly Hills types who invested with a group or syndicate. Before the 1976 reforms, investing in a movie was lots of fun. As an investor, you'd go to cast parties with pretty actresses, get a pass to previews of new releases, and shelter most of your own income from taxes. This was accomplished with a three-way tax break.

You invested your own money, say $10,000. You borrowed $100,000 repayable only out of profits over a 20-year period. No personal liability on the loan. Your $10,000 was called prepaid interest and was entirely deductible. The total investment could be written off fast, creating, say, a $50,000 loss per year. And there was investment tax credit. If the picture was a turkey, the loan was forgiven and the write-offs were no worry for 20 more years, when another tax shelter would have to be arranged to avoid "phantom income" (arising out of the fact that a forgiven debt is treated as a sale of the underlying asset).

The 1976 reforms knocked out all deductions associated with nonrecourse loans on movies. Then the inevitable happened. Americans refused to invest in motion pictures. After all, movies *are* risky. Only 1 in 20 legitimate films make any money. Without the tax shelter, there were no investors. Actors' unions asked Uncle Sam for help. Celluloid processors and producers asked Uncle Sam for help. Popcorn peddlers asked Uncle Sam for help. Uncle Sam came to the rescue. The government decided to become the provider of funds with cheap nonrecourse loans (subsidized by the taxpayer, of course). In 1978, the Small Business Administration licensed Telly "Kojak" Savalas, among others, to borrow $5 million to make movies. But the international film industry is gone from California, a victim of overregulation, union problems, as well as high taxes on both investors and stars. Help came too late. Most American films are now processed in Bavaria. Germany has decided to give German film investors incentives such as the Americans used to give. And they are shot in Spain, which has no union problems or taxes on stars.

Some people wonder why taxes keep getting more burdensome. Every time a shelter is eliminated, another industry flees the country. After they killed off the movie industry, Congress realized that the country lost jobs and tax revenues. To keep the least profitable dregs of an industry in California, the government will now lose money directly by investing directly in the most risky business known to man.

Incidentally, the "old" movie rules still apply to book-publishing ventures. You can finance the publication of a book with a recourse loan from the author. Until Uncle Sam decides to chase the publishing industry to Hong Kong, here is how you can use that gimmick.

Step 1. Find a worthy starving author with a timely book in manuscript form (let's say, Bill Greene's *Welcome to the Tax Revolt!*).

Step 2. Make a deal with the author: You will pay him, say, $100,000, $10,000 cash up front to cover the costs of printing 50,000 copies, and sign a $90,000 note with cash to be paid to the author out of profits. You, the investor, are to get your $10,000 back out of first profits. If the book flops, payment on the $90,000 "loan" from the author is postponed and not officially written off for 20 years.

Step 3. Publish the book and see what happens. If it is a bestseller, you make a lot of money and have to start looking for a new shelter. If it bombs, you write off your $100,000 "loss" over the two-year estimated useful life of the 50,000 unsold copies in your basement. That would be during this year and next year. You'd get $50,000 per year in writeoffs to offset against your regular income. Get it? Book publishing is one of the last places you can use the "nonrecourse" loan to defer taxes into the distant future. Until they change the rules!

Let's now consider that old favorite—oil and gas wells. Start by finding land that is likely to have some oil or gas underneath it. That isn't too hard to do if you have producing wells on all four sides of a site. An unproven site might only cost $25 but could produce a dry hole. Unfortunately, proven sites tend to be fairly high priced relative to their potential, and you might not make much profit drilling there. But you can still get a small tax shelter on a proven site. Here's how it works:

1. Find site.
2. Borrow money for cost of mineral rights, (say, $1,000,000) and costs of drilling well (say, $200,000).
3. As usual, try to borrow more than your actual costs—say, $30,000 extra, which you can take out of the deal and spend, tax free.
4. The cost of preliminary testing, labor, drilling, etc. is deductible in the year spent. So you get to deduct most of your development costs in the year expended—that translates into a "loss" of about $80,000 in Year 1. I assume that certain movable pumps worth, say, $10,000 are above ground and will have to be depreciated over their useful life. In addition you get a 10 percent investment tax credit on all the development costs spent on tangibles (not labor).
5. Assuming that the well produces $25,000 worth of oil or gas per year, just as tests indicated it would, then the unique oil and gas tax shelter gimmick comes into play. The owner-developer of the well gets a 22 percent "depletion allowance" the first year, and 2 percent less every year thereafter until he gets down to 15 percent, which is the permanent depletion allowance. This is a totally arbitrary figure, similar to the depreciation deductions spread over useful life of an apartment building. But the difference in oil

or gas wells is that depletion never gets used up even after you've "depleted" the well 100 percent. In our example, the investor gets about $5,000 the second year, $4,500 the third year, etc. The other $19,500 of oil income is, of course, sheltered by the deductible costs of drilling. There are overflow first-year losses of $60,500 to shelter outside income created by the immediate write-off of expenses.

The depletion allowance is supposed to encourage the development of oil and gas wells and the production of scarce energy. It *would* do that, except for one other factor. The government with one hand gives this depletion incentive, but with the other hand clamps a lid on domestic gas prices at as low as one-sixth of the world price. What happens is that very few people drill for gas. When they do, they take all the write-offs and investment tax credits and then cap the wells, saving proven reserves for a time when controls will be lifted. With expenses, and loans to be paid off, obviously this is a maneuver of benefit only to the extremely rich. In the meantime, ever-increasing proportions of our gas and oil are imported from abroad, and local exploration and production is discouraged. Dollars drain out of the country while our own vast supplies of oil and gas just sit there, unused or undiscovered.

Mining

Mining ventures also qualify for the "depletion allowance." Depending on what you mine, each mineral has its own arbitrarily selected figure for depletion, going from a high of 22 percent for aluminum to a low of five percent for gravel. If you have your own gravel pit or gold mine, you get all the benefits of owning a small business as well as depletion. If you just invest and let someone else operate the mine, there's not as much, but with money borrowed at a low interest rate, good deals like good real estate syndications can throw off a small, fully sheltered cash flow. The big attraction from a tax viewpoint, besides depletion, is the ability to currently deduct all of the initial investment in starting up the venture. Let's take an example of a typical coal-mining deal and see how it works:

The investor agrees to lease coal-mining rights to a certain parcel of land for $100,000, payable $10,000 in cash and, say, $90,000 in the form of a nonrecourse 20-year note carried back by the seller. A bank may lend you $30,000 cash against the lease, and that $30,000 is actually spent developing the mine. Naturally there may be 75 or 100 investors, so these example figures would be multiplied substantially in a real-world deal. For our example, to keep the figures simple we are assuming that you alone put up $10,000 cash for your lease and borrowed $30,000 more. The borrowed money went into opening up the mine. This gives you a $30,000 write-off or deduction in the year of investment. If you were a taxpayer in the 70 percent bracket, you put up $10,000 cash and got a $30,000 write-off. This $30,000 write-off resulted in a $20,000 federal income tax savings. So from your point of view, this 2-to-1 shelter deal gave you the coal mine investment "free," plus a tax refund bonus.

However, like most tax shelters, this one is a tax deferral. Twenty years later, if the venture had gone belly up in Year 1 and the nonrecourse note was forgiven, you as the investor might be faced with the problem of taxable "phantom income" because the I.R.S. could force you to "recapture" the writeoffs taken in earlier years. Most people, and certainly I, believe that deferring taxes for a period as long as 20 years is almost as good as eliminating them entirely. If you can invest your $10,000 cash tax refund in some asset or real estate deal that will increase at a rate of at least 10 percent per year in value, in 20 years you'll have an asset worth over $30,000. Hopefully the coal mine over the years will also have been worth at least $30,000 in tax-free income sheltered by depletion.

At the end of 20 years, who can say what your tax situation will be, whether anyone will even remember the $40,000 write-off you took, or even whether you'll be around? Even more significantly, tax deferred in an era of high inflation is tax permanently avoided: Today $40,000 buys a slightly used Rolls Royce. By the year 2000, it may only buy a Big Mac hamburger.

Imelda's Annuities

One of the fringe benefits that I get out of being a well-publicized author and minor tycoon—besides I.R.S. surveillance—is wonderful entertainment. Not a day goes by when I'm not approached by a salesman or saleswoman who has some new product, service, or scheme. These days, all of them have a tax angle.

In early 1980, a sweet and distinctly foreign female voice on the phone offered me a free lunch at the expensive Carnelian Room atop the Bank of America Building in San Francisco. Suspecting a pitch, but always willing to listen in exchange for a good meal, I arrived as scheduled and was greeted by one of the most gorgeous women I have ever seen. Her name was Imelda, and over a jumbo shrimp cocktail she let me know that she was the district sales manager for one of the "big five" life insurance companies of America. Feeling threatened by a life insurance saleslady, I had to explain immediately that I felt life insurance was the biggest rip-off in the Western world, second only to U.S. Savings Bonds as the worst investment anyone could make.

"I'm quite familiar with your views on the subject, having attended your Tycoon Class and having read your book *Think Like a Tycoon*," she remarked with an enchanting British accent. "But if you will hear me out, I will tell you about a tax shelter plan you'll want to write about and recommend to your students at future lectures." Since she was buying lunch, and I'd have listened to her talk about almost anything just to be able to look at her, I sat back and got this:

Insurance companies are doing fine these days selling a

lot of policies in spite of inflation, because they have adapted to the times and realize that financial planning involves, as its most important aspect, tax shelter and protection against inflation. For those individuals who believe that the stock market or a particular mutual fund or stock from time to time offer investment opportunities, insurance companies offer a plan to get dividends tax free, and get high capital gains if and when the stock goes up.

Assuming that you have $1 million in stocks and are collecting a modest six percent or $60,000 per year in dividends, these dividends are taxed at a 70 percent rate. That would leave only $18,000 income per year on a $1 million investment. Here's how you get all your dividends tax free.

1. Instead of having a million in stocks with no loans against it, take out a margin loan against your stock. This type of loan has no due date as long as the stock is in the account. Let's assume that over a few years' period you'd have to pay about 12 percent interest on a $500,000 margin loan. That would cost $60,000 per year. Obviously, your dividends are thus entirely sheltered. Your $60,000 of dividends is canceled out by your $60,000 of interest. What do you live on? That's Step 2.

2. Purchase from the insurance company a single-payment annuity with the borrowed $500,000. Annuity payments to you might be scheduled to begin ten years later. Under the terms of the annuity contract, your $500,000 will grow in value at about the current prime rate of interest, and you will be able to borrow against the $500,000 cash value at any time to give yourself any spendable funds or any venture capital that you may need. The money borrowed is tax free. The monthly annuity payments when it begins to pay out, are also mostly tax free and last all your life. But you can "borrow" up to $60,000 per year as long as you live, without ever running out of money.

3. I.R.S. regulations say that if you have a "secret in-

tent" or a plan to engage in systematic borrowing against your annuity deposit, they may consider your borrowings as income—thus it is necessary to be unsystematic, and borrow irregularly, occasionally making paybacks of unneeded funds. One can use the annuity account as a sort of savings account, taking out, "on the average," $60,000 per year, tax free.

4. The net result of all this is that, instead of getting $60,000 in dividends and keeping only 30 percent or $18,000, you get $60,000 per year cash tax free in the form of borrowings against your annuity—which you never have to pay back.

5. You can stay in the stock market and borrow more as your stocks go up, increasing your annuity—which, by the way, as a side advantage, is immune from attachment by creditors. You can get over $60,000 tax-free per year for life. And if you feel that the dollar isn't going to be worth much in future years, do it through a Swiss insurance affiliate. You can keep your annuity payable in Swiss francs or any foreign currency. People who took out a similar Swiss-denominated plan five years ago are now getting $200,000 per year in Swiss francs on a $500,000 investment.

Perhaps because I liked Imelda so much, I couldn't find anything wrong with the plan. It was easy enough to understand. Just as in real estate, you could invest in an annuity and get your money out as the value involved went up by borrowing against the fund. Borrowed money is always tax free. In the old days, if you took the borrowed money and put it into tax-free bonds, you could get tax-free interest to live on. But that was changed a few years ago when the I.R.S. passed a regulation to the effect that you can't deduct interest on borrowed money if you own any tax-free bonds. So that led creative minds to open up the annuity gambit: These days, sophisticated investors make a contract with an insurance company. They take your money, and it earns interest at the prime rate. They agree not to pay it out to you for 5, 10, 15, or however many years ahead you want to contract for. In the meantime, you may borrow against not only the funds you gave them but also the interest that is being accumulated tax free for your account. This *is* a way to defer income tax on what would otherwise be taxable interest or dividends.

The only disadvantage I can see is a "real" economic loss resulting from inflation. The prime rate of interest is usually a point or two below the loss in purchasing power resulting from inflation. But for someone who feels that they can pick good stocks (or an investment fund), that will outperform inflation, Imelda's plan seems OK to me. If you want to do it yourself, call up the annuity department of a major life insurance company, and show them this chapter. Ask them to fix you up with an "Imelda Special." If you want it from Imelda herself, write me a letter and I'll forward it to her (she asked not to be identified by her real name in this book).

Rocky's Art Collection

Shortly before he died, Nelson Rockefeller appeared on the Tomorrow Show with Tom Snyder, and announced that he was through with politics. He was going to devote himself to bringing great artworks in the form of reproductions into the American home. The balance of this television program was a pitch for viewers to buy reproductions of various sculptures and ceramics from the Nelson Rockefeller Collection. I wondered why one of the richest men in the world would go into such a schlocky business. Rocky just wasn't the type to be schlocky. I felt that he couldn't possibly have any burning desire to see a reproduction of his personal set of Picasso dinner plates in the home of every truckdriver. "What was Rocky's angle?" I wondered.

Enter Abdoulaye, a six-foot seven-inch African from the Ivory Coast with a novel tax shelter scheme. That day he brought to my home what he called priceless African carvings. He offered me this "sure win" scheme to acquire a great art collection free and to get a tax loss while doing it. He claimed that he had originated the plan, which I have never seen in print before. He claimed to have sold it to the "Great Capitalists of America," including the Rockefellers.

Abdoulaye, the African, would provide the investor with a museum-quality work of art, not necessarily African—he also dealt in Old Masters and Rodin sculptures, and could obtain whatever type of art was desired. Assuming that we agreed on the type of artwork desired, he would set the price, admittedly a bit inflated, but here is how it would work.

- True value of artwork (for example) about $100,000, wholesale.
- His price: $200,000 cash down plus $300,000 in the form of a 5-year note, to be secured by art reproductions.
- Total purchase price: $500,000.

The initial $200,000 was to be borrowed from a bank on my good personal credit. Abdoulaye would keep $100,000 for his efforts and for delivering title and possession of the artwork to me. The extra $100,000 would be used by him to cast a mold or other equipment needed to create a limited series of, say, 2,500 reproductions, which would be advertised and sold as part of the "famous" Bill Greene African Art Collection (Limited Edition Reproductions). I keep the originals and the reproductions.

Abdoulaye would handle production. The marketing of reproductions would be handled by third parties. He guaranteed the sale of enough reproductions to produce at least $500,000—which would pay off my bank loan and my debt to him. The 2,500 reproductions would be sold at wholesale for $200 each, returning $500,000 over the next five years. The first $200,000 I got in cash to pay off my bank loan: the $300,000 balance went 50/50 to Abdoulaye and me. "Once the money begins rolling in on the first reproduction," Abdoulaye said, "You will be anxious to do many deals. Why? Because of the tax benefits."

According to Abdoulaye, since I was buying the art *not as an art investment,* but as the model for a mold from which reproductions were to be made, I could write off the entire value of the artwork purchased in the year of acquisition. That would give me a $500,000 first-year write-off—with no money out of my own pocket. If I were in the 50 percent tax bracket, which he assumed I was, that would give me an immediate $250,000 savings. Since my bank loan was only $200,000, there was no way to lose. Although I would technically "owe" him $300,000, I had a claim against him for $300,000—so even if not a single reproduction was sold, I got the tax write-off and had nothing to lose.

And of course, when the smoke cleared, I got the artwork to keep. He agreed to an appraisal by my consultants both as to the value of the art and the tax viabilities of the scheme.

When I asked my C.P.A. about it, he said he *liked* it. He'd heard "even Rockefeller was doing it" before he died. A great way to accumulate an art collection and get some tax write-offs. The accountant added, "A few years down the line, you can donate the art to a museum, and, assuming that the artwork has gone up in value and you can get a high appraisal for $600,000, you get another write-off of the full $600,000 as a donation." Total write-offs, $850,000. Total cash out of pocket, ZERO.

What that particular tax gimmick relied on is that the property acquired for a particular business purpose—like making reproductions—can be "written off" or depreciated over its anticipated useful life. Because only a "limited edition" was to be made, the useful life of the original was only the acquisition year in which reproductions were made and marketed. Not a bad gambit. If all my reproductions were sold as projected, I'd also make a $150,000 cash profit!

Want to buy a plaster cast of an African antelope? I've got a thousand of 'em in the garage!

Fanny's Stamp Collection

Fanny is one of my avid *Tycoon Newsletter* readers in Florida. Besides investing in properties, she is a licensed real estate agent and in that job makes over $45,000 a year. These earnings would put her in the 50 percent bracket if she hadn't thought up the following little gambit.

Fanny gets her real estate listings by sending out mass mailings to property owners in her areas of interest. These letters merely ask for an appointment to discuss the possibilities, and she gets customer "leads" this way.

Her outlays for postage stamps that she uses in business are about $3,000 per year, but on her income tax returns she shows an expense closer to $13,000. When she is audited, she verifies this $13,000 expense item by showing $13,000 in canceled checks made out to the postmaster in her town, plus receipts for postage stamps amounting to $13,000. If the tax auditor took the time to do so (which he doesn't) and if the postmaster kept records of what was sold to whom (which he doesn't), the result of the most thorough examination into Fanny's affairs would verify that she did indeed purchase on the average of $13,000 of postage stamps each year for the past 20 years.

Fanny tells me she has a way to make risk-free investments of $10,000 per year or more, yielding a tax-free return of over 12 percent per year. At the time she invests the $10,000, she gets a $10,000 tax deduction from her income, and this deduction saves her about $5,000 per year in taxes because she is in the 50 percent tax bracket. The way Fanny figures it, her little scheme lets her salt away $10,000 without risk because stamps are worth their face value, no matter what happens. The gray area (which I consider very gray indeed) comes in because Fanny considers the entire $13,000 she spends on stamps ($10,000 of which she "forgets" in a drawer) a tax-deductible business expense. The appreciation comes from the fact that the particular stamps she buys actually do go up in value each year. Because of the tax aspects, Fanny says she'd have to find a savings account yielding 48 percent per year to equal what she gets from her "secret" technique. Why? Because her 50 percent tax bracket makes her $10,000 investment the equivalent of a $20,000 investment of pretax dollars. Her 12 percent return is thus the equivalent of a 24 percent after-tax return. Since she pays no tax on the appreciation of her stamps, and this would also be subject to a 70 percent "unearned income tax" if it were from a savings account, her $12,000 tax-free return is actually equivalent to considerably *more* than a 48 percent return from a conventional, taxable, interest-bearing security or savings account.

So here come the details of the *Fanny Plan* to earn the equivalent of 50 percent on your money, risk free. Are you ready for it?

During the course of a year, Fanny simply purchases $13,000 in full-page *carefully selected commemorative* stamps issued by the post office. Commemorative stamps are those colorful "special issues" of stamps. They come out several times each month. She pays by check and gets a receipt from the postmaster. She uses a certain portion of the stamps in her business, but the biggest portion goes into her safety deposit box, where she now has $200,000 in face value of stamps. But Fanny says that her particular stamps are worth far more than $200,000 to collectors. The value she places on her 20-year collection is closer to $1 million. Apparently some full sheets of commemorative stamps appreciate in value about in line with the inflation rate, although certain sheets (of greater rarity or artistic merit) go up infinitely more. I can't argue much with Fanny the stamp collector because she seems to have created a nice little retirement nest egg for herself.

But is it legal? My I.R.S. spy tells me that if Fanny prepays her anticipated postage needs in any given year, the mere fact that she bought more than her actual needs doesn't destroy the deduction. In other words, he gives his stamp of approval to the scheme—with this comment: "Obviously, if she does this year after year and *intends* to keep the stamps for their collector's value, the postage expense should be treated as a nondeductible investment outlay. Since it is a question of intent, in my opinion Fanny's scheme is a good one and one that she will probably get away with, but it's also tax fraud—if her secret intentions were known to the I.R.S."

My I.R.S. spy says that the way Fanny could someday get tripped up is if she sells a few valuable sheets of stamps and deposits the check received for payment into her bank account. In a later audit, she might be called on to explain the source of the deposit and pay a tax on it.

When I told Fanny of this comment, she said, "What do you think I am, a dummy? People into coins and stamps do all their deals on a cash or trade basis. I sell for cash when I sell, and I never deposit the money—I use it for meals, trips, and other non-tax-deductible expenses."

"Why do you do it, Fanny?" I asked her.

Her answer was revealing of an attitude I have found over and over and over again: "You can't rely on Social Security or even a husband to take care of you in your old age (Fanny has outlived three husbands). You have to do something. When the government doesn't provide for you, and when the government steals an unfair amount of your earnings in taxes, you've got to fight back. This is the only way I've figured out how to do it. I'm hoping for a few more ideas from the free tax revolt book you promised me in exchange for my postage stamp investment plan."

When I asked Fanny what she would do if the I.R.S. somehow poked their way into her safety deposit box and discovered her fortune in stamps, she said, "It won't happen, but if it does, I'll play the scatterbrained, 50-year-old, helpless widow and say, "Those stamps, those must be the ones I misplaced and forgot to use. I didn't know they were worth anything to collectors, I just like the pretty colors."

If you have a unique or unusual plan for giving the shaft to the I.R.S. vampires, please let me know. If you mail it, your letter will be burned to protect your anonymity. If you phone, I won't tell anybody either. I hope to get lots of far-out ideas like the *Fanny Plan*, and if I use yours, your reward will be a free, autographed copy of my next book.

So if you like this book, or have any comments about any of the ideas in it, please let me hear from you: Bill Greene, P.O. Box 810, Mill Valley, CA 94942. Or phone (415) 383-8264. New ideas are of course welcome!

11.
Foreign
Bank
Accounts

One main tax advantage of keeping a foreign bank account in a foreign currency is that foreign money is not money, as a matter of law. There are U.S. court decisions holding that money, or legal tender, is only U.S. dollars. That leads to a most interesting possibility: You open an account in a foreign country—in Swiss francs, for instance. You are credited with 4 to 6 percent per year interest, just as you would be in the United States by a local bank or savings institution. You started with 100 Swiss francs. At the end of one year, you have 105 Swiss francs in your account. Legal question: do you have an income of 5 Swiss francs? One well-known tax lawyer says there is substantial reason to believe that you received no income. Let's look at why the 5 Swiss francs are not income.

Pretend that instead of 100 Swiss francs you bought 100 shares of American Telephone and Telegraph Stock. There was a five-share stock dividend. One year later, 105 shares of American Telephone and Telegraph are not necessarily worth any more than the 100 shares you originally purchased. No tax is due, nothing needs to be reported to I.R.S. Or assume you bought 99 cows and a bull. A year later, you have 105 cows and a bull. No income is earned until you convert the shares or the animals back into dollars. The 105 cows *could* be worth less in dollars than the 100 cows. Unrealized capital gains or losses are not taxable income! Thus in the opinion of at least one leading tax lawyer, the interest on foreign currency deposits is not taxable income until it is turned back into dollars. If it is not income, it is not taxable, and, more importantly, it may not be reportable on your tax return at all. But the ever-snoopy U.S. tax people put a specific question on tax returns a few years back. It asks whether you have a foreign account or *signature power* over a foreign account. If you checked the "yes" box, the I.R.S. form then directed you to answer further detailed questions about the location of the account and the amounts involved. Yet, curiously, if you checked another box to the effect that you had 25 or more accounts, no detailed information was required. I understand, from a national magazine quoting an I.R.S. source, some 200,000 Americans either checked both the "yes" and "no" boxes and gave no further information, or checked the "yes" box and the "over 25 accounts" box and gave no further information. To be technically honest, I understand many people were advised by their accountants to put a few bucks in 24 or more small foreign accounts so they wouldn't have to give information about any substantial foreign accounts.

Larry Law-Abiding, a friend of mine, did something even more ingenious. He got a foreign friend to accept a transfer of Larry's foreign money. A new checking account was opened in Foreign Friend's name. Then Foreign Friend signed 100 blank checks and handed over the checkbook to Larry. Larry then checked off the "no" foreign accounts box because he neither had a foreign account nor did he have signing power over someone else's foreign account. He just filled in checks and spent them as needed. There is no end to tax avoidance strategies thought up by honest citizens.

The "dishonest" citizens just open a foreign account with cash. They carefully avoid a paper trail between any U.S. bank and their foreign bank. They "forget" about their foreign account at tax return time. This, although possibly illegal, may be a reasonable course.

All governments during periods of international stress or internal rebellion immediately seize the *known* foreign assets of their citizens. The I.R.S., with its two little information request boxes, was able to garner a computerized list of over 200,000 citizens with assets abroad. If it becomes necessary, those 200,000 can be put in concentration camps or otherwise squeezed until they give information about their foreign accounts. France, Germany, and Great Britain—all civilized countries—confiscated the known foreign assets of their citizens as recently as World War II. For many otherwise honest citizens displaced by wars or revolution, a secret foreign account or some buried gold coins meant the difference between survival and starvation. This kind of "dishonesty" is to my way of thinking not dishonest at all. The law of self-preservation takes precedence over any government regulations. It's possible to stay technically legal and check the "no" box with tricks like Larry Law-Abidings' checkbook gambit. But if you check the "yes" box you'll become a "target" and eventually get I.R.S. agents following up what they consider a "lead."

Bank secrecy is usually associated with Switzerland, but virtually all banks outside of the United States and totalitarian dictatorships have a much higher degree of bank secrecy than is available in the United States. In the United States, the lowest form of I.R.S. agent starts any investigation armed with an unlimited supply of mimeographed summonses. These give him access to every piece of paper, microfilm, and other documents concerning you located in the United States. These I.R.S. administrative summonses are tossed at

The I.R.S. passes out summonses and subpoenas
as if they were confetti.

"Go forth to the Xerox. Multiply them
and ye shall be rewarded."

everyone in sight with careless abandon. Once a serious investigation begins, a copy of every bank record about you, every check, Master Charge, Visa, or other credit document you ever signed will be in I.R.S. hands. Agents can find out where you slept and with whom you slept, and will use this information when they interview your spouse. They can and will question and intimidate the payee on every check you wrote. That situation is unthinkable in Europe, where the private citizen still has a considerable right to privacy.

Due to tax treaties forced on most countries of the world by the United States, the I.R.S., if it knows the location of your foreign account can now get at your foreign bank records eventually through its network of foreign agents—but it's much more work and can happen only after formal legal proceedings have been instituted. To get at your foreign records, you must be charged with a serious crime that is also a crime in the country where they are trying to get the records.

Interestingly, tax evasion is not a crime in many countries, including Switzerland. As a result, unless the I.R.S. is willing to ask the U.S. Department of Justice to charge you with something stronger than tax evasion, they can't get your Swiss bank records. Bank secrecy exists in all countries of Europe to a greater or lesser degree. Andorra, Switzerland, and Liechtenstein are the "most" secret. Austria, Luxembourg, and Germany are getting to be more "public" as the United States applies pressure on them.

The thing to remember is that if there is no "paper trail" between you and your foreign account, the I.R.S. cannot find out about it in the first place. Thus, if you are going to have a secret account, do it right. Go personally to open it, armed with a "To Whom It May Concern" letter from your present bankers, identifying you as a good customer and guaranteeing your signature. Open your foreign account with cash or other bearer instruments that can't be traced to you.* Open it in person, not by mail. Do not have any mail sent to you in the United States, because the I.R.S. monitors mail of people on their "hit" list and has a record of the postage meter numbers of all foreign banks. If they are out to get you, they will steam open your mail and photocopy your bank statements. It's technically illegal for the I.R.S. to open your mail, and they can't use any evidence they get this way in court. But they *do* steam open mail, as I know from personal experience.

*A bearer instrument is an unregistered security (such as a U.S. Treasury Bill) that, like cash, can be transferred without endorsement.

12.
Foreign Trusts, the Caribbean Shuffle, Three Flags for Freedom and Lots of Other Tax Avoidance Ploys

Did you know that you, your kids, your wife, or any other American can be made the beneficiary of a foreign trust? If it's done just right and established by a foreigner, you can accumulate any amount of tax-free money abroad in foreign trusts. The catch is that the I.R.S. will attribute any money put in the trust, or earned by the trust, as income to the beneficiaries, unless the American beneficiaries have *no control* over the trust assets. How can you get any benefit out of the trust if you have no control? Generally, control of the assets is left in the hands of a trust department of a financial institution in a tax haven country. Mr. Wong, of course, if he sets up such a trust for you, would personally keep the power to change trustees. If Mr. Wong dies, you might have a letter giving you the power to name the person who can change trustees. The indirect power to fire the trustee bank will generally ensure that the bank acts in accordance with the desires of the beneficiaries. The bank will, as a result, when the time comes, make the desired distributions or transfer of assets. This is an example of not having control for legal or tax purposes but ensuring that your wishes will always be strongly considered. For the life of the trust, all income earned abroad is free of American taxes.

There are several reasons that a person with substantial assets (say over $100,000) should consider moving some assets out of the country into a foreign trust, business, entity, investments, or merely foreign currency bank deposits.

First, the United States is clearly moving toward exchange controls. Right now, anyone can move any amount of money into or out of the country, but if over $5,000 is involved you are obliged to report it to U.S. Customs. Up until a few years ago, there was no reporting requirement. The reporting requirement is the obvious prelude to a congressional finding that Americans have "too much" freedom and should be required to get U.S. Treasury permission before removing their assets to a safer or more profitable place.

Another reason for having assets abroad is that if inflation becomes double or triple digit in the United States, part of your paper wealth can be solidly invested in some other country.

To a Lebanese in 1972 or a Cuban in 1960, or many a German in 1939, foreign assets meant the difference between life and death.

England and many socialistic countries not only tax incomes, but they also tax "wealth." Eventually, the escalating leftist trends in the United States will have to be stopped by a taxpayers' revolt. If that doesn't happen, we'll follow modern England, as usual, and the government will start confiscating the capital of its wealthier citizens. But there's an old saying: "They have to find it first." Wealth the government doesn't know about can't be confiscated. Thus, besides burying gold coins in the back yard, foreign assets or businesses are a good way to conceal assets from a rapacious and thieving government.

Even if the government isn't out to get you with taxes, the trend is clearly to allow unproductive elements of society in America to grab the wealth of professional people through other means. New lawsuits based on bizarre legal theories are causing present-day courts to be compared to Robin Hood. Every medical doctor knows the real risk of being bankrupted by malpractice suits or the high insurance premiums required to protect against them. Everyone who has been through any lawsuit, particularly a divorce, knows what it is to be put through the wringer by litigation. Estate taxes, creditors' claims, probate costs, and many such problems can be avoided by transferring assets to foreign countries, either in trusts or other forms. Foreign assets afford you a degree of protection from Robin Hood judges and juries who want to give your life savings away to anyone who sues you.

For a complete rundown on the latest state of the law involving foreign hanky-panky, I suggest that you look over a book primarily for lawyers, published by the Practicing Law Institute, entitled *Practical International Tax Planning* by Marshall Langer et al. ($30). To order, see the reading list at the end of this book, or visit the business branch of your local public library to get it for free.

Judge Robin Hood giving it all to the plaintiff.

In the event you are wondering about the mechanics of setting up a foreign trust, it could be as easy as this:

To: *Castle Bank & Trust Company,*
Bermuda, Bahamas

Attention: *Trust Department*

Dear Sirs:
I, *Willy Wong,* a citizen of *Hong Kong,* do hereby establish a revocable (or irrevocable) trust of $10,000 to benefit my good friend, *Elsie American.* You have full discretion as trustee to invest said trust fund as you see fit and are instructed to distribute the proceeds to the beneficiary at such time as she reaches the age of 65. During the life of this trust, you may sprinkle and spray interest and principal to meet the needs of the beneficiary at your discretion. I reserve the right for myself or my assigns to remove you as trustee at any time.

Signed, *Willy Wong*
Trustor

Simple, wasn't it?

One master of all this foreign trust sort of thing was and is Harry Margulies, a California tax lawyer who saved his wealthy showbiz clients millions in taxes with a neat gimmick that *New West* magazine (April 11, 1977) called the Caribbean Shuffle.

The Caribbean Shuffle

Step 1. A rich Margulies client "borrows" $50,000 from Anglo Dutch Capital Company in the form of a check. The check is endorsed by the client and "invested" in Del Cerro Associates, a partnership. Del Cerro "owes" $45,000 in interest to World Minerals, which it pays immediately. It also pays $5,000 per year interest to Anglo Dutch.

Funny thing is (or at least the I.R.S. claimed) Margulies personally set up, owns, and controls Anglo Dutch, Del Cerro, and World Minerals, all of which were "paper" or "shell" companies incorporated or headquartered in foreign tax haven jurisdictions, where the I.R.S. couldn't get in to see the books. The I.R.S. said that the only purpose of these partnerships or corporations was to act as dummies or straw men for tax evasion. According to the government, Anglo Dutch never had any real money to make a loan in the first place, and all subsequent transactions were mere paper shuffling. What was the effect of the Caribbean Shuffle for the clients?

Step 2. The client writes and asks for his $50,000 back from Del Cerro Associates, which says, "Sorry, we lost it, we're broke, and we're dissolving. But at least you can get a $50,000 loss on your tax return." So he does. Anglo Dutch provides the client with a receipt for a $5,000 interest payment and a letter of opinion that he can deduct that $5,000 as interest paid. So he does. Total $55,000 in deductions.

Step 3. Tax savings in the 70 percent bracket, about $38,000. Fee to Margulies for all the paperwork, maybe $8,000.

Step 4. But what about the loan the client owes Anglo Dutch? Margulies assures the client that Anglo Dutch will never attempt to collect. The loan stays on the books forever but is never enforced. The client is ahead $30,000. The attorney is ahead $8,000, and Uncle Sam is out $38,000 in taxes.

The I.R.S. didn't like this arrangement or a multitude of similar gray-area deals cooked up by Margulies and a number of attorneys like him, so to put a little fear into their ranks it charged him with conspiracy to evade income taxes. Margulies was hit with 23 counts of aiding in the preparation of false income tax returns. The government claimed it was being defrauded of over $500 million per year by Margulies. Allegedly participating in the Caribbean Shuffle was a colorful group, including many movie stars and unexpected names like Werner Erhard (est), Hugh Heffner (*Playboy*), Angela Davis (radical author), and a few reputed Mafia dons. (Perhaps the only thing the radical right and the radical left can get together on is their choice of a clever tax lawyer.)

At his tax fraud trial, defendant Margulies echoed my sentiment that our present tax system is unfair, oppressive, and corrupt. He said he would be delighted to be put out of business by *legitimate* taxes. As the Margulies trial progressed during 1977, the defendant was able to prove that the I.R.S. had spent millions to hire prostitutes, burglars, and a variety of lawbreakers to investigate him. The government called it "Project Haven," and in this project the I.R.S. clearly engaged in the manufacture of phony documents and perjured testimony. It paid bribes and made "deals" for testimony. Up against a rare defendant who had financial resources to investigate government methods and fight back, these revelations about the illegal activities of the I.R.S. proved them to be perhaps more unsavory and deceitful than anything Margulies had done. The result was an acquittal on all counts for Margulies.

What was the reaction of our politicians? Instead of tossing out the entire Internal Revenue Code, instituting a simplified one-page income tax law, and firing the entire bureaucracy, as common sense would dictate, they hired *more* agents to keep up the good work. At whose expense? The wage slaves, of course. The productive workers and middle classes pay the taxes, the lazy wait for handouts, and the rich have good lawyers to beat the system.

His reputation enhanced by victory, Margulies' tax avoidance practice is reportedly better than ever. Another acquitted codefendant, Quentin Breen, attorney of San Francisco, also increased his popularity.

For you to develop a profitable association with a tax lawyer who will involve you in foreign trust and a web of multitiered foreign corporations, you should have an unsheltered (taxable) income of *at least* $40,000 per year, according to Breen. If you are paying in the area of $15,000 and up in taxes, they can save you money. But you can do a lot of the tax planning on your own.

Protection Against the Continuing Devaluation of the Dollar

Devaluation is one reason we accumulate real estate and big debts. Much responsible opinion in world economic circles feels that the U.S. government, with its unpopular high taxes, perennially unbalanced budgets, and wanton spending on welfare and other giveaways will soon debase the dollar to such an extent that it will become "play money." Like Confederate currency, dollars will be unacceptable anywhere outside of the United States. And even within the United States the shrinking dollar will drastically lose its value until it takes several pounds of paper dollars to buy half a loaf of bread.

Harry Browne and Harry L. Schultz, among others, write books, publish newsletters, and give seminars putting forth a certain pessimistic scenario that has at least partly come true already:

1. The U.S. cost of living rises drastically as inflation hits double-digit proportions. Incomes do not keep pace. Unrest and rioting hit the big cities. The right wing and left wing battle it out for control.

2. Gold investors, people who early on get out of the dollar into yen, Deutschmarks, and Swiss francs, preserve their buying power within the United States. During the bloodletting, they vacation abroad as exchange controls and

213

currency restrictions prevent the flight of other people and dollars abroad. The Iron Curtain and Bamboo Curtain is followed by the Apple Pie Curtain. We end up with a military dictatorship of the right or our own home-grown version of Fidel Castro.

The dollar has, in fact, been devalued substantially in the last few years. The point has been reached where foods, travel, and homes in Japan, Germany, or Switzerland, once cheap by our standards, now cost three times as much as they would in the United States. Inflation is increasing at an increasing rate. Currency controls seem to be inevitable. After taxes and inflation, real incomes are dropping by over 5 percent per year. This has resulted in lowered standards of living for most wage earners. Discontent is rising—but the taxpayers' revolt may, if successful, prevent blood running in the streets. It's easier to vote for a change than to fight a civil war for it. Things can get better just as easily as they can get worse. Some Americans, expecting a real revolution, had enough foresight to buy a ski cabin near Geneva in 1968 when the price was $30,000. Others, expecting a devaluation, put $100,000 into a Deutschmark-denominated bank account 10 years ago. The chalet is worth $150,000 and the German bank account is worth $200,000. Planning for the worst has led many people to both security and profit.

Americans who purchased foreign property or made foreign deposits in politically stable countries acquired *a safe haven and a nest egg* to use in case conditions become untenable at home for any reason. Once exchange controls are imposed, it will be illegal (but by no means impossible) to get assets out of the country. Restrictions just make smugglers out of survivors.

Strangely enough, as taxes on U.S. citizens go up, and U.S.-owned dollars are forced to flee the country, the government is forced to give foreigners tax incentives and other benefits to make it attractive for them to bring their dollars into the United States. For instance, right now, a rich Arab or any foreigner who deposits funds with the Bank of America

214

or Chase Manhattan Bank can get a higher rate of interest than the maximum legal rates for interest payments to a U.S. citizen. When the American gets about 9 percent on his savings account the Arab gets double that on his "certificates of deposit." The effective rate for the American is closer to 2 percent because the affluent American pays a 70 percent U.S. income tax. The tax rate for the foreigner, even if he lives in the United States less than six months each year, is *guess what?—zero.*

Our government *now* discriminates against its own people in favor of foreigners. If *you* as an American buy some U.S. real estate and sell it at a profit, the current state and federal income taxes will take about half your profit. What capital gains tax does the foreigner pay? *Zero!*

Our tax and currency policies closely parallel those of England, following her perhaps a decade later. As a result of her socialism and high taxes, England has already become a colony of the Third World. Foreigners from Iran and Saudi Arabia take all the "cream," and the English are left with only skim milk. In that context, it is not hard to understand why the English tycoon leaves his own country or is not willing to exert himself in England. The British tax structure makes it virtually impossible for him to ever get a fine home in his own country or a Rolls Royce, unless he changes his citizenship and becomes technically a foreigner not subject to high British taxes. The Englishman can literally not even find himself an apartment in London anymore without posing as a foreigner to whom rent controls do not apply. The same thing is starting to happen in America.

Have you been to an international airport lately? Read the signs!

> "It is illegal to import or export more than
> $5,000 in the form of cash, or other negotiable
> instruments without filing U.S. Treasury Form XYZ."

Is that the handwriting on the wall? I'd say it's a clear message of currency controls coming soon to the land of the (formerly) free, home of the (formerly) brave.

For the moment, anyway, there is a reporting requirement but no prohibition against cashing in your chips and leaving the United States. There is, as yet, no enforcement of the new reporting law, and I am aware of no one being searched for "illegal" currency reporting. But by the time this book comes out, those rules may tighten up.

Accordingly, the time to cash in part of your chips is right now—while it's still legal. Following foolish England, the U.S. government appears to be heading down a taxation and regulatory path that will increasingly force its most intelligent and prosperous citizens to flee the country or become criminals by merely attempting to preserve their freedom and economic survival. The United States is likely to go the way of England, where formerly well-off people were, until 1980, restricted to $50 foreign travel allowances. In England, officially reported incomes of over $10,000 per year are taxed into oblivion. In England, all homes of quality are sold to communist diplomats, Arabs, or Third-World wealthy. In England, like America, until a few years ago the population was loyally compliant and unusually willing to pay taxes. Today tax evasion has become the national pastime. All British prices are routinely quoted two ways—half for cash, double for recorded check. A spreading sense that taxes are "too high" and no longer "fair" has produced the same mentality in the United States. We all must become "criminals" to survive and cope.

It's a situation I don't like, but I believe I have a solution.

The Three-Flag Theory

One of the most philosophical tax avoiders I ever met was Paul Harris, a Certified Public Accountant and tax consultant who now makes his home in the totally tax-free Cayman Islands. Paul told me that every person who manages to amass enough money to be called independently wealthy should "fly three flags." By that he meant that one should

216

first fly the flag or become a citizen of a country that does not attempt to tax any of its citizens who live abroad. No country attempts to tax the worldwide income of nonresidents except the United States. Most governments reason that a person who lives outside the country does not get any benefits from taxes spent in the home country and thus should not be expected to pay those taxes. So, according to Harris, the first thing any right-thinking American should do is rid himself of the most expensive passport in the world—the U.S. passport—and become a citizen of a neutral country like Switzerland, Australia, Canada, or perhaps Costa Rica where citizenship can be obtained quickly.

The second flag is the place of official residence. That should be a tax haven country. Tax havens have no income taxes, no military service requirements, and do not interfere with the economic lives of their foreign residents, who by design are wealthy international tycoons. They help the local economy by spending a part of the year there and as seasonal residents spend part of their money for living in the tax haven.

Where are recommended tax havens? For English-speaking people, there are the Bahamas, Bermuda, or the Cayman Islands. All have white sand beaches, palm trees, and cheap, short flights into Miami. If you want to speak English but prefer Europe, there are Gibraltar, Malta, and the quaint English Channel Islands of Sark and Jersey, just off the North Coast of France. They are a quick hover-craft ride away from London. In the Far East, there are bustling British Hong Kong and Portuguese Macao. Africa has English-speaking Liberia, a tax haven run by ex-American slaves.

For the international jet set, there's Monaco (home of Princess Grace) with its famous Monte Carlo Casino. Monaco, population 30,000, has perhaps the largest concentration of international superrich in the world. The climate is like San Francisco, and the language is French. For ski enthusiasts, there's Andorra (between France and Spain) and German-speaking Liechtenstein (between Switzerland and Aus-

*Getting Swiss citizenship—or even a residence permit—
is almost impossible these days, but you can still get in
the back door by getting citizenship or residence in Italy
and then moving to Campione, an enclave that is technically
Italian, but surrounded by Switzerland on all sides.
See you on the Campione slopes!*

tria). A real sleeper is Ireland. Recent legislation in Ireland rolls out the tax-free red carpet, but *only for artists.* These include sculptors, musicians, poets, and authors. For tenors and tycoons, there's the tiny enclave of Campione d'Italia. It is in Switzerland physically, but legally part of Italy. Both border countries ignore Campione, and a pleasant libertarian anarchy reigns.

Tax havens are a fascinating subject, and whole books have been written about the relative advantages of each one—see our reading list. The point is, according to the three-flag theory, one should become a legal resident of a tax haven. To maintain your legal residency in the tax haven, you should figure on spending physically at least a month per year there and probably investing in or leasing property there. If you have a property to share with me, drop me a line.

Finally, there's the third and last flag and your least difficult choice. That's the place you invest money and make money. For most Americans, that's America.

Let's see how the "Three Flags" could work out for you as a former American.

Flag 1 is passport (or citizenship). Your new country of citizenship knows little or nothing about you, and doesn't care where you are or what you do. There are British, Italian, Canadian, Costa Rican, and many other passport holders who have never in their lives been in the country of their technical citizenship. It may surprise you that if either of your parents were some nationality other than American, you may get a foreign passport on application to the local consulate. If you were born somewhere else, that sometimes gets you a new passport. If you're lucky enough to be Jewish, under the Israeli "law of return" you qualify for an immediate Israeli passport by going there.

Flag 2 is your official tax haven residence. The tax haven welcomes you and others like you because you have invested in a home or support the local economy by paying rent on a long-term lease. They love to have you visit and spend your money in their casinos or whatever. By definition, there are no income taxes in a tax haven. Just keep a low profile and don't annoy the locals. They always reserve the right to throw you out without much legal ceremony.

Flag 3 is the place where you make your money. America, as most other high-tax countries, takes an entirely different attitude toward you as a nonresident foreigner. You are no longer a local capitalist to be squeezed and milked. You've been magically transformed into a desired "foreign investor." You are to be wined and dined by government officials—courted with tax incentives not available to mere Americans. Start with tax-free interest from any American bank as an appetizer. Next course: no capital gains taxes. Entrée: government loans and grants to encourage you to set up shop in the United States. Dessert: no taxes on your income or salary if derived from foreign sources. Wow! What a difference a day makes if that day was spent acquiring a foreign passport and tax haven residence. It's interesting that a wealthy "foreigner" actually living in the United States but technically a nonresident gets what amounts to a tax-free pass. Contrast: A U.S. citizen never visiting the United States. but slaving away in Saudi Arabia's 120° F heat for 20 years. He gets no benefits from the United States, yet is *legally liable* to pay up to 70 percent of his worldwide non-U.S. income to Uncle Sam.

As you see, there is no logic or fairness to the present American tax system. The "Three-Flag" theory might make you think about the "value" of being a U.S. citizen and the alternatives available. You should also know that many Americans who acquire foreign citizenship do *not* notify the United States or give up their U.S. passports. They simply stop paying U.S. taxes. This tactic, combined with a very low profile when they enter the United States as foreign tourists on their foreign passports, does not usually produce any unpleasant results. The U.S. passports are saved as a fourth flag for a rainy day.

All this brings us to the final word on tax avoidance, as we try and answer that ultimate question, "How do you cash in your chips?" That's what it all comes to eventually. We die, and concerning whatever we have managed to accumulate during our lifetime, they say, "You can't take it with you." They also say, "You can't beat death or taxes." It may be true that you can't beat death, but taxes—that's a different matter. You *can* beat estate or inheritance taxes. Here are some ways to do it.

1. Before you die, sell all your U.S. real estate, convert to cash, gold, bearer shares, and take those liquid assets together with your family and kids to your tax haven residence.* Unfurl your other two flags and die. You've beaten

---

*Canada is a pretty good place for dying. There is no estate tax, I'm told, and most of the Canadian provinces (like our states of Nevada and Florida) have no inheritance taxes.

income taxes for life, and in death you've avoided *all* estate and inheritance taxes. Just a question of *timing*, wasn't it? Be sure to die with all your assets and all your heirs outside of the United States.

2. If you have some pet project to benefit mankind and if you are not willing to deactivate in some foreign land, you should set up a nonprofit research or educational foundation in America to perpetuate your name—and to carry on some worthy work. Almost anything will do—the Ford Foundation is into the study of government; the Howard Hughes Foundation more into medical research; the Bill Greene Foundation would be for the promotion of individual free enterprise, efficiency in government, and lower taxes. But whatever you choose, even from the grave you control your money and can arrange that it's used for something worthwhile—not squandered by politicians. Best of all, no estate taxes nor income taxes! That's practically taking it with you!

3. For those with under $1 million in assets, the most practical suggestion I can offer is to live well and die relatively poor—up to $150,000 is exempt from estate taxes. While you are building up assets and deferring taxes, live on borrowed mortgage money! You can give away up to $3,000 per person per year to any friends, heirs, or others you want to benefit, long before you die. Whatever's left, spend on yourself. The net result should be that you leave less than a quarter million in real estate equities. If you have a coin collection, quietly place it in the custody of whomever you'd like to have it when you fade out.

I have given you a few suggestions. There is no definitive "right answer" on how to cash in your chips. Some people actually leave their entire estate to the government by bequest—sort of a "thank you" for letting them accumulate wealth during their lifetimes. Others will their money to the poor people of Jerusalem. Whatever you do, if you feel good about it you have the answer. There is no right answer, but *my* answer would not be to give my money voluntarily to politicians of any country.

Avoiding taxes is like making money or anything else. If you set your mind to a certain objective, if you have a goal, and if you work at it consistently and intelligently, you will reach that goal. With that in mind, I tell you that it is theoretically possible to avoid all income taxes during your lifetime and to avoid estate taxes legally at your death.

Death and taxes are not inevitable. Careful study and the "three flags" will solve your tax problems.

Following is the only suggestion I can offer on how to gain immortality.

Cloning

Chicken George and His Fighting Cocks

George G_____ is a Certified Public Accountant from the Bronx who visited Puerto Rico a few years back during a cruise. When he arrived in this quaint Spanish-speaking colony in the Caribbean, one of the local guides dragged him to the local national sport: cockfighting. There George asked a few questions and quickly came up with one of the unique tax avoidance schemes in America.

He formed a limited partnership with his sister and a few other investors to buy a bunch of Puerto Rican eggs. Don't ask me how it's done, but some people can tell which eggs are going to produce fighting cocks. Those eggs sell for slightly more than the ones you get at Safeway. But they are not terribly expensive—let's say that 200 unborn fighting cocks sell for about $200. The big money (mostly borrowed) is spent on the care, feeding, and training of the birds. That may take $10,000 or more—depending on the size of the team you want to end up with. All those costs can be written off in the year incurred.

As the chicks develop, the less ferocious beasties wind up Kentucky Fried. That's about half of them. The remaining birds appreciate at the rate of about $50 per month, per bird. On 100 cocks, that ain't chicken feed! When the valiant warriors are about six months old, Chicken George and his sister sell the birds at fair market value, $30,000, with a no money down installment sale to Chicken George's Subchapter S Corporation. George gets a tax credit for buying "livestock" even though he didn't put up a dime and even though he has already written off their entire cost. Now he can depreciate the fighting cocks over their estimated useful fighting career of two years, at $15,000 per year. They may make or lose money as warriors, but Chicken George has already made it on the tax angles.

The final stage is to resell the fighting cocks to still another corporation or partnership, this time at a great loss—because as the birds get older, their value declines precipitously and they are good only for breeding stock. At each stage, George and his investors get an investment tax credit, short depreciation lives, and 20 percent extra first-year depreciation.

Fighting cocks can be another effective tax shelter.

13.
Tax
Havens

Why doesn't America crack down on the use of tax havens by Americans and foreignized Americans? The answer is simple. The use of tax havens is tolerated for the same reason that the United States does not ban imports and exports: We have become dependent on them!

For instance, some years ago U.S. labor laws demanded by our unions made U.S.-registered ships unable to compete in the international market. From being a major commercial shipping power in the nineteenth century, America's commercial fleet declined to insignificance. By 1950, even tiny Liberia and Panama had bigger merchant marines. What became of thousands of American ships? Their owners formed Liberian and Panamanian companies and transferred registrations of their ships from the United States to Panama or Liberia. Those countries promised low taxes and laws favorable to shipowners. The U.S. government considered forbidding the use of these tax havens by U.S. maritime interests. But that would have brought about a speedy liquidation of all American-owned shipping companies. A compromise was reached. In the event of war or emergency, Liberia and Panama agreed to allow the United States to take over and mobilize "its" ships for the duration of any American emergency. Everyone knew that most Panamanian- and Liberian-registered ships belonged to Americans although the ownership was hidden behind the corporate veil of foreign companies. But an international agreement allowed everyone to keep what they wanted: The tax havens retained their annual registration fees and the prestige of having many vessels bearing their flag; the shipowners got reduced labor costs, more favorable laws and tax savings; the Americans kept a reserve of shipping capacity for use in wartime.

Thus did circumstances bring about the movement of virtually all American-registered shipping from the United States to two small tax haven countries. There is little chance that the status quo will be changed during our lifetimes. And while the United States on one hand tolerates—even supports—tax havens, it has itself become, and is widely advertised abroad as the world's greatest tax haven, successfully competing in this regard with Switzerland. Unfortunately, these highly touted advantages are not available to American citizens—only to foreigners.

Let's look at how the system works. If the United States needs to borrow money, which it does at the rate of over $100 billion a year, foreigners would prefer not to lend unless their interest can be collected tax free. Since most other nations impose withholding taxes of from 15 to 30 percent, the United States gains an advantage by not withholding anything from remittances of American-earned interest to foreigners. To help foreigners avoid taxes, the United States permits American banks and stockbrokers to provide foreigners with secret, numbered bank accounts in any currency—just as Switzerland does. Our government decided years ago to promote the United States as a tax haven and swell place for hot foreign money. This was done to encourage foreign investment in America. The prominence of New York City as a financial center is a direct result of these policies. Several factors keep New York the leading financial metropolis of the world:

1. America has no exchange controls. That means a New York bank may hold currency (for a foreigner only) in any of the world's monies—yen, francs, dinars, or whatever. These currencies or securities may be transferred in or out of the country immediately, without government permission. For the moment, Americans share this economic freedom—but any substantial foreign transactions are supposed to be reported to the U.S. Treasury.

2. There are no reporting requirements on foreign accounts. This means that for all practical purposes, transactions by foreigners in America can be kept secret from both the U.S. government and the home government of the foreign investor.

3. There are no withholding taxes on interest paid out to foreigners by any American financial institution.

4. There are no taxes on capital gains made in America—either short term or long term.

5. America offers many safe and profitable investment opportunities, and promises never to discriminate against foreign investors.

6. Rents on real estate can be exported tax free not because of any special deal for foreigners, but because I.R.S. accounting rules allow depreciation deductions to shelter rents for citizens and foreigners alike.

7. America has a long, unbroken tradition of friendliness to foreign investors. In addition to political stability, we have never confiscated or frozen private investors' funds, except in wartime. And even then, "enemy" funds were always treated with respect, sequestered with an independent administrator, and returned to the aliens at the cessation of hostilities.

*Everyone agrees that the dollar will collapse. The only
question is when? Until it happens, the best strategy is
to keep your money in anything except U.S. dollars.
Borrow dollars, invest in solid assets (land, buildings,
basic materials and foodstuffs, gold and silver coins).
Wait for inflation to wipe out your debt.*

No other country in the tax haven business except
Switzerland offers such a package. Switzerland is in second
place because it is closer to Russia—and this proximity leads
to a cautionary attitude. Some day, communist pressures in
Switzerland could change things! In World War II, even
Switzerland transferred its gold reserves and important records to New York City branches of the big Swiss banks for
safety. There they have remained to this very day.

The slightest hint of a change in these long-established
American practices would cause the withdrawal from New
York of hundreds of billions of foreign-owned deposits. If the
United States even hinted that it was about to become less of
a tax haven, foreigners would certainly try to dump their
U.S. securities and real estate before the rules were changed.
Such sales and withdrawals of capital would doubtless trig-
ger the collapse of all major American banks and a complete
loss of confidence in the American dollar. America would

limp on, but its days as a leader in industry, finance, or political influence would be over. Of course, some people think the collapse is happening now.

A reality of the current international situation is that America as a political entity is already in debt up to its eyeballs. Most of the I.O.U.s of the United States, called "Treasury Bills," are held by American banks. The American banks got the money to lend to the U.S. Treasury by selling certificates of deposit and commercial paper to foreigners. Virtually all substantial deposits are not in the names of individuals but are registered to multinational companies and foreign banks. The reality is that America is acting as a haven for billions and billions of stateless, hot, short-term deposits of unknown ownership. Some of this is, no doubt, American-owned money held under foreign cover. These deposits, in the past, have allowed America to spend more than it makes in taxes. But with a tax revolt brewing, many foreigners now believe that the United States is looking for a way to renege on its national debt. Changing the rules and simply nationalizing everything is not the American Way—although variations on that ploy are being considered. The way the United States does things is sneakier: It attracts foreigners and others to make dollar deposits—"Buy Savings Bonds"—and then expands the money supply to devalue the dollars. It pays back with cheaper, devalued dollars. But next time around investors demand a higher interest rate. The only reason that people keep dollars at all any more is that the high tax-free interest rate works out almost as well as holding other currencies—all of which are bad investments. But all intelligent investors are now looking for other ways to pull out of the dollar and to store wealth. How do you tell? Witness the spectacular rise in prices for gold, art, antiques, oriental rugs, real estate, and any other tangibles. To a certain extent, anxiety about the future status of America as a tax haven and safe haven for investment has produced the current instability of international financial markets. Everybody is nervous, and few long-term investors exist any more.

It seems apparent that American self-interest should prevent any major changes that would precipitate panic selling or panic withdrawals of cash from the Big Apple (New York). "Should" is the word, not "won't," because politicians seldom act in the long-term interests of their country or its citizens. That's why, when I make predictions about the future, I always ask myself, "What would I do, if I were in power, *to get reelected?* What seems to be the *popular* thing to do these days—regardless of how *stupid* or *harmful* it might be to the long-term interests of the country?" When I have the answers to those questions, I have an answer to what the new rules of the game are going to be.

When the popular press begins to rant and rave about the special privileges given to foreigners—and the politicans begin to make speeches about how "obscene" it all is, then you may see the screws tightened. And when that happens, it's "Good-bye, the land of the free!"

Of course, economically speaking, it hasn't been the "land of the free" for Americans for a long time. Not unless the American became a foreigner. What does this all mean to you?

1. Consider becoming a member of the superterranean economy by detaxing or foreignizing yourself, as explained elsewhere in this book.
2. Keep your ear to the ground and be alert for changes in the economy or political scene.

Whatever happens, there's one thing of which you can be sure. If you don't like things the way they are, stick around—things will change! The changes are never "overnight" and can always be predicted well in advance. Whether you profit from those changes or go down the tubes will depend on how well you've paid attention and what moves you have made to take advantage of them.

14.
Expatriation and Multiple Passports

As mentioned, non-U.S. citizens have many tax advantages not available to ordinary Americans. A foreigner, even though he or she may legally live in the United States physically, up to six months each year, is not subject to short or long-term capital gains taxes on deals made in the United States. Interest earned from bank accounts or savings institutions in the name of non-U.S. citizens or corporations is tax exempt. Cash dividends from stocks are "technically" subject to a maximum 30 percent withholding tax, but this 30 percent is taken out only when the dividend checks are mailed abroad. Foreigners who live in the United States as "tourists" simply have their dividend checks mailed to their U.S. homes or to their tax-free U.S. bank accounts. This effectively but illegally avoids the problem of withholding taxes for them. A foreigner always can and will plead ignorance and usually suffers few consequences. Why? Because the government encourages wealthy foreigners to invest and vacation here. This is I.R.S. official policy: "Be nice to foreigners."

A foreigner's salary, capital gains, unearned income, or other income or profits are not subject to any taxes if derived from "foreign sources." Thus a noncitizen could earn "foreign source" money here tax free. He may even work tax free at some salaried jobs within the United States if employed by a non-U.S. entity such as a consulate, government tourist office, or other foreign enterprise.

Any gifts a foreigner makes to anyone are not subject to gift tax if the gift is foreign property, U.S. dollars, or U.S. securities. There is a gift tax on U.S. real estate or tangible personal property—such as diamonds or gold coins. Remember the *giver* pays the tax, not the recipient.

On death, a foreigner's estate is exempt from all estate taxes except for real estate registered directly in the name of a foreigner. Foreign-owned real estate is taxed on the owner's death at a maximum estate tax rate of 30 percent of its value. However, real estate owned through a foreign corporation or trust is not subject to any estate taxes. Thus it is obvious that any well-advised foreigner should never register U.S. real estate in his own name, if he plans on dying.

A wealthy foreigner who would like to live in the United States would obviously do much better tax-wise if he did not become an official legal resident or U.S. citizen. As a resident (someone who officially arrives in the United States as an immigrant), a foreigner is subject to exactly the same taxes as an American would be, with one important exception: The foreigner can avoid capital gains taxes. If a foreigner's investments in the United States go up in value, the alien can leave the country for a year, sell out while abroad, and not be subject to capital gains taxes when he moves back. If an American does the same thing, he is subject to the same taxes as if he never left.

A wealthy foreigner can typically get a multiple-entry visa known as a B-2 visa (temporary or for pleasure). A B-2 is good for life (for all practical purposes) and allows a foreigner to come and go in the United States as he likes on business or pleasure visits. For tax purposes, the foreigner is not allowed to remain in the United States for over 183 days per year—if he does not want to be declared a resident. As a practical matter, foreigners who wish to stay in America more than 183 days and keep their tax-free status need only head for the nearest border (Canada or Mexico), get an exit stamp, and then do a "U" turn back into the United States. By flashing a U.S. driver's license at the border, anyone is readmitted without showing a passport. It is simple for a foreigner to show by passport stamps that he left the states "officially" on, say, January 2, 1981. A year later (this time not showing the passport on the way out) and not getting an exit stamp and getting just an entry stamp in his passport on December 30, 1981, the foreigner can "prove" he was *out* of the United States from January 2 to December 30 (or any dates desired). Americans living permanently in Mexico do the same thing for slightly different reasons. Mexico issues a 6-month tourist card. Americans who live there year round cross the border once or twice a year to pick up a new tourist card on the other side. This keeps them "tourists," free of Mexican taxes.

Most Americans living abroad pay no American income taxes because their first $25,000 of earnings is tax free. This is scheduled to go up to $50,000 in 1981 or 1982. If an expatriate earns more than the exempt amount and doesn't pay U.S. taxes, there is little or no I.R.S. enforcement abroad. Nonresident Americans are supposed to file a special informational return with the district director of the I.R.S. in Philadelphia. Obviously, with bank records and property ownership records beyond the reach of the U.S. taxman, a "low-profile," wealthy, foreign resident U.S. citizen generally *evades* all U.S. income taxes even though theoretically obligated to pay a tax on any income over $25,000.

A foreigner is not subject to the rules governing taxation of foreign personal holding companies or controlled foreign corporations. Thus, it is possible for a foreigner to own a big

233

factory in the United States. He can manufacture "widgets" (or any other product) and sell the product at cost to a foreign tax haven company owned by him—thus assuring that his U.S. operation earns no profits. The foreign corporation can then resell the widgets for a profit anywhere in the world, including the United States, and Mr. Foreigner has effectively (and legally) avoided all taxes. The I.R.S. might try to reallocate some of the profits, but with international corporations involved it's an uphill battle, because the I.R.S. has access only to U.S. books and records.

Enforcement problems of the I.R.S. were illustrated in the amusing case of *Brittingham* v. *Commissioner* (66TC 373, 1976). A wealthy Mexican lady lived in the same apartment in Beverly Hills for about 24 years from 1945 onward. She had a very substantial income and assets in the United States and Mexico. She neither filed nor paid U.S. or California state income taxes for over 20 years. On discovering the facts the I.R.S. gave her a pass on unpaid income taxes from 1945 to 1959, but claimed over $2 million in back taxes and penalties for the seven-year period from 1960 to 1966. She was in the United States on a tourist visa (B-2). When it appeared that she might lose the case, she moved both herself and her assets back to Mexico. The I.R.S., after an expensive legal proceeding, ended up with no defendant and empty hands.

Another chap—let's call him "Our Hero"—was a real estate developer. He made several millions a year and, as an American, paid taxes on it. He went to a tax haven lawyer and worked out his strategy. In our true life story, Our Hero obtained a second passport from another country, in this case England. Unlike the United States, the other countries of the world don't attempt to tax nonlocal income of nonresidents. Thus he was free of any British tax claims. He then established a legal residence in Monaco. How? By simply buying a co-op apartment in Monte Carlo for $50,000 and applying to Princess Grace Kelly's husband, Prince Rainier, for a residence permit. Get the picture? Our Hero, yesterday as American as Apple Pie, Pizza, and Chop Suey is now an Englishman, with a legal residence in tax-free Monaco. This particular chap then formed "Aunt Tilly, Inc." a Netherlands Antilles Corporation that purchased at his cost (Get it? No profit!) a property he had just developed in Florida. The project was a Florida apartment building suitable for condominium conversion. Condo building and converting is what he was doing before he became internationalized. Our Hero used to make $1 million a year, keeping about $550,000 after taxes.

Let's see what happened next. Our Hero had built a nice apartment project for a total cost of about $4 million. It was sold for $4 million to Aunt Tilly Corporation. The rental was tax free to Aunt Tilly Corporation not because of any tax treaty but because under U.S. accounting rules real estate cash flow is sheltered by depreciation on the building, carpeting, fixtures, etc.

Our Hero went to the Miami city planners and received preliminary approvals for a condo conversion and retail sale of the apartments at a price of $7.25 million. Being a generous sort, Aunt Tilly Corporation negotiated a deal with Bob Broker, a local real estate broker, to buy the property for $7 million. Why $250,000 below the probable resale price? Because the Netherlands Antilles Corporation didn't want to be deemed to be "in the business of real estate" or what in the case of an individual might be considered a "dealer." A sale of 400 individual condo units might make the I.R.S. classify Aunt Tilly Corporation as engaged in a trade or business within the United States. It was important for Aunt Tilly to be considered a passive investor. If she was "actively engaged in business," her U.S. real estate income would be taxed at ordinary income rates. Thus Aunt Tilly marketed her condos at a slight discount to a local operator, who in turn peddled them individually to the public.

When the smoke cleared and the Florida property was sold, here is what had happened:

```
Cost of project to Our Hero: .............. $4,000,000
Selling price of project ...................  7,000,000
Profit (paid to Aunt Tilly Corp.) ...........  3,000,000
One-year rental income during holding period
   (Note: There is no recapture of depreciation
   for foreigners!) ........................    400,000
Total net cash realized in one year: ............ $3,400,000
U.S. income taxes ................................ Zero
```

Compare zero with approximate taxes if Our Hero paid ordinary income taxes as a U.S. resident real estate developer. The tax would have been about $1.7 million, or about half of the profit.

Naturally, getting the legalities arranged the first time was not cheap. Lawyers and others had to be paid. Our Hero indicated to me that these were his approximate expenses:

```
Initial consultation with lawyer regarding
   expatriation and second passport ............... $20,000
Cost of British passport .........................      10
Cost of Monaco resident's permit and
   related documents .............................     100
Cost of setting up Netherlands Antilles Corporation,
   including legal opinion from United States lawyer
   on nontax status .............................  20,000
Netherlands Antilles tax on Aunt Tilly Corp. ......... Zero
Misc. expenses (down payment on co-op apartment in
   Monte Carlo, travel) ..........................  20,000
                                                  _____
Total cost of internationalizing ................... $60,110
```

Because the tax cost of not internationalizing would have been $1,700,000, Our Hero was very pleased with the results.

There are few court cases involving Americans residing abroad, because the I.R.S. has virtually no power to serve papers on or enforce money judgments for back taxes against Americans. There is even less power over "former" Americans. The I.R.S. tries to scare people by saying it will claim taxes for up to 12 years after expatriation—but a low-profile expatriate has little to fear because the I.R.S. simply isn't all that efficient. One of the biggest loopholes in the American tax system is the fact that a *balance sheet* is never required of an individual taxpayer. The I.R.S. still has no right to know what your assets are or *where* they are. As a result, the American who disappears abroad for a few years and reappears as a "foreigner" with pots of gold is generally not called on to explain the source of his good fortune. In fact, as a wealthy "foreigner" the returning expatriate is treated better than a "mere" citizen. With this background, here are a few hints or possible strategies to consider:

How does one go about giving up U.S. citizenship? First off, formally renouncing U.S. citizenship in my opinion is probably a *bad* idea—particularly if you haven't found another country that will make you a citizen and give you a passport. Even when you do get a second passport, it isn't necessary to renounce U.S. citizenship.

The whole process of obtaining a second passport has been made to appear very mysterious, and one financial and tax haven consultant reportedly charges $30,000 to obtain new passports for rich Americans.

I did my own study of the subject by merely phoning all the consulates in San Francisco and asking what the requirements were for getting a passport of their country. Here is what I learned: Any citizen of the United States who has foreign-born parents may have a very good chance of obtaining a foreign passport from his ancestral home country by merely applying for a passport and producing his parent's birth certificate, his parent's marriage certificate, and his own birth certificate. The fees are usually very small, ranging from about $12 (Great Britain) to $48 (Philippines). I would suggest *not* getting a Philippine passport, because that is the only other country in the world that attempts to tax the worldwide income of its citizens. The Philippine passport is relatively easy to get—but must be renewed every two years, and at that time the consulate renewing the passport will try to negotiate you out of about $2,000 per year in income tax. Interestingly enough, when an American passport is renewed abroad, there is *no* questioning about whether you paid U.S. income tax. One cautionary note: A *naturalized* (not native-born) American who obtains a foreign passport is taking a big chance. If he is found out, his American citizenship may be formally revoked. How do the Americans usually find out? If a routine customs search on entry to the United States yields two passports, the U.S. passport is automatically confiscated! But, in general, a foreign consulate will *not* tell the United States that you have applied for (or have been granted) a foreign passport. Consular officials of most countries tend to be very friendly, helpful types, and will give you straight answers on what if anything they report to the host country. If the possibility of the United States finding out about your second passport bothers you, you might consider applying for your new passport at an embassy *outside* of the United States while on a vacation in, say, Mexico City or London. But that is probably not necessary. Most countries maintain legations in New York City because of the United Nations—and those legations tend to be quite tight lipped and uncooperative with U.S. governmental authorities except in the case of serious criminals, dope dealers, bank robbers, and so on.

Suppose you *don't* have a foreign parent? Even a grandparent may do. Ireland will issue an Irish passport to Americans of Irish ancestry. Or religion may do it for you. Israel will give you a passport if you can prove that your mother was Jewish. When I asked the Israeli consul why, I got this cryptic answer: "You can never be sure who your father was." A Catholic just may be able to get a Vatican passport—but that one is very tricky. It's easier for priests.

Interestingly enough, if you, as an American-born individual, obtain a second passport because of birthright or religion you do *not* lose American citizenship. The people I asked about this at the U.S. State Department were very hazy. Probably in the next edition of this book I'll be able to get you a case citation—but it appears that the decision in a recent immigration case involving an adult holder of two passports set forth the American position that an American-born citizen *can* be a dual national. Up until recently, the U.S. State Department view was that dual nationality was possible only up to age 18. Adults had to make a choice. But now the old rule appears to be on the way out.

Ireland is a perfect tax haven for artists.

Ireland will issue a passport to anyone who can prove that they had one Irish parent or four Irish grandparents. If you are a talented artist, writer, sculptor, poet, or intellectual—Ireland will give you a free pass on taxes for life if you make it your legal residence. Not a bad deal if you're into leprechauns, four-leaf clover, high-spirited women, and good whiskey!

Then, of course, there is the third possibility—that your ancestors came from a place like the U.S.S.R. or Algeria, where you wouldn't want their nearly useless passport even if they gave it to you. Or perhaps you just can't make it on family background, or religion. Well, all is not lost; getting a second passport just gets more expensive.

Suppose you want a Mexican passport. According to the Mexican Consulate, it is impossible for someone not born inside that country or who did not have a Mexican parent to get a Mexican passport. I pressed him. He indicated that maybe one or two passports per year were granted by special application to the President of Mexico. I pressed further: "How does one go about making special application?" The next thing I knew I was in the office of a prominent Mexican-American immigration lawyer in Los Angeles. His view was that for a fee of $10,000 payable in advance, a Mexican passport was assured "in about six months." Having dealt with Mexican lawyers before, I knew that if I were seriously interested in a Mexican passport I'd want the money held in an escrow account in America until the passport was delivered. Whether this particular gentleman could actually deliver the passport I'll never know—but there's an old saying that applies in Mexico and almost any other country in the non-English-speaking world: "If you've got the money and a good lawyer, you can get anything you want out of a government." Thus it is usually possible to get a passport through extralegal channels if you are able to find an attorney who specializes in such matters. I'm sorry to say that corruption in high places makes everything possible.

The mechanics of getting a not-exactly-kosher passport seem to follow this pattern. Every country has a few states or provinces where a courthouse burned down and the records were destroyed. Your lawyer arranges for a few affidavits to be signed, and in due course a bogus birth certificate, wedding certificate, or other appropriate documents are prepared to replace the "lost" vital statistics. A passport is issued based on the birth certificate and other documents, which no one can ever prove are false.

Another method, totally illegal, is simply getting the birth certificate of a child who died in infancy—or a person you are sure never had a passport in his own country—and simply building up a new identity for yourself based on the name and birthdate of the deceased. If for instance you studied French in school and are pretty good at it, you should be able to assume the identity of a dead French person. Naturally you'd apply for the passport in France. If a question came up about your accent, you'd better have a good story ready—such as, you attended the American School in Paris and that's why you sound like a Yankee. The beauty of this method is that you can do it alone—without the help of a lawyer. Just be sure that birth and death certificates are not cross-indexed in the community where you are trying to pull this one off.

All things considered, if you can afford it, getting a well-connected, corrupt immigration lawyer is probably your best bet. Why? If he is on a "contingent fee," you only have to pay if he gives you the results you want—and if there is a slip-up, the lawyer gets the heat and will probably be better able to smooth things over than if *you* got caught making some blunder in a foreign country.

Italy is a country where a good lawyer can work wonders.
After World War II, most courthouses were burned down and
records were destroyed. In Italy, taxes are set at very
high rates, but few people pay taxes. There are a lot of
communists there, but if I had to live under communism,
Italy would be my first choice. Italian communists are all
Catholics, which is unusual in itself. But they share with
their right-thinking brothers a real joy in living,
loving, and eating. The men are romantic, the ladies
are tigers. People don't take themselves too seriously,
and you just can't beat Milano for great grand opera.

241

Obviously, the names of these lawyers are not bandied about in books like this or the public press, because their usefulness would be at an end if a crusading journalist in their own country produced the headline story "Crooked Shyster Makes Millions in Phoney Passport Scandal—Foreigners Made Citizens, for Big Fees!" If I knew any names and addresses, I couldn't publish them here. But with a little determination on your part, you should be able to get all the foreign passports you want. I recommend that you try to do it legally!

OK. Now we shall assume that you, Jack or Jane Armstrong, the all-American boy (or girl) have an American passport, but the foreign country to which you've applied for citizenship wants you to turn it in for the new passport that they will give you. This assumes you are trying to get a legal passport based on foreign ancestry or religion. There are two ways around this problem, but because they are a little "gray" I'd prefer anyone with the specific problem to send me a stamped, self-addressed envelope with a $20 bill and ask for the sheet I intentionally left out of this book, entitled "How to Legally Hold Two American Passports." I didn't want 100,000 copies of this page floating around, because the "loophole" under which two American passports can be legally obtained would be too rapidly closed. It will probably be closed anyway in the 1980s but hopefully later rather than sooner. In any event, you can trade in your *extra* U.S. passport for your new *foreign* second passport.

What was the point of all this time, trouble and expense to get a second passport? Self-preservation. There is one thing you can be sure of in this ever-changing world: *Your government regards you as a natural resource to be taxed, regulated, and possibly sacrificed in the national interest.* But the national interest may not be your interest. Good Americans, Japanese by ancestry, lost all their property and were incarcerated in concentration camps in World War II for no crime other than that they were Japanese-Americans. German-Americans got a similar shafting in World War I. As

242

I write this book, persecution is being undertaken against Iranian-Americans. Germans of Jewish ancestry were once murdered in Germany in 1941. Polish people who were children of wealthy Poles were murdered by communists in Poland in 1948. Christian Lebanese were murdered by Moslems in Lebanon in 1968. Left-wing French liberals were murdered or deported by France in 1943. Americans are being murdered or kidnapped all over the world—just because they are Americans.

Whatever you are, your turn will come to be persecuted. It is only history. With luck, you may never have it happen during your lifetime—but if persecution and subjugation don't happen to you, they *will* happen to your children, your grandchildren, or your great-grandchildren. In the United States during the era of George Washington, over one-third of the population was forced to leave America. They were the Tories who supported England. A hundred years later, another third of the American population was displaced in the American Civil War. Millions of Americans who chose the wrong side were forced to move to Mexico, Canada, South America, and Europe.

Just because during our lifetimes America has been free of civil strife or terrorism is no guarantee that this will continue. The odds are against it. Although I do not wish to raise any specters of gloom or predictions of the end of America, you should be aware that historically we are *due* for another major upheaval. Since it is relatively easy to establish a second citizenship in a neutral country and a safe haven in peacetime—but almost impossible once the bombs start falling—doesn't it make sense to work out a sensible contingency plan well ahead of time?

Even the Boy Scout motto is "Be prepared."

15.
Sovereign
Immunity

Even better than having a foreign passport and a foreign corporation to make your activity (whatever it may be) tax free is to operate with *sovereign immunity*. It is an established principle in America that if a foreign government owns and operates a business within the United States, the profits of that business are entirely tax free. Under this provision, the Soviet Union can and does broker shipping deals, speculate in grains, etc., through its New York office. It pays no income tax whatsoever on its huge profits. Any communist country can run a bank, hotel, or other profit-making company in the United States without being obliged to pay the 50 percent income tax that Americans must pay. Obviously, this means they are at a great competitive advantage. Not only communist countries get this privilege, of course. Any small country that makes investments in the United States has this tax-free status.

Older methods of tax avoidance are obsolete when compared with the newest weapons of the superterraneans.

How can *you* get it? Simple. Make friends with Chogdal of Sikkim or the dictator of Paraguay. All kings, emperors, etc., are, in effect, just businessmen struggling to stay afloat, as well as sovereign heads of state. You might be able to arrange to channel your money and time into investments held in the name of a foreign government.

Don't think this isn't already being done. John B. Smart,* an expatriate from Utah and other places, recently cultivated a friendship with High King Tupoo of Tonga (an obscure island republic in the South Pacific). A few years back, Tonga had nothing to its name but half a dozen coconut trees. Now it's emerging as a major international developer of hotels and casinos. The money for these projects, channeled through Tonga's Bank of the South Pacific, in-

---

*A name I made up. It is not intended to be any real person, living or dead.

volves much more than a few coconuts. Since Smart runs the bank, I'd guess the money belongs to him and his associates.

For you to pull off a similar coup, just organize your own group of investors and find a Tupoo who will let you wheel and deal under his banner of sovereignty for a small cut of the tax savings or profits. A fringe benefit will be that, as a diplomatic representative of a sovereign state, you personally cannot be sued or arrested. When U.S. officials tried to arrest Smart for tax evasion, he reportedly flashed his Tonga diplomatic passport and told the American tax men to fly a kite. According to a story in the *London Times*, that is what they had to do.

If you are a good Catholic, the idea may have crossed your mind to combine national sovereign immunity with religious exemption from all inspection, control and taxation. Sorry, you're just a wee bit late on that one. A burly American in his fifties from Al Capone's town of Cicero, Illinois, has already convinced the Pope to let him run the Vatican Bank. The Vatican Bank is reputedly the world's richest and

Consulates and embassies pay no taxes!

most swinging private bank (going by the official title of the Institute for Religious Works). The Vatican Bank maintained a low profile in its international wheeling and dealing until recently when it attracted unwelcome publicity by backing an alleged underworld character in his alleged attempts to control and loot a chain of American and Italian banks.

Attaining sovereign immunity is a pretty far out concept. But I did want to raise your consciousness to the possibilities, and let you know of one other method of attaining sovereign immunity: Conquest! In 1979-80 a French soldier of fortune who had been serving various African dictators decided that he would simply take over a whole country. With a handful of mercenary friends, in a short coup d'état he named himself King of Comoro, an Island in the Indian Ocean. Activities like this are not played up very much in

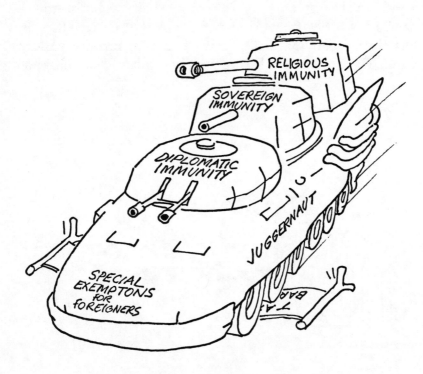

The hard-core tax avoider can't be stopped by conventional tax barriers any longer.

the American press because the United States government does not want to encourage too many imitators. But many individualistic Americans set up their own sovereign states several times a year—either by conquest or by settlement. One of my favorites is the Republic of Minerva formed recently by some Los Angeles Libertarians on an uninhabited coral reef in the South Pacific. They issued coins, stamps, passports, and proved to be a great annoyance to the I.R.S. They were an even greater annoyance to Mr. Smart and the Tupoo of Tonga who declared war on them and captured the coral reef back. The government of Minerva now plots a recoup from exile, back in the Los Angeles Embassy of Minerva.

Perhaps taking over a country by force of arms is too tame, too 19th century for you. How about taking over a *Planet?* Well, if not a planet, then at least a *satellite.*

16. Reaching for the Stars

As I was starting this book in 1979, I received a call on the phone from one of my colleagues. This was his idea: "Let's put a satellite into outer space."

"Sounds like a good idea, but what would we do for encores."

"No joke," said my friend (I'll call him Reverend Hype), "Hear me out."

"In the Caribbean and in Africa, and in most of the world, there is a big market for the *Word of the Lord.* NASA (National Aeronautics and Space Agency) has a deal whereby they will launch and place into orbit a private communications satellite for only a few hundred grand. My thought is that we pop for the satellite and a launch. Then we can beam out programs of hope and inspiration to all the masses of the world, who are hungry for spiritual guidance. My own message of 'Prosperity through Giving' could be a ten-minute

251

spot 24 hours a day. The way it works is that our ground station in New York would transmit programming to the satellite, and those programs would be simulcast in different languages all over the world on a 24-hour a day basis."

"Isn't there one thing you are forgetting, Reverend Hype?" I asked.

"What's that?" the Reverend asked.

"Simply that most people around the world are poor folks and they don't have TV sets."

"You don't know the facts, man! In the Third World, all you need is one TV set per town, and since there isn't much to do, all the brothers and sisters will come into a tent or an igloo to watch TV every night. They might even pay admission! We give them a big-screen TV and a satellite receiving station—one per town. Every community in the world will buy it on credit. We finance the project through the World Bank or some Japanese development bank that wants to push sales of their television receivers. Maybe we can get the host country to guarantee all or part of the installation costs."

"Why would a poor government want to pay anyone for beaming religion to their people?" I asked.

"We give the local government an hour of prime time each day to broadcast their local propaganda messages. And, if they want it, we can let them do some local programming, too. We give them whatever they want!"

"How does this operation make any money?" was my next question.

"We make it coming and going: First, I figure we can place 5 million satellite receiving stations each year for at least 10 years. After that we'll have the replacement market. Our cost will be around $100 million a year, but the profit from each receiver should net around $1.7 billion per year just from installations. We should get another billion in rentals of our programs from existing cable and pay TV systems."

"Gee, Reverend, figures like that sound stratospheric—I never hear figures like $1.7 billion outside of Washington, D.C.," I commented.

The preacher went on: "And there's more. Much more revenue will be coming in from our programming. We'll sell time to all the radio and TV missionaries and visionaries. Religion is the world's biggest business—bigger even than marijuana and cocaine. And it's legal! The market is just unlimited."

"Why would all those people buy time on your satellite?" I wondered aloud.

"We're talking about beaming the message of the Lord right out of the heavens, right to the people who need it. Every receiving station would have a minimum of 5,000 viewers. If we have 20 million stations, we'll have a loyal audience of over 1 billion people every night. Donations from the viewers will roll in from all over the world to support this kind of mission.

"Our congregations in the more affluent countries will send in more (tax-deductible) donations to get the message to the folks in the boondocks. Religious TV is already grossing more than the commercial channels."

I didn't need to ask, but I did anyway: "Reverend Hype, what's the tax status of all those billions you stand to make?"

"I don't make anything, boy. As you know, I'm the head of my own church. The Church of Prosperity. My church owns everything, and I'm just the servant of the Lord. Of course I like personal prosperity, but I've had all I need for years. The billions in sales, grants, commissions, and donations just will go for more bibles, satellites, and any other projects I dream up. Religion is tax exempt. Our product never wears out and can be sold again and again. I get excited just waking up in the morning when I think of all the possibilities.

"Wanna be our lawyer and financial consultant, Greene? I'll give you 5 percent of the gross receipts—should net you $5 million a year for starters."

"Not right now—but I'll mention your idea in my new book as an example of superterranean thinking. If Werner Ehrhard could do billion-dollar promotions with est and Ron

Hubbard could do it with Scientology, I don't see why you can't pull it off."

(*Author's note:* Religious TV satellites have now been launched by NASA. My friend's financial projections turn out to have been very much on the *low* side.) The whole world is getting the message of *Prosperity Through Giving*. They are giving a lot of tax free donations to Rev. Hype and his colleagues.

17.
The
Super-
Terraneans

Offshore Corporations, Multinational Operations, and Other Fancy Tax Angles Used by Rich Folks to Avoid Taxes

As recently as 1974, the subject of foreign tax havens was taboo. No matter how hard you searched, there was nothing in print in the way of a "how-to" book. It was OK, even respectable, to use foreign tax havens, but wealthy individuals of the world could only find out how to use them with the help of a savvy and expensive international lawyer. These lawyers and Certified Public Accountants who specialized in international tax avoidance were always well known "in the profession." For a time, it was a small and select group.

The economy of many a small country was based on the use of that country by rich foreigners as an "offshore" center of financial activity. The prime example of such a country used to be Switzerland before they succumbed to U.S. pressure and discouraged tax haven business.

Prior to 1962 it was possible for an American (for instance) to merely incorporate in a foreign country, channel his profits to a foreign corporation, and totally escape U.S. taxes on his income. Such simplicity obviously meant profitable business for lawyers who specialized in such offshore incorporations and kept the mechanics a trade secret. It also meant that during the 1960s more and more attorneys would try to get into the act until even a manufacturer of undies in Des Moines felt the need for an offshore corporate base.

Putting it into what I call "baby talk," this is how an Iowa ladies'-underwear manufacturer would use a tax haven. Remember, this was under the "old" rules. They were changed in 1962 and changed again in 1976.

Let's say that on December 31, 1960, the factory owner produced 100,000 panties at a cost of $100,000. He sold the panties all over the world for $3 each, or $300,000 in total. His profit was obviously $200,000. As a U.S. citizen and taxpayer, he had an income of $200,000, and in 1960 paid a state and federal income tax of over $100,000. After reading an article about offshore tax havens, he went to his local lawyer and said that he too wanted to pay no taxes ever again, legally. The lawyer, having been recently deluged with literature about lawyers' seminars on international tax planning, pulled out his file and referred the client (let's call him Mr. Undy) to the world-famous international tax specialist, Mr. Solomon Grundy, in London. These names are all fictitious, of course.

Mr. Undy flies to London, and Mr. Grundy tells him that for a substantial fee he will set up a tax haven "offshore" corporation in a small country like Liechtenstein or the Bahamas.

"What does that mean to me?" asks Mr. Undy.

The lawyer replies, "Essentially, I write a letter that asks the government of the Bahamas to please issue a sheet of paper or 'charter' that says a corporation has been established in the Bahamas. The name of the corporation is 'The Undy International Corporation.' The only shareholder is Mr. Undy. The only officers are Mr. Undy and a local Bahamas lawyer (whom we shall call Mr. Bahama). For another fee, Mr. Bahama will open a bank account for the Undy International Corporation and will do whatever you tell him to do. The Undy Corporation will be the alter ego of Mr. Undy.

"Let's suppose (just to keep things simple) that all your undy sales were just to one store, the Gallerie Lafayette of Paris. And let's suppose further that each year you shipped the Gallerie 100,000 undies, and they sent you a check for $300,000. Now you will vary the procedure slightly: You sell the 100,000 undies, at cost, to the Undy International Corporation. Undy International resells to the Paris store for the usual $300,000."

"But how can I do that?" interrupts Mr. Undy. "Undy International Corporation is just me."

"No," says Mr. Grundy. "Under international law, the Undy *Corporation* is a separate legal entity—a new individual—separate and apart from you, even though you own all the stock, and even though you are the only officer. Your employee, Mr. Bahama, will merely send you an order on Undy International stationery for 100,000 undies. On behalf of Undy International, Mr. Bahama will promise to pay you $100,000. Eventually, Mr. Bahama will send you $100,000 and will deposit $200,000 in the corporate bank account in Freeport, Bahamas.

"But," says Mr. Undy, "how can I make any money that way? The panties cost me $100,000! If I sell them for $100,000, I break even. I can pay my employees and my rent, but my business doesn't make a dime!"

"Of course," replies lawyer Grundy. "That is exactly what you want. On your 1961 U.S.A. income tax, you merely report that you had a break-even year. For the sake of good form, you might wish to create a small profit by selling at a tad over cost to your foreign corporation."

"So far, that's great," grunts Undy, "but how do I get to enjoy my $200,000 profit? Can I ask Mr. Bahama to send me a check? And how about Undy International Corp.—don't they have to pay any taxes?"

Grundy leans back in his easy chair. "Question One: If you get a check sent into the United States from Undy International, you'll have a tax problem. If you call it a dividend, you have to pay a U.S. tax. If it's a salary, you'll have to pay a tax. So one of the best uses for the foreign money in your corporation's account is just to leave it abroad. Invest it in stocks, bonds, interest-bearing accounts, or perhaps build a new undy factory somewhere else in the world. Build an estate for your children and grandchildren! Of course, Undy International could always buy a yacht or a limousine and furnish it to you—for business use, of course. That would be tax free. They could even finance a skiing vacation or other business trip for you and your family. But suppose you want cold cash? If Undy International deposited $100,000 at a foreign bank, I'm sure that any bank would be willing to lend you $100,000 individually if the loan were secured by the corporation account. In international finance, this is called a back-to-back loan. Of course, borrowed money would be tax free to you back in the United States.

"Your second question was about the tax status of Undy International. Undy International, being a company incorporated in a tax haven, doesn't pay any taxes. Why? Because that's the whole point of a country setting itself up to be a tax haven. The tax haven country charges a small fee each year. Local lawyers, like Mr. Bahama, get to earn fees for performing various services for foreign companies. The foreign companies do no business in the tax haven but use the tax haven as a conduit for business transactions. Advantages to the tax haven country are that local lawyers, hotels, and banks get business and accounts that would otherwise never be attracted to what is usually an out-of-the-way place with few natural resources and not too much going for it. In the United States, for instance, the state of Delaware is a domestic tax haven that is actually used by many non-U.S. citizens as a corporate tax base. Its annual charge and tax on corporations is nearly the lowest in America, and its secrecy laws and business laws are very much in favor of corporations— not in favor of individuals who sue corporations. So, like Delaware, offshore or non-U.S. tax havens usually provide a degree of secrecy, favorable business laws, and minimal tax burdens."

"So," says Mr. Undy, "My foreign corporation is nothing more than a sheet of paper or a charter and a lawyer who puts a plaque on his door along with hundreds of other different plaques. 'Undy International Corporation' is essentially a mail drop and a bank account in the Bahamas. How about if I die while there is a big balance in the corporate bank account?"

Mr. Grundy: "Your representative, Mr. Bahama or his successor, could be given death instructions, and the funds will be disposed of according to your wishes, without any tax imposed by the Bahamas. Naturally, there will be no report to the U.S. tax authorities. Tax havens usually have secrecy laws, and if Mr. Bahama told the I.R.S. anything, his own country would put him in jail and take away his license to practice law."

"Are there any disadvantages to setting up a tax haven corporation such as Undy International?" Mr. Undy asked.

"As always, there is a risk that the U.S. laws could be changed and that you might have to report ownership of foreign corporations—or the United States might pass some law that would make your corporation's earnings taxable to you (note: This is what happened in 1962). Another possibility is that the government of the Bahamas could go leftist, and all local bank accounts could be confiscated. This problem could be avoided by keeping your accounts in a third place— like London, England—and keeping an eye on current events so that you can move your funds quickly, and your corporation to a more hospitable environment in the event of undesirable changes in government. (Note: A leftist regime took over the Bahamas during the 1970s, with the result that a large portion of Bahamian tax haven business has moved to Bermuda and the Cayman Islands.)

"How about fees and costs?" asked Mr. Undy.

"To set up an operation that will avoid $100,000 in taxes, I'll arrange it for 50 percent of the first year's tax savings, and 10 percent of the tax savings in future years," offered Mr. Grundy.*

"One final question," queried Mr. Undy. "Suppose I set up this operation and the I.R.S. challenges it. Can I go to jail?"

"Surely not," said Mr. Grundy, banging his shoe on his great mahogany desk for emphasis. "I will, as part of my $50,000 package deal, write you a legal opinion that (this was the rule prior to 1962) the earnings of Undy International may be accumulated indefinitely and without limit, and that they are nontaxable to you as an individual and need not be reported or mentioned on your stateside income tax returns. Such a letter, from a respected international lawyer such as myself, will indicate your good faith and be conclusive evidence in any court of law that you did not intend to evade taxes—only to avoid them legally with generally accepted, court-sanctioned methods."

"Boy oh boy!" exclaimed Mr. Undy. "You certainly have a silky-smooth, quick answer to every question."

"What do you want?" muttered Lawyer Grundy. "I should learn to stutter?"

In the 1960s and 1970s, as every small businessman and professional tried to become a member of what I call the "superterranean economy," the Practicing Law Institute in New York began giving tax-shelter seminars for lawyers. People

---

*Fees are always subject to negotiation, but setting up a tax haven operation from America will run at least $25,000 with a first-class lawyer. If *you* know the laws and have the contacts, actual or hard costs involved are well under $5,000. At my home in Mill Valley, California, about twice a year, I give seminars I call *"Advanced Tax Avoidance,"* where for the price of a deluxe dinner I go through the mechanics of setting up tax haven operations.

were realizing that if they could keep only 15 percent of every extra dollar they earned, it was logical to spend 85 percent of their time and money on tax avoidance. After all, an hour spent to earn $100 only got you $15. But an hour spent to save $100 on taxes brought home the whole $100. The fees charged by lawyers and accountants were astronomical, but always less than the taxes would have been. Because of the big fees, the professionals wanted to learn all they could about tax havens and international tax planning.

One of the men who taught these seminars was a lawyer named Marshall J. Langer. He published his lecture notes, and they became the landmark book, *How to Use Foreign Tax Havens*. No responsible authority had ever written anything of value on this once-taboo subject. But before the ink had dried on this book, the laws of the land were drastically altered and the old simplicity of tax haven use had vanished. Perhaps I.R.S. agents had attended his seminars. The main changes were new "reforms of 1962." They made an American shareholder of a closely held foreign corporation taxable on the worldwide income of the foreign corporation *whether or not that income was distributed*. This meant that new ways to avoid taxes had to be created by the experts. Every lawyer and tax expert knows that when one loophole is closed, another dozen or so are created. Some loopholes are unintentional and best kept private. Others are deliberately created by Congress to encourage "socially desirable" activities. These include expanded imports, factory construction in Puerto Rico, and exploration for natural resources. To keep American-owned enterprises viable in the jungle of international competition, Congress grants virtual tax exemption to the foreign branches of U.S. banks, insurance, and shipping companies. The 1962 reforms meant that Americans operating through tax havens had to get into the officially encouraged sector of business operations, give up control, or look for new loopholes. Sometimes the best course was a combination of all three options. In the loophole department, the multitier holding company came into its own

261

after 1962. Lawyers found that if an American was a controlling shareholder of a profitable foreign corporation, he would be assessed directly on the earnings as if the foreign corporation didn't exist. But if a second tax haven corporation was formed to own all the stock of the first one, the second one—being just an owner and not taking any profits or dividends—could be kept unprofitable. Obviously, the American owner was not subject to any tax on profits because the corporation he owned directly didn't make any profits. But the I.R.S. saw through this, and the law was changed again to include "indirect" ownership. This led to the formation of strange new forms of ownership such as the Guernsey Trust and the Liechtenstein Stiftung in which no one except the lawyers running the operation could be sure who owned anything or what was really going on.

A good insight into all these operations and the historical background can be obtained from the latest version of Langer's *Tax Haven* book, now called *Practical International Tax Planning*. This book is recommended reading for anyone who earns over $50,000 per year.

Mr. Undy earned over $50,000 per year. When he heard about the 1962 tax reforms and received a written suggestion from Mr. Grundy about forming a two-tiered corporation, he took the next plane to London, and was granted an audience with the high priest of international tax planning. He asked, "How does a two-tier corporation work?"

Grundy told him, "Any U.S. citizen now has to report on his tax return the ownership of any foreign corporations in which he has a controlling interest. The U.S. citizen also has to report any foreign bank accounts over which he has control or signature power. The new rules provide that any income earned by controlled foreign corporations (with a few exceptions just mentioned) would be attributed to the owner, whether or not he received any distribution of money.

Poor Mr. Undy! After only one year, was he undone? Far from it! Lawyers have a way of solving any problem (for a fee). Thus the multitier multinational operation was born.

262

We rejoin Mr. Undy in Mr. Grundy's office. "A fine kettle of fish you've gotten me into," says Mr. Undy. "My tax return asks me what foreign corporations I control and what bank accounts I control. If I lie and don't mention Undy International Corporation, that makes me guilty of tax fraud. And with $200,000 a year involved, I just don't want to tell the I.R.S. a lie that will enable them to go back over my tax returns at some future time and put me in the pokey."

"Not to worry," intones Mr. Grundy, the famous London solicitor. "Here is what we have done for all our clients. We set up another corporation for you in Panama, and that Panamanian corporation holds all the stock in Undy International (Bahamas) Corporation. I will own the stock in the Panama Corporation, which we shall call Grundy Holdings (Panama) Limited."

"What's the purpose of that?" asks Mr. Undy.

"So that you can truthfully say that you don't own or control any foreign corporation," answers Mr. Grundy.

"But I do control you, don't I?" asks Undy. "So I'd still be lying on my tax return if asked if I controlled any foreign bank accounts or corporations."

"That's where the third tier comes in," explains Lawyer Grundy. "We set up a trust on the Island of Jersey in the English Channel, and the trust has no assets, only an option to purchase the Panamanian shares. Trust me! When the smoke clears, you can answer all the I.R.S. questions truthfully, and they will never get a clue as to what you are doing. Having an option to purchase control is *not* control. Whatever laws, rules, or regulations the I.R.S. passes, we shall think up ways to allow you to continue to avoid taxes. Of course, all the extra paper work will *cost* you more. But with even a 50 percent tax rate, we can still save you plenty of money on taxes! Besides, I'll link you up with some of my other clients, and you'll actually make money in new deals."

Grundy went on: "I will create such a network for you—of companies owning companies, trusts controlling partnerships, and a web of foundations, and other business

263

entities so complicated that even you will not be able to understand what is going on."

Mr. Undy protested, "What's the point of creating all this paperwork—and, besides, I *want* to understand what is going on."

Grundy then became very profound, and with rapture in his voice and folding his fingers he told Mr. Undy the *Big Secret:* "Frankly, Mr. Undy, you don't have a choice. Either you give me and the accountants financial control of your operations—and you join the ranks of the *multinationals*—or you go back to being a small-time manufacturer of underpants in Des Moines, Iowa. You can go back to Iowa and pay out most of what you make in taxes. Or, you can let me handle your financial affairs, and you get everything you want. I have other clients in South Africa, in Australia, and in Luxembourg. Their interests can be merged with yours. We will go public by selling stock to offshore insurance companies. You'll make millions. We can have licensing agreements, barter transactions, forward hedging of currencies. We can do things you have never dreamed of. There is a world out there, Mr. Undy, a world you have never glimpsed. It is a world you have never even imagined. It is the world of the multinationals. Private companies with bearer shareholders more powerful and more permanent than most countries. I will create trusts that no creditor or tax collector can penetrate or take away from you. You can be an important part of all this. Thank heaven you came to me in time. What will it be, Mr. Undy, small peanuts in Iowa—or the stratosphere?

Mr. Undy paused. New vistas opened to him. He glanced at the papers on Mr. Grundy's desk. A leather-bound black volume had been imprinted with the title: "Expansions, Mergers, and Acquisition Plans: Undy Universal (Liechtenstein) Aktiengesellschaft." Mr. Undy had a vision of himself sitting with that volume at a great mahogany desk in New York or London. Hundreds of little dwarfs were scampering around the office wearing sweatshirts imprinted "Zurich Gnome." A sexy gorgeous Danish secretary with tremendous breasts was taking dictation. In his daydream, a message came over the intercom. "Your Lear Jet is waiting to take you to the conference with Mr. Kashoggi in Mecca."

Mr. Grundy interrupted the revery: "What will it be, Iowa or infinity?"

On that day, Mr. Undy joined the growing ranks of the *Superterranean Economy.*

*"Your Lear Jet is waiting to take you to the conference
with Mr. Kashoggi in Mecca."*

18.
Form
Your Own
Corporation

Recently there have been some full-page ads in the papers promoting ordinary corporations as the "ultimate tax shelter." It may not be the "ultimate," but by forming a corporation one can *reduce* taxes from 50 percent to 17 percent. Here is how the tax reduction feature of your own corporation would work.

A corporation is considered a "legal person," just like a human being. But corporate incomes are taxed at a different rate from individuals. The corporate tax rate is 17 percent of the first $25,000 of earnings, 20 percent on the next $25,000, and 30 percent on the next $25,000, 40 percent on the next $25,000, and 46 percent on amounts over $100,000 income per year. The obvious logic is that, if you are a self-employed plumber in the 50 percent tax bracket, you can form a corporation to handle the retail pipe sales (or some segment of your business earnings, say $25,000 per year). Presto, your tax is lower: 17 percent instead of the 50 percent people rate.

To eliminate taxes entirely, you can then use the accumulated income in the corporation to contribute to a variety of allowable "tax-free fringe benefits" for you, your employees, and your family. These include health insurance, pension plans, company cars, group life insurance, educational programs, and so on. Only owners of corporations can provide these tax-free to themselves and their employees.

If there is any money left after the fringe benefits, the corporation pays a tax on remaining net profits at a low 17 percent rate. One can also look around for existing corporations in similar businesses that carry forward large tax losses. By merging, you can totally shelter your corporation's earnings with the carried-forward losses of an unrelated entity, a "shell corporation" you purchased from someone else. An individual can't create tax losses like that, either.

The main disadvantages of incorporating are

1. It costs money. Although you can do it yourself for $50 to $75, a "service" will do it and provide you with a registered office for about $200 per year. There are also minimum annual state fees, although these can be kept to under $200 per year in most states.

2. If you are an employee of your own corporation, the Social Security tax will amount to about 12 percent of whatever salary you pay yourself, as opposed to about 8 percent if you are self-employed. But the increased cut to Social Security can be avoided by making sure the corporation doesn't pay you anything except director's fees, fringe benefits, reimbursements for expenses, and dividends. None of these are subject to Social Security tax. If no salary or wages are taken, you can actually use a corporation to totally avoid Social Security taxes.

3. The double-taxation feature: The corporation pays a 17 percent and up tax on its earnings, but when these earnings are paid out to you as dividends you are taxed on the dis-

268

tributions as *unearned income* at a 70 percent tax rate. Moral: You can't form a corporation and expect to save any taxes by just passing cash through it. You do save taxes if you set up fringe benefit plans or if you want to use accumulated profits taxed at a low 17 percent rate to expand or wheel and deal. Generally corporations help the self-employed or professional, but are not of much use to real estate investors, who get a much better deal without them.

Everything You Need to Know About Corporations (and a Little Bit More . . .)

To understand what a corporation is, let's start at the beginning. Before there were any such things, we had Merrie Olde England, and life was filled with many of the same events still going on today. There were births, marriages, and deaths. There were storekeepers, butchers, bakers, and candlestick makers. But there were no corporations, because none were needed. Then one day some explorers discovered Africa, India, America, and a few other little places—and it wasn't long before many people realized that a lot of money could be made by establishing plantations, settlements, and large-scale industrial enterprises. But few people in those days had enough money to own more than a few merchant ships. Even kings and queens didn't have enough capital to start and maintain mines, ranches, and so on 10,000 miles from home.

And so it came to pass that the kings and queens of those days were approached by bright, ambitious chaps who proposed a deal. Someone went to the King of England and said, "King, if you give me a charter, sort of a monopoly, on all the exports of furs from North America to Europe, I'll give you 10 percent of the profits."

The King thought about it and said, "Wow, that's a swell idea. I don't have to put up any money, and I get a piece of the action."

The King scribbled a note saying "Eggbert Entrepreneur is hereby authorized by me to raise cash from the general public by selling shares in a new company—a corporation operating under Royal Charter with the official protection of our Army and Navy—said corporation is to have the *exclusive* right to set up trading stations in North America with the idea of making profits in the fur trade. The name shall be the Hudson Bay Company."

Early corporations were always chartered by the sovereign or king to engage in trading, exploitation of mineral deposits, or other business activity that required more money and personnel than the normal delicatessen on the corner.

Years ago corporate charters were granted by kings so that private individuals could raise money to engage in some monopolistic activity that was made illegal for everyone else. The king got a piece of the action. Today, you still have to give the sovereign a 50 percent share of profits, but, instead of a monopoly, the government gives you enough rules, regulations, harassment, and paperwork to drive you nuts.

From the start, the general public was offered an opportunity to invest in "shares" of the corporation. In England, all corporations ended their name with the word "Limited" or "Ltd." to distinguish them from partnerships or sole proprietorships in which the owners were personally liable if anything went wrong. The new form of enterprise, the corporation, was liable for damages due to negligence, failure to perform a contract, etc.—but only up to the assets of the corporation. Liability for the officers and shareholders was *limited.* The concept of limited liability was, and still is, an important consideration. Another feature of the corporation was its perpetual life. Officers could die, retire, resign, or be fired—but the shareholders would elect directors every year. The directors would appoint the officers, and the officers would run the company—forever! The Hudson Bay Company, Ltd., was started about over 300 years ago, and it *still* runs trading posts in Canada. As might be expected, they are called *department stores* these days. I'm not sure if the Queen of England still owns 10 percent—but it's possible. When shareholders die, their heirs inherit the shares.

Some corporations made a lot of money for their shareholders. Others went into bankruptcy. Things got more complicated over the years, but the basic idea was always the same: Any individual could apply to the government (any government) for a corporate charter. With the application, the promoter of the corporation-to-be submitted a plan telling the government what sort of business he intended to go into, how many shares he intended to sell, and where a representative of the corporation could be found. This form of application to start a corporation is called *articles of incorporation.*

I could include sample articles of incorporation, but they are very standard forms that can be obtained at any stationery store catering to lawyers. Lawyers buy an "incorporation kit" for about $10, fill out the forms, and charge the client $750. You can buy your own kit. If you are going to form a corporation with under 10 acquaintances who will be investing, you really don't need a lawyer. A small informal operation like this is called a *close corporation.*

A charter is issued as a matter of course to all applicants who pay a small incorporation fee to the state. Whatever state you live in, you can get a free copy of your local corporation laws, fees and costs, sample articles of incorporation, and full instructions on how to form a corporation. Merely write to "Office of the Secretary of State, New Incorporations Department, Your State Capital, Your State."

In many states, a corporation can be a one-man (or one-woman) operation. In California, for instance, one person can be the president, secretary (who keeps the records) and treasurer (who signs the checks). That same person can be the only director and the only shareholder. In other states, two or three individuals are required to form a corporation: but these can be nominees, and after the charter is received for all practical purposes you can have a one-man show in any state . . .

Any name not already in use may be given to the new corporation. Most states will try to collect an extra fee from you by asking you if you want the name you have chosen "held for you." Forget it. Names are not important, and if the name you want is already taken then just get another one. You can generally find out by phone if the name you want is available. Also, most law libraries and business libraries have an annual publication listing all the corporations in the state alphabetically.

A *resolution* will be required when your corporation does something like enter into a major contract, open a bank account, or give you the tax-free fringe benefits mentioned on the first page of this chapter. For instance, if you are going to buy yourself a car your corporate resolution should make it clear that the car is being purchased by the corporation, in the corporate name, and is to be used for business purposes only. If your company is going to adopt a plan to pay all your medical bills, health insurance, life insurance, or educational expenses, the I.R.S. requires some formalities. The proper

RESOLUTION of the Board of Directors of........Gorgonzola.&.Motsarella,.Limited........

at a meeting duly called and regularly held at the office of the Company in.....Georgetown,....................

.Cayman.Islands...on the....10th.......day of.....January............................19.81...

RESOLVED:

1. **That** CANADIAN IMPERIAL BANK OF COMMERCE, in this resolution referred to as "the Bank", is hereby appointed the banker of the Company;

2. **That**(¹)........Morton Motsarella, Gordon Gorgonzola........

    or any....one....of them, is/are hereby authorized for and on behalf of the Company from time to time:
    (a) to make, sign, draw, accept, endorse, negotiate, lodge, deposit or transfer all or any cheques, promissory notes, drafts, acceptances, bills of exchange, orders for the payment of money, contracts for letters of credit and forward exchange, whether or not an overdraft is thereby created in any account of the Company; also to execute any authority to any officer of the Bank to accept and/or pay all or any drafts, bills of exchange or promissory notes on behalf of the Company; also to execute receipts for and orders relating to any property of the Company held by or on behalf of the Bank;
    (b) to do all acts and things and execute all documents requisite to give security to the Bank upon all or any real or personal, immovable or movable property of the Company, whether by mortgage, hypothecation, charge, pledge, assignment, transfer or otherwise, including, without limiting the generality of the foregoing, security upon accounts receivable, bills, notes and other negotiable instruments, securities (as defined in the Bank Act), warehouse receipts, bills of lading, security under Section 82 or under Section 88 of the Bank Act, and mortgage security under the Bank Act, the National Housing Act, or any other Act; and
    (c) to execute the Bank's form of agreement as to the operation and verification of the accounts of the Company; and also to execute any agreement with or authority to the Bank relating to the banking business of the Company whether generally or with regard to any particular transaction.

3. **That** any one of the following(¹)........Morton Motsarella or Gordon Gorgonzola........

    or the then acting PRESIDENT or SECRETARY/TREASURER

    is hereby authorized for and on behalf of the Company from time to time to negotiate or deposit with or transfer to the Bank (but for the credit of the Company's account only) all or any cheques, promissory notes, drafts, acceptances, bills of exchange and orders for the payment of money, and for such purpose to draw, sign or endorse the same, or any of them, or to deliver the same, or any of them, to the Bank endorsed with the name of the Company impressed thereon by a rubber stamp or other device; also to receive all paid cheques and other debit vouchers charged to any account of the Company and to execute the Bank's form of receipt therefor.

4. **That** all acts and things done and documents executed on behalf of the Company as hereinbefore authorized may be relied upon by the Bank and shall be valid and binding upon the Company and whether or not the corporate seal of the Company has been affixed to any such document.

5. **That** the Company shall provide the Bank with a certified copy of this resolution and a list of the names of the directors, officers and employees of the Company authorized by this resolution to do any act or thing, together with specimens of their signatures, to be acted upon by each branch of the Bank with which any dealings are had by the Company until notice to the contrary or of any change therein has been given in writing to the Manager or Acting Manager of such branch.

    Certified a true copy of a Resolution passed by the Board of Directors of the said Company at a meeting duly called and regularly held on the.....................10th.................day of...January..........., 19.81....and recorded in the Minute Book of the proceedings of the said Board of Directors.

    Dated the........................10th.................day of.....January........................19.81....

SEAL

Morton Motsarella
PRESIDENT

Gordon Gorgonzola
SECRETARY

(1) It is preferable that official positions be designated rather than the names of those authorized to sign. /& Treasurer

273

forms can be obtained (free) from your local Gestapo* office. To get the federal tax advantages of a corporation, you are expected to actually have documented shareholders and director's meetings—even if just you are involved. This is called "observing the formalities of the corporate form." Receipts and disbursements are expected to be transmitted in and out of the company checking account.

One of the main advantages of operating with a corporation involves a little-known loophole that I have never seen in print—even in the books that tell you how wonderful it is to incorporate. I am reluctant to mention it—but if you promise to keep it a secret, here it is:

As an employee of a corporation, you can, by resolution, set up a pension plan. Into this plan you can deposit up to 25 percent of what the corporation pays you. The deposit into the pension plan (which is just another bank account) is deductible to the corporation, but not taxable to you until you take it out. What a lot of people don't know is that this type of retirement plan can be dissolved at any time—without any tax penalties (Internal Revenue Code, Section 401A). This means you can legally divert income in your high-income years into a fund that has a life all its own. You can wheel and deal with the pension fund, even lend your pension fund money or borrow money to put into the pension fund, and here is where the *big news comes in:* You can put your best deals in the name of the pension fund, and make millions, billions, and trillions in capital gains, interest, and even corporate dividends—*all accumulating tax free* until you close out the pension fund.** I hope I am being clear—because being able to do what I have just told you puts you into an even better position than we were before 1962. As you know

---

Editor's note: Mr. Greene was carried away. He means "I.R.S.," of course.

**When you liquidate the pension fund by paying yourself the money, you simply write yourself a check from yourself as trustee. This distribution is taxed as "ordinary income." But a distribution of money you lent to the pension plan is a tax-free "return of capital."

from my chapter on tax havens, before 1962, all you had to do was set up a corporation outside of the United States, channel your profits into it, and you were not taxed until distribution was made to you. These days, you can do the same thing domestically by setting up a corporation in any of the 50 states, having the corporation set up a pension fund, and then making deals in the name of the pension fund. All profits made by the pension fund are tax free. When you want the money, you just dissolve the pension fund. You can be the *sole trustee!*

The only problem or trouble I can see with this is that it's almost inevitable that the I.R.S. will change the rules of the game just as soon as they get a copy of this book. But who can say?

If you are going to take advantage of this, I strongly urge you (if any substantial bucks are involved) to get yourself a good C.P.A. to assist you in "observing the formalities" and doing it right. In case your accountant doesn't know where to look, the rules of the game are obtusely set forth in the Employee Retirement Income Security Act of 1974. This can be found in the Prentice-Hall or Commerce Clearing House loose-leaf digests of the tax code which are in every business library or law library.

Doing tax-free business as the trustee of your own pension fund must be the biggest sleeper in the tax code. Maybe Congress knew what it was doing and figured that, with the Social Security system about to go bankrupt, it would be nice if there were a few people with retirement plans they could actually live off in retirement. Inflation will make the conventional retirement plans of most companies, the I.R.A.s, and the Keogh retirement plans that Congress has generously allowed you to invest in, just about worthless, too. They are worthless because they offer no inflation protection.

An incidental advantage of the superterranean pension plan is that it is not subject to attachment by any creditors—judgment or otherwise—while it is in effect. For a medical doctor paying exorbitant malpractice fees, it seems that placing assets in your own personally managed pension fund could offer a way of becoming judgment-proof that is a lot cheaper than the more than $20,000 per year being charged for insurance.

After talking up all these advantages of incorporating, I want to end up with the disadvantages of incorporating.

1. Corporate records are not subject to the Fifth Amendment right to refuse to supply incriminating information. So the I.R.S. or any adversary in a lawsuit will be able to demand and obtain all these records from you. The financial records of your pension fund can also be subpoenaed.

2. It is expensive and time consuming to file the many required documents: state and federal income tax returns, annual statements, etc.

3. Annual state franchise fees are usually between $100 and $200. You'll probably end up needing a registered corporate agent and/or occasional legal advice, which will run another $200 to $500 per year.

Setting up corporations and giving advice on pension plans is not my field—so please don't even ask me for a private consultation on the subject. But one of the better books on the subject has been put out by my friend Dr. Richard R. Sylvester. It's called simply *Tax Planning: Strategy, Tactics, Decisions & Actions.* If this book is not available in your local bookstore, I have a supply. The price is $19 plus $2 for shipping and handling.* If you are unhappy with it for any reason, just return it and I'll send your money back. It is more technical than this book and goes into more detail. Sylvester will consult on an individual basis with clients. He specializes in tax planning, bankruptcies and pensions. His telephone number in Los Angeles is (213) 472-5336.

---

*This is the 1981 price. All prices subject to change due to inflation.

19. Beating Social Security Taxes

Are you ready for another selection of nifty ways to beat the taxman? Let's explore the absurdity of our tax system and show you how to take advantage of more esoteric tax shelters you can create for yourself.

I call the Social Security "social insecurity" because a lot of money is deducted from your paycheck during your lifetime without your consent. The money could have been profitably invested to return a princely sum each month during retirement. But what does the Social Security system give you today? Barely enough money to rent one room in a slum with a share of the dirty bathroom down the hall! Certainly not enough money to stay alive with dignity and comfort. Social Security dumps old folks in rocking chairs and makes them human garbage. Social Security is not nearly enough to pay for real needs, and the politicians have the nerve to call that "social security." Whatever it is, in the near future Social Security deductions are going to be taking up to 15 percent of a wage slave's earnings. Yet the future Social Security check will probably buy even less when a wage slave is forcibly retired.

Here's how to beat that particular form of legalized theft. If you are employed by someone else and earn wages, you can become a minister or a member of a religious group opposed to public insurance. That gives you the right to file I.R.S. form 4361, an "Application for Exemption from Self-Employment Tax for Use by Ministers, Christian Scientists, etc." By filing this application with a separate statement that you are conscientiously opposed to any form of public insurance, you get the exemption for life and don't have to file every year.

Form **4361** (Rev. March 1978) Department of the Treasury Internal Revenue Service	**Application for Exemption from Self-employment** **Tax for Use by Ministers, Members of Religious** **Orders and Christian Science Practitioners**	File in Triplicate with Internal Revenue Service

Documentation required by Specific Instruction Item 4 MUST be attached to this form. Before filing this form see General Instructions.

1 Name	Notta Taxpayer	2 Social security number 000-00-0000
Address	123 Brotherhood Drive	
City or town, State and ZIP code	San Francisco, CA 94107	

3 Check ONLY ONE box: ☐ Christian Science practitioner ☒ Ordained minister, priest, rabbi ☐ Member of religious order not under a vow of poverty ☐ Commissioned or licensed minister (see Item 7)

4 Date ordained, licensed, etc. 5-14-78

5 Legal name of ordaining, licensing, or commissioning body of religious order
Church of Freedom

Employer identification number 25-0000001

Address
c/o Bishop Bill Greene, Box 810

City or town, State and ZIP code   Mill Valley, CA 94942

6 Enter the first two years after the date entered in Item 4, above, in which you had net earnings from self-employment of $400 or more, some part of which was from services as a minister, priest, rabbi, etc.; or as a member of a religious order; or as a Christian Science practitioner . . . . ▶   1978   19

7 If you are applying for the exemption as a licensed or commissioned minister, and your denomination provides for the ordination of ministers, please indicate to what extent your ecclesiastical powers differ from those of an ordained minister of your denomination and attach a copy of your denomination's by-laws relating to the powers of ordained, and commissioned or licensed ministers.

Caution: Form 4361 is not proof of any of the following: (a) the right to an exemption from Federal income tax withholding and social security tax; (b) the right to a parsonage allowance exclusion (section 107 of the Internal Revenue Code); or (c) assignment by your religious superiors to a particular job.

8 I certify that, because of my religious principles, I am conscientiously opposed to the acceptance (with respect to services performed by me as a minister, member, or practitioner) of the benefits of any public insurance which makes payments in the event of death, disability, old-age, or retirement or makes payments toward the cost of, or provides services for, medical care (including the benefits of any insurance system established by the Social Security Act).

I certify that I did not file an effective waiver certificate (Form 2031) electing social security coverage on earnings as a minister, member, or practitioner.

I hereby request an exemption from payment of self-employment tax with respect to my earnings from services as a minister, member, or practitioner, pursuant to the provisions of section 1402(e) of the Internal Revenue Code. I understand that the exemption, if granted, will apply only to such earnings. Under penalties of perjury, I declare that this application has been examined by me and to the best of my knowledge and belief it is true and correct.

Signature ▶ *Notta Taxpayer*   Date ▶ March 3, 1979

Note: The exemption is granted only if the application is approved by an appropriate Internal Revenue officer, and Copy C is returned to you marked "approved."

For Internal Revenue Service Use	COPY A To be retained by Internal Revenue Service
☐ Approved for exemption from self-employment tax (see Caution above) ☐ Disapproved for exemption from self-employment tax	

By ....
(Director's signature)   (Date)

You have a legal right to file this form, but unless you
are a minister of an organized established church, the I.R.S.
will probably discriminate against you and cost you more
in legal fees than your tax savings—even if you win.

Some court cases have held that opposition to Social Security must be the "official view of a recognized sect," not just your personal viewpoint. One way to get around this is to actually join up with the local Quakers (Friends), Christian Scientists, Jehovah's Witnesses, or set up your own Universal Life Church. Having your own church may be useful in other ways, so a step-by-step method of becoming another Moses, Mohammed, or Martin Luther is outlined in the next chapter "How to Form Your Own Church."

Briefly, how about becoming a minister? That's easier than falling off a log. You just send $2 to Kirby J. Hensley, Universal Life Church, Modesto, CA 95351, plus a self-addressed stamped envelope. He'll make you a minister of the Universal Life Church. Of course, you have to believe in what is right, and believe that every person has the ability to decide for himself what's right. That gets you an official card of ordination. In case you wonder if that makes you a "real" minister, the answer is that I harbored similar doubts when I was ordained by Reverend Hensley, founder of the Universal Life Church. He gave me the authority to ordain others. Since that time I've founded my own Church of Freedom and become a saint in the Universal Life Church (attested to by a genuine engraved certificate), and I hold regular services for at least three people, including myself, as required by law I've ordained many other ministers at $2 a head, and I've performed two marriage ceremonies fully recognized by the State of California. I was assigned a state and a federal religious tax exemption number from the Universal Life Church. If California and the Feds recognize me as a minister, then I guess I am one.

You might well ask, "Isn't this some kind of a tax-evading sham that the I.R.S. could knock out if they took you to court?" The I.R.S. has tried to knock out the U.L.C. and its subsidiaries, many times. They lost because courts are very unwilling to say that anyone's beliefs are insincere. If we profess a religious belief, the I.R.S. must give you and me the same benefits they give to a Catholic priest, a Jewish rabbi, a Quaker, a Christian Scientist, or Billy Graham. That benefit is a total exemption from Social Security withholding, plus other tax benefits.

Are my beliefs sincere? Between you and me, *they are.* I am conscientiously opposed to Social Security, which, like most taxes, is nothing more than theft. It takes a lot of hard-earned money and gives back dollars worth a lot less than the dollars paid in.

Do you recall that in the chapter "Pay No Taxes Ever Again, Legally" I told you that most senators, congressmen, Presidents, and governors don't pay any income taxes? They don't pay Social Security, either. They know how to use good loopholes, and they know a bad deal when they see one. Do you think they are all members of the Universal Life Church? Nope. They have something even better going for them. They just passed a blatant law exempting all politicians from the Social Security system. Can you believe that? All state and federal legislators and public officials are exempt from Social Security. It's true. Guess who else is exempt?—All *employees* of the Social Security system. They too know Social Security is a total rip-off. So there you have it. The politicians who set up Social Security won't have any part of it, and the employees of the system don't want any part of it either. Does that tell you anything?

Don't even begin to question the sincerity of my conscientious opposition to any government-administered insurance scheme. The people who set it up and the people who run it are all conscientiously opposed too!

Once you have become a minister or have formed your own church, you've got to convince your employer not to withhold Social Security deductions from your paycheck. This can be accomplished in most cases by writing your employer a letter such as the following:

Dear Mr. Employer,

This will inform you that I am a *minister* of a religious establishment whose members have declared their conscientious opposition to public insurance (Social Security). Accordingly, please do not withhold any funds from my paycheck designated for Social Security (Federal Insurance "Contribution" Act). The necessary forms to obtain an irrevocable automatic exemption for myself have been filed with the federal government. Copies are enclosed herewith. I hereby agree to hold you harmless against any liability to me or to the federal government in connection with your cooperation in this regard.

Sincerely,
Elfrida Employee

The method outlined here is, in my opinion, entirely legal, ethical, and moral. But it has a very definite risk that you should be prepared to assume. *The big almighty I.R.S. computer in the sky may classify you (along with several million others) as a troublesome subversive element and a tax protester.* This is clearly a violation of your constitutional right to freely exercise your religious beliefs, but when the time comes to pull the lottery tickets for audit, you may be right up there with me. And, once audited, you can count on the I.R.S. giving everything else you did an extra close look. You may beat them, but what's a legal victory if your lawyer's costs are more than your tax savings?

Thus, all in all, if your income is derived from employment in a standard wage-slave job, I'd think twice before filing for an exemption. It is sad, and unconstitutional, that the very form that you have every legal right to file will probably target you as an object of political persecution for your religious beliefs, regardless of how sincere they may be. Too bad, but true. The I.R.S. doesn't care much about constitutional rights.

If you are self-employed, you can get all the benefits of withdrawing from the Social Security system with none of the risks just outlined. The reason is there is *no form to file,* and thus no red flags going up in the I.R.S. computer. Here's how you do it.

You form a corporation in whatever state it is cheapest to do so. In the West, that will be Nevada. Call it "Yourname,

Form 4029
(Rev. June 1974)
Department of the Treasury
Internal Revenue Service

Application for Exemption
from Tax on Self-Employment Income
and Waiver of Benefits

To be filed in duplicate
with the Internal
Revenue Service

Name of taxpayer

Social security or identifying number

Number and street or rural route

City or town, State, and ZIP code

Before you file this form, please read General Instruction A, Who May File.

I certify that I am and continuously have been a member of ....
(Name of religious group)

....
(District and location)

since .... and as a follower of the established teachings of that group, I am con-
(Day)   (Month)   (Year)

scientiously opposed to accepting benefits of any private or public insurance which makes payments in the event of death, disability, old-age, or retirement or makes payments toward the cost of, or provides services for, medical care (including the benefits of any insurance system established by the Social Security Act).

I request that I be exempted from paying self-employment tax on my earnings from self-employment, under section 1402(h) of the Internal Revenue Code.

I waive all rights to any social security payment or benefit under Titles II and XVIII of the Social Security Act. I understand and agree that no benefits or other payments of any kind under Titles II and XVIII of the Social Security Act will be paid based on my wages and self-employment income to any other person. I certify that I have never received benefits or payments under the above Titles, nor has anyone else received these benefits based on my earnings.

I agree to notify the Internal Revenue Service within 60 days of any occurrence which results in my no longer being a member of the religious group described above, or in my no longer following the established teachings of this group.

Furthermore, I understand that if any tax exemption under section 1402(h) of the Internal Revenue Code ceases to be effective, this waiver will also cease to be effective, but only to the extent that benefits can be payable only on the basis of my self-employment income for and after the first taxable year in which the exemption ceases to be effective, and my wages for and after the calendar year beginning in or with the beginning of such taxable year.

The first year I became subject to self-employment tax was .... (Show "NONE" if you were never
(Year)
subject to this tax).

The name, title, and address of an authorized spokesman of my religious group are as follows:

....
(Authorized spokesman)   (Title)   (Address)

Under penalties of perjury, I declare that I have examined this application and waiver and to the best of my knowledge and belief it is true and correct.

Signed .... Dated ...., 19..........

For use of Internal Revenue Service

☐ Approved   for exemption by ....
☐ Disapproved   (Director's signature)   (Date)

Copy A—For Internal Revenue Service

282

Instructions

A. Who May File.—You may apply for exemption from payment of self-employment tax if you are a member of a recognized religious sect or division, and as a follower of that sect's established teachings, you are conscientiously opposed to accepting benefits of any private or public insurance payments in the event of death, disability, old-age, or retirement, or payments towards the cost of, or to provide services for, medical care (including benefits of any insurance system established by the Social Security Act). Before you are granted an exemption, the Secretary of Health, Education, and Welfare must determine that—(1) the sect or division has the established teachings referred to in the preceding sentence, (2) it is the practice, and has been for a period of time which he deems substantial, for members of this sect or division to provide for its dependent members in a manner he deems reasonable in view of the general level of living, and (3) the sect or division has existed at all times since December 31, 1950.

B. Do Not File.—You are ineligible for this exemption if:

(1) You received benefits or payments under Title II or Title XVIII of the Social Security Act, or if anyone else received these benefits or payments based on your wages or self-employment income, or

(2) You were subject to self-employment taxes for taxable years ending before December 31, 1967 and you did not file this form on or before December 31, 1968.

C. When to File.—If you first become subject to self-employment tax for a taxable year ending on or after December 31, 1967, file this application on or before the due date of your income tax return for that taxable year. If you miss this filing deadline contact your local Internal Revenue office.

D. How to Indicate Exemption on Form 1040.—When filing Form 1040, write "Exempt-Form 4029," on the self-employment tax line of Form 1040.

E. Where to File

If your residence is located in:	Use this address:
New Jersey, New York City and counties of Nassau, Rockland, Suffolk, and Westchester	Internal Revenue Service Center 1040 Waverly Avenue Holtsville, N.Y. 11799
New York (all other counties), Connecticut, Maine, Massachusetts, New Hampshire, Rhode Island, Vermont	Internal Revenue Service Center 310 Lowell Street Andover, Mass. 01812
District of Columbia, Delaware, Maryland, Pennsylvania	Internal Revenue Service Center 11601 Roosevelt Boulevard Philadelphia, Pa. 19155
Alabama, Florida, Georgia, Mississippi, South Carolina	Internal Revenue Service Center 4800 Buford Highway Chamblee, Georgia 30006
Michigan, Ohio	Internal Revenue Service Center Cincinnati, Ohio 45298
Arkansas, Kansas, Louisiana, New Mexico, Oklahoma, Texas	Internal Revenue Service Center 3651 S. Interregional Hwy. Austin, Texas 78740
Alaska, Arizona, Colorado, Idaho, Minnesota, Montana, Nebraska, Nevada, North Dakota, Oregon, South Dakota, Utah, Washington, Wyoming	Internal Revenue Service Center 1160 West 1200 South St. Ogden, Utah 84201
Illinois, Iowa, Missouri, Wisconsin	Internal Revenue Service Center 2306 E. Bannister Road Kansas City, Mo. 64170
California, Hawaii	Internal Revenue Service Center 5045 East Butler Avenue Fresno, California 93888
Indiana, Kentucky, North Carolina, Tennessee, Virginia, West Virginia	Internal Revenue Service Center 3131 Democrat Road Memphis, Tenn. 38110

If you are located in:	Use this address:
Panama Canal Zone, American Samoa, Guam	Internal Revenue Service Center 11601 Roosevelt Boulevard Philadelphia, Pa. 19155
Puerto Rico (or if excluding income under section 933) Virgin Islands: Non-permanent residents	Internal Revenue Service Center 11601 Roosevelt Boulevard Philadelphia, Pa. 19155
Virgin Islands: Permanent residents	Department of Finance, Tax Division Charlotte Amalie, St. Thomas Virgin Islands 00801
Foreign country and have an A.P.O. or F.P.O. address	Internal Revenue Service Center for your permanent home State
Foreign country U.S. citizen and those excluding income under section 911 or 931	Internal Revenue Service Center 11601 Roosevelt Boulevard Philadelphia, Pa. 19155

Inc." or anything you want. A charter will cost you well under $200. Then open a corporate bank account. Channel borrowings, rents, fees, commissions, and all money you want to report as gross income through the corporation. Then you pay all business expenses out of that same account. If you are into real estate, your deductible expenses can always be arranged to be more than your annual income, so there will be no tax. But there will, hopefully, be a cash flow. This cash flow you simply pay out to yourself as a dividend whenever you need money.* On your annual tax return, you elect to treat the corporation as if it didn't exist by declaring it to be a Subchapter S corporation. When you elect to do this, as you can with any closely held corporation, the corporation is exempted from all income taxes. Any company income or losses pass directly to the owner(s). Best of all, if the distributions to you are called *dividends*, not *salary*, they are not subject to Social Security tax. (Section 211(a) Social Security Act, S.S. Reg. #4, Sect. 404.1054, S.S. Claims Manual 1507.5, I.R.S. Reg. 1.1402(a)-5).

The I.R.S. could conceivably argue that the "dividends" were really salary and should be taxed accordingly, but your reply would be that, if you collapsed the corporation and pretended it didn't exist, there wouldn't be any income to pay salaries, because the corporation (due to depreciation and borrowing to pay debts) is, and always will be, operating at a loss. It is being operated as a legal tax shelter.

Until the laws are changed, there is nothing the I.R.S. can do to you. Because U.S. congressmen and senators often channel their non-government earnings through Subchapter S corporations, they are not anxious to close this loophole nor to have any of their own money go into that bottomless pit of Social Security.

If you are audited, as a backstop, you could flash your

---

*If for some reason you prefer not to declare a *dividend*, you may choose to call a distribution to yourself a "*director's fee.*" These fees are also exempt from Social Security.

minister's card to the I.R.S. agent and tell him that, even if the I.R.S. wanted to fight about your Subchapter S treatment of the deduction, you are conscientiously opposed to Social Security for religious reasons anyway. The agent will probably have had enough of you and will give you a pass. The collection of Social Security is not a high-priority item for I.R.S. agents, who don't believe in the system either. Yes, you guessed it. The I.R.S. employees didn't want to be covered by Social Security, so they are exempted, too.

20.
How to
Form
Your Own
Church

There has been lots of talk and publicity about a religious exemption and many requests made to me for exact details on how to form your own church. Rather than give out second-hand information, I decided to investigate and organize a church. Now I'm able to give an authoritative report.

Forming your own church does work. It can save you not only income taxes but also real estate taxes and Social Security taxes. Not to mention the prestige, influence, and spiritual satisfaction it may give.

The basic theory behind a religious tax exemption is that the tax law, as it stands, gives traditional Catholic priests, Protestant ministers, and Jewish rabbis certain tax advantages over other wage slaves. These same tax benefits accrue to you if you choose to call yourself a preacher, minister, guru, or religious adviser. The only requirement is a sincere belief in your religious calling and at least two other

Nobody in Hardenberg, New York, pays taxes. Even the tax assessor's house is a monastery of the Universal Life Church.

people who are willing to be in your congregation and act as the board of directors of your church. Naturally, you don't have to call it a *church*, because the name is not important. Any religious institution and its officers qualify for the tax breaks. You can call your church a Zen Center, the Cosmic Temple, or anything you want.

What are the tax breaks? Locally, if the county assessor gets an application for religious tax exemption, stating that you are converting your home to a regular place of worship, you get an exemption from real estate taxes. Near where I live a group of rich psychoanalysts claimed that some expensive land overlooking the Pacific Ocean was to be their open-air Zen meditation site. They got the exemption. It saves them $30,000 a year in taxes on their former picnic grounds. In Hardenburg, New York, the whole town declared themselves to be ministers. Every home became a monastery or church. Nobody pays real estate taxes in Hardenburg. Thus, until the laws are changed and churches of the established religions are also taxed, forming your own church seems to be a viable gimmick to get a local real estate tax exemption.

There are plenty of tax breaks at the federal level, too. The taxpayer with a small business forms a church and donates his business to the church. The church, as mentioned, can be any three people, including a spouse, grandma, grandpa, and the kids. The church then opens a bank account. All business earnings go to the church bank account. The church then provides its leaders (and needy members) with tax-free "allowances" to pay rent, mortgage payments, taxes (if any), furniture, food, housekeeper, repairs, etc.

How do you "form a church?" There are two ways. The most traditional is to write to your local state capital as follows:

Secretary of State
Department of Corporations
State Capital
Your State
Dear Sirs,

Please send me necessary forms and instruction books to assist in the formation of a nonprofit religious corporation to be known as the *Joe Smith* Church. Please let me know if the proposed name, "*Joe Smith Church*," is available for use by my congregation.

Sincerely,
Rev. Joe Smith
The Joe Smith Church

In due course, you will receive from the state all the necessary forms and instructions on how to use them. Although state laws vary, the costs involved will run from nothing to about $50 for a charter. A charter is a sheet of paper issued in response to your application, noting that under state law the Joe Smith Church is now a legal entity, much like a corporation, registered in the state, and entitled to do all things that churches normally do. That includes owning property in the church's name, receiving income or donations tax free, and owning and operating your former radio station, publishing company, or whatever business you may choose to transfer to the church. Any business can be owned by the church, but if the income generated by that business is to be tax free, it must be church-related. For example, the church could own a radio station making inspirational broadcasts. If the profits from donations to the station are used to propagate the faith, they are tax free. Naturally, the station can pay living, travel, and other allowances to any church leaders and can pay ordinary taxable salaries to technicians and other employees. Brothers, sisters, monks, or others committed to the church can receive tax-free lodging, food, and allowances.

On the Joe Smith Church letterhead, once you have your charter you can request a state sales tax exemption number, which is granted as a matter of course. Similarly, you request a federal tax exemption number. Federal tax exempt status may be a little harder to get. The Feds may actually send someone out to make sure you are meeting the technical requirements for a church—a genuine congregation of at least three people who have regular meetings. But, beyond that, state and federal government people are bound under present laws and decisions to take your word for it that your religious beliefs (whatever they may be) are sincere. If they challenge you, it's up to them to disprove that you are a bona fide religion. This is an almost impossible task.

Because the Prophet Mohammed had only his wife and a couple of kids in his congregation before Islam became the world's largest religion, and Jesus had only 12 disciples for some years, the U.S. courts will not use size or the mode of religious expression in determining the merit or legal sufficiency of your church. Thus, as long as you didn't tell people that you were forming a church solely as a tax dodge, you and your church stand in the eyes of the law with the same dignity and rights to tax exemption as a Catholic bishop and his cathedral.

In Philadelphia, the Society of Friends (Quakers) holds meetings that are down-to-earth discussions of moral issues. Their services bear little resemblance to the rituals of most Christian churches. But they are a recognized sect that has been around for centuries. Each member is considered a minister, and they are conscientiously opposed to serving in armies or paying Social Security taxes. At the opposite end of the spectrum, San Francisco's Church of Satan, as might be imagined, has rather peculiar beliefs and practices. Yet all churches have the same legal status.

The fastest way to form your church is to write the "Modesto Messiah," Reverend Kirby J. Hensley, Founder, Universal Life Church, Modesto, California. If you send the U.L.C. a $50 donation, he will ordain you as a minister and immediately charter your church as a branch of his "mother church." You'll be deluged with literature from Kirby on what you can and can't do legally. That's how the folks in Hardenburg, New York, got through the paperwork so quickly. Reverend Hensley's Universal Life Church and its offshoots have reluctantly been recognized by most states and many foreign countries. After a long legal battle, federal tax-exempt status was confirmed in 1974. With the U.L.C. charter, you can open a bank account and start church operations immediately. You can file (or not file) tax returns as a minister. Get full details on how to take all the benefits of being a clergyman by buying a minister's tax preparation guide, sold at any store dealing in religious supplies. Because many church benefits may be no longer classed as income for tax purposes, filing a tax return may not be legally required.

If you plan to file conventionally for church incorporation with the state, and fight with the Feds over your tax-exempt status, I'd say that you should think twice. You might be opening the door to harassment. During 1978, the I.R.S. staged massive raids on the Church of Scientology, confiscating all the books and records they could lay their hands on. A few years before that, they raided Reverend Hensley's Universal Life Church in Modesto and confiscated his small bank account. The way the system works, the I.R.S. can do most of its damage before a court case finally comes up. If and when the church wins (as it usually does), there is no recourse against the I.R.S. for the high legal fees and damage to your reputation the agents have done.

Starting a church under the auspices of the Universal Life Church means that the battle has already been won for you. No government agency need have any record of your church's existence. They don't know if your church has any assets, nor where those assets are. Best of all, under the present rules, they can't force you to tell them, either. The basic premise of the Universal Life Church is that every individual has the right to live a good life according to his own moral conscience. As a result, Reverend Hensley is very big on personal freedom and very much opposed to government interference in his or your religious and financial affairs. He's easy to identify with and will not let the Feds see his records. So the fact that you have formed a Universal Life church is almost as secret as having an account at the Union Bank of Switzerland.

The following clipping is an example of the sort of column you might find in an issue of the *Universal Life Church*

News. The paper is mailed out free to registered Universal Life Church ministers and holders of church charters. I think it is good, reliable information, and so does my lawyer and accountant. It is certainly a lot more reliable and truthful than the rubbish we get from many agencies of our own government.

The questions foremost in peoples minds are taxes, how much higher will the government up taxes, and how people will be able to pay them? Why should I pay taxes to support people who won't work. These are all serious questions. Ones that need immediate answers. The economy is suffering, our faith in government is almost nil. It seems there is nothing to look forward to. There is something that we can do to at least correct part of our troubles. When we see elected government officials, ie governors, attorney generals, assessors, school superintendents, as low as elected officers go or to the President of the United States, breaking or using the law to discriminate against   American people it is our duty to report it to their superiors and to the American people. If it still continues the next step is to vote them out at the elections.

It has been the policy of the Federal Government to actually promote organized religion by granting it almost total tax immunity. All income that accrues to a non-profit church corporation is tax exempt (with the exception of unrelated business income). There are about six different kinds of church income, five of which are totally tax exempt.

1) DONATION INCOME - All money and property donated or willed to a church or otherwise received from its church members is tax exempt. A church may perform any type of services or engage in any business activity for the benefit of its members without paying taxes on the income.

2) FUND RAISING ACTIVITY INCOME - Whenever a church sponsors a fund raising activity and charges admission, the income is tax exempt. All income that is generated by various church members by donating their services in return for contributions to their church is tax exempt.

3) PASSIVE CHURCH INVESTMENT INCOME -

All income earned by a church via its own investments in stock, bonds, rental properties, bank accounts, etc. is tax exempt. A passive investment is any investment that does not require day to day management and supervision by the directors of the church.

4) CAPITAL GAINS INCOME - Any income or profit realized by a church from the sale of church owned assets is tax exempt.

5) RELATED BUSINESS INCOME - Any income that accrues to a church from a business venture that can be justified on the basis that the business is related to the mission of the church is tax exempt. Several examples of related business income can be found throughout the Catholic Church with regard to the radio and television stations that the church owns and operates. Churches are also engaged in publishing as well as the life insurance business. The Lutheran Church maintains a $3 billion insurance fund exclusively for church members.

6) UNRELATED BUSINESS INCOME - Churches can own and operate any kind of business. If the IRS can prove in court that the income from a particular business venture is not related to the overall mission of the church, then it can force the church to pay taxes on the income. The most famous and recent example of this is when the IRS finally forced the Christian Brothers Winery to pay income taxes on the revenue they received from the production and sale of liquor related products.

Watch following issues of the UNIVERSAL LIFE for more information regarding taxes and the clergy.

Before you send in your $2 to me or to Reverend Kirby J. Hensley of the Universal Life Church, you might want to know more about this organization. According to Hensley, his church is the fastest-growing religious organization in the world, with over 20 million card-carrying ordained ministers, each of whom is adding on the average another five or six members a year. At that rate, everyone in the world will be a minister of the U.L.C. by next May. Bishop Hensley is a simple and inspired individual—and someone who stood up to the I.R.S. and told them where to go. He personally told me that he is opposed to religion getting any tax breaks, but as long as "organized religion" gets tax immunity he feels that everyone with a storefront church or open-air meditation center should get the same breaks. Just as I put out a newsletter when the spirit moves me or when I get disgusted enough with the politicians and the I.R.S., so does Reverend Hensley put out his newspaper, *The Universal Life*. If you sent in for a minister's card or church charter, you'll be on their mailing list for the paper. Incidentally, they never bother you for contributions! But they sell, by mail, marriage certificate forms, doctor of divinity diplomas, certificates of sainthood, and will, in fact, print up a certificate with anything you want on it. You can be an archbishop or even an archangel! Here's what the basic minister's card looks like:

Universal Life Church, Inc.

Headquarters: 601 Third Street, Modesto, California 95351
Telephone (209) 527-8111 or 537-0553

Credentials of Ministry

This is to certify that the bearer hereof

Name __REV. Bill Tycoon Greene__

Address __P.O. Box 810__

City __Mill Valley__ State __CAL__ Zip __94942__

is ordained by Universal Life Church, Inc.

SEAL

PRESIDENT — KIRBY J. HENSLEY, D.D.

Universal Life Church, Inc.

Headquarters: 601 Third Street, Modesto, California 95351
Telephone (209) 527-8111 or 537-0553

The Universal Life Church, Inc. certifies that the bearer of this credential, whose name and address appears on the face of this card, is a legally ordained minister in the Universal Life Church, Inc. This certificate of ordination is granted for life, and the holder hereof is entitled to perform all ministerial services, such as: baptismals, marriages, funerals, and to conduct church meetings. The holder is entitled to all the privileges and considerations usually granted a minister.

The Universal Life Church, Inc. assumes no responsibility for actions by the holder hereof, for use of this credential for any purpose other than for which it is issued.

For the dedicated servants of the Lord, dealing with the I.R.S. has to be one of the most frustrating aspects of the ministry. Calls or visits to the I.R.S. "taxpayer service" are always confusing. Each I.R.S. officer one speaks with has a totally different answer to the same question. But the I.R.S. does have a free "official" publication recently known as Publication 17 *(Tax Guide for Ministers and Religious Workers)*. You can get it by looking up "U.S. Government" in your local phone book (white pages) and finding the subheading, "Internal Revenue Service." There will usually be a toll-free number to call. I suggest that you ask for Publication 17 by number *and* by title. Also ask for a list of all other publications designed to help taxpayers. They are free and may provide some guidance. Remember, of course, that they are written by the *enemy* and they are not designed to help you pay less tax. They are often written to mislead you into paying more tax than may be necessary.

Once you have decided to serve God, it is your *duty* to use your time and the material abundance the Lord bestows on you in *his* service. There is no question that *you* as a minister, teacher, rabbi, priest, guru, or whatever your title— there is no question at all that you can do a lot better in using money for the Lord's work. The government wastes money, and the political leaders of all countries are at best *amoral.* It is my personal prayer that *you* as a religious leader will always work for maximum freedom of the individual. Maximum freedom implies *toleration* by you of differing religions and viewpoints. And consistency requires that if you seek to reduce your tax paying to zero, you should also refuse government aid, government "assistance," and government regulation insofar as the law allows.

Here are some of the things that you, as an ordained minister, should know. An *ordained minister* is considered "self-employed" by the I.R.S. for Social Security purposes (Internal Revenue Code 1402[e]). To become an *ordained minister,* recognized by the I.R.S. you must be recognized by the state in which you live as being legally authorized to perform all of the ecclesiastical duties normally expected from a religious leader. These duties include presiding over circumcision rites, communion, baptisms, weddings, funerals—and, of course, regular religious services. The I.R.S. will accept *either* state government standards or the rules of your particular church in recognizing who is authorized to perform these duties. As previously mentioned, you may form your own religious institution by filing with the state of your residence and later applying to the I.R.S. for tax exemption. If you are on the board of directors of the church you have formed, you simply write yourself a letter ordaining yourself.

The Universal Life Church makes things considerably easier. Bishop Kirby J. Hensley will ordain you by mail for $2 plus a self-addressed envelope. Once you are an ordained minister, you can ordain others. Because I am ordained, I often ordain as many as 50 or 60 people at my Sunday meetings in Mill Valley. I prefer not to do my ordinations by mail because I like the ceremony and the good feelings of doing it in person—but if you'd feel more comfortable getting your minister's card from me, that's fine. Don't forget, the $2 "free-will offering" and the self-addressed envelope—to Reverend Greene, Church of Freedom, P.O. Box 810, Mill Valley, CA 94942.

If *only you* are involved, and if you are self-employed, you are not subject to Social Security "self-employment tax" if you are opposed to public insurance on conscience or religious principles. Should an auditor ever question the reason why you filed a Form 4361 (Application for Exemption from Self-Employment Tax for Use by Ministers, Members of Religious Orders, etc.) *Never, never, never* state that you did it to *save on taxes,* or that you *didn't want to be bothered calculating your Social Security taxes.* If the auditor notes *that* in his little black book—you have *blown your cover.* The facts that you *do* save on taxes, and that you don't have to be bothered with the calculations, flow naturally from your decision—but that original decision must have been made or based on purely religious reasons. Remember, the I.R.S. is just like the Catholic church: They care not so much *what* you do, but *sin* or the lack of sin stems from what you were *thinking* at the time. So be sincere. Think the right thoughts for I.R.S. and you won't go wrong. As I was saying—if just you are involved and you are self-employed, there is no particular reason to form your own church. But if you are a homeowner or renter and you wish to take advantage of the *parsonage allowance,* and if other people in your sphere of influence also wish to be exempt from Social Security taxes, there are a few things you should consider.

As a minister, any money or cash that comes your way as a donation or as earnings from your regular job is still *taxable income.* It may not be subject to Social Security tax, but it is still subject to state and federal income taxes. There is only one exception to this: If a friend, relative, or parishioner makes a gift of money to you with no expectation of future services, and not in compensation for past services, that gift is nontaxable, and need not be reported on your tax return. Here's how a *church* differs: Any money coming into a church bank account as a result of donations, services you have performed, or the sale of religious or related materials is *tax exempt.* If the *church* employs people beside yourself, their wages are not subject to Social Security withholding. Your own church can give you money (tax free to you) to pay for your home and living expenses. This unique tax benefit is available *only* to ministers, and is known as the *parsonage allowance.* Let's look at how the whole process works.

First off, the Internal Revenue Code (Section 107) provides that a minister or religious worker in the employ of a church can get a tax-free cash allowance for the fair rental value of a furnished home, including garages, and utilities. Sorry, maids and butlers *cannot* be included! The amount that the minister is to get must be *designated* in advance, says the I.R.S. What does that mean? It means that when you own or rent your own home, the board of directors of your church, before it pays you a cent, should have a regular meeting and, at that meeting, adopt a resolution something like this:

Official Resolution

It having come before the board on *December 31, 1983,* that under existing laws and regulations, our Minister is not subject to federal income tax on a parsonage allowance paid to him as part of his compensation, provided that said allowance is designated in advance;

And the board having considered the estimate of our *Most Reverend Alibaba* of his annual expenses; A motion was made by *Charles Godlove,* and seconded by *Helen Heavenly;* and this resolution was unanimously adopted by the Board of *the Church of Freedom (Universal Life Church);*

Be it RESOLVED that Reverend *Alibaba* shall receive a total remuneration of *$49,000* for *1984,* allocated:

$20,000 Designated parsonage allowance
$10,000 Expenses for office supplies and part-time help
$10,000 Automobile expense
$ *5,000* Travel, entertainment and educational expense
$ *4,000* Religious materials, subscriptions, books

(signed) *Tillie Treasurer*
Entered in the Official Minutes Book on *Dec. 31, 1983*

Technically, if this resolution or "designation" of parsonage allowance is not made in advance, the minister loses the benefit of the allowance. There has been the suggestion, by the unscrupulous, that it would be a simple matter to backdate such a document if you forgot to do it at the beginning of the year. But I would not recommend such finagling. After all, it was reasoning like that which got Richard Nixon into such hot water. He backdated documents and always took short-cuts. It is up to you to do things right in the first place. Ministers have a duty to set a good example for politicians, lawyers, and judges!

But, as usual, I have been saving the best news for last. Suppose you have formed a church. One way or another, you channeled income to your church. The church, of course, pays no income tax on any income or donations stemming from its religious activities. You pay no income tax on your parsonage allowance or on the various expense allowances you receive. Naturally, the expense allowances must have been spent, and you must have receipts to show that they were spent on the items for which they were designated. But the parsonage allowance does not have to be spent on your home. The only requirement is that it be fair rental value of the home (plus furnishings, utilities, repairs, upkeep, etc.). Obviously, if you already own your own home, your expenses may be only $2,000 per year for taxes and utilities, but your parsonage allowance of $20,000 would yield you an $18,000 tax-free windfall. Regardless of what profit you are making on the parsonage allowance, you are also allowed to *deduct against your income as an itemized deduction* the taxes and mortgage interest paid on your home. Lawyers call this a "legal double-dip." You get reimbursed (tax free) for an expense, but you are still allowed to deduct it! (see Rev. Rule 62-212.)

21.
Tax-Free
Barter

The I.R.S. would, of course, love to tax the air you breathe at $1 million a gulp if we let it get away with it. Thus it is no surprise that the I.R.S. position on barter deals is such that it has often tried far-fetched theories to try and collect taxes on barter deals.

What this means is that the I.R.S. would like to see trades taxed like this. For example, you have an old outboard motor you were about ready to junk. Thus it had a value to you of zero. Your friend had an old power mower he was about to junk, thus it had a value to him of zero. But you were planning on going out and buying a new outboard for $600. You traded. The I.R.S. would be delighted if you and your friend both reported an extra $600 of income from barter transactions, because that would represent the "value gained" to each of you. Of course, you just might choose to value your swell outboard at $400, and the junky old power mower you received at $20, taking a $380 loss on the deal (which could be done only if the item obtained was used in your trade or business). And what if your friend did the same thing? The U.S. Supreme Court in an old case ruled that both of you went overboard: "It is presumed that value received is the same as value transferred." What this decision means is that when you trade personal nonbusiness property for other personal nonbusiness property there is no tax. But personal nonbusiness property traded for a product or service used in your trade or business may give rise to a deduction! I'll explain how this works in a few seconds. But first, how about where you trade your personal services for an item of property you get in trade? There the I.R.S. thinks they have you! They consider the value of item received as taxable income. As you see, making a regulation is easy—but enforcing it can be very tough. A brand new item listed in the *Sears Catalog* is easy to value. But a used, damaged, or inoperable item is almost impossible to value, except as junk or scrap metal. Services that are listed in a price list issued by a professional association are easy to value—but "consultations" can be anywhere from free to $2,000 per hour. Because some things are impossible for the I.R.S. to appraise, how can you best take advantage of the confusion? Here are a few rules.

Trade Unwanted Items for Needed Business Products or Services

Try to trade personal things—old toys and attic goodies, unwanted presents, etc.—for expendable or depreciable things to be used in your business. Value the necktie you got from your mother-in-law at its $45 cost. Why not? It's new—you never wore it! Value what you get—the 1,000 sheets of stationery or whatever—at the highest advertised price you can find: $45? The judge said that value received is presumably equal to value paid. On your tax return, take a business expense deduction. You are allowed to pay deductible business expenses with personal property. Keep ads, written memos from a third party, or some "evidence" of how you arrived at the high valuation of what you traded out and what you got in return. If you pay a lawyer's bill with your Rolls Royce—deduct the fair value of the Rolls!

Services for Property

If you trade your professional services for goods, unfortunately you won't get very far valuing your services and the trade received at a high price—property received constitutes business income. So the idea is to value what you receive in exchange very low. You should keep a record and report at least a nominal gain from any exchange for your services. You are a lawyer, and you help a friend through an audit. He gives you a camera. The I.R.S. will maintain that your "income" was the fair value of the camera. Keep in mind that a new Nikon has a definite market value. An unfinished, old, or broken camera would have a very low value. Failure to report any income from trades for services—particularly if you are known to be actively doing that sort of thing—constitutes tax evasion and is a crime. But reporting a low value such as an $18 broken camera received in exchange for an $18 consultation could, at worst, result in an "honest disagreement" with the I.R.S. and an assessment for additional taxes if the I.R.S. decided to make a "federal case" of it. If you bring a broken camera into court, they will look like ninnies if they try to value it at $1,800.

Business Property for Property

The 1031 exchange is used a great deal in big business transactions, and can be a source of great tax savings. You can do a 1031 exchange and shelter your capital gains entirely. The subject is so important that I have devoted an entire chapter to it in this book. Read it at least twice and see if in your particular business you can do a 1031 exchange with something other than real estate.

Nonbusiness Services for Nonbusiness Services

If you trade your services for somebody else's services—for example, sailing lessons for haircuts—technically there is taxable income to both sides. The I.R.S. would, no doubt, like to say you got $100 in sailing lesson income in exchange for two haircuts, which cost you nothing to give. Net taxable income to you, $100. Net taxable income to your friend, $100.

But these individual deals would be so hard to trace and follow up that they have always been simply overlooked by the I.R.S. If you want to be technically correct—both parties should record the transactions as an exchange of gifts or as business promotion. Or else value the haircuts and sailing lessons very low!

Barter Clubs—Dangerous!

Warning! Beware of some barter clubs. Bartering has become big business. It is difficult to imagine the I.R.S. getting much out of a major crackdown on flea market wheeler-dealers. There are simply too many of them. They are too disorganized. They are not listed anywhere on computer, and the transactions are too small. There is no record of flea market sales or exchanges. Further, every deal uncovered would be open to arguments over valuation. But *organized* barter-exchange *clubs* are long overdue for a series of midnight I.R.S. raids. Many organized barter clubs work this way—with slight variations;

A sporting goods dealer joins up, pays $1000 to the club, and is credited with $1,000 worth (or some agreed amount) of "trade." It is understood that if another member of the club comes in to his store and presents a "trade check" he is bound to honor it as if it were cash. The sporting goods dealer may spend his check like dollars on anything—a hotel suite in Hawaii or with any other club member offering a desired service or product.

The barter clubs offer a directory of members together with the product, services, and prices. The directory makes it convenient for the members to make deals—and for the I.R.S. to get a list of targets for investigation. The way some clubs promote membership is that Mr. Sporting Goods is told he can write off the merchandise he sells for trade checks as a business or promotion expense. But the goodies he buys with his checks for his personal use are not going to constitute taxable income. The I.R.S. will not go along with this if they find out about it. They will treat the trade checks as if they were dollars.

For about 10 years, increasing numbers of small business people have been using these barter clubs—getting expense write-offs on their inventory and reporting no corresponding income on purchases. The problem is, some clubs act as banks or clearinghouses for the trade checks. They keep detailed records of who spent what, where, and when. The I.R.S., to discourage these clubs, can grab the records, move in and claim tax fraud. They will probably be successful in forcing Mr. Sporting Goods and others like him to take as income the fair value of the hotel accommodations and other goodies he bought. Unlike the flea market and other subterranean economy deals, in some of the barter clubs there is no problem for the I.R.S. to prove "value received." The trade checks are issued as the equivalent of U.S. dollars. If records show you spent $10,000, that is your untaxed income. If you are going to join an *organized* club, be sure there are no central records of the deals between members. If there are, be sure that *your* records tally in a reasonable way with club records. To avoid tax fraud charges, declare some barter income. Better yet, if you are involved in formalized club trading and if you are not paying your taxes, change your ways. Either get legal or be an intelligent criminal and join the subterranean economy. Don't make barter deals with paper trails!

As a general rule if you want to avoid an eventual audit, stay out of any barter club that acts as a central bank, keeps records, or has you listed in any sort of directory.

22.
Barter and Incomplete Transactions

You can barter for tax-free vacations. Assume that you want to go on a vacation to Berlin, Germany (or anywhere else in the world) for four weeks. If you rented a hotel suite and car in Berlin, it might cost you $2,000 a month. And if you sublet your place back home to help defray the cost of your vacation, that might bring you, say, $1,000 in rent. The rental income would be taxable, but the rent you pay out would not be deductible (unless your trip was for business purposes). How do you change all that? You can advertise in a Berlin newspaper:

> **VACATION EXCHANGE DESIRED**
>
> Two-bedroom house in Las Vegas, U.S.A., available for July exchange. Want Berlin home or apartment. Write Angela American, Las Vegas.

You would probably hear from several very friendly exchangers. You would take over their car, house, and friends for the summer and keep your cash outlays to less than one-tenth of what they would have been. Instead of having taxable income from your sublet, your entire stay in Berlin would have had no tax consequences whatsoever. If the exchanger in Berlin was a Wachamacallit Distributor, he might be accommodating enough to "invite you" to Berlin for a business conference and give you a contract to become the American marketing agent for wachamacallits. In this case you'd take a tax write-off for the airlift both ways to Berlin. You would even make a few bucks peddling wachamacallits in the United States. If there doesn't seem to be much market for them after you have made well-documented efforts to sell them, it's no great loss—except on your tax return.

To make exchanging homes and living abroad (or in different parts of the United States) easy, the Vacation Home Exchange (subscription about $20 per year) will let you list your place and will send you a thick list of similarly inclined individuals. Their address is 350 Broadway, New York City.

Next, we'll talk about a gray area—bartering and flea markets. You can, of course, also barter for things or services. If you are a doctor, dentist, or lawyer, or if you can provide any useful services whatsoever, you can always trade at least some of your services for some of the things you need. When Carlos the doctor needs his teeth filled, if you are a dentist you might suggest that you will do his family's teeth as a gift. "It would be nice," you casually suggest, "if Carlos delivered certain medical services to my family also as a gift." Result—no tax consequences. Just be sure to have the proper "gift intention." Why? Because the I.R.S., if it finds out about the services trade will look for your secret intentions. A gift of goods or services is not taxable to the recipient, but in rare instances they have tried to tax trades. As a rule, they have bigger fish to fry and won't bother the individual trader.

As a practical matter, there is no way for the I.R.S. to find out about your trades unless someone tells them. Then the I.R.S. has the problem of valuing the trade and proving your secret intention to avoid taxes.

Household furnishings you do not want can, by law (Internal Revenue Code Section 1031) be traded for other household furnishings you do want. If you went out to earn $950 to spend on a new dining room table you'd have to earn maybe $1,500 in taxable income. Naturally, you would not get any tax benefit for an expenditure on a new table for personal use. But if you already had a table, acquired earlier as a gift, trade, purchase, or whatever, you can trade it for another table or something of "like kind" you want. Section 1031 of the Internal Revenue Code allows you, within broad limits, to exchange things you own for things you want.

The trouble is, that procedure is very cumbersome. Technically, if you just sold furniture or things you owned at a flea market and kept the money or bought something else, if the sale made a profit you'd have a taxable gain to report. But because sales of personal furniture, old TV sets, and so on are generally at a loss, most people do not keep records of what they paid nor of what they received. Further, the I.R.S. does not have as one of its priorities tracking down unreported flea market proceeds. Why do you think that flea markets are such a big business today with 10,000 people filling your local convention hall every weekend? Simple! They have become a part of the subterranean economy. People will always find a way to cope. The answer to high, inflation-bloated prices, the answer to sales taxes that people don't want to pay, the answer to the question of how to earn a tax-free second income? For millions of people, an answer is the weekend flea market. If you haven't been to one, try it. Anything you desire can be bought or sold for cash. No receipts, no guarantees, no checks, and *no tax!*

Another Artful Dodge – The Sunbelt Switch

This is a "gray" area that some find useful. Assume that you are a home owner. Your residence is a typical upper-middle-class three-bedroom, two-bath model that has appreciated (in Los Angeles, anyway) from $50,000 four years ago to $175,000 today. You have furniture and appliances that could cost about $25,000 to replace. But the only tax benefit you get out of the place is a deduction for your annual real estate taxes and possibly your mortgage interest. That isn't bad—it beats no deduction at all—but here is how you might get an additional $12,000 or more in deductions.

Contact friend (let's call him George) across the street. He owns another $175,000 "sunbelt special" furnished comparably to yours. You do a tax-free trade with George, drawing up the papers so that you "buy" his place for $175,000 on the same day he simultaneously "buys" your place for $175,000. You each "buy" the other's furnishings for $25,000. He takes title to your place, you take title to his place. No tax on that deal. Then you lease from him at a fair price—say, $400 per month. He does the same with you. The "Sunbelt Switch" will now create big losses for tax purposes that you didn't have before. You still live in the same place. Every month you swap checks with George; $400 comes in and $400 goes out. But there is one big difference. You are now a renter where you live, but the owner of investment property across the street.

The $100 per month you and George used to each spend on a gardener wasn't deductible. Now it is. All maintenance, repairs, painting, etc. can now be deducted as a business expense. You couldn't have done that with expenses on your own residence. But you can get all sorts of business deductions for those garden hoses, bags of fertilizer, and other things needed to keep up a home. Naturally, you want George to spend just about the same amount as you do to keep the house you "rent" in equally good shape. Best of all, you can now depreciate the structure and contents of your new rental property. Let's have a look at how the "new" deductions might work out for you:

310

Annual Loss on Investment Property

Depreciation

Cost of land	$25,000	
Cost of building	$150,000	
Useful life of building	20 years	
Annual depreciation: 1/20th of $150,000		$ 7,500
Cost of furnishings and appliances	$25,000	
Useful life	5 years	
Annual depreciation: 1/5th of $25,000		$ 5,000
Repairs and maintenance (pool, gardener, etc.)		$ 4,500
Total deductible expenses		$17,000
Less: Rental income for year		(4,800)
Net deduction for tax purposes*		$12,200

The only problem that I can foresee with the Sunbelt Switch is that the I.R.S. (if they found out what you were up to) would invoke their godlike powers and claim that the transaction was entered into without any real business purpose but just to avoid taxes. If they raise that issue and take you to court, you'll definitely have a hassle. Still, this gambit is much better than many others, because an inventive mind like yours could no doubt think up a few very *good business purposes* for you to switch houses. Obviously, you should develop some correspondence or memoranda supporting that "sincere belief" on your part. As I have said, the I.R.S. makes up rules as it goes along for its own benefit and will *always* presume that you had the "improper" intention to beat them out of taxes. It is up to you to cast every transaction you go into as a pure business transaction, never done for solely personal pleasure or tax benefits. Finally, I want to caution you that I regard the Sunbelt Switch as so "gray" that I strongly urge you to have a lawyer or C.P.A. help with its implementation—if it appeals to you.

---

*If your "only purpose" for doing this was to save taxes, you don't get the deduction!

The $1,000 Nickel

A San Francisco lawyer told me about this one. Whenever he gets a complete pass—an acquittal—for one of his heavy-duty dope dealer clients, this attorney expects and gets a $10,000 bonus. But he only pays a tax on 50 cents. How does he do it (legally)?

It appears that there are certain rare American coins—technically still in circulation as legal tender—but they are worth up to $1,000 and more to rare coin collectors. My friend, Terry, the lawyer, tells his client, "My fee is 10 nickels, but only very special 1843 nickels, of which very few were ever minted. They happen to have them in stock at Ajax Coin, and they may cost you $1,000 apiece." (This is a fictitious coin, date, dealer, and price.)

Cocaine Charley always pays Terry, the dope lawyer,
with $1,000 nickels.

Terry then puts the nickels into his rare coin piggy bank, which by now must be worth several (untaxed) millions. The transaction is reported as a petty cash item, and he carefully documents the receipt of "50 cents from Cocaine Charley." According to Terry, this tax avoidance ploy is perfectly legal. Other lawyers feel that, if found out, Terry would be subject to tax on the fair market value of the coins. Now, if Terry wants to "spend" the nickel, he either pledges it for a loan with a coin dealer, or he makes a gift of the coin to someone else with the "hope" that the recipient will make a gift to him of the "something" he needs. Terry says that, because he dumps the coin into a piggy bank with regular coins, he has demonstrated his intention to accept the money as face-value nickels and not collector coins.

As with all tax avoidance ploys, I'm sure that Terry would much rather pay a reasonable tax on his income than go to all this bother. But at today's high tax and inflation rates, most lawyers, judges, and everyone else has to have their own "cute" pet schemes.

Whether this same technique can be used with stamps is another question. Even uncanceled stamps are not legal tender, and the government wouldn't have to accept unused old postage stamps in payment of taxes. But they *would* have to accept your old U.S. coins, and they couldn't give you credit for any more than face value.

As a result, Terry says that if his "retirement plan" is ever challenged, he'll make a grandstand play in court by offering to pay any tax due by turning over his entire piggy bank. The I.R.S. would be forced to accept it and compute the tax based on the face value of the coins—at least that's what Terry says.

Terry tells me that he likes proof coin sets, old real silver dollars, and 1909 VDB pennies. According to him, the value of rare American coins tends to increase far faster than the inflation rate so he doesn't mind keeping the coins forever, as a trouble-free investment. The I.R.S. knows about Terry—but they haven't bothered him yet.

The Research Writeoff

Here's another little gem! The Internal Revenue Code Section 6230, 6231, 6233 allow an individual (or company) to write off in full in the year of the expense all costs incident to the research and development of a new product, process, formula, invention or similar property. "Incident" expense is a little looser than "ordinary and necessary." Merely reading the code might not give the average person any ideas for saving on taxes, but it gave *me* plenty. Let's suppose you liked yachts. Step one: Dream up an idea for a new type of yacht—for example instead of being constructed of standard Fiberglas, you'll use steel strands to give the hull extra tensile strength—or perhaps a variant design to make it go faster, or any idea that would make your boat an improvement over existing yachts. Step two: You form "Oceanic Research & Development Corp." for $50 and then borrow $350,000 to build a prototype. Step three: Built it, test it on a cruise to the Caribbean. And step four: Write off the entire cost of building and testing the yacht on your current year's income tax return.

Naturally, being a Tycoon you will try to market the yacht or your steel-belted process (which you patent). You hope to make money on the invention or new model, but if you don't you still own an expensive yacht, you had a shakedown cruise that cost another $25,000, and unlike most yachtpersons, you were able to write it all off as a legal expense in one year.

One friend (who happened to like scuba diving and eating lobsters) decided that what this country needed was a better lobster tank for home and restaurant use. He developed said tank at great cost (all deductible) and is now selling a comfortable number of tanks each year. He tells me that he had to purchase hundreds of live lobsters and make many trips to their natural habitat to observe them under water. All these expenses were "incident to" developing his product.

Income That Isn't Income

An award for personal injury, or a court award or settlement in a defamation or slander case is not income.

Imagine that you're a housepainter. The guy who hired you, Mr. X, owed you $18,000 for work. Your taxes on this income might be as high as $9,000—net to you only half of what you earned, or $9,000. But imagine these possibilities: on the last day of the job, Mr. X called you "a rotten S.O.B. and a lousy housepainter" in front of three of your friends. You then filed a suit against him for $50,000 for defamation. You settle quickly for $18,000. Pay the lawyers on both sides $1,000 each. You then keep the entire $16,000 tax-free, and you're way ahead. Only Uncle Sam would be $9,000 behind.

Naturally, you could not have intended or secretly planned to save taxes by this method, but if it happened to work out, well, that's just good planning. The same tax advantage would result if you received an injury to your back on the last day of the job and settled that negligence claim with Mr. X for $16,000.

The Kookie Keogh

At the present time, the law allows owners of small businesses or the self-employed to take a percentage of their income and divert it tax-free into a retirement fund for themselves. When you quit working, you pay yourself back the money in the so-called Keogh Plan trust fund or retirement fund, mostly tax free. The problem with most of these retirement plans for the self-employed is that the money diverted from salary income goes into the pension fund. It is then "invested" in savings accounts and stock market mutual funds that do rather poorly. The result has been that the guy who wanted to retire found that his "nest egg" after inflation had far less purchasing power than he contributed, even with the tax-free accumulated interest added.

A few highly innovative doctors and dentists did something unconventional with their Keogh Plan tax-free contributions. They bought fine art, which they kept in their homes on the wall to look at. Another fellow I know bought classic cars and rented them to period movie producers for tax-free income.* One gent bought antique furniture. Others expanded their stamp and coin collections or made other similarly unconventional investments in "collectibles." People with these Kookie Keoghs obviously do far better, investment-wise, than people with ordinary retirement funds, but the big problem with these plans is that you can put away tax-free only up to 15 percent of your taxable income. That means, by necessity, you must *have* a fairly substantial taxable income. Since our objective is to have very little or no taxable income, and thus little or no tax to pay, the Keogh Plan, whether Kookie or otherwise, has no place in the thoughts of a serious tax avoider.

The Incomplete Transaction

I've never seen this concept written up or discussed anywhere, but the very best accountants use it for billion-dollar deals involving their billion-dollar corporate clients. Let me give you a homey little example so you can use it yourself. You bought property X—a building, can of peas, or oil painting for $1 a few years back. You are selling X to someone else this year at an astronomical profit. Say the selling price is $10,001. That would create the liability for a capital gains tax on your $10,000 profit. But here is how the tax can be avoided.

The $10,001 paid by the buyer is called an "escrow deposit." It goes to a third party, not to you—but it is agreed in advance by all parties how the money is to be invested until it comes out of escrow. Let's say it is to be placed in $10,000

---

*Payment was for "wear and damage," not for use.

Swiss franc bonds earning 5 percent annual interest. The contract for sale gives the buyer the right to possess and use X for five years, during which time he has the unconditional right to give the property back to you and take his money back out of escrow. Of course, in your heart you may hope that the deal is so good for the buyer he wouldn't do that. But on paper at least you have an *incomplete transaction*, and the $10,000 isn't really "yours" for five years. It's invested just the way you'd have invested it, but for tax purposes it isn't yours, and your interest isn't taxable income. There is legal authority in the famous Starker 3 case for the position that the deal can even be converted from a sale into a tax-free trade for another oil painting or building if in the course of the next five years you discover something similar ("like the kind") to what you just sold. You'd instruct your buyer to take title to the new like-kind property and pay for it with the money in escrow. As a final step, your buyer deeds the new property to you "in trade" for the X you sold him, and he takes title. The escrow account is closed out. The net result of all this is that you can "sell" something, pay no taxes on the profits, keep the proceeds invested as you wish, and look around for a new investment until you find it. This procedure enables you to take a good offer when it comes along, but to treat the transaction for tax purposes as tax-deferred. What if in a year or two you just want to take the cash out of escrow—perhaps because you have found a good tax shelter deal of unlike kind? All you do is get the buyer's agreement to wind up the transaction. The escrow agent pays you the money. The buyer gives up his right to rescind. The escrow company will always follow changes of instructions coming from *all parties* to a deal. Question: What if the fifth year creeps up on you, and you don't have a trade or a new tax shelter deal? It's a gray area, but I'd say just extend the escrow and the exchange privileges for another five years. This gambit, as far as I know, is legal—but unless you are already a lawyer or C.P.A., be sure to get professional help engineering this one.

How Tuned-In Tycoons
Get Their Kids Through College Free

This is not, strictly speaking, a tax avoidance gimmick. But you should know that one could write volumes on government giveaway programs. For any parent with kids about to go to college, remember: Scholarships, fellowships, research grants, and academic prizes are tax exempt. The Department of Health, Education, and Welfare has more than $3 billion a year to give away as tax-free grants to college students. The only requirement for one class of these giveaways (forget good grades, aptitude, or anything else) is that the potential college student was not claimed as a deduction by his parents on their income tax return for two years prior to getting the grant. Further, your child can't live at home for more than six weeks in the year prior to receiving the grant. The theory, I suppose, is to assure that the handouts go to homeless waifs who are not supported by their parents. As a matter of planning, instead of an allowance, pay your kids a tax-deductible salary in high school. Don't take a dependent's deduction for your kids in the two years before they start college. In their last year of high school, encourage them to move in with their boyfriends or girlfriends. That way Uncle Sam will pay for their college education, and you won't have to. Write to the Department of Health, Education, and Welfare, Washington, D.C., for a free booklet covering educational grants and scholarships. The rules keep changing, but any kid can find a handout if he makes the effort. Scholarships are always tax-free income!

There are many types of federal tax-free grants as well as private scholarships available to students in almost every field. If your children are sophomores in high school, it isn't too early to encourage them to visit the local scholarship and financial aid office of a nearby college to make sure that they get an early start. The all-important game for students is getting in early on the federal handout gravy train. Also remember that the Air Force Academy, West Point, the Naval

Academy, and the Coast Guard Academy are but a few of the totally tuition-free institutions of higher learning that your children (male or female) can apply to these days. *There are far more handouts available than qualified recipients who apply for them.*

All scholarships, fellowships, and research grants are tax free to the recipients and tax deductible to the donors. But the I.R.S. will disallow something as blatant as your own family business giving generous scholarships to your own kids. But here's a hint. How about your family business setting up a scholarship program that just happens to benefit the kids of your friend Al. And maybe Al supports a research fellowship that just happens to benefit your kids. Just a suggestion. If the I.R.S. finds out you planned it to work out that way, it's disallowed, but if it just happens to work out that way. . . .

The Mail Order Business

The mail order business isn't exactly pure fun, but it too can also offer good tax shelter. My neighbor Gladys silkscreens nasty sayings on T-shirts and sells them by means of ads and direct mail. Her large family is always shirted to a "T." Her little home business pays all family expenses and makes $30,000 a year besides. She and her husband never pay income taxes. At the end of each year, all profits are invested (deductibly) in more and more supplies, shirts, advertising, postage stamps, and other inventory. Let's hope that when she decides to cash in her chips by liquidating her inventory of 10 million T-shirts there is still a market for them.

In my own case, not satisfied with my sound studio and I.B.M. equipment, I wanted to write off my groceries and beer, so I began giving "Tycoon Classes" at my home, which included beer and a free lunch. That gives me the right to stock up on pâté, Heineken's, olives, and all my favorite delicatessen snacks—shared with students at Tycoon classes. The "business supply" inventory *you* build up is written off as an expense, even before it is used.

You can go into virtually any venture and create business write-offs. Suppose you like to raise Japanese goldfish. Normally any money you spend on this as a "hobby" would be nondeductible. But if you merely print stationery calling yourself the Joe Smith Yokahama Koi Fish Hatchery, you can deduct the cost of the stationery, your equipment, and basic stock of fish. You can even take an investment tax credit on the aquariums and pumps. All you have to remember is that, to avoid the disallowance of your expenses in a later year as a hobby, you should arrange your financial affairs so that the Smith Fish Hatchery can have a profitable year now and then.

The Installment Sale Gambit: How to Beat the Capital Gains Tax

The installment sale method of deferring capital gains taxes is not recommended by me to anyone who'd like to become a tycoon. In time of high inflation, it never pays to be a *banker* and have people owe *you* money. Reason? Inflation annually robs you of 20 percent of your purchasing power. Taxes take another 20 percent. For example, if you have $10,000 in profits due you on an installment sale and if the note due you bears an exorbitant 40 percent interest you will get a check next year for $4,000. On $4,000 of interest income you'll probably pay a combined state and federal income tax of $2,000. Inflation will eat up at least another $2,000 of your purchasing power, thus a tremendous 40 percent interest rate, lets you barely break even.

The Installment Sales Revision Act of 1980 which allows a seller to spread his capital gains tax over a long period of time, and to take any percentage "down" (eliminating the old 29 percent down payment rule), is in my opinion a piece of garbage. Installment sales in general are not worth the serious consideration of any seller of appreciated property. But there is one exception: Some folks have thought up a clever and apparently legal (!) way of getting 100 percent of your cash sales price shortly after the day of sale, totally free of any capital gains tax. The seller can then invest the money immediately in some real estate deal or other arrangement to outperform inflation. Here's how the game works. The buyer agrees to buy your property at a $10,000 profit to you. He agrees to pay you $10,000 at a floating interest rate with interest payments to be every six months, but no principal payments for 25 years. The buyer then puts up $10,000 cash at a local bank in a savings account to secure his payment. The interest rate floats at whatever the bank is paying on this deposit. The seller (that's you) then borrows the money from the same local bank (remember—borrowed money is never taxable) secured by the deposit. When the smoke clears, the buyer has, in economic reality, paid $10,000 cash for your property. But from your point of view as the seller you never got the $10,000 cash. You merely borrowed the $10,000 secured by the $10,000 deposit. A complex maneuver perhaps, but just one of the many circumnavigations used by clever capitalists to beat the I.R.S. out of what many people feel is an unjust capital gains tax. This form of tax avoidance is called "deferral" of income, and eventually 25 years later when you close out the $10,000 deposit and pay off your loans the capital gains tax will have to be paid, unless of course you extend the deal another 25 years. But one of my mathematician friends calculated that at projected inflation rates, the capital gains tax that will be due in 25 years will be less than one cent in current purchasing power.

23.
Spreads
and
Straddles

Butterfly Spreads Are Not Margarine!
Straddles Are Not
for Cowboys or Sex Fiends.

Millions, possibly billions in taxes have been saved without any of the fanfare or publicity given to oil and gas, cattle raising, and movie productions. That is probably why, until recently, the I.R.S. overlooked the practice of generating "paper losses" with stock market and commodity straddles and spreads of various types.

According to an article in *The Wall Street Journal*, a cassette tape prepared for internal distribution at Merrill Lynch (the world's largest stockbroker) tells their salespeople: "Tax straddles or spreads enable us to create for reasonable cost the capital gains and losses we need to materially change the tax liability of high bracket taxpayers." That is what a tax straddle does. By making a deal that will "lose" money this year and "make" money in a future year, you can create a "paper" profit or loss when needed, virtually on demand. Most stockbrokers are very accommodating and will arrange these deals for any customer. I will go into some detail about tax straddles, not only because you can still use them if done discreetly, but because they will give you ideas of your own about how to create artificial, but legal, losses that will defer income taxes into the distant future. This story of how losses and gains can be "manufactured" and how the I.R.S. is feebly trying to get them disallowed will be useful to you in developing your own tax strategems.

Let's go over a simple example to get the basic point across. On June 1 of this year, assume that sugar prices had just quintupled in the past six months. Some people think that the price of sugar will double again in the next six months, other people think that it will go down by at least half. You don't really give a hoot about sugar but you *would* like to get a tax loss of $500,000 to offset the half-million profit you made this year on, let's say, a building you sold for all cash. Or perhaps you'd like to avoid a tax on the big commission you earned this year.

You purchase a contract from Merrill Lynch or any accommodating commodity broker, expiring January 2 three years hence, obliging you to buy and to sell 1 million pounds of sugar, at $1 per pound. Without going into a great deal of explanation of how the commodities market works, or even dealing with a real situation, let's just assume that you correctly predicted that there would be a violent fluctuation in the price of sugar and people would *either* make a lot of money or lose a lot of money, depending on whether they are "long" sugar (that is, obliged to buy it at today's price) or "short" sugar (that is, obliged to sell it at today's price). Do you have the picture? If you were a true sugar speculator, you'd probably only take *one* position, either "long" or "short," depending on whether you felt the price of sugar would go up or down. But you took two positions that cancel each other out.

The I.R.S. has nothing against you being a speculator. If you make money, it taxes all of the profits, and if you lose money it lets you deduct *part* of the losses. That's fair, isn't it? Trust old I.R.S. to be fair.

You may already know the general I.R.S. rule that if you enter into a transaction not for a possible profit, but *only* for tax reasons, then you are not supposed to deduct *any* of the loss. The I.R.S. wants you to prove a primary profit motive, not just a tax savings motive on any deal you go into.

Of course, the I.R.S. is obviously being unrealistic. In an era of up to 70 percent federal taxes and 15 percent state taxes, your motivation, if in proportion to the distribution of potential profits is going to be 85 percent to benefit the government with only 15 percent for you. According to their Alice-in-Wonderland way of thinking, the investor should be penalized if his main concern is to maximize the tax-free portion of his profits, one way or another. What I'm trying to say is that if the vast majority of any profit made (85 percent) has to be earmarked for taxes, then the primary consideration in any investment *has to be* the tax consequences and not the profitability. Yet the I.R.S., by its rule, insists that this motivation be cleverly concealed in every instance.

Bearing all that in mind, it's now December 31 of this year, and, just as you thought, sugar is either down to 50 cents per lb. or up to $1.50 per lb. It doesn't matter which, because with your straddle you are both long and short sugar. You will have exactly equal profits or losses in each contract, regardless of whether sugar went up or down. Assume in our example that as of December 31 profit will be $500,000. (Note: The profit arises because you contracted to buy 1 million pounds of sugar at $1 per lb. If sugar is later selling at $1.50 per lb., you take delivery, pay out $1 million, and simultaneously sell the sugar to someone else for $1,500,000. This gives you a $500,000 profit. In the real world of commodities, this is all done on paper, and you never physically see the sugar.) The loss is also $500,000. (Note: The "loss" is taken in much the same way. When you sold short, 1 million pounds of sugar at $1 per pound, you made a contract with someone to the effect that you would deliver 1 million pounds of sugar at a dollar a pound, whether the market price later went up or down. When the price went to $1.50, you "covered" the short sale, which means you bought sugar on the open market for $1.5 million and simultaneously sold and delivered the same batch of sugar for $1 million. Thus, you lost $500,000 on the short sale.) Under the terms of your contract, you *must* close it out, that is, take your profit or loss on both contracts within three years. But you can also close out either the long or the short contract early.

In our case, you'll close out one before December 31 of the year in which you need the loss.

Why would you close out just half of the contract? Easy! So you could pick out the losing contract and close it out near the last day of the year, thereby *establishing for tax purposes the loss you need*. But you wouldn't have to come up with $500,000 out of your pocket because you'd close out the *other* account early in the new year and use your profit to cover the loss. Or you could repurchase the losing contract and repeat the whole project the following December.

There wasn't much of a profit-making purpose to that exercise, was there? From the start with a straddle, it appeared almost guaranteed that you couldn't make anything, because whatever amount one contract went up, the other would go down exactly equally. And, of course, Merrill Lynch or any other broker who set up the deal for you got their (roughly) 1 percent commission on each side of the contract.

But look what it did to your tax picture. A $500,000 loss is booked or recorded *this* year. The fact that you had an equal profitable transaction on your account isn't visible on your tax return in the year you take the loss. So unless the I.R.S. looks at several years at one time there is no way for them to find out that you did a tax straddle. Thus, straddles in any volatile stock or commodity permit someone to shelter profits or shift profits and losses from year to year at minimal cost.

What about the $500,000 profit you book the next year? Sometime during the following year, you'll have to come up with another scheme to keep deferring that profit into the future. But even if you don't shelter it, you have had the one-year *use* of up to $450,000 in state and federal taxes you didn't pay—all for a 2-point commission. ("Point" is Tycoon talk for "percentage points.")

Most tycoons believe that paying no taxes by deferring income or profits is an act of faith in the continuing irresponsibility of government and continued inflation. A personal tax can be allowed to accumulate indefinitely—just like the national debt. Eventually the tax liability will be disposed of in the same way that tycoons feel the government will dispose of the national debt—by settling it for some amount less than the amount due, defaulting on it, or most likely, by allowing inflation to make any present-day debt seem like a miniscule sum when the dollar is devalued to a tiny fraction of its present value. In any event, if the I.R.S. did discover your straddle scheme, the most it could say is, "Your intention in making the sugar deal was clearly

to avoid taxes and not to create any real possibility of profit."
It would disallow the loss and also (taking their usual generous position), disallow out-of-pocket expenses such as commissions and the fees paid to your tax lawyer or C.P.A. for
setting the deal up. To cast a little fear into the populace, it
might even criminally indict you, your stockbroker, and
your lawyer as it did with some straddlers in New York City
in May of 1978. But, of course, the I.R.S. will lose (as it did) if
the defendants have any kind of intelligent lawyers representing them. Why? Because the I.R.S. assault is based on the
idea that it can ascertain a trader's secret heart of heart intentions. To find someone guilty of a criminal offense, a jury
must conclude that the trader's *only* motivation was a tax
evasion. If there were *any* business reason for the transaction
and any way the trader could have made a profit, even in the
most bizarre imaginable circumstance, the taxpayer must be
given the benefit of the doubt.

If I were the defendant on our sugar deal case, one defense would be that I intended to make a profit this way: If
sugar went up, say, 50 percent to $1.50, I would first close
out the $500,000 *profit* account. I would then have the op-
portunity to make another $100,000 profit on my remaining
contract if, for instance, sugar prices dropped from $1.50 to
90 cents, or 10 cents below the original contract price. In
other words, I could claim I was looking for a "whipsaw" motion in the price of sugar so that I could at an early stage close
out one contract at a profit. Then I could wait and see until I
could close out the second contract at a profit as well. One
could reasonably claim that tax considerations were of
minor, secondary, importance—or had nothing whatever to
do with the deal. (Note: Interestingly enough, $600,000 in
earnings after maximum 15 percent state and 70 percent federal taxes would amount to a net of 15 percent or $90,000. A
$600,000 loss, by sheltering other income from the same 85
percent tax rate could be worth $510,000 in net tax savings
to a high-bracket tax payer. The point is that, with a high
rate of taxation, business losses can be much more profitable

than gains, and it is logically to be expected that wealthy business people would be much more interested in the tax angles of a deal than in producing a product or service at a profit. At an effective tax rate of 50 percent, a real gain or a paper loss produce the same net. At an effective tax rate of *under* 50 percent—say, 20 percent—it is only worthwhile to make profitable deals. Obviously, any income tax rate over 50 percent is counterproductive. Will someone please tell that to the politicians?)

Because you know that the I.R.S. (if you are audited) is likely to try to make a case out of your "secret intentions to create a paper loss," it is obviously prudent to show no tax avoidance motives, but only profit motives in your correspondence or communications with other people. When I began the straddle deal, I would have taken the precaution of writing my broker a letter explaining my intention to make a profit on both contracts. I'd have mailed a detailed explanation of the same strategy to my grandmother in Akron, as well. With carbon copies of my early intentions clearly spelled out, the fact that my strategy didn't work and I didn't gain anything from the deal (except a tax loss) can't support the I.R.S.'s criminal or civil case. In real life, people really do invest for profit but often end up with nothing but a loss. Even when you make a "capital gain" by selling something at a profit, after taxes and inflation these days almost everyone takes a real loss if they liquidate. That makes it sound economics to never sell or close out a profitable position but to keep it open and appreciating forever. The tax-conscious investor always does just that. He closes out losing positions and takes losses at the end of each tax year. Unrealized profits can be locked in with so-called "put" options.

The straddle technique can be employed to carry forward profitable securities positions indefinitely. Why it's called a "butterfly spread" no one knows for sure, but it seems that when diagrammed a certain way the arrows and dots in a straddle with two stop-loss orders resemble a butterfly with open wings. Most of the big New York Stock Exchange members will arrange straddles or spreads for you for only the cost of commissions. It can involve selling treasury bills short and buying Fannie Mae government notes* long, or buying and selling commodities long and short with an assortment of different dates and commodities all carefully calculated to allow you to have losses every year end and to carry forward profits indefinitely.

Actually, the concept isn't too different from buying up 100 shares of every stock on the exchange and then, at the end of each year, selling all losers but keeping all winners indefinitely. Losses are tax deducted annually. Profits are carried forward indefinitely. As in real estate, you live on money borrowed against your unrealized gains. (Of course, we all know the gains are not real gains usually—price appreciation is just a reflection of the inflation rate, and in fairness, shouldn't be taxed at all.)

How does it all end for the straddler? Up until the 1976 reforms, the strategy of letting profits ride had a very happy ending. You died (as all of us will someday). Your heirs took over the appreciated assets without capital gains taxes. There was an estate tax, of course, but it was at a much lower rate. The assets were valued "net" as of the date of death (less debts). So you were able to fade off into the sunset, escaping any tax on accumulated profits. But in 1976 they attempted to change the "ultimate loophole." Through a complicated formula, the unrealized capital gains of a deceased are supposed to be taxed on death, just as if they were sold. But that, in practice, will amount to more than a 100 percent tax and if enforced the government will end up owning everything in one generation. Why? Because if you bought the X apartment building, for instance, or shares of the X corporation for $1, 30 years ago, and it's now worth $100,000, you've most likely refinanced it. When you die, there's $85,000 in secured loans. The I.R.S. disregards loans.

---

*Government-guaranteed bonds secured by mortgages.

So with taxes of $50,000 due on X, also loans of $85,000, it would mean the heir would have to pay $135,000 (a $50,000 tax and an $85,000 loan) for assets worth only $100,000 on the market. Any heir in his right mind would say, "Take it all, I.R.S. Let the government have everything. Let's be as they are in Russia." Realizing that this is exactly what started to happen in 1978, the I.R.S. temporarily suspended the operation of the new rules on inherited property. So it looks as if you can still avoid taxes as long as you live by deferring them. As of now, your heirs won't have to pay any taxes on the gains you deferred. Let's hope it stays that way. For the moment, you can still die happy, knowing that with spreads, straddles, and refinancing, you've been able to beat the I.R.S., even from the grave!

24. Outwitting the I.R.S. Computer

Many people are intimidated by the fact that the I.R.S. in its news releases often refers to the fact that it has purchased from I.B.M. and others great monster machines. At the touch of a button, they supposedly can assemble documentation on everything you spent and everything you earned. The I.R.S. would like to have you believe that it controls infallible, know-it-all, beeping monsters just like Santa Claus in the children's song:

He knows when you are sleeping,
He knows when you're awake,
He knows when you've been good or bad,
So be good for goodness' sake!

Fortunately, the level of I.R.S. efficiency has a long way to go. In the computer game, they say, "Put garbage in and you get garbage out." In other chapters, I have mentioned that "honest mistakes" can reduce the computers to hopeless inefficiency, and maneuvers such as filing phantom returns could bring the I.R.S. to a grinding halt. But computers may get more efficient if we let them. If you hate the idea of being spied on, here are some of the things you can do to make the big I.R.S. computer a useless spewer of scrap paper.

As I learned when I received printouts of my first computerized mailing lists, a computer is downright stupid. Imagine that you have on a list "Herbert Z. Glockenfarber" at a certain address. At the same address is "Herbert Z. Lockenfarber" and "Herbert Z. Bockenfarber." One look should tell you that these are all the same person. You would consolidate your list by ascertaining the right spelling and eliminating redundant listings. But a computer with millions of names treats slight variants on spellings or addresses as separate people. It has no intelligence, and with a little help from you it can be defeated.

What does this mean to you as an individual in search of privacy? If you don't want the I.R.S. to know whenever you open a bank account, get a credit card, apply for a driver's license, etc., use a variant of your name. Spell it differently. Incorrect classifications will be helped along if you vary and transpose your social security number digits as well. Close out your bank accounts at least once a year and open new accounts. Get some mail in a post office box, and change addresses every year or so. It's much better if they press a button on the computer to separate out all the rich folks, and the computer thinks you are 50 different people earning $1,000 per year instead of one person earning $50,000 per year. Instead of merely getting an "unlisted phone number," which can be traced by any government official or detective, get your phone listed under a totally fictitious name. The phone company doesn't care—as long as their bills are paid. And there is nothing illegal about using a variety of names. Have a different accountant do your taxes each year. Does all this sound childish? Perhaps this advice does not fit your situation. But the more you can confuse the other side, the better.

If you get mail at a post office box,
and change it once a year, the enemy can't
keep track of where you are or what you're doing.

In many parts of the world—like most of Europe, for instance—survival depends on keeping a low profile. Europeans are much more "private" than we Americans. A multimillionaire's home in Italy will look much like the home of a blue-collar worker, from the outside. In never-ending battles with the taxman and government regulators, Europeans discovered it's best if the government doesn't know you exist. Keep the enemy confused, and they may leave you alone.

In the future, we can expect a higher level of violence in society than in the past. In coming years, it will get harder to be "law abiding" and easier to be a criminal. There will be more respect and admiration for criminals than for government people. The federal bureaucracy will continue to grow into a repressive organism regulating and taxing every activity and detail of human life. As more and more people have reasonable gripes, more and more will drop out. A few bandits will get guerilla training and sophisticated weapons. This will be the justification for more regulation and "gun control." We had a good look at the future when the S.L.A. had the whole country in turmoil for almost a year. Ten not-too-bright "urban guerillas" murdered a school superintendent, kidnapped a newspaper heiress, robbed banks, stole cars, and got away. They were protected and sheltered by the public and made the subject of heroic poems and folk songs. As the Los Angeles police surrounded their burning "last stand," millions of Americans watched the shoot-out on TV and cheered for the S.L.A., *not* for the cops.

*When the fuzzy-thinking leftists set out to blow up all
the wealthy property owners or capitalists, they won't
find you if you've been operating under an assumed name.
There is nothing illegal about using an alias—
so long as your purpose is not to defraud.*

Time and time again the bandits of today become the government leaders of tomorrow. Our political system is very accommodating to fuzzy-thinking leftist revolutionaries. New leaders who were brought up as Black Panthers do not have much sympathy for property or business owners. Our best protection is being inconspicuous. Pose as an agent or manager for the owner if you own property. Keep real estate ownership listed on public records in the names of "fronts." Any title company office will show you how to use land trusts, straw men, or holding agreements. Be like one of the richest men in Nevada. A chap who just died there, named Redfield, owned thousands of parcels of real estate. Almost all were in different fanciful names. Real estate brokers in the West knew that if you looked up a chunk of land and it was registered in the name of "Gideon Q. Aardvark," it probably belonged to Redfield.

That's why today if you want to buy property in my town and the property is in the name of Loco N. Cabeza, you might want to talk to me . . .

25.
Beat
the I.R.S.
with Its Own
Rules

The I.R.S. has for the internal use of its agents, a manual called *The Policies of the Internal Revenue Service Handbook.* If you want a guide to what you can get away with, and how to do it, consult this book! It's the only way you will know how the bureaucrats will respond to whatever you did. Where can you get this little gem? Formerly it was not available at all to the public. You had to get it from a former agent in private practice. This led to a black market in unauthorized copies of the handbook and to some taxpayers having a big advantage over others. But under the Freedom of Information Act (one of the best laws ever passed), private publishers got hold of it, and today you can find this formerly secret I.R.S. handbook at most business libraries. One version is published by Tax Analysts and Advocates, 732 17th Street, NW, Washington, DC 20006 ($99.50); another is published by Commerce Clearing House, 4025 West Peterson

Avenue, Chicago, IL 60646 ($130). It's a fat loose-leaf book, and the price includes update sheets of all changes or additions made during the year. Because of the relatively high price, unless you are an accountant or tax lawyer, you'll probably want to refer to it at the library rather than get your own copy. Let's look at the sort of tidbits you'd learn from the manual.

Late Filing

Let's say that you were broke and owed a big tax. Paralyzed by fear, too much drink, and/or problems with your mother-in-law, you didn't file a return until it was *very, very* late. From reading the manual, you'd have learned that fear, lack of funds, or family problems is not considered an acceptable excuse. According to the book, if all you have is a lame excuse the I.R.S. collection agent is duty bound to go after you not only for all taxes due but also for hefty penalties. But let's say you were smart enough, just before the filing date, to consult the handbook. Here's what you'd have found: A 60-day extension for filing—without penalty—is yours for the asking! If requested before the filing date, the I.R.S. will automatically, in writing, grant a 60-day extension for *any* reason. If you want an extension of six months, that will be granted for any *good* reason. What's a good reason? The handbook gives you a list so you can take your pick. if your real reason isn't on this list, don't try it because any other excuse than those given isn't a *good* reason by definition.

Here are the reasons you can use successfully to request an extension of up to six months. Why? Because the handbook says so! There will be no penalties if you use any listed reason or a combination of these reasons for obtaining an extension. There will be an interest charge of 7 or 8 percent per annum on the late balance when ultimately paid—but with a 16 percent true inflation rate, you certainly are better off (if you have a substantial tax due) always taking the maximum extension you can get away with. Here are the acceptable reasons for the I.R.S. to grant you a six-month extension.

1. Death or serious illness of the taxpayer or his immediate family
2. Unavoidable absence of the taxpayer from the locale of his usual business
3. Loss of records due to fire or other casualty
4. Inability to calculate the tax due for reasons beyond taxpayer's control (a change in the law or unresolved court case, perhaps)
5. Ability to file or pay that has been materially impaired by civil disturbances
6. "No money to pay"—an excuse *only* if the lack of funds resulted despite the exercise of ordinary business care and prudence (in other words, the I.R.S. doesn't think much of the inability to pay excuse)

Suppose you want to take *more than* six months to file or to pay? The handbook says, "In no event will an extension by granted for more than six months unless the *taxpayer is abroad.*"

If you want to get a long extension from the I.R.S. or settle debts for 20 cents on the dollar, your best bet is to head for another country that has no extradition treaty and negotiate with the I.R.S. by letter.

341

Obviously, you better pack your bags for Mexico or somewhere outside of the United States and send your request for an extension in from some foreign spot—if you need more than six months to get it together.

The handbook also covers many of the most common excuses people give for not paying taxes and instructs the agents how to deal with them. For example, "I gave the papers to my *accountant*, and the accountant didn't get it done on time." The agent is instructed to ascertain whether the taxpayer got the materials to the accountant before the due date, and then to determine if the accountant—for reasons beyond the accountant's control—couldn't prepare the return on time. Only if both factors were present will this be considered a good excuse. (Better you should pack the bags for Mexico!)

Can You Give the I.R.S. a Bad Check? What Happens Then?

The agent is instructed to give the taxpayer notice, and if within 10 days of getting the notice a new, good check is supplied, the I.R.S. will accept payment without penalty if any reasonable excuse is made. The bad check gambit is probably good for an extra couple of months of delay.

Auditing

How long does the I.R.S. have to go after you? The statute of limitations on tax returns is three years from the date it was filed. But according to the handbook, the I.R.S. must start its audit early. If you don't hear from the I.R.S. within 20 months after the filing date, you are probably home free on that year.

Informers

The I.R.S. manual indicates that anonymous tips will *always* be checked out if seemingly reliable information involves illegal activities *and* tax evasion. Paid informers and purchased evidence are used regularly. The main sources of information considered reliable by the I.R.S. are underworld contacts and undercover agents. Because publicity regarding the use of informers generates *unfavorable public reactions,* agents are instructed not to issue news releases or advertisements to solicit tattletales. Recruitment of informers may be done privately. If an informer materializes on his (or her) own and asks for advance compensation, the agent is instructed to get the information up front and file a request for a reward on Form 211, which must be signed by the stoolpigeon. Rewards can be paid after the information has been evaluated and determined to be worthy of compensation. Form 211 and the statements of informers are theoretically not public record and cannot be obtained, even under the Freedom of Information Act. (Just like the Inquisition—any enemy or ex-lover can denounce you and trigger an extensive investigation without risk of having to back up the accusation. The only way to change this is for you, my readers, to send the I.R.S. a fantasy about the illegal activities (dope

I.R.S. agents have been directed not to
advertise publicly for finks . . .

but are encouraged to maintain underworld contacts
and keep known criminals on the payroll as informants.

dealing or bribe taking) of a federal judge in your area. After enough judges are bothered by enough I.R.S. snoopers, perhaps then they will put an end to these practices. Better make your tips anonymous!)

Compromising Past Due Taxes for Twenty Cents on the Dollar

Suppose you've had all sorts of extensions, and paid with a bad check, and now the I.R.S. comes to you with a big bill, plus interest and penalties. According to the handbook, if you do not pay promptly agents are instructed to levy on any assets or sources of income you may have. That includes Social Security benefits, pensions, or any assets known to them within the United States. If your source of survival is public assistance, they can grab that too. But because of possible adverse publicity, the agents are instructed not to grab the welfare checks of little old ladies or cripples who have no other source of income. In other words, hardship cases get a pass if there is danger of bad press. But if the taxpayer has no apparent source of income and no reachable assets subject to being grabbed by the I.R.S., the agent is instructed to suggest that the taxpayer make a compromise offer or agree to a time-payment plan.

If the taxpayer resides or has moved abroad, the agent, in effect, is instructed to settle a claim as quickly as possible for the best he can get—and not to attempt to analyze or assess the taxpayer's total financial picture. This is in recognition of the fact that the I.R.S. for all practical purposes has no extraterritorial powers and can't do much to anyone who has taken himself and his assets across a foreign border.

From your point of view—if you want to make a compromise on the best possible terms for yourself—plan on doing your negotiations from a safe haven abroad. That will give you your best bargaining stance, according to the handbook.

It should be noted that if you intend to skip the country while owing a lot of taxes, don't broadcast this idea to anyone. As long as you have any assets in the United States and are rumored to be liquidating with plans to leave, the handbook provides for a "jeopardy assessment": The I.R.S. can tie up all bank accounts, stock holdings, and real estate it knows about if it has reason to suspect your imminent departure.

If and when you do visit Mexico or Brazil, your strategy should be to negotiate a settlement as soon as possible while abroad—if you ever intend to come back. Because if you don't make some compromise, you'll still owe the full amount, plus interest and penalties, when you get back. The usual three-year statute of limitations stops running while you are outside of U.S. jurisdiction. The interest and penalties keep running against you. But the I.R.S., not sure that you'll ever return, is under orders to grab what it can and settle fast. Twenty percent on the dollar is about as low as they will usually go.

Before the handbook was released a few years back, the I.R.S. tried to avoid making it public with the defense that it would reveal the weaknesses in the system to the general

345

public. As you may have noticed from the few hints on these pages, *it sure does!* Check out the handbook yourself for more revelations.

Many people in the I.R.S. will get gray hairs from this chapter and from the next. A turncoat I.R.S. agent, when he heard about my book, called me and said, "I'll show you how to bring the whole system tumbling down in a matter of a few years."

"Show me," I said.

"Show me," I said.

26.
The
B.O. Ploy

Back in 1913 when the income tax law first went into effect, it was promoted to the voters as a levy to soak the superrich only. Even for the superrich, the tax promised a minimal 2 percent of net income. A senator of the era, when asked if the rate couldn't someday go up to as much as 20 percent and be used against the common folks who voted it in replied, "If rates ever got anywhere near 20 percent, an outraged populace would most certainly toss any congressman foolhardy enough to vote for such an increase right out on the street." Unfortunately, as with all politicians' predictions, this one was forgotten once the people voted in the income tax. Tax rates spiraled out of sight, and today the wage slaves pay most of the taxes. "Soak the Rich" schemes always soak the middle class.

Instead of just being a method of financing necessary operations of government, as originally intended, the income

347

Form 1040.

INCOME TAX.

THE PENALTY
FOR FAILURE TO HAVE THIS RETURN IN
THE HANDS OF THE COLLECTOR OF
INTERNAL REVENUE ON OR BEFORE
MARCH 1 IS $20 TO $1,000.
(SEE INSTRUCTIONS ON PAGE 4.)

List No. ....

.... District of ....

Date received ....

File No. ....

Assessment List ....

Page .... Line ....

UNITED STATES INTERNAL REVENUE.

RETURN OF ANNUAL NET INCOME OF INDIVIDUALS.
(As provided by Act of Congress, approved October 3, 1913.)

RETURN OF NET INCOME RECEIVED OR ACCRUED DURING THE YEAR ENDED DECEMBER 31, 191....
(FOR THE YEAR 1913, FROM MARCH 1, TO DECEMBER 31.)

Filed by (or for) .... of ....
(Full name of individual.) (Street and No.)

In the City, Town, or Post Office of .... State of ....
(Fill in pages 2 and 3 before making entries below.)

		INCOME		TAX	
1. Gross Income (see page 2, line 12)	$				
2. General Deductions (see page 3, line 7)	$				
3. Net Income	$				

Deductions and exemptions allowed in computing income subject to the normal tax of 1 per cent.

4. Dividends and net earnings received or accrued, of corporations, etc., subject to like tax. (See page 2, line 11)	$				
5. Amount of income on which the normal tax has been deducted and withheld at the source. (See page 2, line 9, column A)..					
6. Specific exemption of $3,000 or $4,000, as the case may be. (See Instructions 3 and 19)					
Total deductions and exemptions. (Items 4, 5, and 6)	$				
7. Taxable Income on which the normal tax of 1 per cent is to be calculated. (See Instruction 3).	$				

8. When the net income shown above on line 3 exceeds $20,000, the additional tax thereon must be calculated as per schedule below:

				INCOME.			TAX.	
1 per cent on amount over $20,000 and not exceeding $50,000....	$				$			
2 " " 50,000 " " 75,000....								
3 " " 75,000 " " 100,000....								
4 " " 100,000 " " 250,000....								
5 " " 250,000 " " 500,000....								
6 " " 500,000								
Total additional or super tax					$			
Total normal tax (1 per cent of amount entered on line 7)....					$			
Total tax liability....					$			

tax laws became a tool for achieving political or social goals. During the bootlegging era, I.R.S. criminal powers were used to "put away," on tax charges, those "undesirable elements" who supplied the public taste for booze—notably, Al Capone. Nixon used the I.R.S. to harass his political enemies. The I.R.S. today still spends much of its enforcement budget persecuting unpopular people or religious sects like the Moonies or the Scientologists. As long as a politically weak or unpopular sect is involved, nobody seems to mind.

The most important rule in tax avoidance is *Keep a low profile.* Don't flaunt your wealth. Don't try to get your financial success touted in the popular press. Don't do as I do. Do as I say.

Let's say you discover a perfectly good way to make money and shelter it by some tax loophole or gimmick. If you blab it around and get written up in the papers, the I.R.S. task force will be out to investigate you. If other people use it successfully, within a couple of years Congress will righteously close the loophole. That is why I have many second thoughts about publishing this book and giving away a lot of my pet schemes.

Before we get back into the nitty-gritty of it all, let me give you another bit of advice. Don't expect your typical lawyer, C.P.A., accountant, or tax preparer to give you much in the way of creative tax-saving advice. You have to adapt tricks you learn here and elsewhere to your personal situation and ask the professional if he or she thinks they will work for you. You personally have to be alert to tax-saving opportunities, the possibility of creating deductions, changing taxable income into nontaxable cash flow, and creating the sort of tax-sheltering investment situations that I talked about in the *"Pay No Taxes Ever Again, Legally"* chapter and elsewhere. If you marry a C.P.A. or a tax lawyer, you may get some help with your taxes, but short of living and sleeping with a tax adviser you can't look to anyone but yourself for discovering and implementing basic strategies. Where besides this book can you get ideas? I suggest the Thursday front-page column in *The Wall Street Journal*, *"Tax Report."* Dow Jones has also published a small paperback digest of tax reports from the past few years. There's a monthly newsletter, *Tax Angles*, P.O. Box 2311, Landover Hills, MD 20784. The cost is reasonable. Mention Bill Greene and they'll send you a sample for $2. In my reading list, there's a lot of tax-oriented material. You can also take a tax course after you've finished Accounting 101.

The best tax gimmicks you'll think up yourself! They may be variations on basic themes discussed here, but used in such a manner as to fit in with your unique situation. They will be best kept to yourself after being cleared as "probably legal" with your accountant. By the way, try to get that accountant's opinion in writing. Later, if you are ever charged with "criminal" tax fraud, the fact that you requested and relied on an accountant's opinion will go a long way in clearing you of any criminal intent. The tax laws are so obscure, so lengthy, and so full of varying interpretations that with any degree of caution, being indicted for criminal tax-evasion is almost impossible. I understand from a *Wall Street Journal* article that in a nation of about 100 million taxpayers, an estimated 90 million fudge to a greater or lesser degree. Yet in the entire United States only about 500 convictions per year come down for those who plead not guilty and fight their case through the courts. That works out at about .00005 percent of the tax evaders of this country being convicted. Not bad odds. And of course being convicted doesn't mean you'll spend any time in the pokey. There are many suspended sentences, pardons, or paroles.

The interesting fact about those who are convicted is that virtually *all* were indicted on the evidence of *informers* who fell into two basic categories—disgruntled employees who'd been fired, and ex-wives or ex-lovers who felt they had been jilted. The trial testimony of these informers reads like a broken record.

Informer: "Mr. Tax-Cheater over there *told me* he intentionally was not going to report certain cash income he received, but because of my special relationship I can tell you how much he got, from whom he got it, and what he spent it on." The informer then goes on to explain in detail. The informer's evidence is duly corroborated with documents, photographs, and other testimony. Sometimes the other testimony is unwillingly extracted from other friendly witnesses who were offered a pass on their own tax shenanigans if they'd help put Mr. "T" away. That's the usual sordid way the I.R.S. gets convictions: paid informants and pressured witnesses. It's a nasty little system you must never become the target of. Moral of the story—don't intentionally fail to report taxable income you actually get, and don't create substantial deductions out of thin air. More importantly, whatever you do, don't brag about any tax-cheating you do to your girlfriend, trusted business associates, or anyone else. At some later time, their vindictiveness over a real or imagined wrong could put you into the soup.

If you keep a low profile keep your affairs private, and are not an I.R.S. target there is little risk of going to the pokey for tax-evasion.

To avoid criminal penalties, all you need is just one court case (out of the millions of court cases dealing with tax matters) that supports your position, even obliquely. If you can't find a case, a law review article or tax lawyer's opinion will do. Last and least, *anybody*'s opinion, such as a reporter in the *PoDunk Star* saying that a certain way of reporting or not reporting a transaction was legal, may suffice to show that you were acting on what you thought was reliable advice. The Bible is full of enough parables and advice to support virtually any moral position. Since the Internal Revenue Code is many many times as long, and many times more parabolic and confusing than the Bible, a reading of any code section applicable to your particular situation will likewise be subject to many varying interpretations. With that, let's see how to beat the I.R.S.

With a low profile and instructions to your accountants to prepare your tax return to avoid any "red flags," the day may never come that you are audited or criminally investigated. But if you have done anything to be worried about (and who hasn't), my good friend Ollie the lawyer says that high-level criminals are never nailed for tax evasion anymore, because they have learned a few secrets about criminal tax fraud cases. These secrets I now pass on to you.

1. Most tax convictions involve informers. The easiest case for the government to prove is "conspiracy to evade." The pigeon gets a pass and a promise of a reward. Typically the pigeon did the same thing you did perhaps as your partner or spouse. If the pigeon will testify to your tax evading intentions as an "unindicted co-conspirator," the government case is hard to overcome.

This unpleasant situation can be simply avoided by doing anything questionable solo—all by yourself—and not telling anyone your secret intentions. Don't have any partners, and don't brag about your tax avoidance techniques. As I said several times, informers are almost always disgruntled employees or ex-lovers. Remember, the I.R.S. doesn't care

I.R.S. informers are almost always disgruntled employees or ex-lovers. But the I.R.S. also uses paid burglars, pimps, prostitutes, and other sleazy scum.

much what you do, they are more interested in your state of mind—kind of like the Catholic Church. They feel sin is as much in the mind than in the act.

2. The second largest reason anyone is convicted is that they give the I.R.S. information on themselves either directly, or by leaving incriminating documents with their accountants. Rule: *Never, never, never* talk to an I.R.S. agent directly. Always be insulated by your accountant, or if things get serious, by a tax lawyer. That way you won't put your foot in your mouth. The I.R.S. manual is full of dirty tricks designed to entrap you. No matter how much an I.R.S. agent smiles, he is never out to help you. No matter how friendly he seems, he is out to take your chips, or put you in the pokey. That's what he's paid for. That's how he gets his promotions.

Never permit your accountant to retain in his or her office any work sheets, original ledgers, memos of conversations, or any of your records whatsoever. There is no accountant-client privilege, and I.R.S. agents can swoop in at any time and grab your records from your accountant's office.

Another way people give the I.R.S. enough information to hang themselves is by giving the I.R.S. a paper trail resembling a superhighway. With enough papers and records, the I.R.S. can select and choose from thousands of documents. With unlimited documents, the I.R.S. could probably build an adultery case against the Pope if it had a mind to. Because none of your records are in the hands of any third person (except your lawyer) you might take the following steps: Don't use Master Charge, Visa, or any other credit card for personal expenses. Always pay and accept payment in barter or cash only. If you must use checks, fill them out and endorse them with light blue or yellow Pentel pens. Bank-copying equipment is not sensitive enough to copy light-colored inks, and the I.R.S. will only be able to subpoena blank copies of checks.

3. Fight the I.R.S.'s requests for records or information at every step of the way unless their agents offer to compromise their claims or drop their criminal case in a way totally acceptable to you. Many taxpayers fall over and play dead at the slightest pressure from the I.R.S. Others plead guilty to something they're innocent of, just to avoid a trial. If investigating you costs the I.R.S. a lot of time and money, you may be harassed for a time, but eventually you'll be given a pass. If you don't give the I.R.S. any cooperation or any records at all and if it goes to court, it will be obliged to claim that every expense you claimed was fraudulent. You may be accused of concealing huge amounts of "unreported income." When the government takes this shotgun approach, you can always prove that 99 percent of the government's case is hot air. The questionable 1 percent remaining will be a percentage of error every juror can identify with. No taxpayer can substantiate every deduction and document every deposit. Without a lot of specific information to narrow a case down to several clear instances of intentional fraud, the government can't win a case against you.

4. Politically, in my opinion you should inform your senator and congressman that debtors' prison was abolished in every other civilized country shortly after the time of Charles Dickens. Governments should have no more right to coerce cash out of its citizens by threat of jail than any creditor should have to jail any debtor. If enough citizens took the position that civil penalties should be the only penalties available to the I.R.S., the I.R.S. would cease to be an organization that can be used to terrorize people who have unpopular political views or who are the targets of "selective enforcement."

The I.R.S. should be totally divorced from all functions except fairly and impartially collecting taxes. The I.R.S. is now in the business of chasing ex-husbands who are behind on their alimony and putting suspected felons in jail for tax evasion when they could not be convicted of anything else.

The I.R.S. certainly *is* in the business of harassing its critics. I know *that* from personal experience. All of these functions, to my way of thinking, are improper and should be taken away from the I.R.S. Besides getting this country back on the road to freedom and privacy, reducing the I.R.S. criminal investigation division by 100 percent would save the U.S. Treasury hundreds of millions of dollars each year.

The B.O. Ploy

Let me give you another hint that seems timely at this point. Just like us, I.R.S. agents respond to painful or unpleasant situations by getting them over with as soon as possible. Remember, I.R.S. agents are human too. That may seem hard to believe in view of their high-handed methods, but a friend of mine discovered a ploy that is worth passing on at this point.

When an audit of his return was scheduled, Kinky began wearing the same clothes for two weeks. He did not wash, and by the time the interview was scheduled, he smelled

The B.O. Ploy

"You're the swellest-looking I.R.S. agent I ever met. How about a date tonight?"

very ripe. To top it off, just before his audit he had a bowl of garlic soup. When the I.R.S. agent asked him to prove up a few questionable deductions, good old Kinky moved in close to show him the papers. Whenever the agent tried to move to the opposite side of the room, Kinky just moved right in there and breathed on him. Result? Audit prematurely terminated. No changes in Kinky's return.

Other ploys I have heard of involved an inability to concentrate on the I.R.S. agent's question due to an irresistible sexual attraction. This can be particularly effective if you make disconcerting passes at an agent of the same sex and he or she isn't inclined in that direction. The danger is that the agent may take you up on it, and you'd better be prepared to follow through. Kinky got his nickname after a male agent took him up on his advances a few years back. That was when he decided to develop severe B.O. for the next encounter.

27.
How to
Bring Down
the System

What can *you* do to bring down the system? This is the chapter the I.R.S. is worried about. I know it is worried because I have had the cooperation of several I.R.S. turncoat employees. They told me that a recurrent nightmare of I.R.S. bigwigs is that most people will eventually find out just how weak and vulnerable the system is. The tax collectors worry that the man on the street will learn that he is being conned and that he can fight back effectively. When that happens, the tax system becomes impotent, and, as in Italy, nobody pays.

The American system of taxation depends on voluntary compliance: voluntary filing and voluntary paying. Once even a substantial minority of taxpayers fail to file or refuse to pay, there is no mechanism to collect from or prosecute more than the tiniest minority. According to information from the I.R.S., there are under 300 convictions per year.

There are also about 900 plea bargains—usually for suspended sentences. Yet a report of the General Accounting Office (July 11, 1979, by Daniel Harris, one copy available free from General Accounting Office, Rm. 1518, 441 G Street, NW, Washington, DC 50548) indicated that at least 6 *million* (that's 6,000,000) people who *should* have filed income tax returns failed to file. Ninety percent of these people never got so much as a follow-up letter from the I.R.S. Why? Simply because the I.R.S. does not have any budget to pursue nonfilers. With about 90 million people filing returns in America and the vast majority of these applying for refunds, it is plain that if 6 million don't even file, the government already has a problem that is too big for it to handle. But tax rebels who have done their own research estimate that the number of nonfilers who owe taxes is somewhere between 18 and 24 million individuals. Regardless of who is right, *you* should know that total noncompliance is a fast-spreading epidemic the government can't begin to cope with except by issuing false news releases lauding the success of their mostly imaginary enforcement programs. The truth of the matter is that between nonfilers and tax cheaters of one kind or another, there may be close to 100 million American individuals and businesses who don't pay their proper taxes. With 300 convictions per year, you can see that the odds of a run-of-the-mill nonfiler or tax cheater going to the pokey are around 300,000 to 1.

What you may not know is that for several reasons it's a far better strategy to *not file any return* than to file a *false* return or a *blank* signed return. If you can get off the computer so that the government doesn't know where you are or what happened to you, it is virtually impossible for the I.R.S. to even *start* an investigation. A filed tax return generates its own leads—there may be omissions, errors, or comparisons with prior years to establish a fraud. At least there is an address where they can look for you. But failure to file gives no such leads. Getting off the computer can be as simple as moving from your present address and not giving a forwarding address to the post office. Naturally, you should not continue to be listed in the phone book, either—at least under your old name. An extremely interesting book, *The New Paper Trip*, 160 pages, published by Eden Press, Box 8410, Fountain Valley, CA 92708 ($10) shows how to establish a new identity for yourself. It suggests, amusingly, that if you don't want to move, you can just change your name and Social Security number (through a variety of legal or illegal methods), and purchase a rubber stamp "DECEASED." By stamping all incoming mail you don't want and dropping it in a mailbox, you can effectively "kill" your old self and become someone new. The "paper trip" will give anyone who wants it a fresh start.

Assuming you don't file a return after taking some steps to drop out, and assuming that you are found, did you know that simply not filing, even if "willful," is a misdemeanor, not a felony? There is a big difference between the two. A misdemeanor is something like spitting on the sidewalk, driving without a seat belt, or repairing your leaky faucet without a permit. The *maximum* punishment is a small fine and less than one year in the county jail. Typically, nonfiling is not prosecuted. A Certified Public Accountant friend of mine has a gross income in the hundreds of thousands. He failed to file a personal return for a number of years. When this year an I.R.S. agent finally came in to visit him, all the C.P.A. got was a polite suggestion to file his last three years of returns within the following six months. His only excuse was that he was "too busy" to file.

There are a host of reasons why different Americans feel a sense of outrage at the "system." In my own case, it was the fact that I was singled out for I.R.S. harassment because I gave a lecture on how to save on taxes, using real estate. Until it happened to me personally, I was blissfully unaware that any totally innocent individual could be financially ruined, deprived of reputation, and be utterly helpless— without any recourse against government. But this could happen only if he were ill-informed and poorly represented!

359

That experience made me a rebel and ultimately led to this book.

Even more outraged was Irwin A. Schiff, who had to rate Number One on the I.R.S. "enemies list" after he sold about a hundred thousand copies of his book *The Biggest Con—How the Government is Fleecing You.* He gave regular seminars on how and why not to file income tax returns. He probably nets over $100,000 year. He publicly announced year after year that he was filing a blank or "Fifth Amendment" tax return and was not paying a dime in income taxes, federal taxes, state sales taxes, or any other kind of taxes. After years of going on national TV talk shows and being the most visible, flagrant tax evader in the United States, he was finally brought to trial in 1979. The result was a sentence of six months. This was appealed and eventually reversed. As of 1981 Schiff was still a free man and still refusing to pay taxes. That's what happened to a guy the I.R.S. had dead to rights and just couldn't ignore!

Thus you may begin to see that the risks of not filing are not so bad. If you keep your tax rebel thoughts to yourself and do not broadcast that your nonfiling is a deliberate and intentional act, then, as a low-profile nonfiler, the worst that would happen is in most cases you'd be *asked* to file a return for the last three years. And that's only if and when they find you. The only way you can be found is if you leave a paper trail. The way to cover your tracks is fully explained in *The Paper Trip.*

Let me stress right here, before I go on to talk about other things, that not filing *is illegal.* It is risky. It *could* even land you in jaul. The odds are overwhelming that you'll never serve a day, but not everyone wants to break the law—even if there is *no* chance of getting caught. I am in the more conservative school and would rather avoid taxes by using the many *legal means* available.

In my opinion, most people now in the subterranean economy could generate enough expenses and write-offs so that they could file tax returns and stay legal. Nobody who reads this book should ever have to pay taxes. Obviously, staying legal requires more time, effort, and record keeping. But going underground is something like being a fugitive. Do you really want to live under an alias? The choice is yours, and this chapter and this book is here to show you some alternatives.

Revolt is a serious business. Before becoming a serious rebel, and risking your freedom, you'd better ask, "What am I doing, and why am I doing it?" A few years back at the Wharton School of Finance in Pennsylvania, I got to know a number of wealthy Cuban kids—that was in the pre-Castro days. Many of them were for "revolution against tyranny and torture under Batista." They supported Castro during the late 1950s. The next thing they knew was that their hero had won, their parents' property was confiscated, and in order to live a decent life or practice their chosen profession they were obliged to move to exile in Miami. Today, most of them are Cuban-Americans who never expect to return to a Cuba that has no use for them. Going further back, to the 1930s and the Hitler era, the vast majority of Hitler's earlier supporters who were members of a group known as the "Brownshirts" or S.A. were all murdered shortly after their leader came to power. They all wanted to overthrow the Weimar Republic—a weak ineffectual democracy plagued by inflation and in many ways similar to the United States of America today. Look what happened then! Before that, after the 1917 Russian Revolution, the leading supporters of Lenin, including a character named Trotsky, were all snuffed by Stalin when he came to power. In more recent times, I had an Ethiopian student as a tenant. He was always parading and carrying signs demanding the overthrow of Haile Selassie. It seemed to me that if his parents could afford to send him as a student in the United States, he had to be a very lucky and upper-class African indeed. I asked him about the possible loss of his privileged status in the event there was a successful revolution in his homeland. His answer was something like, "Anything would be an improvement over the present regime." I heard very much the same thing from young Iranians in 1979. Well, both Ethiopians and Iranians got their revolutions. But when the new regimes took over in both countries, women's rights, free speech, the right to own property, the right to travel—all the things that those students took for granted—were immediately suspended. Whatever tortures, executions, injustices, and other complaints the students had were miniscule discomforts compared to what happened under the new regime.

That is why at this point I want you to think very seriously about what will replace the present system and present tax structure if blatantly illegal methods of avoiding taxes are successfully used by the majority. If the vast majority of the American population evade the tax law and become "outlaws," the American Dream as we know it could evaporate in a move to the far right under a Hitler. Or we might end up in an authoritarian socialist state with a Mao Tse-Tung. If that's what you want, fine! But if you want the maximum freedom for everyone, I think the Libertarian Party* will serve a useful purpose. As it grows in numbers and influence, I predict that most of its ideas must (within the next 10 years) be adopted by the major parties. Possibly the Libertarians will replace the Republicans as the second power base in the United States. And because Libertarians are universally opposed to the income tax, it is likely that this tax will be abolished or drastically limited.

Why am I bringing all this up? Simply because in my opinion, the taxpayers' revolt is gaining momentum and much more is happening than the man on the street realizes, or the government dares to admit. But if we don't want to wake up one morning with power in the hands of some despot it is necessary not only *to rebel*, but also to *support an alternative form of government*. To rebel against a system

---

*The author, Bill Greene, is a Libertarian, and in a close race for the Libertarian nomination for Vice-President of the United States (1980) he was narrowly defeated by "none of the above" and Ed Koch who became the candidate.

you don't like without supporting a program to enhance individual freedom is irresponsible. A government can only stand so much pressure before it evaporates and resigns. That creates a vacuum. Highly organized well-armed juntas often move into a political vacuum. The U.S. government is currently under a great deal of pressure and is probably more unstable than any knowledgeable person cares to admit publicly. The tax revolt is just one aspect of this. Today there are probably more people opposed to our form of government and its taxing policies than in support of it. But as yet there has been no way to measure that opposition except by Gallup and Roper polls. These show that the vast majority of people have little or no confidence in their political leaders. They yearn for a charismatic "leader" and that puts the republic in a vulnerable situation.

The tax revolt is here, partly as a result of loss of faith in government, and partly for economic reasons. In recent years, most people have come around to the view that inflation is caused *solely* by government, and is a form of hidden taxation. If wealth is being taken by government at the rate of 15 to 25 percent per year through inflation, and another 60 percent or more through federal, state, and local taxes, most people feel this is simply unfair. They are unwilling to work from Monday through Thursday just to pay taxes. Almost everyone has a personal gripe against government. Some feel that it is madness to spend money on atomic weapons and missiles when we already have enough to blow up the world several times over. Others feel that Americans are simply overgoverned, overregulated, and unfree. They don't want to support a bureaucracy in Washington that keeps getting bigger, more oppressive, and more interfering with every aspect of their personal life. Many individuals don't wish to be told what medicines or drugs they can take, what foods they can eat, when and if they can travel abroad, etc.

As a result, they become tax strikers. They refuse to pay taxes, to serve in the army or to support the government in any way, shape, or form. Some extremists blow up toilets in the Capitol Building, others even want to blow up people.

I don't believe that violence or killing is ever productive, and even not filing a required return is too risky for my blood. For anyone close to me, I'd always advocate staying within the law. Stretch it, yes. Skirt around it, yes. But do it legally. Don't put yourself in a position where they've got you by the you-know-what. Your choice may be otherwise if you are young, foolish, and want to be considered a hard-core member of the tax revolt. If you feel a moral obligation to express your outrage and indignation, you may want to be like Irwin A. Schiff. But I am sure he had a lot of sleepless nights, a lot of worry, and a lot of suffering as a result of his conviction. Personally, I think the guy ought to get a medal. But what he got was a long trial that no doubt cost him every penny he made from his books and lectures—and his savings. Lawyers do not come cheap.

Personally, I don't want to be a hero. Or a pioneer either. But I admire those who, like Schiff, are both. A strong moral stance against taxation puts you in the same league with Washington, Jefferson, Ben Franklin, and Patrick Henry. We sometimes forget that the "Fathers of our Country" were nothing more than a bunch of tax-rebels. Up to the year 1764, the vast majority of American colonists were proud to be British subjects and citizens of the most powerful and civilized nation then existing. There were always a few malcontents who objected to regulations that limited the production of finished manufactured goods in the American Colonies, but there was virtually no thought of armed resistance, or any real resistance to the mother country.

In 1764, the British Parliament passed the Sugar Act, which prohibited Yankee ships from obtaining molasses directly and tax-free from the growers in the French Caribbean. The Sugar Act provided that the colonists would have to purchase their sugar from England. British processors would add their mark-up, and the Crown would add a tax. Prior to the Sugar Act, the New England colonies and the South had little in common. But the Sugar Act was a serious economic blow to both areas. Yankees from wealthy Boston and New-port picked up molasses in Santo Domingo and Cuba. They brought it back to New England where it was processed into rum. The rum and other local products were taken to Africa and traded for slaves. The slaves were then brought to the American Southland. The Sugar Act might have destroyed this lucrative trade triangle—but the Yankees ignored it and became smugglers on a vast scale. With the most prominent Americans forced to become "outlaws," it was not long before fired-up patriots like Patrick Henry wrote that England would "drive us to extremities . . . hostilities will soon take place; and a desperate and bloody match it will be."

King George of England, when he heard of the fuss in America, took a hard line and imposed additional taxes to make up for the revenue lost by the smuggling. Next all the colonies sent delegates to a First Continental Congress in Philadelphia. Britain regarded this as treason and issued an ultimatum to submit. At that point, Pennsylvania's John Dickenson reflected the thoughts of many Americans when he wrote (in 1768), "Those who are taxed without their own consent . . . are slaves. We are therefore *slaves.*" Of course, in those days, black slaves were not even considered human beings, and the 1776 Revolution, at least insofar as many Southerners were concerned, was fought to preserve *their* source of cheap slaves. But the rhetoric was all about British oppression, tyranny of taxation, and the use of force against good citizens.

The revolution followed! Most historians agree that as of 1776, at least one-third of the American colonists were "Tories" or English loyalists. Another third had little or no property, nothing to gain or lose, and were quite apathetic. A tiny minority of middle-class individuals were *really* upset, and less than a third of the rest of the American colonists were in favor of following their lead and breaking away from England. The small minority became the "Fathers of Our Country."

That in a nutshell is the story of the American Revolution. It has some parallels to the present situation. Do I have to spell them out? *When enough activist people get angry, you get a revolt!*

A revolt is a *successful* rebellion. The high-toned moral stances and posturing may come, but the root of the American Revolution was simply that some powerful folks were squeezed economically, and unfairly. These days—more than at any time since 1776—the same thing is happening.

In colonial days, when a rum smuggler was caught or when a tax striker went on trial, American juries often refused to convict. This was a source of great annoyance to Britain. Until recent years, people indicted for tax evasion seldom beat the rap because the people by and large supported the system. Today, it may be breaking down. Most fair-minded judges and juries find it increasingly hard to mete out a severe sentence to people who feel that taxes are unjust and for that reason refused to pay.

Most judges and jurors will have to *agree* that taxes are unfair and unjust. Anyone with eyes can see that the wealthy don't pay taxes. The politicians don't pay taxes—nobody except poor Johnny Lunchbucket pays taxes, and even he is going to wise up.

So, if you want to be a tax rebel and a hero, the risks these days are not as great as those faced by earlier Americans (such as Nathan Hale: "I regret that I have only one life to give for my country"). You won't get hung, you probably won't even ever go to trial, and if you do, you can get national publicity with the "Nuremberg Defense" that Schiff at the last minute in his trial decided *not* to use.

"What's the Nuremberg Defense?" you ask. Just after World War II, our own government in the Nuremberg Trials of Nazi war criminals enunciated the principle that every citizen has a duty to oppose a government that acts in an immoral way. That new and novel principle of international law was used to convict Nazis who defended their conduct by saying, "I was only following the law of my country and doing my duty."

The prosecutors from the United States said at Nuremberg that a citizen can't just blindly follow laws or take orders but must first apply universal standards of moral judgment. This was a very dangerous stance for any government to take—but the United States took it, and predictably now it has returned to haunt the U.S. government. It happened first in Korea and Vietnam where the other side tried Americans for war crimes using the Nuremberg standards set by the United States itself in 1946. It is an "ultimate weapon" for use by tax rebels. If ever brought before a judge, your most powerful argument is to say that after World War II the United States condemned to death people who followed "the law" and now, when our government finances abortions; makes war on far-off innocent people by supporting vicious dictators, torturers, and murderers; breaks treaties with old friends; and destroys basic liberties with forced busing or whatever gripe you feel outraged about, we must not support our government in its erroneous and immoral policies. Say, "The only way I can express my opposition is by not paying taxes to carry out morally repugnant policies." Judges and juries find it very hard to mete out a severe sentence, or any punishment at all, to people who feel very strongly and conscientiously about a particular moral issue. As a result, most sentences—to those two or three dozen morally indignant tax protesters (out of millions) brought to court involve a suspended sentence or an alternative to jail—such as doing some socially useful work.

This sort of Nuremberg defense—similar to being a conscientious objector to military service, will work *only* if you are *sincere*. If you are not paying taxes just because you are an irresponsible deadbeat or a person that a judge or jury perceives as being without any socially redeeming features, you will lose. So don't embark on the outlaw life unless you feel that you know what you are doing and why you are doing it. In the final analysis, you have to be willing to risk a few months in jail in support of your principles. Once you have made that decision, you are invulnerable and invincible.

Like Patrick Henry, Joan of Arc, or Nicolas Copernicus, whatever "they" can do to you is very little. You will be a hero, and many of the organizations listed at the end of this chapter will flock to your aid. There are far more of "us" rebels than there are of "them" tax collectors, and we are the productive, thinking people of America. The ultimate power resides in us!

Now that you are all pepped and prepped, what else can you do? Schiff used to recommend to his followers that they file a Fifth Amendment return. Some people still sell "kits" showing you how to fill out such a return. What you are supposed to do is object to each and every line of the return on the grounds that you cannot be compelled to be a witness against yourself (according to the Fifth Amendment to the U.S. Constitution). As a result, you say you are not going to give the I.R.S. any information that might later be used to prosecute you. That was Schiff's position. At his trial, the judge found this argument to be "frivolous." Summarizing the court's position, he couldn't let Schiff get away with turning in a blank return because that would mean no one in the United States would be obliged to file tax returns. And that would destroy the power of the government to tax. It was obvious to me before the trial that the decision had to come out this way against Schiff. After all, the federal judges are paid by checks issued from the U.S. Treasury. The U.S. Treasury is fed mainly by income taxes. If a federal judge ruled in favor of Schiff, he'd be ruling himself out of a paycheck and out of a job. The cards were stacked against Schiff, and even if his argument were legally sound, no federal court could buy it. Schiff now says it makes more sense not to file a return at all. I would agree and go a step further: Unless you insist on being a hero and perhaps a modern-day martyr, don't file and don't keep a high profile. By staying invisible, you have the best chance of not being bothered at all. The I.R.S. as a rule only prosecutes vocal tax rebels. It has never heard of the Constitution or freedom of speech. Of course, modern-day martyrs don't get thrown to the lions any more.

They don't even get tortured physically. They have to spend a lot of money on attorneys, maybe get burglarized by the I.R.S., and eventually get a little rap on the knuckles. The rap on the knuckles is just a small fine and a misdemeanor conviction—at the very worst. There is the possibility that, as the majority of taxpayers go this route, the government may change the law, as King George did, and throw the book at one luckless person to scare the rest. As I have said many times, and now will repeat again—the odds may be one in 300,000 that it will be *you* but before becoming a tax rebel you simply *must* make the decision that it's worth going to jail for. If you are not terrified of prison and not intimidated by the opposition, your odds of emerging unscathed are greatly improved.

Incidentally, if you work at a job for a salary, your taxes are automatically withheld. There is no advantage to not filing if you have a refund coming. So you may want to tell your employer that you have a lot of allowances or dependents. Thus there should be no withholding. It's a misdemeanor (Internal Revenue Code 7205) to file a false withholding certificate—but if you have a sincere belief that you won't have to pay any income tax, it is *not* punishable to file a W-4 form with your employer so that no taxes will be withheld from your salary. Two recent acquittals in this area were in *U.S.* v. *Friend*, U.S. District Court, Arizona, No. 79-13 May 22, 1979 and also in *U.S.* v. *Forinash*, U.S. District Court, South Dakota, No. CR 78-40040-001, April 2, 1979. But don't go wild! One fellow filed a paper indicating that he had 90 children when he had none. This was so blatant that he was convicted of the misdemeanor. But allowances are different from dependent deductions, and you might well be wrong "in good faith" by taking too many allowances that cover things like expected casualty or depreciation losses. In any event, you deserve to know that by merely giving your employer a W-4 form (obtainable at the post office) you can prevent the I.R.S. from getting hold of your money. If you are pretty sure that your income properties or business activities will generate sufficient tax losses to shelter your salary income, do it! Why let the government have the use of your money when you can put it to far better use yourself.

How to Exasperate the I.R.S. and Get Them to Leave You Alone!

The whole I.R.S. is a poorly organized paper processor. If you don't create any paper record of income for them to find, its agents won't know what to do about you. If you create too much paper that doesn't relate to your income, they won't know what to do about you.

First and most important, if you ever get a call on the phone or in person from government agents, DON'T TALK TO THEM! They are the enemy. Don't answer any questions. Don't even give them your name! Say that they must give you their calling card, their identification papers, and the reason they want to see or talk to you. Say that if the person they are seeking agrees to talk to them, you will let them know after discussing it with your lawyer.

If the agent visiting you identifies himself as a special agent, *get a lawyer fast!* And make sure he's a tax-law specialist. Read the book *Criminal Tax Fraud—Representing the Taxpayer Before Trial* (see reading list). It's the book your lawyer will read before he tries to defend you. You might as well know the enemy at the start of any confrontation.

If you decide to give any co-operation at all, do everything by mail. Never answer any questions orally unless you tape-record the conversation. I.R.S. agents will lie about what you said. And never let the I.R.S. see or copy your original documents. Only show them photocopies. The I.R.S. has been known to alter, steal, or "lose" originals.

Don't worry about proving your income. The I.R.S. will have to accept whatever you tell them or find paper evidence of income you didn't report. Just be sure you can support (with receipts) your claimed deductions. Don't get yourself in the bind of having more receipts for cash payments than the income you reported—unless you can prove you started with some savings or extra cash at the beginning of the time period under audit.

At every stage of your dealings with the I.R.S., delay and postpone, Delay and Postpone, DELAY AND POSTPONE! Appeal. Appeal! APPEAL! If you think an agent has been impolite or has overstepped his authority, write to his boss, "The Commissioner, I.R.S., Washington, D.C." Make waves! Send a similar but freshly typed letter of complaint to the regional commissioner at the place where you filed your return. Send similar but freshly typed letters to your congressman, your senator, and the President. Throw in all your complaints about unfair taxes, inflation, and government wastefulness in general. Tell all the politicians you'd never have voted for them if you knew you were supporting a bunch of I.R.S. gestapo agents. Stir up some trouble! If the agent makes a decision or comes to a conclusion that you don't like, write him a brief letter stating that you wish to appeal his decision to the next highest authority. Have a lawyer represent you. If you lose, appeal again. There are several levels within the I.R.S. and several levels of courts once you exhaust the I.R.S. internal procedures. If you are known as a "fighter," the compromises offered to you will get better and better at each level. In the few disputes I have had with taxing bodies, they were always tough as nails at first—but if I had the patience and took a reasonable position supported by some case law, they usually gave up, long before the case got beyond even the first or second appeal. The I.R.S. knows that most of its selected victims start out feeling guilty and paranoid, and as a result I.R.S. agents feel they can get away with anything. But if you know your rights and have done your homework, *you* are David and they are Goliath.

This is a suggestion you might think is unusual—but I strongly urge you to audit (that means sit in on for free) if possible the tax law classes at your local law school. You may be able to do this without signing up or paying for the class. But, if necessary, a class in taxation is worth paying for. A law school course is much better than the H & R Block course, which is essentially how to fill out tax forms, rather than law. But taking an H & R Block or other tax preparation course isn't too bad a way to start. Just as in making money, or any endeavor, *knowledge is power.* If you don't have time for a formal course (often given at night), there are some excellent books and tapes around. I'd recommend my own two tapes—"Pay No Taxes Legally" and "Advanced Tax Avoidance." For reading matter, one of the best all-around reference books is the *Commerce Clearing House Master Tax Guide.* (Write: Commerce Clearing House, 4025 W. Peterson Avenue, Chicago, IL 60646, or visit any law bookstore or business library.) The price of this book is a real bargain: under $10! The trust departments of major banks usually have a supply of the paperback version on hand, and they give it away as a freebie to lawyers and accountants. You might be able to wangle a free one by calling the trust department and passing yourself off as a good customer or a soon-to-be-admitted lawyer. Perhaps the best tax avoidance book ever written, not in most libraries, and available only by mail, is Sylvester on *Tax Planning* (309 pages, hardcover, $24.95; order from Bill "Tycoon" Greene, P.O. Box 810, Mill Valley, Ca 94942 or by phone with VISA/MC 415-383-8264). This is a scholarly book full of unusual tax cases and usable ploys all supported by detailed citations. Lawyers and CPAs love it. So will you.

Why Procrastination and General Obnoxiousness Is a Good Tactic in I.R.S. Dealings

Promotions in the I.R.S. go to agents who make the most money for the "service" in the shortest amount of time. Thus if you prove to be a monumental time waster, they may rapidly tire of fiddling with your case. Here are a few thoughts to get them to leave you alone. Basic I.R.S. techniques involve intimidation, surprise, and trickery. Don't let yourself be threatened, caught unaware, or tricked into releasing information or documents. They believe that everyone is so scared of them that no matter what demands they make, taxpayers will buckle under immediately and give them what they want. At the beginning of any audit, if the I.R.S. agents want to see or check on just one reasonable item, it is probably a good idea to let them see it. But if you feel that they just want to go on a fishing expedition through your records, ask for a formal letter setting forth *what* they want and *why* they want it. Also request a complete transcript of your file under the Freedom of Information Act. That gambit alone will cause delays of two or three months. Remember, an I.R.S. subpoena is not a court order. You *can* refuse to show your records!

Never set foot in an I.R.S. office, and never allow them to set foot in your home or office. If your returns are prepared by an accountant, be sure he returns all paperwork, notes, and your complete file to you after working on your annual returns. Your accountant's file should contain *only* a carbon copy of the tax return he signed as preparer. All worksheets should go back to you. If the accountant won't cooperate, get a new accountant. The I.R.S. can and will seize any client records left with any accountant.

You have an unconditional right to refuse to produce any of your own paperwork. It is up to the I.R.S. to prove that you had an income greater than or deducations less than those reported. They must also prove that you *willfully* did not pay a tax due to get a criminal case going. If they disallow your deductions, you can always *produce* your shoebox full of receipts to support them.

At the risk of being repetitious, I'd like to let you see a sheet printed by some tax-hating Libertarians who also put out a tax newsletter. Some of their ideas seem a little *far out* to me, but have a look. The following pages should be good for future reference—and a few laughs.

101 MORE Tax Gambits
(That the IRS Hates to Face!)

★ Do you have a very large check you want to cash without running it through your bank? Take or mail the endorsed check to the bank the check is drawn on and ask for two cashier's checks each for about half the amount. (Note: US banks are required to notify the IRS anytime you cash a check and withdraw more than $10,000 in currency.) Now go to another branch of the same bank a few days later and break one of the cashier's checks into two smaller ones; repeat with the other large check a few days later. Continue doing this until the final cashier's checks are each under $10,000. A variance of this is to ask for $5000 or so in cash everytime you break a larger cashier's check into a smaller one. Later cash the smaller checks at various branches on different days. You now have cash; the gestapo has no record of the transaction; and the banks have made a few dollars in fees.

★ Problem: How to get $100,000 cash from the sale of your house out of the country and to your foreign bank or investment without letting the US government know what you're doing. The Law: you must fill out a special form anytime you take $5,000 or more cash or checks out of the country on a given day. If you take or send $4,999 out, no form is required. First open up your bank account (by mail if necessary) with a foreign bank with a common sounding name. "Swiss Bank" would raise eyebrows; "XYZ Canadian Bank" would be acceptable. You go to the major banks in your area, purchase cashier's checks under $2,000, scribbling an illegible signature or different name. You then send up to $4,999 per day in cashier's checks to the bank. Of course, your account with the bank with the innocent sounding name is in the Cayman Islands, Bahamas, or Switzerland.

★ Problem: How to let money, valuables, etc. pass to heirs, or to persons who will put it to good use when you die and yet avoid having the tax collector take a large slice. First get everything—property, land, stocks, bonds, savings accounts, bank accounts, etc. out of your name and into the name of some ficticious organization, founda-

tion, or church. For property, sign off on deeds, and have them notarized—the grantee can be inserted later, the same with stocks, etc. Then store everything in a safe deposit box in a city, distant from where you live (preferably in a country with banking secrecy). The box is in the name of some organization, foundation, or church, with you as the signer to get into the box. Ask for an extra signature card to change officers. Sign off on the signature card and either have the heirs sign on or arrange to have the card and a letter of instructions given to them after your death. You arrange for the heirs to recieve the keys by some other means or through another person who does not know where the safe deposit box is. Remember: when the banking collapse comes, the large multinational banks will be the first to fold and getting access to a safe deposit box in them may be difficult. Also larger banks may have a central index of names of persons with access to boxes, thus making it easier for the government to determine where your assets are kept.

★ The IRS can subpoena your bank statements and the front and back of your personal and business checks. Consider closing your bank account.

★ Change banks at least once a year. Do not necessarily pick the bank closest to your office or home.

★ When paying bills, pay with money orders or cashier's checks. Purchase them from different banks. This way you can pick what you want to show the IRS.

★ When someone pays you, try to cash his check at his bank if it is near by. That way your bank will not have a copy of the check to show the IRS if it subpoenas your account.

★ If you must deposit the check to your account, cash the check at your bank, don't deposit it. This makes it much more difficult to locate a copy of it later.

★ If someone pays you on a check drawn on an out of town bank, endorse the check, send it to the bank with in-

structions to prepare a money or cashier's check to you, deduct their fee, and return it in the postage paid envelope. You can then cash the cashier's check at the nearest branch of that bank. The effect is that only you know what your gross income is. The IRS can subpoena your bank records, but they will come up empty.

★ Pay cash when you can. Always get a receipt.

★ Keep a garbage box. Each year photocopy your receipts to tie in to your reported expenses. Then throw the receipts into the garbage box. This will build up after a few years. If you are audited, you can throw the box of receipts at the gestapo auditor. (Be sure to mix up the receipts after he leaves each day; this will cost him an additional 2 hours and .003 ulcers.)

★ Audit tips:
1. The IRS agent must generate a certain dollar volume for each hour of work. If you can run up their time they may want to get rid of you.
2. Keep them on the defensive.
3. NEVER set foot in an IRS office and never allow an agent to enter your office or home.
4. Do everything by mail; keep original documents and send photocopies to the agent.
5. Never provide more than is specifically requested.
6. Don't try to prove your gross income just provide support for your expenses.
7. Appeal to every level; appeal by mail —it costs the IRS more to write a letter than to make a phone call.
8. Remember—they may not give up easily this time, but you can be so obnoxious and persistent that in the future it will cost more to audit you than they can ever hope to recover.
9. EXAMPLE OF A LETTER TO THE INTERNAL REVENUE SERVICE SHOULD THEY EVER CHOOSE TO AUDIT YOU:

Dear Sir:
Regarding your request to audit certain parts of my tax return:
The following request is made under the

Reprinted with permission from FREEDOM TODAY, PO Box 11242, San Francisco, CA 94101, (415)665-3348, membership $24/year.

Federal Privacy Act:

1. Why was this return selected for audit?

The following request is made under the Federal Privacy Act and the Federal Freedom of Information Act:

2. If your answer to number 1. cites a combination of factors, state the limits for each and where my return was placed in relation to the IRS limits.

3. If the decision was made by an IRS employee, state his name and title.

4. Your reqest for information was not clear. I will not provide all my records. However, I will provide you with substantiation for individual items if you will use the descriptive title I used in my return and the respective dollar amount.

5. Will the IRS reimburse me for my costs of photocopying appropriate records for this audit? If you refuse, state the statute under which you refuse.

6. Will the IRS reimburse me for the services of a bookkeeper, accountant, or attorney to comply with your audit requests? If not, cite the apppropriate statutes.

Sincerely,
/s/

(You should be able to take up to two yrs. before they can finally assess you.)

★ Always tape record all conversations with the gestapo, but tell them first. This upsets them.

★ When they call, say, "I do everything by mail; send me a letter." If a phone conversation takes over 10 seconds, they have the upper hand. REPEAT: "Send me a letter; I do everything by mail." and hang up.

★ Sovereign Immunity is the doctrine that the State is sovereign and you cannot sue it without its consent. Try refusing to provide the IRS any information until the auditor waives any defenses of sovereign immunity and consents to being sued if he commits any tortious act. Also insist that the US Attorney waive sovereign immunity for the US Government.

★ Remember—IRS agents have to generate at least $100 per hour in additional taxes to justify their work. If you're difficult, they will go after the easy pickings (i.e. other taxpayers) first to meet their "quota".

★ The IRS is required to give you notice if they issue an administrative summons for your bank records to your bank. You can delay this for many months by seeking an injunction from the Federal Court. An example of the pleading is available from Citizens Courtroom Workshop, 110 West C St., Suite 1010, San Diego, CA 92101. The cost is $10.

★ What if the IRS wants to ask you questions about your tax return? If you were a bank robber or other criminal you could ask the government to contact all government agencies to see if your telephone were being bugged (18 USC 3504). It is arguable that it would apply in a civil case as well. They MUST tell you if your telephone is bugged before you are required to give any information. There's another year down the drain. Only a masochistic gestapo agent would continue after you. Copies of the petition/pleading are available for $10, also from Citizens Courtroom Workshop.

★ Buy and read Harry Brown's book, Complete Guide To Swiss Banks.

★ Dark red check paper is difficult to distinguish from ink when microfilmed.

★ Commercial Light Blue Illustrator Non-reproducing Very Fine pen will not reproduce on microfilm copies of checks. (Available at art supply stores.)

★ Whenever you open a new bank account, you are always asked for a banking reference. A notation is made on your signature card of this information. Your new signature is sent to your old bank for comparison and return. Your OLD bank also makes a notation on your old signature card referencing the bank at which you are opening your new account. The government can subpoena your old bank signature card and follow you to your new bank. Therefore, when the new account clerk asks you where you bank now or banked previously, just say,"I don't have a bank account." You will get a funny look, then a smile as the clerk reaches for your cash to open the new account. No one turns down new business.

★ If you keep a safe deposit box, don't keep it in the bank you do business with. Don't even keep it near your house or office. As an added precaution, keep the box under the name of some fictitious organization or business

with your signature as the only signer.

★ If a bureaucrat calls you asking to look at your books for an audit, stall, stall, stall. The longer you stall, the less likely you will finally get audited. If you're assessed, you don't pay. You also save lawyer and accountant fees. Common stalling techniques:

1. Don't answer any letters asking for records or appearances—wait for a bureaucrat to call. (2 month delay.)

2. When he calls, tell him "Please put your request in writing, listing what documents you want." Don't let him give them to you over the phone. (1 month delay.)

3. Ignore subsequent letters until he calls again. (1 month delay.)

4. When he calls again, say that you haven't had time but you will start to accumulate them. Use some variation of this line for the next six months: e.g. out of town on vacation or business; been sick; records must be in the attic or in storage, still looking for them; swamped with business; etc. Be strong, don't be intimidated—stall for a full six months.

5. Next, bring your accountant or attorney in if you are willing to pay their fees—explain that their job is to stall, stall, stall. You may have to explain to them how to stall; some CPA's never do understand that they do a better service for their client by stalling than by assembling all the records. Insist that the accountant or attorney stall for a full 4 months or more. Give them copies of items 1. thru 4. above.

6. If necessary have the attorney or accountant switch handling the bureaucrat over to the other, e.g. your attorney finally tells the bureaucrat that he doesn't have time or that you are delinquent in paying him and he can do no more work until he's paid. When the bureaucrat calls you, tell him your accountant is now handling everything and to call HIM. (3 months.)

7. Another stall: have your accountant turn everything over to another accountant not in his office. (4 months.)

8. After the stalls, start with the letters to inquire why you are being audited, the bureaucrat has now used up 15 hours of his direct time over a 2 year period; he will now probably misplace your file back in central files. NEVER TELEPHONE A BUREAUCRAT to find out what's happened to him or when he's coming out. WOOPS!—The Statute of Limitations just expired on your case. No bureaucrat is interested in you any longer.

There is no accountant-client privilege. The I.R.S. may not look at any of your papers in your possession.

Phantom Returns

A "phantom return" is a fictitious return filed by a fictitious person. To do a maximum damage to the I.R.S., it should request a reasonable refund of between $500 and $5,000.

For our 102nd tax gambit, let's look at the possibilities of the "phantom return." If the 100,000 readers of this book each filed 10 phantom returns, the I.R.S., sent off on a million wild goose chases, would be brought to its knees in a single year. I can't advise you to do this because it's illegal, and I might be found guilty of some sort of conspiracy, so I will talk only of the possibilities revealed to me by my secret spy friend within the bowels of the I.R.S. Criminal Investigation Division.

The internal policy of the IRS is this: On receipt of any average-looking tax return that is mathematically accurate, if a refund is requested the I.R.S. will *refund the amount requested immediately.* They do not verify the authenticity of the attached W-2 forms (showing the amounts withheld).

Armed with this valuable and still current knowledge, a few dozen inmates at a high-security federal prison filed bogus tax returns with bogus W-2 forms, using their correct names. Within a few days, their refund checks arrived. They used the funds to hire a top-notch lawyer. He got some of them out. The whole caper was not discovered until many years later when hundreds of prisoners had so many U.S. Treasury tax refund checks that an employee at the prison store got suspicious, checked further, and learned that the cons had bilked Uncle Sam to the tune of a million dollars or

more. The lawyer who told me the story said that in his opinion, the U.S. Treasury had to be losing at least a billion dollars a year from this gambit alone.

When I asked why the government didn't check W-2 forms against the originals filed by the employers, I got an answer that nearly floored me: Forms filed by employers, banks, and other payers of income and dividends—the forms that are supposed to be cross checked against the income we report—the forms that make us believe Big Brother is watching us—these forms are routinely fed into *giant paper shredders.* Only in rare instances are a few pulled at random and spot checked. The government is thus *unable* to verify whether most people claiming refunds are entitled to them. As a result, all refund claims are paid.

When the "convict story" leaked out to the press and was reported in a few antiestablishment papers, the I.R.S. indicated that they were instituting special secret procedures to detect those situations. But I checked recently, and my lawyer friend said that his convict clients were still applying for and getting tax refunds. But now the refunds were being

Possibly a billion a year is paid out by the U.S. Treasury to convicts and others who file phantom returns in order to get "refunds" of taxes never paid.

mailed to friends on the "outside," only because prison officials were on the lookout for tax refund checks in convict mail. Presumably the secret procedures involved telling the wardens of federal prisons to get suspicious if inmates spend over $50,000 at the company store.

That leads us to what you can do.

Being a very conservative and honest fellow, I'd never try to collect a tax refund that wasn't honestly due me. That would be stealing. But I think it would be kind of fun to help the I.R.S. get deeper into the morass from which there is no exit. Now I'm not suggesting that you file 10 phantom returns with made up names, addresses, social security numbers, employers, etc. And I'm not suggesting that you have even more fun by filing phantom returns for *really* big amounts, like $15,000 or more, using the names and addresses of people you are not too fond of ...

But if you did play a dirty trick like that, you can be sure that the already overworked I.R.S. investigators would start to go crazy. If the I.R.S. never tried to get back the refund, they would now have on the computer a taxpayer who failed to file in the following year. Out go the collectors. No such person. No such address. Or if one of your most unfavorite people got and cashed a refund check—imagine the results of an investigation into the affairs of a guy who filed *two* tax returns in one year—one of them totally bogus.

Someone with access to a computer, word processor, or even an automatic memory typewriter like the one I'm using could prepare a reasonable-looking return, and then retype it a hundred times, each time changing a digit of the Social Security number, a digit of the address, an initial in the name. Even one person working with modern equipment for just a day could strain the resources of the I.R.S. to the breaking point. And what would the Phantom have to lose? With no real malicious intent to make any money on the deal and all the best motives—there isn't much risk. If you were caught, the news media would have a field day and most judges would have a good laugh and treat you as a prankster. Another misdemeanor!

And just imagine a bunch of bureaucrats faced with the problem of cross-checking millions of returns and false leads where most of the material needed to do the job has been eaten by the giant shredders. Oh, the frustration you could reap!

Now I wouldn't tell anyone to do such a thing. I might go to the pokey myself if I did. But I certainly wish that a Phantom or two, or ten, or a thousand would show their outrage. Just as the fabled Captain Krunch discovered that by blowing into a crackerjack whistle he could tie up all the long-distance circuits in Los Angeles, the Phantom Tax Return Filer could become a folk hero. Three years after the gambit, he could write his memoirs. With prosecution barred by the statute of limitations, you could end up like Captain Krunch—he was hired by the Telephone Company at an exorbitant salary just to keep him out of Ma Bell's hair. Maybe the I.R.S. vampires would pay you $90,000 a year to stay away from your typewriter. Is it inconceivable? Not when our government pays lots of people not to do things. Farmers get billions not to farm. The unemployed get billions not to work. Why shouldn't you get something for not filing phantom returns?

Enough of phantasy, fun, and phantoms. Back to reality!

*Some people have good times sending the I.R.S.
on wild goose chases.*

28.
Cashing and Stashing Your Chips

Sooner or later, you'll want to cash in your chips. Conventional advice on cashing in your chips is called "estate planning," and that is all about avoiding taxes on your estate when you die. Nobody talks about cashing in your chips *before* you die, when you can still enjoy them. And those estate planners seldom mention one of my plans—the Three-Flag Technique—that lets you fade away taking your estate with you. Who said you couldn't take it with you? You can and you will!

After you have made your real estate millions during the next few years, you should cash in your chips gradually. Sell an occasional property when your depreciation from other deals amply shelters the cash. Or you can withdraw cash annually by refinancing properties you already own. These two moves should provide much more than the cash you need to live on. A part of what you draw out of real estate should be invested in what I call "pleasurable diversification," prefer-ably abroad. I say "abroad" because, while not a prophet of doom, I feel there is a substantial chance that personal prob-lems or political changes could have very negative conse-quences for us in America.

Our present socialist-tending "system" constantly erodes our personal freedoms. The freedom to make, keep, and dispose of money we have earned is more and more lim-ited. Because of the probabilities, in my opinion one should regularly cash in part of the chips, long before the casino cashier closes down. I use the gambling analogy because the only technique in gambling that seems to work for me is the pocketing of a portion of each winning bet and taking those winnings totally out of the game. The real estate business in the United States is much like gambling. The game is very hot now. Everybody is winning. But if you keep all your winnings riding on new bets, in the same game it's only a matter of time before you lose it all. There are two reasons you will forfeit all your chips in gambling or in real estate: (1) A string of bad debts as the table cools off; and (2) the casino changes the rules, making it impossible to quit as a winner.

A series of bad bets or investments is easy for anyone who's been around a while to visualize. Cost overruns, law-suits, bad bets, and generally unexpected predicaments take their toll. When I made my first real estate investments in California, I tried to buy secluded cabin-type properties perched high on hilltops or ridges. They were often reached by dirt roads—preferably in a secluded grove of redwood trees, with creek, sundeck, and magnificent view. My theory was that the rarity and Thoreau-like quality of these proper-ties would command very high rents. It worked out fine for several months. I had 100 percent occupancy in my dozen cabins. That sort of full occupancy was absolutely necessary, because with the big mortgages I was supporting, anything less than unusually high rents with 100 percent occupancy wouldn't have provided enough cash to service the loans and pay expenses. Because of excellent and secluded locations, these cabins were not accessible to public transportation and could only be reached by car. Who would have predicted (before it happened) the immediate obsolescence of the automobile when the Arabs embargoed oil exports in retaliation for our helping Israel? And if you had predicted that situation, would you have thought that four of my tenants would leave and that there would be no market at all for secluded rental properties? But that's exactly what happened. For a time there were four-hour waits for gas, and you could only buy three gallons at a time. Tenants who had to commute long distances to work by car just couldn't make it. They had to move out of my places. My loans went into default. At the time I considered selling off one of the properties to raise enough cash to keep the rest afloat. But there was no market at a price that would have yielded any more than the exact amount of the loans.

With hindsight, it is easy to say that that situation couldn't last forever. But at the time we didn't know that gas rationing wouldn't be a permanent thing. It was pretty hairy, and the only thing that saved the Bill Greene infant empire was an end to the embargo a few weeks after it began. I hung on to all my properties, not because of any crystal ball, but only because I couldn't sell them. There were no buyers. I should have bought more property for no money down at bargain prices when everybody else was panicking, but I had neither the nerve nor the money to support unrentable properties until things got back to normal. The point is, no matter how smart you think you are, totally unpredictable things can happen—and *will* happen. Your best-laid financial plans can be thrown into a complete disarray. That is why you need diversification and reserve.

Diversification should be fun! You have been working for financial freedom. After a few years, you have it. The only problem then is to discover what turns you on. One friend of mine (male obviously), bought a modeling agency in Paris. It came with its own building containing what the French all a *chic penthouse*. The agency also brought him in contact with a lot of very chic women. Now he spends increasingly large amounts of time in his Paris digs—doing whatever it is that bachelors who own modeling agencies do. He tells me he has finally found happiness. The travel to and from Paris and all related costs of staying happy are deductible as ordinary and necessary business expenses.

Another lady I knew was always interested in art history and, between you and me, social climbing. She took her rather substantial real estate profits and two years ago remodeled a historic castle in southern France, near Geneva. Some of her chips went into an inventory of old master paintings and drawings. She is phasing out of American real estate and now spends her time cavorting with new jet set friends she met in her Monte Carlo and Geneva art galleries. For her, dealing in fine arts was tax deductible happiness.

A foreign business with a small return on investment, high pleasure quotient, and fiscal privacy is what turns me on. I'd like to own the Club Mediterranean in Tahiti—or a similar resort in the Caribbean. But, whatever you do with your chips, if it's outside of the United States it can be placed beyond the reach of the taxman and other predators as well. Most noncommunist foreign countries permit a far greater degree of financial privacy than is common in America.

Generally, foreign holdings should not be registered in your own name or ascertainable from any public records. This is accomplished by having your real property held in the name of a reliable local law firm, a bank, or a corporation set up by you. Corporate shares and other securities in Europe are typically in "bearer" form so that no outsider or snooper can ever ascertain with certainty who owns what.

Until you decide what foreign investments appeal to you, consider buying gold coins and storing them in a safe-deposit box in a traditionally neutral country. There is no reporting requirement on your income tax return for stashes of valuable coins. They tend to rise in dollar value with inflation—remaining constant in their purchasing power. By using borrowed dollars to acquire gold coins, you can get the same benefits of leveraged investment in real estate. Gold has a low pleasure quotient, however, and doesn't produce any income to pay interest charges while you hold it.

Another temporary place for money is a bank account in a foreign "hard" currency. Unlike gold, you don't have to physically collect it when you need it—but you can write a check and cash it anywhere in the world your bank has a branch or correspondent.

When secret foreign bank accounts are mentioned, tax evasion is what many people think of first.

Naturally, if the U.S. government does not know that you have 20,000 Swiss francs ($10,000) deposited in a savings account in Zurich, Switzerland, they can't tax the 5 percent or approximately $500 per year interest that this account pays you.* But tax avoidance is not a reason to open an account abroad. Good real estate investments in the United States should enable you to make money both legally and tax free. The 5 percent interest you can get on a Swiss savings account doesn't amount to much. But the fact that Swiss francs are not depreciating as fast as the dollar allows you to store a greater amount of purchasing power than if you kept your money in dollars.

Keeping a foreign vacation home in Canada, Mexico, or the Caribbean, stocked with a year's worth of provisions, and a safe full of gold and silver coins, won't help you evade taxes, but can help ensure that the good times aren't over for you in the event of problems at home. Thus, having fun in

---

*Although as mentioned in another chapter, foreign currency credits, until converted back into dollars, probably do not constitute taxable income in any event. I.R.S. regulations cover corporations and traders in foreign currency—but an individual, in my opinion, is in a different category.

foreign playgrounds and preserving the economic freedom you have worked for, not tax evasion or profit, is the reason for cashing in some of your chips early and moving them abroad. Quick-changing regulatory or tax systems and novel legal theories could make a self-sufficient professional person poor in a matter of days. In view of these uncertainties, each responsible person owes it to himself and his family to divert (as soon as he can afford it) enough assets to establish and support himself in a different part of the world. Of course, my rule is that you should regularly enjoy your second-life retreat or foreign vacation home once you've established it. That's what I mean by cashing in your chips and taking them with you.

Once you are independently wealthy, your money or assets abroad do not have to earn the maximum return, or any return at all. Secret foreign holdings or even domestic diversification, can be considered merely *insurance* against bad times we hope won't materialize. We don't have to go back to Nazi Germany to recall situations where a safe-deposit box full of gold coins in Switzerland meant the difference between life and death. During the Nazi period, if an "enemy of the German Reich" already owned property in the United States, he might get a resident's permit. He lived. Without assets outside Germany—or enough coins to bribe his way out—he died.

A similar situation happened in Lebanon only recently. When I visited Beirut in 1969, the town seemed more prosperous than Miami Beach. Whites, blacks, Christians, Moslems, and Jews, rich and poor, seemed to be getting along well. The Lebanese government was committed to *de facto* neutrality—staying out of the frequent wars the rest of the area kept waging against Israel. Beirut was like a little bit of America, an oasis of toleration, capitalism, and general prosperity, with lots of people like you and me owning rental properties, motels, and doing very well, thank you. All at once some poor slobs with guns, who had always been out of sight and out of mind, broke out of Palestinian refugee camps. Smoldering discontent turned into gunfire and bombs. *Poof!*—it was all over. The good life for the Lebanese middle class ended in a few days. Everybody's property was bombed and burned. Insurance companies went bankrupt. The banking system broke down. The Lebanese pound, which had been touted as one of the strongest currencies in the world, became worthless. Many Lebanese had friends, homes, and investments in Paris, London, and New York. They moved and left the fanatics to kill each other. And 300,000 civilians who couldn't leave were killed in the cross-fire.

The same thing happened before that in Cuba. To a lesser extent, it happened in 1976 in Mexico when the peso was drastically revalued downwards. A rich Mexican creditor became a poor Mexican overnight.

Don't make the mistake of thinking that the United States is a "bastion of capitalism." Remember how a few kooks in the Symbionese Liberation Army paralyzed California with only half a dozen terrorists. Imagine what would happen if all the American radical left groups (or, for that matter, the crazies of the far right), with thousands of adherents, got organized and decided to change things by force in the United States. Things *would* change. In any civil strife, almost *everybody* with political consciousness, property, reputation, or even humanitarian impulses eventually gets hurt. The valued citizen of yesterday becomes the refugee, the human garbage of tomorrow. It could happen in America! Today the creditor class *is* being wiped out by taxes and inflation. Landlords in New York have been ruined by rent controls. Even in good times, there is a treacherous world out there.

Now for some more gloom! The possibility of marital problems is another very good reason to have some foreign assets. Perhaps you are living in conjugal bliss right now. But, statistically, the odds are 75 percent that you won't be in 10 or 20 years. You may wake up one morning to find that your bank accounts are tied up by a court order, your busi-

A secret stash of gold coins, stamps, silver, diamonds,
and strong foreign currency is immune from the grabby
hands of ex-wives, Robin Hood judges, or the I.R.S.,
not "legally"—just practically!

ness property is being operated by a receiver, and your spouse is living with her new divorce lawyer in *your house.* The cost of a divorce could send you to a basement apartment with junkies shooting up inside your foul-smelling hallway. *Poverty!* All you have worked for destroyed!

Pretty heavy, eh? How nice it would be to have a secret reserve fund across the border and be able to tell your wife's lawyer, "Take her. Take the heavily mortgaged real estate. Take it all, and God love you, you got what you deserve." You then take your favorite kids and join your money in Tahiti where a little grass shack and a little brown French girl are waiting at the Club Med.

Lawsuits are brought every day in the United States. All the liability insurance in the world will not save you from serious financial difficulties if a plaintiff proves that something you did was *intentional* (uninsurable) or if your insurance company weasels out, as they did on me once.

Let me tell you the story. Horace once rented an apartment from me. He didn't say anything about plans to set up a dentist's chair and do fillings in his front room. If he had told me, I probably wouldn't have cared as long as he paid the rent on time and as long as the drilling didn't bother the neighbors. But I didn't have a hint about Horace's dentist business. Being insured by a $3 million "All-Risk" liability policy, I thought it would cover me against "all" risks, just as the title said. As you probably guessed, the dentist pulled a few wrong teeth (or at least a patient claimed he did). A malpractice suit for $2 million was brought against Horace. He turned out to have no license, no money, and certainly no insurance of his own. Under a novel legal theory, I, as owner of the building, was also sued for negligently renting a dentist's office to an unlicensed quack.

Notifying my insurance company to defend me was easy. But their letter to me was a surprise:

Dear Mr. Greene,

We regret to inform you that your policy covers you for all risks arising out of your ownership and operation of *residential* property, but specifically *excludes* liability for persons claiming damages for injuries arising out of *commercial or professional* use of the premises. Accordingly, we decline to defend you against this claim, for which you are not insured.

(Signed) Your friends at_____

Thanks a lot!

The case cost a bundle in attorney's fees. It was settled out of court by me paying another bundle. Who'd have thought that I'd be liable for a tenant I didn't know was an amateur dentist, pulling the wrong teeth from a patient I'd never heard of? Although I later learned I could have obtained a "Waiver of the commercial or professional exclusion" at nominal cost, that information came $20,000 too late.

The point is that there seems to be no way of completely protecting yourself from ruinous lawsuits that could cost every penny you have. The private insurance that comes from having a secret stash is the best insurance I can think of. In case you are still not convinced that there is no protection against lawsuits in which the awards have gone out of sight and the rules keep changing, let me tell you the story of actor Lee Marvin.

Marvin knew that wives in California have a way of stripping their husbands of cars, houses, bank accounts, and everything else when they want to go off with a new boyfriend. So Marvin didn't get married. He had girlfriends. When he broke up with one of them, she sued for divorce. Her theory was that, since it is no longer fashionable in California to get married, the 2 million women living in sin should get the same divorce rights as wives. Decision: The girlfriend gets it.* Good-bye Marvin's money. Except perhaps for his secret Swiss bank account!

Then there may be economic difficulties of a short-term nature. Assume you don't get sued. You and your spouse are happy. There is no revolution. But you are in a real estate deal where you bought a bargain property with a short-term loan. You had expected to borrow long term from another lender, but money all of a sudden, unexpectedly, got tight. Stocks you owned went down at the same time. You know if you hold on it will all work out eventually, but for the moment you need $10,000 fast to keep things afloat. What a relief it can be to have your foreign bank issue a letter of credit or make a loan secured by your secret stash. It bails you out of troubles at home. Your foreign assets provide financial strength to be held in reserve for any emergency.

Troubles with the I.R.S. may well put you in the hole for crushing legal fees, even if you are completely innocent of everything they accuse you of. Although the risks of actually going to jail for tax evasion are minimal, the I.R.S. has awesome power to ruin you while your case grinds through the bureaucratic mazes. This was discovered by many political enemies of the Nixon Administration. Let us assume that

_____
*As of 1979, the Marvin case was modified, and the girlfriend was limited to a "moderate" rehabilitation allowance of over $100,000!

you did nothing illegal and were not a political target. But an ex-employee or competitor, jealous of your success, files a false "tip" with the I.R.S. The tipster says you have evaded taxes on gambling ventures. That "evidence" or false tip is enough to send armed I.R.S. special agents swarming over your office books and your bank accounts. They interview ex-wives, business associates, employees, and everyone you ever wrote a check to or called on the telephone. They speak with all your friends, relatives, competitors, colleagues, and enemies. With their questions, affidavits, summonses, badges, and guns, they thoroughly intimidate *everyone* you know. They ask about your activities in gambling, prostitution, and dope, and throw in murder and extortion for good measure—as if they were proven facts. Within a few weeks, only your bravest and truest friends have anything more to do with you. This intimidation is exactly what happened to me when the I.R.S. learned that I planned to publish this book.

Wouldn't a coffee plantation in Brazil be nice? Even if you never used it, if the flak got too thick or the game got too rough, a safe haven—a home away from home—might be just the place to vacation and let things cool off. Brazil, Switzerland, and a number of other countries feel that the

The prudent businessperson will keep his own bank or at least some money abroad for a "rainy day."

American I.R.S. is far too heavy-handed. They will not extradite accused tax evaders, as a matter of policy. Tax evasion is not considered a crime in most civilized countries, but rather a form of political protest.

If there are problems at home, a warm and friendly welcome that you've arranged for in advance will give you many happy returns.

29.
Last
of the
Honest
Taxpayers

Contrary to I.R.S. news releases, the last "honest taxpayer" vanished from America some time during the Nixon era, when it was disclosed that the Internal Revenue Service was used to harass and intimidate the political enemies of that administration. Enemies were defined as those movie actors, celebrities, or just plain folks whom Nixon, his F.B.I. director, or his aides considered a threat to society. It was discovered by the politicians that the tax laws were such an incomprehensible morass that virtually any citizen could be arbitrarily audited, accused of tax fraud, and financially ruined, regardless of how hard he tried to be an "honest taxpayer." And if John A. Citizen could be selected for arbitrary enforcement procedure, why bother trying to be honest? This attitude was reinforced by regular disclosures that the leading political figures of our day through the use of legally allowable gimmicks paid no taxes whatsoever. Ronald Reagan (cattle-breeding programs), Jimmy Carter (peanut warehouses), or Richard Nixon (outright fraud), paid no income taxes at all, even though their publicly funded salaries and allowances ran to six figures. Further disclosures during the 1970s indicated that average senators or congressmen and many state legislators enjoyed effective incomes of up to half a million dollars a year in salaries, benefits, and fringes. But a large number of them also paid no taxes whatsoever. Then there were the disclosures that dozens of very rich people who made over $1 million a year legally paid no income taxes. Finally, a number of university professors began to focus on the "subterranean economy." Through careful, scholarly economic analysis, they proved what many of us had suspected all along: That at least 1 out of 10 people got off the government computer entirely by having no bank accounts and insisting on cash payments for the services they performed as independent contractors or small-time wheeler-dealers. Members of the subterranean economy paid no taxes. If you add to them the million or so "tax rebels" who file blank returns, then you can no longer accept the myth pushed by the I.R.S. that the United States is a nation of happy and honest taxpayers. Not with 20 million nonfilers! Voluntary compliance has been dead for years. The facts seem to indicate that, today, everybody who can cheat on their income tax *does* cheat. The only people who pay "their share" (which turns out to be *far more* than their share) are the poor wage slaves who work for a living. They find that the greater part of their earnings are automatically deducted for Social Security, unemployment insurance, state, federal, local property taxes, and hundreds of other taxes. Is any relief in sight for them? How has the government rewarded these good citizens? It devalues the dollar with a planned inflation, literally robbing the wage earners of their stored sweat. The money that you sweated for, earned, and saved is eroded at the rate of 10 to 20 percent or more each year by inflation. The government talked about stopping inflation. But how they cause inflation in areas clearly controlled by them can be seen from the increasing cost of postage. The cost of mailing a first-class letter has been increasing at an increasing rate—outpacing inflation. Did greedy businessmen or union leaders do that? No! State and local taxes have been increasing for a decade at a *compounded* rate of over 16 percent per year. Thus is it any wonder at all that more and more people are dropping out to join the subterranean economy and pay no taxes. Others achieve the same result by becoming tax rebels. Many of the wealthy and productive—a trickle now becoming a flood—are leaving the country entirely! Some 250,000 of our best people emigrate each year to seek tax relief and more fairness in some other country. It certainly is no wonder that when I give my tax avoidance lectures I get a turnout of thousands of people from a small ad. Everybody is sick to death of confiscatory taxes that keep going up and that are unfairly and selectively enforced. People don't want government money squandered on programs that almost nobody needs or wants. But when we elect politicians like Carter who call the tax system a "disgrace to the human race," they proceed to complicate the tax code even more.

There is nothing I'd like better than to be able to identify with a government that I feel shares my concerns for providing a land of opportunity where the American dream, financial independence (through the acquisition of wealth and property), and the making of honest business profits was once again regarded as a desirable thing; a government that would stimulate our free enterprise system instead of forcing every small business to keep half its personnel occupied just coping with government red tape and taxes. We all are working Monday through Thursday, either paying taxes or filling out unnecessary forms forced on us by unnecessary people.

To such a government, I'd be delighted to pay a straight 10 or even 20 percent of everything I earned with no deductions, no incentives, no loopholes. I'd be happy to work every Monday for an honest government, if I could work Tuesday through Friday for myself. But, the other way around—the way it is now—four days out of five are either spent working for the government to pay taxes or are wasted by me with lawyers and accountants just in unproductive coping—trying to figure out how taxes can be legally avoided or how government giveaway programs can be best used. I don't like it, and I don't think anyone else does. To be forced into such a kowtow position vis-à-vis government is distasteful. Governments should tax or burden all people equally. Why should the welfare recipient pimp in New York City be able to drive a Rolls Royce, collect cash from his "girls," and spend his tax-free days lolling and selling heroin at a sidewalk cafe any more than the multimillionaire or the politician? He too should work one day a week for the government. And if someone doesn't pay money taxes, maybe there should be the opportunity to give one day per week of personal useful services in lieu of taxes. I am saying that, if there is to be any meaningful tax reform, everybody without exception should do their part, and that means agreeing on something like a 10 percent across-the-board tax for everyone, with no exceptions. Those who don't earn enough money to pay any tax, or don't want to pay, should contribute to their country with services. Taxes today are grossly unfair for the middle-class working stiff, who has had all the burdens forced on him. Government lets off the unemployed classes entirely. Why should someone get welfare or aid to dependent children, etc. with no contribution?

The system clearly is unfair and needs reform. There seems to be no way for the average citizen to do anything about it, even if he sincerely believes, as I do, that there is nothing wrong with paying a reasonable amount of tax that will be used to promote the legitimate purposes of government: the protection of life, liberty, and property rights, as guaranteed by the Constitution. I am fed up with supporting vast bureaucracies.

The billion-dollar Drug Enforcement Administration guarantees solutions worse than the problems. Pot smokers were hurting no one, except perhaps themselves, but now lethal paraquat sprayed on Mexican marijuana plants threatens to poison hundreds of thousands of young Americans, to poison the land, and to poison Mexican tomatoes that we buy at a local grocery store. Personally, I feel if an adult wants to smoke pot, or for that matter, drink Drano, they should perhaps be warned of the dangers but then be allowed maximum freedom to drink or smoke their way into oblivion. In other words, I for one, do not want my tax money spent on poisoning my kids with paraquat, supporting hundreds of thousands of undercover agents, policemen, judges, jailers, and so on. Over the last 20 years, the multibillion dollar antidrug program has managed to cut off 5 or 10 percent of the drug traffic while over 90 percent gets through. I say, make it and every other "victimless crime" legal. Tax dope along with alcohol and tobacco and make it a revenue producer instead of a bottomless pit for consuming our national wealth.

Don't we learn anything from the past? During Prohibition, the illegality of booze made it more attractive and probably increased consumption. People who wanted to get a drink got their alcohol one way or another. But there was more death and poisoning from bad bathtub gin. The same is true of cocaine, heroin, and pot today. Those who want to try it will get it. It may be adulterated and filthy and illegal, but they will get it and use it because that's the way people are and always have been. If you want more promiscuity, make sex illegal! Make any popular activity illegal and you'll get more, not less of it. A few hundred years ago, banning coffee shops in Vienna turned that city into the coffee-brewing capital of Europe. I don't want my tax money used to support an army of public servants devoted to preventing other people from having what they regard as a good time, even for their "own good." It's a losing battle!

Then there is the new Department of Energy. What a joke! Take a bunch of schoolboys and schoolgirls out of their college teaching jobs. Be sure their experience in the real world is limited to managing their lunch money. Make sure that few, if any, have ever met a payroll or run any sort of business. Then give them *more tax money than the combined profits of every oil company in America* with the job of regulating the oil companies "in the public interest." And people wonder why gas lines form and prices triple. What has the government accomplished? It has forced the oil companies to divert resources from producing and distributing oil into coping with federal functionaries on a one-to-one basis. After services are disrupted and prices are forced to be much higher than they need to be, the government will hit the oil companies with an excess profits tax that will divert more money away from producing energy. Where will the money go? To hire more *federales* to disrupt the economy even further. The Department of Energy doesn't produce a drop of oil—but it spends more than oil company profits to raise prices and disrupt normal flows. I get angry over conditions like that!

I am sure that you have your own particular gripe. I am sure that you know of some idiotic government program. Why doesn't someone *do something?* You elect a candidate, and the next thing you know they are co-opted by the system. Taxes get higher, regulation gets worse, government spending increases. The country continues its slide downhill.

Why?

The eternal paradox, coming up, will explain it.

30.
The
Eternal
Paradox

Although I have been ranting and railing about those bad politicians in the state capital and in Washington, D.C., the truth of the matter is that they are people very much like us. And people like us, the vast majority of Americans, have many moral issues and other ideas we agree on.

We believe that old people, sick people, young mothers, the mentally or physically disabled should not be allowed to starve to death as they do in India.

We are proud that when we visit a foreign country, our embassy is the biggest and best in town. It's *nice* that Americans were first on the moon and it would be just swell if we had the best space program.

Nobody wants a bunch of dope addicts shooting heroin in hallways and then burglarizing our homes to get the money to support their habit.

We resent the Arabs, Ralph Nader, and the oil companies, (or whoever) making our cars so expensive to drive. And we certainly like open spaces, clean air, and attractive public buildings.

As a result of these and many other generally accepted beliefs, we are willing to have a government restrict our freedom "for our own good," and we are willing to pay taxes. Whenever a poll is taken and people are asked if they are in favor of free public libraries, free parks, old age pensions, free public schools, medical assistance, and so on—the vast majority are in favor. We also, for the most part, support space exploration, and we feel that something should be done about drug abuse. We are against price gouging by the oil companies, and all the other problems facing an urbanized, complex, and very rich society.

If you were elected to public office without any particular training in the Libertarian way of solving problems *by leaving them alone,* you might very well have the belief that almost all problems can best be solved by government intervention, government regulation, and government takeovers of industries that are not performing as well as they might be. If, after government intervention things got worse instead of better, you probably would believe in good faith that the solution was *more* regulation, *more* tax money, or *more* diversion of control from the private to the public sector.

Let's look at a few homely little examples.

Years ago in a certain U.S. city there was a tragedy. Several children burned to death in the home of a babysitter who (although she should have been watching the children) neglected her charges. There was a fire and they burned to death. The newspapers and others clamored for a law. Laws were passed. Licenses were needed to offer childcare. Special training and examinations were needed to get the license. A sprinkler system was required. If anything went wrong at other preschools after that, new laws were passed. A kid fell down some stairs. Thereafter babysitters had to do their thing only on ground floors with no steps in their homes. The amount and type of food, toys, activities were all regulated down to the most minute detail. Charges were regulated and limited, and fines imposed if there were any deviations. Eventually there were no childcare facilities in the city. They had been regulated out of existence. Because there was a "need," daycare centers costing much more than private facilities were established at tax-supported facilities. Mothers who took their children there had many complaints—but there were no alternatives. Taxpayers grumbled a little, but the facilities only added half a percentage point to their property tax. Who could be against children? Everyone accepts the status quo.

What's the point?

The point is that government, as usual, went too far.

Trying to solve a problem, the city in question made it impossible for a mother to entrust her children to an individual of her own choosing. The city, responding to thousands of pressures like this, went from a budget of under $1 million twenty years ago, to $60 million today. It went from being a minor tax collector to the point where 5 percent is added on to the price of every hotel and motel room in the city, and 25 percent is tacked on to every parking bill, not to mention several hundred other new taxes on everything except breathing. The city is now contemplating its own income tax on wage earners within the city—to be able to provide "needed services." Those taxes just sneak up on you— and all for very good purposes!

The same thing is true at the federal level. Needs will always expand to soak up available funds. Millions and millions of dollars were appropriated to provide assistance to the Cuban and Vietnamese refugees as they arrived in the United States. Who could refuse to vote them a paltry few million?

But when your ancestors arrived at Plymouth Rock to face a cold and hostile environment, was there a social worker there to greet them? When Columbus landed, did the Arawaks appropriate 10 tons of wampum and put him on welfare until he could get "adjusted"? When the millions and

401

Mr. Columbus, let me welcome you to America!
Hilda Rainwater, your social worker will arrange for your
language lessons and weekly classes in "social adjustment."
Pick up your unemployment check at tribe headquarters
every Thursday. After six months, you qualify for welfare
benefits, Medicare, and Social Security.

millions of poor Germans, Jews, Irish, and Polish arrived from 1895 to 1910, there was *no* welfare. There were *no* social services. *None were expected.* But people got along. They worked. They showed some of the pioneer spirit that made this country great. They prospered!

That doesn't happen as much any more.

America began to follow postwar England down the tubes with lower productivity, lower standards of living, and a generally slower pace and less demanding life. There's no secret why. If you give people money not to work, they won't work. If you reduce incentives to produce wealth, people will lay back and let someone else do it.

Much of what happens in America can be predicted from what happened in England a few years earlier. Since World War II, the English socialist "do-gooders" had political control. They believed in meeting "social goals" and "human needs." As a result, there was overregulation of business, excessive welfare programs, socialization of medicine and industry. Accomplished at the cost of massive inflation and the lowering of productivity, once-mighty England foundered economically, landing in the position of a third-rate power.

America's Democrats during most of this period followed the British. Whatever mistakes they made, *we* made a few years later. Now that England has turned from socialism to a conservative political party, perhaps the same thing will eventually happen here. When hard-money conservatives take over, there will be unquestionably fewer handouts for the poverty class. Unemployment goes up, taxes go down, social services are cut. If the program goes on long enough, inflation is eliminated, and the economy recovers—eventually. The price may be riots and violence.

What will happen in the United States in the next few years?

My predictions: The "human needs" people will stay in the background after the 1980 elections, probably led by Teddy Kennedy. There will be no meaningful tax reforms and under the Reagan Administration there will be just a few hand-outs. We shall witness unsuccessful attempts to stem inflation with wage, price, and rent controls. A black market in goods and services will develop. Tax avoidance will replace baseball as the national sport. Laws and taxes will become more oppressive for the middle and employed classes and the economy will undergo a very severe recession during 1981-1985. The government will be faced with increasing crime, drug use, and tax evasion.

The government, as well as the public, will feel they have "lost control" of the economy. All sorts of experimental legislation will be tried. There will be rationing of gasoline and some scarce foods. There will be currency controls so that money can not be exported without permission. The government will be forced to cut down on welfare and Social Security payments. This will not be done in an honest, staightforward way: They will quietly fiddle with eligibility requirements in order to cut out recipients who have little or no political clout.

So, if you want a prediction, it's this: Things like unemployment and inflation are going to get a lot worse before they get better. The tax revolt people—the same people who want less regulation and more free enterprise—are going to be heard, but they will be largely ignored during the 1980s. But we will snap out of the welfare state sooner or later, or there will be economic collapse. So here it is: More and more taxes, rent controls, oppressive and restrictive laws for a time. Then a big swing toward conservative economic policies. Much pushing and shoving. Great instability! What will happen after that? . . . Your guess is as good as mine. Because the American public is impatient for fast, simple solutions, politicians who want to leave the patient alone until it cures itself will probably not last long. Even though this may be the only intelligent route. That's why you should take an active role in the taxpayers' revolt.

Coming up—"Who's Who in the Tax Revolt." With luck, you will find a niche in the tax revolt that feels good to you.

31.
Who's Who in the Tax Revolt

Howard Jarvis
and the American Tax Reduction Movement

The big name—the guy who made the cover of *Time*—the fellow that the public identifies with the tax revolt—is Howard Jarvis. Many in the movement are probably jealous of him. He has managed to grab most of the publicity, the headlines, and the major credit for the passage of Proposition 13 in California. He also has a personal mailing list of all the big contributors in the country. Once you respond to one of his urgent pleas for a donation, you will get a cascade of mail asking for more money. I don't mind, and I send him a couple of bucks now and then. There is no question that Jarvis has put together an efficient lobbying machine with a great deal of clout. In many elections where Jarvis put in his two cents, the fuzzy-thinking-leftist candidates were given the bum's rush by the voters.

There is something about this crusty old guy that appeals to almost everyone except maybe Jane Fonda. He has had friendly representatives in Congress introduce his pet bill, the American Tax Reduction Act. This bill would limit government expenditures to 18 percent of the gross national product, cut all income taxes by about half, and index all tax rates to inflation. Indexing would prevent taxes from taking a bigger chunk of an individual's income each year just because of inflation. The Jarvis proposal is considered "radical" by most legislators and as a result has generated little support. Of course, Proposition 13 (which cut California real estate taxes by 60 percent) was considered "superradical" before it passed. If you want to support this legislation, write to your congressmen and senators and tell them you will never vote for them again unless they write you that they are in favor of this legislation or give you a darned good reason why they are opposed to it. Howard will certainly be happy to get any donations you care to give. His address is Howard Jarvis, Suite 350, 6333 Wilshire Blvd., Los Angeles, CA 90048.

Jarvis has been fighting for tax reduction and spending limits for years. He's in his seventies, made his personal fortune in real estate, and now works full time to support candidates in favor of more tax cuts. A demagogue with little intellectual depth, he is just what's been needed to stir up the silent conservative majority in mid-America. His program is my favorite!

Phil Crane
and Americans to Cut Taxes Now

Phil Crane, as you know, is a Republican, a conservative, and was a candidate for the Republican presidential nomination in 1980. He's also the head of a group known as the American Conservative Union. Somehow I distrust anyone who would stay in the political party that gave us Richard Nixon. I also distrust conventional politicians who seem to make a lot of promises but when elected always deliver "M.S."

("More of the Same"). Crane has a bright and witty economist on his staff—Milton Friedman, Ph.D. That will mean "More of the Same Piled Higher and Deeper," since they don't offer much but inspiring conversation.

These gents are in favor of a constitutional amendment to limit tax increases in any one year to no more than the percentage increases in the gross national product. That means leaving tax rates pretty much as they are with the present disastrous effects of inflation continuing.

Crane's suggestion is that you send a tea bag (symbolic of the Boston Tea Party) to any legislator or congressman that you feel is squandering too much taxpayers' money. My suggestion is that you send Crane a tea bag and tell him to quit thinking small and to team up with Jarvis, Koch, or Clark and offer us some meaningful tax cuts. His address is Phil Crane, 316 Pennsylvania Ave., SE Washington, DC 20003.

Ralph Nader
and the Tax Reform Research Group

For our fuzzy-thinking leftist readers, we give you Ralph Nader. Nader was the man most responsible for those annoying buzzers in your cars. He'd have air bags in there to smother us if we let him. He single-handedly has brought about more burdensome, useless, costly legislation than any other human being. He has multiplied the paperwork and necessity for forms and permits to unheard-of levels. And now that tax reform has become popular, he wants to get in on that. Oh well, at least part of his program is interesting— although it doesn't focus on saving us any money. The T.R.R.G. is currently lobbying for:

1. Publication of internal I.R.S. operations. (I guess he hasn't heard that other people have fought and won that fight.)
2. More notice to taxpayers of their rights. (I'd rather

rely on someone other than an I.R.S. agent to tell me my rights.)

3. Low-cost legal representation for middle-income taxpayers. (Does that mean "raise everybody's taxes" to have the government pay the lawyers on both sides of every case?)

4. Give citizens the right to sue the I.R.S. for wrongful damages. (Even though that one might give me $10 million, I'm against it. If everyone started suing and collecting damages from the I.R.S., where would it come from? Nader doesn't tell us—but it would come from our tax money!)

The trouble with fuzzy-thinking leftists is that they promise us $5 and later charge us $10 to collect it. Nader puts out a monthly newspaper and other publications. You may want to write him at P.O. Box 14198, Ben Franklin Station, Washington, DC 20044.

Ed Clark
and the Libertarian Party

Third parties in the United States have usually come and gone quickly. But the fast-growing Libertarian political movement seems to be capturing popular support because it is so much in tune with the mood of the times. They have a number of amusing—and serious—ideas. They put forward candidates in most elections. The membership usually consists of the brightest and most interesting assortment of people you could ever hope to meet. Most Libertarians are individualists and would never be in a political party. But this one is different. Libertarians want to abolish the income tax!

They also believe that in every political election the ballot should contain, along with the candidates' names, a space marked "None of the above." That way the voters could refuse to elect any of the bad apples usually running. Because of those two ideas alone, I had to join up immediately!

Not too long ago, at the Libertarian Convention in Los Angeles, I ran for the nomination for Vice-President of the United States of America. Also on the ballot were Edward Koch (brother of Charles—see next section) and "none of the above." In a heated election, I lost not only to Koch, but also to "none of the above." And I still feel becoming a member was a good idea.

Ed Clark, a Los Angeles lawyer, is a sincere, intellectual, soft-spoken gentleman in his late thirties. He ran for President in 1980. If elected, he would have disbanded about 99 percent of all government agencies. There was no chance that he would win. But there was no chance that Norman Thomas the Socialist would win, either. Thomas ran several times during the 1920s and 1930s and every single plank in his third-party platform eventually became law. Teddy Roosevelt would probably be a Libertarian if alive today! You should join the Libertarians. I guarantee you'll have lots of fun with vital, creative people. They'll be people like you who will have read this book. You can make a major contribution to changing the course of American history. Being a Libertarian means that you are the cutting edge of social change—in favor of limited government and maximization of individual freedom. The party is small enough so that you can get to know the movers and shakers by their first names. I'll personally look for you at the next convention! To join the Libertarian Party (national) and participate in lots of activities, find the local chapter in your phone book (white pages) under "Libertarian Party."

Charles Koch
and the National Taxpayers' Union

There are about 1,000 registered lobbies in Washington. All of them want more government money and more support for their particular "thing." The National Taxpayers' Union wants less spending, less waste, less government. Less means more to Charles Koch (pronounced "Coke.") More of what's important, anyway, and that's *freedom*. The N.T.U. is a first class well-run organization with about 80,000 members. The N.T.U. figures that for every dollar contributed they have saved taxpayers over $150,000. I believe it!

The N.T.U. supports the passage of a constitutional amendment requiring a balanced budget. Thirty states thus far have backed the call for a national convention. Thirty-four states are needed. The project needs the boost of more dues-paying members and supporters. Another proposed amendment would limit income taxes to a maximum of 25 percent.

The N.T.U. has been instrumental in bringing about serious consideration of moves to deregulate the airline and trucking industries.

The N.T.U., by exposing waste and fraud, claims to have brought about the elimination of projects and proposed expenditures that would have cost taxpayers over $150 *billion!*

The N.T.U. supports local communities in moves to cut local taxes. They aided the Proposition 13 battle in California with staff and funding.

As Ben Franklin said, "Either we hang together,
or we hang separately."

In complete contrast to the extroverted Howard Jarvis, Charles Koch is a shy, quiet, and very wealthy self-made man who personally owns one of the larger industrial conglomerates of the world. He makes few public appearances. Unlike many industrialists who don't look beyond their own bailiwicks, Koch gives generously to N.T.U. and provided financial support for the organization before cutting taxes became the fashionable fad it is today. A $15 membership in this organization brings no further pressures for donations and includes a subscription to the *Dollars and Sense Newsletter*, which contains some good tax-saving ideas for individuals. Send $15 to National Taxpayers' Union, Dept. G, 325 Pennsylvania Avenue, SE, Washington, DC 20003.

Heroes and Martyrs

If you were a baseball buff, it just wouldn't do if you had never heard of Babe Ruth, Joe DiMaggio, or Willy Mays. Likewise, at any gathering of tax resisters you'll hear these names mentioned:

- Vivien Kellems, Newberry Road, East Haddam, CT 06423. This lady has been a leading tax rebel for years. She owes part of her fame to the fact that she beat the I.R.S. (*U.S.* v. *Kellems*, U.S. District Court, New Haven, Conn, Case 13.665) by pleading the Fifth Amendment privilege against self-incrimination. It wanted her books and records. She appeared in response to an I.R.S. summons but refused to produce any papers. Since she won, she's a hero.

- Karl Bray, late of Salt Lake City. Bray had a talk show in Salt Lake. He was also an early Libertarian. He organized tax protest rallies and eventually was sentenced to six months in prison. There he organized the prisoners to become tax rebels. He is a saint and martyr of the movement.

- Marvin Cooley and Vaughn Ellsworth, P.O. Box 60, Mesa, AZ 85201. Both have served time for their tax revolt activities. Both are still dissidents. Ellsworth sells a lot of his "5th Amendment Income Tax Return Packet" for $5. I

411

wouldn't recommend using it. But it has some interesting information, and if you are an activist "rebel" and want to hang in with this group, you might want to get in touch.

- Jack Matonis, publisher of *Citizen's Strike Newsletter*, P.O. Box 2885, Fullerton, CA 92633. Send him a dollar plus a self-addressed stamped envelope for an interesting sample newsletter written by a Libertarian lawyer.
- Rene Baxter, publisher of the *Freedom Fighter*, a newsletter of the tax revolt, P.O. Box 204, Trail, OR 97541. Send $2 for a sample issue.

I would like very much to expand this section in later editions. If you know of any newsletters or organized groups, please send samples and news clippings along to me. Most of the people I have named are not wealthy. If you are going to correspond with them, always send a stamped, self-addressed envelope and a donation of a couple of bucks.

32.
Survival
Insurance

One thing about owning property, having big bank accounts, sitting on top of the world financially—even in the best situation, a few mishaps can wipe out the biggest portion of your wealth. Thefts, divorces, lawsuits, an unexpected revolution, or a string of bad business deals should be regarded as *probable* in a tycoon's career, not just *possible*. But in the roughest of times there is something harder to lose than money. It's the stuff between your ears. Spell that knowledge—training—brainpower—*a second skill*.

Do you want the best survival insurance? Then understand that you're on the edge of a socialist abyss. The fuzzy-thinking-leftists of the world want to grab your private property. They may succeed in your lifetime. One thing you can do about it is to develop a second skill that even socialist society will find worth preserving. It doesn't matter what it is, but *be prepared* to earn a living in a different social system.

Develop a skill that is saleable. Be a plumber, brewer, doctor, secretary, deep sea diver—whatever turns you on. When the chips are down, it will be a protective covering and may save your life.

During the communist takeovers all over the world most capitalists and aristocrats were worthless to the "new order." But many of those who blended in with the working class until the shooting was over did fine. They later escaped to the West and started over again. Next time there may be no West to escape to. The best you can do will be to go back to being a wage slave.

As Maurice Chevalier said when asked if he liked old age, "It's not great, but certainly beats the alternative!"

But forget the world communist revolution for a second. Suppose you lose all your money or you get on the next White House enemies list and must leave the country. A needed trade, another language, and a foreign passport should be something you obtained in advance. Once you are rich, regardless of how good or stable your immediate environment may seem, spend a little time establishing safe havens and the means to get there. You'll survive with your second skill. With foresight, you'll also have local funds and property stashed at the end of your escape routes.

Finally, I shouldn't even have to say it because it is obvious: Your odds are enhanced by staying *healthy*. If there is no political trouble and you simply go bankrupt, you can make a comeback if you are in good mental and physical shape. To survive, prosper, and enjoy life is hard if you are feeble-minded or sick. If your life at home just goes along smoothly without any problems, you will enjoy life more (and for a much longer time) if you keep in good shape. Watch your diet and exercise every day. Never stint on time or money to improve brain power or physical stamina.

Personally, I'm into making money now only for the fun of it. I have more than I need for my simple lifestyle. Likewise I'm into tax avoidance for the fun of it. As you can guess, I don't approve of a socialistic America and don't want to contribute to it. Finally, giving the I.R.S. agents a good run for their (or should I say *my*) money is just one more challenge. The system by which Americans make money and are taxed is only "unfair" if you don't know the rules and how to bend them. Here's hoping that this book will help you play the game by the rules, legally, successfully, and enjoyably.

If you've noticed any glaring errors in this book or have any comments or suggestions at all, please write me, Bill Greene, P.O. Box 810, Mill Valley, CA 94942. I'll try to answer personally, and if I use your ideas or corrections you'll get a present from me—either an autographed book, a cassette recording, or something. Remember, I give a series of live lectures throughout the country, and expect to be publishing a lot of follow-up material in the *Tycoon Newsletter*, which you can get *free* for one year. Send me $2 (cash, please) for postage and handling. I'd also like to get *your* comments about this book and suggestions that will make the next edition even better. Please keep in touch so that I can share all the latest information with you! If you have a burning personal question and want a personal answer, drop $20 cash in an envelope to me. I'll do my best to help you out. I used to reply without charge, but the number of queries lead to a fulltime office and secretary, so I have to cover my costs. Please don't ask me complex tax code questions. I'm not a C.P.A.—just a real estate guy who has gotten into an argument with the I.R.S. and wants to even up the odds for working folks.

33.
Final
Thoughts
...and a Poem

In 1913, few people opposed a minimal income tax that 99 percent of the people would never have to pay. But a few opponents of the original income tax law suggested that once such a tax was made legally possible, the tax rates might go up. One congressman suggested that a 10 percent upper limit be imposed on income taxes lest some day taxes be imposed at the unthinkable heathen level set by the Arab conquerors of Europe in the period 700 to 1400 A.D. What was that level? Twenty percent!

Senator William E. Borah of Idaho rose to the Senate floor and expressed outrage at such a suggestion. Who would ever be permitted to impose such a confiscatory heathen rate? Any congressman or senator who would vote for raising the income tax rates would certainly be out on his ear in the next election. The people of the United States would never stand for it. He went on to say that a 10 percent limit on income tax would be unnecessary, since that might encourage the rates to rise to the unthinkable level of 10 percent.

As we all know, the unthinkable level was reached only a few years later in World War I, and the confiscatory level of 20 percent was far exceeded when by World War II the highest tax rate was 90 percent. After each war was over, tax rates dropped—but only slightly. A Congress and government accustomed to having billions to spend could never go back to mere millions—*not unless YOU vote for congressmen, senators, or elected officials who believe in the tax revolt!*

Lawyers always love the process of governments raising taxes and toughening up loopholes because it means more business for them. I once remember talking to Percy, a partner in a major accounting firm. He was a lawyer, a Certified Public Accountant, and the branch manager of the Hong Kong office. In those days, the Hong Kong tax was a simple 10 percent of all local income. Period. Foreign corporations could incorporate with a simple form and keep their charter alive for a few hundred dollars a year. Yet Percy the lawyer-accountant was thinking of moving away from the prospering center of free enterprise.

"Why?" I asked.

"Because things are so simple here that nobody needs good lawyers or accountants."

Percy had just been transferred from India, which he called a "paradise." I always had thought of India as a place where poverty, bureaucracy, and high taxes combined to choke the life out of a nation of otherwise productive and enterprising people.

"That's exactly why it is a paradise for lawyers and accountants! Where the government really puts the screws to people, everybody needs us to show them a way out. That means high fees and high status for us. Here there are no loopholes, and almost everybody willingly pays the 10 percent tax."

This chance meeting and conversation convinced me that, for the most part, lawyers and accountants are eager accomplices in creating an economic and taxing system that is terrible for the individual and economic suicide for a nation. They like a system that benefits lawyers, accountants and politicians. How sweet it must be for a lawyer to be elected to the legislature, pass a law that only he can understand, and then be paid handsomely to show people how to evade or avoid the law.

Our present system is absurd! It gets more absurd with each passing year. It is no good for the country and has already sapped our vitality, our virility, and it is leading us into the decline experienced by all other countries that have attempted to create socialist utopias at the expense of their productive leading citizens.

What can we do about it? We can demand of our elected representatives a chance to vote on the income tax. Why should I or any of my fellow citizens be bound by a 1913 law that I and they have never had a chance to vote on at the ballot box. We can oppose all new taxes, especially the insidious Value Added Tax, or V.A.T., that has been adopted in England.

Remember—the original 1913 income tax amendment was promulgated as a soak-the-rich measure. Taxes were limited to 1 percent on incomes over $3,000, in an era when $3,000 was equivalent to about $50,000 in 1980 dollars. The highest tax bracket was reached at $500,000 when the income tax reached 6 percent. Only people who earned the equivalent of $10 million per year in today's currency had to pay at the highest tax bracket of 6 percent. Today, plumbers, waitresses, and good carpenters find themselves saddled with the highest tax bracket of 50 percent. "Soak the rich" has become "Soak yourself." Would you vote for income taxes today if given a choice? Write your congressman and senator. Tell him you'll never vote for him again unless income taxes are reduced to 10 percent maximum.

In all my books, there have been some swell poems. For those who were expecting another inspiring piece, you won't be disappointed.

Here is this year's bid for the Nobel Prize in Literature:

Bill Greene's Ode to the Tax Revolt

Oh, Income Tax, how I hate you,
At the bottom—that's where I'd rate you.
I'd tramp through jungle, snow, or gale,
I'd even spend a year in jail,
There's no place I wouldn't look
Be it magazine or book,
For a hint or a tip
To avoid your nasty grip.
If I pay a tax before I die,
May my soul not fly to the sky,
But downward, downward should I vector
Till I'm in *hell* with the tax collector.
And when his hands go in my pockets,
I'll chop them off, and ascend with rockets.
Up in heaven there, I'll rendezvous,
With the gang who beat Internal Revenue.*
On my gravestone may this be shown:
   Here Lies Bill Greene;
   As a poet, he wasn't glorious.
   But as a tax rebel, he made us VICTORIOUS!

---

*Will you be there?

About
the Author

by Boswell Orwell

What kind of person is Bill Greene, this popular Pied Piper of wealth accumulation and tax avoidance?

William Greene spent his first few years in a fourth-floor slum walk-up in Chicago, where his father was a socialist-leaning state representative in the Illinois legislature. Graduating from a substandard public high school in Chicago, Bill reasoned, was no way to get on in the world. So, at the age of 13, Bill Greene won a scholarship to Francis Parker, an exclusive private school. In high school, he assessed what he considered his liabilities: He was financially poor, he came from the working class, and thought of himself as physically weak and unattractive. He believed that the only way he could match the achievements of his classmates was to try harder. Mediocre at sports, at the age of 14 he decided that wealth was to be his stepping-stone to success, fame, and happiness.

With making money his goal, he read biographies of tycoons. He made his first real estate deal while in high school. Bill acquired a small parking lot in Chicago when he was 15. Then, as a 16-year-old stockboy at Brooks Brothers, he began to dress like a banker (with factory seconds the store manager gave him). At 17, he searched around for a reputable college that would spare him four years of "useless" liberal arts and set him on a fast track to financial freedom. Applying first to Harvard, he learned that Harvard Business School demanded an undergraduate degree as a prerequisite. But the Wharton School of Finance in Philadelphia (University of Pennsylvania) accepted him right out of high school and gave him a hefty scholarship as well. To speed things up, he registered at Wharton under two different names and took so many courses that although his deception was uncovered he was still able to graduate at the age of 19 in record time. He was a stock market millionaire at the age of 22, broke at 24, and a multimillionaire two years later and ever since.

Chutzpah, or "push," is a quality that has made many people successful—and with this quality Greene is very well endowed. At any gathering, he takes center stage and talks enthusiastically for hours about his main interests: real estate deals, history, art collecting, and Libertarian politics. He's a man of unusual drive, an engaging sense of humor, and obvious intelligence. But, contends Greene, it doesn't take brains to make money. Success in money-making, or politics, is always *inversely* related to IQ, he quips: "The dumber you are, the better your chances of being rich or a congressman."

Earlier in life, Greene dated many daughters of the superrich. "But," notes Greene, "rich girls tend to be spoiled and demanding."

At 42, he is a happy man, presiding over a large, rural hilltop estate overlooking the San Francisco Bay. A beautiful and attentive Filipina wife lives with him in connubial bliss.

His American headquarters, also a busy office, is always full of attractive secretaries, electronic office toys, and sophisticated security and alarm systems. He lives, for tax reasons, at least six months of each year outside of the United States.

Greene obviously enjoys wealth, but doesn't spend much. Although his California hillside nest is three times the size of a normal home, it is simple redwood log outside and "laid-back" inside. Greene claims that 95 percent of his furniture was free—from his rental properties—things that tenants left behind when they moved. He strives for minimum overhead and never buys anything at retail. Greene trades his books and lectures for goods and services. He considers conspicuous consumption a waste of time and money. His dress is casual: studied shabbiness, even by California standards—more tenant rejects! Bill's manner is direct, honest, and informal. He is of average height. Like a Trappist monk, his hair grows thick and brown in a half circle below the bald top of his head. Greene laughs easily.

Looking back at his only spending spree some years ago, Bill says, "It was not a success!" He bought a new Rolls Royce convertible and a Jaguar sedan. "They were terrible! The cars always were breaking down. I'd take one to the garage to have the electric windows fixed. The day I drove it out, the radio wouldn't work. Then the engine would conk out. One day I was in a shopping center and somebody opened a car door into me. With a Rolls' aluminum body, what would be no dent at all in another car required an expensive specialist. That put the Rolls in the garage for four weeks. And it cost $1,800 for an itsy-bitsy dent. The happiest day of my life was when I got back into a truck."

During this early affluence, he also hired a Japanese housegirl and a formal butler. "The butler was homosexual, and I had to listen and suffer along with all his love problems. The housegirl always had something wrong with her teeth so I ended up looking after them—spending all of my time driving her back and forth to the dentist."

After dumping the Rolls Royce and the servants, he decided to simplify his life by driving cheap, dependable trucks and doing his own cooking and housekeeping. He moved to Africa, then Hong Kong. He has several homes.

Nonconformist though he is, his economic principles sound as though he would like to repeal the Sixteenth Amendment (income tax) and give the post office back to the Indians. But, uncovering loopholes in the American tax system makes him glow. He describes his favorites: "Real estate is an absolutely wonderful game under today's tax code. Because of the tax incentives, America is the only country in the world that has (or had, until recent rent controls and the environmentalists) an abundant supply of modern housing. In almost every other country in the whole world, the opposite is true. In a place like Copenhagen, Denmark, there is a twenty-year wait for a couple to get an apartment. In Geneva or Tokyo, a single-family house is unaffordable. There you have no tax benefits. With rent controls and limited opportunities for profit, there is no incentive to build anything but office buildings or expensive resort cabins for tourists.

"In America we have wonderful tax benefits given to real estate owners. They are serving their purpose. We have more roofs—more covered space per capita by three or four times, than any other country in the world except maybe Canada. Go to Germany, or Switzerland, or Japan, or anywhere in the Third world. There is no hope whatever of an individual working family acquiring their own decent home without a government handout. The tax incentive system here (what some people call *loopholes*) has led to an abundance of privately owned, privately financed rental properties and owner-occupied homes. In many other countries, all cheaper apartments or houses are state owned or taxpayer subsidized."

On inflation, Greene says, "the home that a few years ago was $50,000 is now $125,000 and going up 20 percent a year. Don't forget, though, the salary that was $10,000 a few years ago is now $25,000. People have to work fewer hours in this country to own a home than in any other. And when you talk absolute prices, that $125,000 Mill Valley house is $1 million in Zurich, or Monaco. Go to Tokyo and say, "I would like to buy a house, any old house, what's the cheapest?" They will say, "Well, $1 million." The reason is high demand and rent controls, no tax incentives to build. So in most countries nobody except the superrich can own a single family home. That's what's going to happen here.

"Before I gave these Tycoon Classes, people used to come to me to find out my "magic formula" for getting rich. There is no magic formula. You just have to learn about inflation and how to play the tax game. I learned those rules back when I was a kid at Wharton, and I did very well once I put my mind to it. But if you're in an area that is going to have rent controls and you're owning apartments, you'll lose your shirt unless you're nimble enough to sell out in time by converting to condos. There are lots of pitfalls in real estate, but I've tried to cover most of them in my book, *Think Like a Tycoon.*

When asked why he is willing to share his money-making, tax-saving secrets with those who pay a modest fee to attend his seminars or buy his books, the answer is frank. "I like being a celebrity! And every time an ex-student tells me about his or her latest scam or deal, I get a real kick." The reason he *started* giving his Tycoon Classes, however, is quite interesting: Feeling lonely and abandoned following a collapsed love affair, the inspiration came to him to advertise. He announced a course in the local paper: "Making Money in Real Estate—for Single Women." The course was advertised as "How to Become a Lady Tycoon." The price was, get this, *free!* With lunch included! Just like today, it was taught four years ago at his mountaintop estate in Mill Valley. He hoped to meet some sexy, materialistic ladies who would share his interest in making real estate deals. On opening day, 35 women showed up. So did eight gay men. Since the men offered no competition for the ladies he wanted to meet, Bill was delighted to let them stay. Many a present-day gay real estate tycoon in San Francisco got his start at a Bill Greene Tycoon Class. They are among Greene's staunchest supporters. The demand for free classes was such that he began to charge for his classes. Greene now gives them for $350 and up in various locations in California, and free ones at San Quentin and other prisons. Thousands have now taken his Tycoon Class. Most graduates own several income properties. But one of his inspired prison students once escaped, robbed a bank "to get working capital," and is now back behind bars. "You can't win 'em all," sighs Greene.

When Bill Greene completed his first book, *Think Like a Tycoon*, he found no publisher willing to touch it, nor any bookstores who would retail it. So he did some creative thinking and asked local hardware stores to take them on consignment. Fifteen thousand copies sold like hotcakes at $17 a crack. Now most sales are by word of mouth and he gets 40 or 50 orders every day from all over the world. Greene's third edition, revised for 1980 and now $11, was dedicated to "Chip and Dale," two I.R.S. agents who shadowed and investigated him for two years. For a time, they stood outside his wrought-iron gates, tapped his phone, infiltrated his tycoon classes, and kept him under surveillance. After jousting with his lawyers and accountants annually for several years, they seemingly *gave up*—finding nothing illegal in what he does or teaches.

When not giving classes, Greene cherishes his privacy, reads a great deal, enjoys classical music and his children. He writes poetry, paints, and has just finished a new workbook, "How to Acquire Distress Property." He has half a dozen pretty young women at his home editing and typing his books, newsletter, and lectures. Greene rises at 8 A.M. and usually works past midnight. He appears on talk shows several times a week, where he gives financial advice for the blue-collar worker. He also lectures at state and federal prisons on how to beat the system legally.

Is Bill Greene a modern-day Pied Piper, leading us wage slaves out of the financial woods into a tax-free paradise, or is he getting us into a dangerous game that will take us down the tubes?

"If the I.R.S. eliminates depreciation and the states impose rent controls," Greene admits, "this double punch from the government would send real estate investors out of residential real estate and into gold coins in a flood unseen since the days of Noah's Ark. Safe, unproductive activities like stamp and coin collecting would monopolize the time of previously productive people." Greene adds, "Real estate and construction could become, for all practical purposes, a nationalized or subsidized industry, as it is most everywhere else in the world. We'd have new public housing projects proceeding with the 'efficiency' of Amtrak or the post office." Greene feels that the real estate game—with high untaxed profits—probably will be over in our lifetime unless a less socialistic, more Libertarian philosophy takes hold in America during the coming two decades.

"In short," says Greene, "the free enterprise system is now being taxed and legislated out of existence. But what might be the twilight of capitalism can still be the best years ever for ambitious, hard-working people who get into real estate and other good tax shelter deals now." Tax avoidance is here to stay. It's America's major industry. At least that's what he tells us!

A copy of Bill Greene's $11 book, *Think Like a Tycoon*, can be ordered by mail or phone on an unconditional money-back guarantee. His newsletter is free. Send two dollars cash for postage and handling. Greene can be reached at P.O. Box 810, Mill Valley, CA 94942. Phone (415) 383-8264.

Readings

Reading List

These first four books are the most highly recommended and may be ordered during 1981 for the price indicated direct from Bill Greene. After 1981, and in the case of all other publications, it is suggested that you make mail or phone inquiry to determine current prices and availability.

Think Like a Tycoon, by Bill Greene, P.O. Box 810, Mill Valley, CA 94942. Order by mail with a check or Phone (415) 383-8264, with Visa or M/C number. If you liked *Tax Revolt,* you'll love *Think Like a Tycoon,* by the same author. It concentrates on how to make more money. You can worry about saving on taxes later. Full of cartoons and Bill's zany stories. They will show you how to make a million dollars. $14 includes postage, handling and a year of Bill Greene's *Tycoon Newsletter* ("Make More Money & Pay Less Taxes").

How to Pay Zero Income Tax—Legally, by Dick Lee. $16, hardback, 114 pages. A very helpful little volume aimed at the real estate investor. We use it for our own tax seminars, where the author is often a guest speaker. So it must be good. Available from Bill Greene, Box 810, Mill Valley, CA 94942.

Tax Planning, by Dr. Richard Sylvester, hardback, 309 pages. $24.95. May be ordered from Bill Greene, Box 810, Mill Valley, CA 94942. Because this book is simple to understand, yet has full code and case citations, it has my highest recommendation. Sylvester shares my philosophy that merely *reducing* or deferring taxes is not worth the time or effort. We must *eliminate* taxes by legal means. Sylvester has a scholarly approach. His book is required reading for tycoons seriously interested in making more money and keeping *all* of it.

Hazard Unlimited: The Story of Lloyd's of London, by Antony Brown, Davies Publishing, London, England, c/o Bill Greene. $14 covers cost of book plus postage and handling. Recommended for those with a net worth of $1 million or more, and who might consider joining Lloyd's. Lloyd's earns lots of money and provides tax shelter too.

Master Tax Guide, Commerce Clearing House, 4025 W. Peterson Avenue, Chicago, IL 60646. $7.50. A 500-page "Bible" of federal tax accountants. CCH publishes a number of books, educational cassettes, and newsletters, primarily for lawyers and accountants. All very helpful. Especially good is their cassette course, "Fundamentals of Partnership Taxation," by Kess, for $27.

C.P.A. Examination Review Outline, by Gleim & Delaney, Wiley Publications, P.O. Box 561, Hayward, CA 94543. Phone (415) 886-2482. On the East Coast, 605 3rd Av., New York, N.Y. $20. For hard facts, well presented, pound for pound, this is the best buy you'll ever get in a book about accounting and tax law. Over 1,000 pages of well-indexed material. Exceedingly nitty-gritty. This book is used by accounting students to prepare for the C.P.A. examinations. It has not found its way into the hands of the public. Want to be able to interpret the tax code and do your own accounting? Highly recommended.

Far Out Reading

Income Tax Law for Ministers and Religious Workers, by B. J. Worth, P.O. Box 725, Winona Lake, IN 46590. $3.25. Mr. and Mrs. Worth won't show you how to set up a church, but they do the income tax returns for many ministers, missionaries, and priests. This 50-page paperback is very helpful in ascertaining the special benefits available to the religious.

The Paper Trip I, by Anonymous [Who Else?]. If you want a consciousness-raising experience about the ease of entry into the subterranean economy, or if you are just into so much debt and trouble that you'd like to drop out, the *The Paper Trip* and other publications of Eden Press, P.O. Box 8410, Fountain Valley, CA 92708 are for you. In *Paper Trip* you learn how to disappear, get new identification including passports and Social Security numbers, job references and credit cards. Eden Press publishes rather amazing materials for the underground economy, including books on home-made weapons, survival/ camping techniques, being a fugitive, staying free, and so on. *Paper Trip* is $12.95. Ask for a free catalog of other stuff, too.

The Biggest Con, by Irwin Schiff. $6. If you feel guilty about *not* paying taxes, this book is a fast cure. Years ago Schiff decided that since the federal government was being run by a bunch of crooks, it would be criminal for him to pay taxes. The government has tried to put him in jail for this since 1973 but has not succeeded. He was convicted in 1979 but got off on appeal. Schiff presents a very convincing argument that if private citizens got together to do what the government has been doing they would all be guilty of a conspiracy to defraud the public. For some eye-opening, unusual views, send $6 to Freedom Books, P.O. Box 5303, Hamden, CN 06518. Phone (203) 281-6791.

Complete Guide to Financial Privacy, by Mark Skousen. $10. Alexandria House Books, 901 N. Washington St., Alexandria, VA 22314. If you don't want the I.R.S. or your ex-wife to know what you are doing, this book is an excellent investment. The title says it all.

Criminal Tax Fraud, by Crowley. $30. Tricks of the trade used by high-priced tax lawyers to keep their clients in the chips and out of the pokey. Despite the high price of this book, for those worried about I.R.S. persecution it is the best investment you'll ever make. It shows how *not to get caught,* the basic rule being "Keep your mouth shut" when the I.R.S. comes to call. Don't give its agents any leads, clues, or ex-lovers to interview. Though written for lawyers, it reads like a novel and is very *funny.* Get it! Also get on the mailing list for the Practicing Law Institute's many seminars and publications on tax shelters, international tax havens, real estate, etc. Write Mrs. B. G. McDonald, Book Sales, Practicing Law Institute, 810 7th Avenue, New York, NY 10019.

Trade and Tax Profiles: Bermuda, Bahamas, the Caribbean, by Touche Ross International. 119 pages., paperback. Available free from Touche Ross, C.P.A.s, one of the big five tax-accounting firms, at 1633 Broadway, New York, NY 10019. This is a summary of the law, tax policies, investment incentives, and legal tax haven benefits available.

Practical International Tax Planning (Former title: *How to Use Foreign Tax Havens*), 1979, by Attorney Marshall J. Langer, The Practicing Law Institute (B. G. McDonald, Book Sales Manager), 810 7th Avenue, New York, NY 10019. $40.00 includes postage and handling. If you have a high net worth and want to get fancy, this book will provide you with many useful ideas. The author explains concepts used by wealthy individuals and corporations to reduce taxes with "offshore" operations. Aimed mainly at lawyers.

How to Profit from Offshore Banking, by A. V. Laurins. Published by the author. 211 Sutter Street, No. 607, San Francisco, CA 94108. Phone (415) 346-3208. A thin and expensive paperback book with 154 pages at $20. But Laurins has discovered a loophole: An American can get a foreign bank charter (with a little help from his friends) and thereafter earn money tax free, abroad. If this is your bag, any information you can get on the subject is worth the price.

How to Profit and Avoid Taxes by Organizing Your Own Private Bank in Saint Vincent, by Jerome Schneider, $15 paperback, 155 pages. WFI Publishing, 2049 Century Park East, Los Angeles, CA 90067. Phone (213) 533-8700. Like the Laurins book, this one zeroes in on a small Caribbean island that has set itself up as a tax shelter. It offers some unique possibilities for high-income-bracket people who can afford about $20,000 to set up a bank, and $5,000 a year to keep it running.

How to Save Money by Incorporating in a Tax Haven, by Paul Harris, Box 613, Grand Cayman Island, British West Indies. $16.00 postpaid. The ex-president of a Cayman Island bank gives 200 pages of fact-filled information on all the tax havens of the world: geographics, risks, costs. Definitely good reading if you are thinking of leaving the states for a little grass shack on a coral beach permanently or temporarily.

Newsletters and Other Publications

Bill Greene, editor and publisher, *Tycoon Newsletter.* At $2 per year, this has to be the bargain of the century. The catch is that Bill only puts out a newsletter when he feels there is something important to say. Also, he doesn't want checks. If you want to risk $2 to be on the mailing list, you pays your money and you takes what you gets. Write "Tycoon," P.O. Box 810, Mill Valley, CA 94942.

Mark Skousen, editor, *Personal Finance,* $48 per year (24 issues). Mention me (Bill Greene) and send $2 for a sample issue: P.O. Box 2599, Landover Hills, MD 20784. Aimed at the hard money enthusiast (coins, gold, and Swiss francs), it's far more intelligently written than most of the doomsday-predicting publications. Some ideas could be worth far more than the cost of a subscription. Ideas on real estate tend to be too general or too impractical (Example, Aug. 1979: "Now is the time to invest in single-family homes in Rhodesia/Zimbabwe"). But stuff like that does tend to open your eyes beyond the city limits of your own home town. They are on top of current events, and their analysis of trends is penetrating. I'm sure that physicians and dentists go right out and buy what is advertised: diamonds, gold, books on tax avoidance and coin collecting. But these ads are a good way to see how the winds are blowing. The best material on taxes finds its way into the highly recommended sister publication, *Tax Angles* (below).

Mark Skousen, editor, *Tax Angles*, $30 per year (12 issues). Sample $2. A truly excellent service and good value for money. It's a 4-page newsletter, and unlike most of them, which are 89 percent B.S., this one often has usable hard info. Same address as above.

Ruff Times Newsletter, by Howard Ruff. Check price by calling toll-free (800) 642-0204. While not much about taxes, Ruff's informative newsletter has all kinds of investment (and some tax-saving) advice. To get a view of what's happening that is different from the standard media, you might ask for a sample copy, and subscribe if you like it.

The Forecaster, by John Kamin. Newsletter and various publications by this fellow are as good as anything being put out. His specialty is coin investing, always a favorite in times of inflation and high taxes. Although coins offer no tax shelter, people who deal in coins do it on a cash or trade basis. Send $2 for a sample to *Forecaster*, 19623 Ventura Blvd., Tarzana, CA 91356.

Mark O. Haroldsen, publisher, *Financial Freedom Report*, $36 per year and well worth it. You may subscribe through me, Bill "Tycoon" Greene, P.O. Box 810, Mill Valley, CA 94941. Visa or Master Charge by phone (415) 383-8264. This fat monthly magazine is the largest circulation real estate periodical in America. Aimed at the "embryo" tycoon, it has inspirational success stories, lots of "how-to-do-it" tips, and interesting ads for real estate deals and business gadgets unobtainable elsewhere. Some have said that Haroldsen makes more money talking and writing about it than doing it. They are probably right. But Mark *did* very well in real estate before he turned his interest to writing his best seller *Wake Up the Financial Genius.* He's found a *need,* and he fills it very well. Highly recommended.

A. D. Kessler, publisher, *Creative Real Estate,* $27 per year, sample issue $2.75 if you mention Bill "Tycoon" Greene. Box 2446, Leucadia, CA 92024. This monthly magazine is aimed at the "Big Shot" tycoon who already owns a million in property—or the broker who handles very big deals. I get some of my best ideas from this publication. But it's technical and definitely not for the beginner.

David Glubetich, publisher, *Impact Real Estate Reports,* $59 per year. Very useful material. Not quite for the novice aimed at by Haroldsen, and not as stratospheric as *Creative Real Estate.* Each month Dave does a different report. Write Impact Publishing, 1601 Oak Park Boulevard, Pleasant Hill, CA 94523. Get a sample report for $5 from among these titles: *Converting Single-Family Homes to Office Buildings, Syndications,* or (my favorite) *Using Options in Real Estate.*

Index

438

439

440

Think Like a Tycoon
Confessions of a Real Estate Tycoon

From California, this underground best seller has helped thousands get a handle on their time, politics, money, tax problems and love life.

Mill Valley author Bill "Tycoon" Greene, 42, tells his story: "Life wasn't worth living, nobody loved me. I was down to $200, a Rolls Royce, a butler, a mansion and one maid. Poised on the Golden Gate Bridge, I was ready to jump. Then 'He' spoke to me. Soon I had no butler, no maid and one old truck. I grew a beard, wrote poetry and got a hot tub. I accumulated a million dollars worth of property for 'no money down.' That year (in real estate) I earned more money than the presidents of General Motors, DuPont and Xerox, *combined*. Read my book to find out how I went from despondency to social acceptability, big bucks, tax refunds and an absolutely fabulous sex life. Find out how and why I teach San Quentin cons and single girls to be Tycoons. Learn how *you* can become the first tycoon on your block."

"Enthusiastic ... Entertaining! Mercifully clear of pseudopsychological hype ... Sticks to making money in real estate. Well worth the time of any potential investor." —*Money Magazine*

"Greene shows anyone with self discipline how to own a million dollars worth of real estate within a short period." —*LA Herald Examiner*

"Your appearance stirred up more audience response than any in recent memory." —*Producer, NBC TV Tomorrow Show*

"A Darned Good Book! Five years of experience in two hours of easy reading. Send me 10,000 copies for my friends and subscribers."
—*Mark O. Haroldson, author of the best seller:*
How to Wake Up the Financial Genius Inside You

"Your tongue in cheek chapter on how to bamboozle your banker' had the entire board of directors at [one of America's largest banks] convulsed with laughter all day. The truth really hurts. It's required reading for all officers." —*Chairman of the Board*

HOW TO ORDER:
Visit your favorite bookstore or call 415-383-8264 anytime. Have your Visa or Mastercharge card ready. Place your order for THINK LIKE A TYCOON. Or, mail a $16 check to Bill Tycoon Greene, Box 810, Mill Valley, CA 94942.

ALL BOOKS SOLD WITH UNCONDITIONAL
MONEY BACK GUARANTEE.

Take the Tycoon Class at Home!

Now, at a fraction of the price of the "live" seminar, you can get 11 hours of cassette tape and all the study materials from the Bill Greene Tycoon Class for home study. This home study course includes all the major topics covered in the weekend class. It includes:

Eight Cassette Tapes (each covering more than the title indicates) attractively packaged in a booklike album,

"Think Like a Tycoon"   "Buying Your First Investment Property"
"Finding Super Deals"   "Pay No Taxes Ever Again, Legally!"
"Getting Organized"   "No-Money-Down Deals"
"Advanced Tax Avoidance"   "Trade Up Tax Free—1031 Exchanges"

The Tycoon Class Workbook, a fat reference manual you will refer to hundreds of times in your real estate dealings. Contains forms, vital tax information, negotiating tips, and almost everything you need to know about investing in real estate. This is the newest, updated edition.

Landlording, by Leigh Robinson, a book so good that Bill wishes he had written it himself. It is fun, easy to read, and contains all you need to know about handling tenants, managing property, and keeping your books and records straight.

The Realty Bluebook, the Bible of real estate. No real estate agent leaves home without it. Not sold in stores, it was previously available only to professionals in the business. It contains forms, checklists, everything you need to know about the technical aspects of real estate.

Think Like a Tycoon, by Bill Greene, an epic on making money and avoiding taxes. It is 240 pages long, profusely illustrated, helpful and humorous. This book should become a national bestseller. Before the general public can buy it, it is available only to friends on our mailing list. If your order is received in the next 15 days, you will get a personally autographed preview copy that may be a collector's item once the book is nationally advertised.

The total cost of the home study course is $200 plus U.P.S. delivery. Many students felt the personal contact with dynamic and inspiring Bill Greene was an essential part of the Tycoon Class experience. But the written materials are exactly the same and the cost of the home study course can be deducted if you take the "live" course later.

Anyone who receives a home study course and does not agree it's worth far more than its cost, can return it undamaged, within two weeks for a full refund.

The next step is up to you. No salesman will call on you and give you a sales pitch. The Tycoon Course will change your life drastically for the better, but you must give *yourself* the push. YOU must get off your fanny and move! Get the home study course on a no-risk trial basis.

The materials in the Home study course are available separately, too!

See our price list and order form at the end of the book.

Price List

Complete Home Study Course
     Includes 8 cassette tapes, *Tycoon Workbook, Landlording, Tycoon Newsletter* for 3 years, *Realty Bluebook, Think Like a Tycoon,* and UPS delivery $200
     Or Order Separately
Think Like a Tycoon .... $16   *Landlording* $15
The Realty Bluebook .... $16   *Individual Cassette Tapes* (each) $13
SPECIAL INTRODUCTORY TALK: "Buying Your First Investment Property," on cassette. General summary of the Tycoon Class with detailed instruction on how to use the standard offer form (included). This tape will be included as a gift to all those who order the Home Study Course.
THIS TAPE ALONE - Special $9
The *Tycoon Newsletter* is $20 per year. It is FREE to all who have read and enjoyed *Your Personal Tax Revolt* Please send $2 cash for postage.

Order Form

Send order to Bill "Tycoon" Greene, P.O. Box 810, Mill Valley, CA 94942
Please send me:

_____*Complete Home Study Course,* $200 each.

_____*Think Like a Tycoon,* $16 each Hardcover

_____*The Realty Bluebook,* $16 each

_____*Landlording,* $15

_____"Buying Your First Investment Property," $9 each

_____Individual Cassettes, $13 each (designate titles desired)

_____Free Sample Newsletter, 1 year (Send $2 cash to defray postage cost)

_____*Your Personal Tax Revolt,* (this book) $16

_____*How to Buy Distress Property* (Reference Workbook) $55

Name _____

Address_____

City/State/Zip _____

Check enclosed_____Charge me_____

Visa No. _____

Master Charge No._____

Expiration Date _____

Total of your order _____

Postage (add $1.50 for each item) _____

TOTAL ENCLOSED_____

Please use billing address of your card when charging merchandise.
Phone orders accepted with charge orders at (415) 383-8264